SATHER CLASSICAL LECTURES
Volume Twenty-three

From HOMER to MENANDER

From
HOMER
to
MENANDER

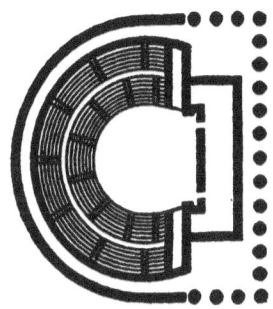

Forces in Greek Poetic Fiction

by L. A. POST

University of California Press

Berkeley and Los Angeles

1951

University of California Press
Berkeley and Los Angeles
California

Cambridge University Press
London, England

TO FIVE GREAT TEACHERS

Francis B. Gummere

Rufus M. Jones

Charles R. Lanman

H. W. B. Joseph

Gilbert Murray

PREFACE

THE AIM of my work is explained in the first chapter. Excellent books on Homer and on Greek tragedy, taken separately, are obtainable. No one, however, as far as I know, has since Aristotle considered Greek epic, tragedy, and comedy from a single point of view, studying fiction as essentially a representation of forces in action. Menander in particular has not been given the place that he deserves as successor to Homer and the tragedians. Secondly, the study of Greek fiction from Aristotle's point of view almost forces the student to combine with his criticism of poets a reconsideration of Aristotle's *Poetics* or *Theory of Fiction*. My views on this point are summarized in the last chapter of this book. Those whose main interest is in the philosophy of fiction are advised to read the added ninth chapter first. The earlier chapters may then be read as supplementary and illustrative material. Still a third project has intruded here and there. I should have liked to add a tenth chapter dealing with fiction as a force in history and discussing the place of fiction in personal and social dynamics. This proved to be a task too great for my powers. Nor would a single volume, let alone a chapter, be enough for such a theme. In preparing my lectures, however, I had the project in mind and was concerned not to divorce fiction from history, nor the history of ancient Greece from that of the rest of mankind.

Except for omissions, the first eight chapters of this book are substantially the lectures that I gave as Sather Professor of Classical Literature at the University of California in the spring of 1948. It is a great privilege to participate in the lively and varied intellectual activity of that great university.

I am deeply grateful to Professor W. H. Alexander, Chairman of the Department of Classics at the time of my visit, and others who smoothed the way and gave me the most friendly welcome. To Professor Alexander, and to Harold A. Small, Editor of the University of California Press, I owe a debt for careful editing. Professors L. A. MacKay and J. E. Fontenrose read my typescript

and made valuable suggestions. For other helpful hints I am indebted to Professors H. R. W. Smith, Harold Cherniss, Alan R.
Thompson, and the late Max Radin, and to others more than I
can remember. I have learned much from my students at Haverford during thirty years, and also at Bryn Mawr in the spring of
1945. Professor Ralph M. Sargent of Haverford College read and
discussed many chapters of my book with me. Last and most important is the friendly criticism that I have received from Professor
L. R. Shero of Swarthmore College. In the preparation of this
book he has corrected my information, my grammar, and my
style, has verified most of my references, and has helped with
proofreading and indexing. He has saved me from innumerable
errors and infelicities. For such as remain I alone am responsible.

L. A. Post

Haverford College

CONTENTS

I
The Pattern of Success:
Homer's *Odyssey*

It will readily be granted, I imagine, that fiction is not only itself a force in human life, but that it is also of all arts the most capable of presenting to the imagination a representative model of human fate. It alone may hope to include in the imitation of life all the forces that move men from within or act upon them from without. Such forces help to determine the destiny of individuals and of nations. The part played by fiction in educating and inspiring leaders of men and their followers has varied greatly from nation to nation and from age to age; hence a historical study of fiction as a force has an essential contribution to make to philosophy of history. Indeed some comparison of the parts played by fiction in different times and climes must, I suppose, necessarily be included in any really dynamic study of history. We must distinguish the dramatic or the dynamic from the pictorial in history as in art. History may be presented as a tapestry that displays no more than eternal artistries of circumstance or as a theater of full life, a never-ending sequence of interacting forces: some material, some moral, and some—the religious, spiritual, or philosophic—that operate on the level of inspiration or creative imagination.

Such a dynamic study of history, which would include the dynamics of fiction as a force in history, lies beyond the scope of my ambition. But in studying the aesthetic of forces in a particular field of fiction it is necessary to have the larger import of such analysis in mind, for it is the significance of the larger field that lends authority to the cultivation of the smaller plot. In fact, it will be necessary from time to time to throw out for inspection occa-

I

sional obvious-seeming generalizations about life and history as well as art. Still, my main concern at the moment is with fiction as the art that depicts all the potentialities of human life. Great fiction, as opposed to the merely frivolous, confronts us not only with a picture of such potentialities but also with an assessment of them in terms of value, whether spiritual or practical. In fiction we see men moving, but also moved and acting or suffering; at the same time we ourselves participate with the actors and respond positively or negatively to the author's assessment of values. Thus the aesthetic of fiction becomes highly complicated, for it involves an adequate appreciation as well as awareness of all the forces that are depicted in fiction as present in life. Fiction, of course, has many artistic elements besides the dynamic, but it is the forces seen and felt in fiction that relate it most closely to life and make it important morally and philosophically as well as artistically. This must be my apology for the attempt to study forces in fiction apart from other elements.

In fact, a study of forces in any field of fiction presupposes an interest in philosophy as well as in history. Many questions must be kept in mind even if no final answer can be discovered. What is the relation of fiction to scientific or historical truth? What is its relation to social and political concepts and to the moral patterns of life? What is its relation to the creative insight of seer, artist, or philosopher? Fiction, like other literature, may convey information, give pleasure, or transport the hearer or reader to a new world of the imagination. Great fiction may even use the power of imagination to dominate past and future, shaping them to new purposes. Such imaginative influences have their effect on behavior and result at times in a complete transformation of the ruling interest of one man or another. The varieties of literary experience are akin to the varieties of religious experience and have a similar impact in human life. Fiction may contain much or little of philosophy or history. Its power to influence the imagination is both greater and less than theirs, for what it lacks in truth, it makes up in art, and, as Aristotle knew, there is often philosophical truth in fiction, even when it is most lacking in historical truth. The distinction between fiction and history or philosophy is not always easy to make in practice, for there are borderline cases.[1]

The forces that we find illustrated in fiction are the forces of life, but their pattern is at the same time an artistic pattern. Hence the study of forces in fiction is a contribution primarily to aesthetic analysis, however profitable the study may incidentally be for history and philosophy as well. Art has a language of its own addressed to our aesthetic sense even when it depicts the issues of life, as they are fought out on many an unregarded battlefield. It makes us aware of them by intuition rather than by logic or by personal experience. Still, both the impact of experience and the clarity that comes with logical analysis are required before we can see clearly in its proper focus the true pattern of a work of fiction. Moreover, it will not do to focus our attention either on a field that is too large or on one too small. It so happens that the field of Greek poetic fiction recommends itself particularly to one who would, in spite of the formidable difficulties of the task, attempt, at least in one area, to study forces in fiction and fiction as a force.

In the first place, we have in Greek poetic fiction works and writers among the greatest in all literature. The perfection of Homer's art as seen in his two epics, the *Iliad* and the *Odyssey,* has been almost axiomatic among critics. The tragedies of Aeschylus, Sophocles, and Euripides, though only a small number of them are still extant, reached approximately the same level of greatness as the epics of Homer. Their greatness is sufficiently apparent in the works that survive. Our appreciation of the tragedians may be too narrow or otherwise inadequate because so much of what they wrote is forever lost to us, but enough remains to indicate their quality. Even less, unfortunately, remains of Menander, of whom we have not a single complete work. In his case, however, our study takes on added importance, for it is dealing with less familiar material. We shall see that in his plots he avails himself of all the resources of tragedy as far as the depiction of lively characters is

[1] For notes to chapter i see pages 273–276.

concerned, and that he is as much concerned with morals and personal insight as his predecessors. Though he wrote comedy and though in his characters the influence of Aristophanes and Old Comedy in general may be seen, he is as serious and as realistic in his assessment of the forces that move men as are the writers of tragedy. He too exercises a magic that transports the reader and produces great fiction, by which I mean fiction that fills men with wonder, introduces them to strange new aspects of life or new attitudes toward life, and so endows them with new interests and new insights. The dominance of later writers by Homer gives a unity to Greek fiction that is not easily paralleled in other languages, yet each work and each writer has a particular individuality. In technique and in the attitude of writers toward the problems of human existence, it is, however, possible to trace a single line of development from birth through life to decadence.

Greek literature developed naturally and undisturbed because in the great period it was little influenced by the outside world. We can hardly hope to trace the influence of other cultures even in the case of Homer, with whom our knowledge begins. He appears as an isolated phenomenon. His work was a mighty force in creating the European world that we know, but no amount of study can tell us what created him. We know practically nothing of his life or of any previous Greek literature. We know of his environment hardly more than we can deduce from the *Iliad* and *Odyssey* themselves. Fortunately the clarity and precision of Greek creative writing are such that we can usually be fairly certain what effect Homer or one of the dramatists intended to produce even when we have no evidence but his work. Certainty is, however, increased when we consider the whole course of development in one view. Furthermore, concentration on the fictional rather than the poetic aspects of poetic fiction may also suggest new interpretations even of authors whose works have been analyzed before in books without number. The very compression required in order to include so many works in one study may perhaps of itself serve to eliminate what is extraneous and expose only essential patterns to view.

It is well that we are not overwhelmed by the very bulk of Greek work; the total amount of poetic fiction that has come down to us is hardly more in bulk than we have of Plato and less than we have of Aristotle.[2]

We shall find that the total impact of our authors, in spite of exceptions, is highly moral in its intention. Menander will appear in a new aspect to many when his work is seen as a culmination of the fictional development that shows itself in Homer and the tragedians. Even in the case, however, of much-studied writers, the extent to which they are moral and philosophical in their approach may come as a surprise to those who have been taught to look for appreciation of beauty rather than of goodness and truth in the Greeks. Matthew Arnold imposed upon his generation a distinction between Hebraism and Hellenism that served his propaganda but may be misleading and unfair to the Greeks. He identified man's "moral side and the current of force which we call Hebraism." From this it is natural to infer that Hellenism emphasizes sweetness and light at the expense of good morals. Actually, of all artists the Greek writers were furthest from advocacy of Art for Art's sake. They were concerned not merely with goodness and truth, but also with social welfare as they conceived it, and with the excellence of individuals. It is true that Puritan views about lying and fornication are not shared by the Greeks. Still, however we may disagree with the leniency of their system in any particular case, the point is that they did have a system and that they were strict in applying their principles. Certainly their fiction is rich in moral patterns.[3]

It is a further advantage in studying the Greek development that we have the *Poetics* of Aristotle to serve as a guide to the Greek attitude toward fiction. While for the most part he treats of the technique rather than the philosophy of fiction, his analysis is particularly applicable to Greek fiction and is instructive by its very omissions and confusions. On the other hand, a study of the works with which he deals will provide much material for criticism of the *Poetics* itself. Paradoxically the work of "Longinus" on the sublime will concern us less in spite of its more philosophical and valuable approach, for Longinus is interested only in the sublimity of short passages and has little or nothing to say of the transporting effect of the total pattern of action or suffering as worked out in epic or drama. Aristotle on his part believed that a tragic plot should strike terror even when a mere summary of the story is given. Modern critics are far from agreeing with him, for physical horror, as we see it in the ancient or the Elizabethan theater, no longer interests us greatly. We prefer to it in tragedy the presentation of morally and socially significant conflicts or challenges to complacency. There are many other points in Aristotle's analysis of Greek epic and tragedy that will provide occasion for disagreement. Hence in this study we shall from the start be laying a foundation for criticism of the *Poetics* and for a new approach to philosophy of fiction.[4]

Though we shall endeavor to be more philosophical, if such a thing is possible, than Aristotle, we shall largely agree with him in disregarding the poetical side of Greek poetic fiction. As he points out, there is also prose fiction, and the elements of fiction are the same in prose and in poetic fiction. The scope of our study will accordingly be much the same as that of Aristotle's. He was familiar with far more Greek tragedies than we are acquainted with, but most of what he says is well illustrated in works that have survived through the ages. He was inevitably unacquainted with the work of Menander, since Menander's career began as Aristotle's ended. Yet Aristotle's analysis is readily applicable in the field of New Comedy. In fact, he may have had more than we can know to say of New Comedy in the second book of his *Poetics,* long since lost, in which he treated of comedy. He included in comedy not merely plays whose chief purpose is to excite laughter, but also such epics and tragedies as have happy endings. But in any case Aristotle includes some discussion of comedy in the extant *Poetics.* We shall not, however, follow him in discussing Aristophanes and other poets of Old Comedy, but omit them, for we are concerned with the serious depiction of human action as it leads to success or failure. The characters of Aristophanes are often realistically depicted, and one of them, Lysistrata, is treated seriously from beginning to end of her play, but the patterns of action in Aristophanes have a delightful logic of their own that refuses to be bound by realistic considerations. His characters have a freedom that removes them from our world of responsibility. Strepsiades and Dionysus do not interest us personally. They are puppets animated by the poet's thread of argument, not moral but comic agents. Similarly the dialogues of Plato, which have the form of fiction, as Aristotle points out, do not demand consideration here, since the fictional element in them is altogether secondary to the philosophical.

Prose fiction in fact never reached in ancient times a high standard of psychological or philosophical interest. The Greek novels of Roman times are fairly effective in a rhetorical and pictorial fashion, but the adventures that they relate better illustrate the caprices of fortune than the active lives of intelligent human beings. In Latin we have much better novels by Petronius and Apuleius, but their effect is rather to entertain than to guide. They are better demonstrations of the varieties of folly and sin in the external world than clues to the complex labyrinths of inner experience. The Lady Murasaki, who in Japan wrote *The Tale of Genji* about the year 1000 of the Christian era, produced at last a great novel with psychological overtones and a reasonably realistic picture of high society. Yet not until the last two hundred years did prose fiction in Western civilization enjoy a position of respect. Indeed, fiction belongs now to prose as emphatically as in the best days of Greece it belonged to poetry. How recent this development is, will at once be apparent to anyone who studies the pious tradition which a century ago largely forbade the reading of prose fiction unless its moral or religious instruction was preponderant. In the early part of the nineteenth century the bluestocking Hannah More read the narrative poems of Walter Scott but refused to waste time on most of his novels. So it was in many religious homes of my youth. Certainly it would be waste of time

to study the pattern of action in Greek prose fiction in the hope
of finding scenes of psychological or philosophical import. Such
scenes are confined in Greek to poetic fiction.[5]

It is, however, not alone the quality of Greek epic and drama
that makes them particularly worthy of attention. The importance
of Homer and the dramatists was exceptionally great in their own
world, and they have thus become important factors in the European world and wherever the influence of European civilization
is felt. The Greeks were largely self-educated. They learned much,
to be sure, from earlier civilized peoples, but, being always children, as the Egyptian priest remarked to Solon, they played with
what they learned and discovered new possibilities in the old material. Though dependent on others for their start, they soon improved beyond recognition any art or science that they took over.
They combined the theoretical and the practical to an unusual
degree. They were more realistic than the Hindus and more specu-
lative than the Chinese. They were less hampered than most by
superstition and dogma. They were skeptical of prophets and never
accepted, as the Semites did, the authority of divine and unchange-
able codes of law. They had their gods and their codes, but felt
a singular freedom in their great period to criticize and revise
them. Political organization in Greece was likely to be local and
temporary. Religious organizations operated under secular management and never became dominant. Thus literature and art were
free to create their own conceptions of the gods. While the poet
was limited in one direction by the need to please his audience,
his influence over that audience was not disputed by kings or
priests. Except in Crete, Homer was the great educator of Greece.
His imaginative creations were not censored, and in the realm of
the imagination, once he had won supremacy in fiction, it was long
before he could be challenged by writers in other departments. Pindar might criticize his glorification of Odysseus, the historian Thucydides might scale down his estimate of the greatness of the Trojan war, and philosophers might castigate his immoral stories of
the gods; Homer was the man in possession. The sharpness of

Plato's attacks on the influence of Homer and tragedy is our best
evidence of the part that they played in his time in shaping the
popular mind.[6]

In the end, philosophy and history became independent and authoritative guides of life, and fiction ceased to be a medium for
Greeks who had a new view of life to communicate. It was inevitable that, with the growth of historical and geographical knowledge and the greater accuracy and profundity developed by scientific and philosophical thinking, fiction should sink in its function
to the level of entertainment. At the same time the poet could
no longer speak to and for the whole people. I do not suppose that
there was ever a time or place where popular poetry was produced
by the whole community. The material for works of the imagination may be slowly accumulated like scientific knowledge of facts,
but to create from such material a single organic unity is the work
of a gifted individual. When that individual, however, in his creative work is aware of the existence of an audience that he may
hope to thrill by his picture of men and events, he becomes conscious of hidden motives and possibilities in his audience and
makes them in a sense participants in his own inspiration. In the
best period of Greek literature, writers were or hoped to be leaders
of the people. They took upon themselves unlimited responsibility
to deal with moral and political problems. If they were to succeed,
they had to be aware of the fundamental assumptions of Greek
society, and to base the expression of their new insights on already
existing foundations. Thus the development of Greek literature
went hand in hand with the development of the Greek people until
the privileges of empire passed from the Greeks to the Macedonians. From that time till now literature has been, with some exceptions, in retirement. It speaks to individuals or to groups, but
not to nations as a whole. It acts as a leaven, to be sure, but it has
lost the grand manner.[7]

In the eighth century before Christ the Greeks were just becoming conscious of themselves as a people. Their cultural life was
without form and void; the work of creation was still to come. In

other nations the work was done by warriors, statesmen, prophets, philosophers, or priests. In Greece it was a poet who legislated and prophesied and determined the bent of social growth. His inspiration can be traced even in the historian who belittled and the philosopher who denounced him. We need not trouble ourselves to inquire who the poet was. We have the *Iliad* and the *Odyssey;* their artistic unity forbids us to suppose that they had more than one author each. Nor is it likely that Greece at this period produced two great men whose thoughts and imagination could achieve masterpieces with so little individual difference of manner or outlook. *Iliad* and *Odyssey* are twin stars and must be studied together. It is easier to believe in one genius called Homer, as the Greeks did, than in two. The argument from design is, to be sure, not convincing when we are confronted by something imperfect. When, however, we find a work of art so well designed that changes in the fundamental pattern would destroy its total effect, the conclusion is forced upon us that the work had a creator. We need not pursue here the subject of origins, since we are interested in the finished composition. The materials available were an important factor, but genius has a way of transforming base metal into gold with rearrangement of its patterns. The product is on a different level spiritually from the ingredients. Whatever Homer took from other men in the way of folklore or legend or myth was reshaped by him to suit his fictional purpose. He is great, not as a repository, but as a dynamo.[8]

He first, as far as we know, realized the possibilities of fiction. Since it uses words as a medium, it can include thought and tell us whatever can be told about the inner life of a man. Aristotle includes dancing among the arts of action, and some paintings and sculptures convey strongly a sense of motion or struggle, but dancing must omit intellectual interests from its sequences; and the timeless quality of painting and sculpture deprives them of the possibility of showing cause and effect in a complex development. Thought and calculation of consequences are a large part of responsible living, and thought must be conveyed by symbols. In general, the only symbols that art has been able to use effectively to show a man's thoughts are words. To know a man we need to know his interpretation of life. Men may be aware in a situation of much more than is visible to the eye; the remote fact or the disembodied ideal is often a vital force in reflective action. Hence it is impossible to create complete characters without the use of words. To feel the difference between wordless and verbal arts we need only reflect on the difference between Homer's descriptions of the pictures of life that adorned the shield of Achilles and his own representation of life itself.

As Aristotle noted, fiction—at least Greek fiction—is primarily concerned with what characters do and suffer. Furthermore, it often puts the question why they do and suffer what they do. For this reason fiction is bound to create an environment for its characters, a world in which they live, a world that may be contemporary or archaic, romantic or realistic, intimate or public. It will be at the same time recognizably like the common world of men awake, and yet somehow transformed by the author's imagination. Thus the characters will not merely be interesting in their psychology; they will face events and make decisions, and when decisions are made they will undergo the ordeal of success or failure. Either human actors will meet in a clash of wills and aims, or men who have no conflict with each other may find themselves at odds with fortune. Thus a pattern of action results from the interaction not only of characters but also of events not planned by anyone. The complete pattern of men and events is formed in the imagination of an artist who aims at a total effect that is artistically right. It must be right, however, not only for him but for his audience if it is ever to come alive in a world of action; and to be right for his audience the forces in it must be so presented that the audience will feel them as the author intended, laugh where he wished them to laugh and weep where he meant them to weep, and understand the import of decisions.

The artist may show life as it is, was, will be, ought or ought not to be, must be, has been, or could be if only something were different. When he represents events, his picture of life is philosophical so far as it is thought out, and religious so far as it involves a search for ultimate security, and faith in something as surely good. Even if life is bad, it is at least good to know the truth about it. There is a fundamental difference between the psychological reality of characters and the philosophical creation in art of a total universe of action. Either psychological insight or philosophic depth is enough to make a work of fiction great. The Greek writers had both. They also wrote in verse and thereby achieved on occasion a special sublimity of mood and at all times a verbal pattern that elevates their work above the commonplace. The rhythm of their verse often conveys a sense of life apart from the meaning of the words. Greek dramatic verse is frequently rhetorical or lively rather than poetical in the modern sense. It celebrates the normal rather than the eccentric in human experience. In any case, the verse of Greek fiction is a medium for depicting action and serves practical ends. Consequently it bears little resemblance to the pure poetry of modern times. No doubt the ancient poet had less command of theory than the modern, but he made his meaning clear.

It will help us to get the range of our material if for once we disregard chronological order and study the *Odyssey* before the *Iliad*. The *Odyssey* is not only a sequel but a complement to the *Iliad*. In both poems the poet considers it his function to stimulate the passion for glory and to hold up ideals of glorious conduct for emulation by later ages. In the *Iliad* he glorifies a warrior, Achilles, and shows how he gloried not only in military prowess and in adherence to the precepts of honesty and honor, but in passionate loyalty to his friend Patroclus even after death. In the *Odyssey* it is a woman who is glorified because of her loyal love for a husband who has been twenty years absent and may be supposed to be dead. The theme of loyalty and courage as the true glory is the same in both, but the shifting of attention from one sex to the other produces great changes in environment and in the pattern of action. There is another great difference in that the glory of Achilles is displayed in contempt for death. The soldier must compete for honor without hope of other reward than glory itself. His dead friend cannot be restored to him, and the *Iliad* has, as Aristotle says, a tragic plot. He calls the plot of the *Odyssey* in contrast ethical and complex. It is complex because it has recognition scenes and because the tables are suddenly turned for the suitors when Odysseus is recognized.

The ethical plot is a plot that was common in Greek tragedies and popular in the theater, but Aristotle distinguishes tragedy proper with its unhappy ending from the kind of story in which all turns out well in the end. He calls this kind of plot—the success story, the pattern of trouble and deliverance or misunderstanding and clarification—ethical, I suppose, because it is the success of good characters only that is insured, while bad characters are in some way punished. The effect might thus be supposed to be highly moral. At any rate, Aristotle distinguishes the plots proper to comedy and tragedy, though Greek tragedies often have happy endings and differ in practice from comedy only in their treatment of character. Unfortunately this has led to a certain ambiguity in the meaning of the word comedy ever since his time. Such comedies as Dante's *Divine Comedy* and Shakespeare's *Winter's Tale* are not particularly comic, but they end happily and thus satisfy Aristotle's criterion. When a tale is actually treated in a comic spirit, it is quite possible to have a success story that ends happily for bad characters, like the Punch and Judy show. The immorality is part of the comedy. Aristotle notes the inferiority of comic characters, but implies that the characters who win out in the success story of tragedy are not inferior. But he knows a tragedy, the *Orestes* of Euripides, in which one character at least is inferior. He means, no doubt, that the general effect is comic. You obviously may have a burlesque of a tragic story or may present with tragic seriousness a story of success in which success is preceded by tragic dangers and decisions. Longinus lays down the rule that sublimity is as closely connected with suffering or emotion as pleasure with *ēthos*.[9]

Now *éthos* is a very elusive word in Greek. It means good character, character of any kind, and normal life. The *Odyssey* is pleasurable as the *Iliad* is sublime. The later poem gives us scenes from common life; it depicts character in unemotional scenes; and it affords a model of normal morality. The *Odyssey* makes up by extension in time and space what it lacks in intensity.

Once we admit that the success story should be moral, we are committed to an interest in correct sentiments rather than in noble fury, in the usages of polite society rather than in the rude conflicts of men in a state of nature. Homer goes further, however, by depicting more than one kind of life. The Cyclopes have no state at all, and there are many peoples with strange ways that a wanderer might be tempted to adopt, notably the Lotus-eaters and the Phaeacians. In describing the latter, Homer seems to be as insistent as Plato was, later, on the danger to morals involved in isolation and control of the sea. It is here that the climax of temptation comes for Odysseus. It is characteristic of Homer to make his good woman more tempting than any bad woman could be. Nausicaä is an unmarried Andromache, and like Andromache she tempts the hero in Book 6 of his poem. As Andromache tempts Hector to forget honor and refrain from battle, so Nausicaä tempts Odysseus to forget his wife and refrain from further perils by sea and land. The bad women who tempt Odysseus are the nymphs Circe and Calypso. When he resists, their power yields to the behest of the gods, who are alert to further the cause of morality. Odysseus risks not only his life but his virtue more than once in the course of his travels. Homer would never have suggested such a sentiment as "Be good, sweet maid, and let who will be clever." It is only the clever Odysseus who succeeds in being good and so returning to his wife. Odysseus' cleverness may indeed strike us sometimes as being inconsistent with plain honesty, but Homer justifies him by giving him a god in his own image to guide him. Athena directs not only his actions but those also of his wife Penelope and his son Telemachus. She tells all parties what she thinks is good for them, and encourages Telemachus to find out for himself what news of his father he can. As she explains, a young man needs to see the world and meet difficulties for himself. In fact, Homer is rather fond of pointing out alternatives to make the rightness of a decision conspicuously clear. The *Odyssey* is a guide to ancient etiquette, a comedy of manners in which manners are not at odds with morals.[10]

It divides easily into parts A, B, C, and D. In D, Books 13–24, we are in Ithaca and all the gods are united in support of Odysseus and his family against the usurping suitors. In A, Books 1–4, and B, Books 5–8, the gods support Odysseus, but have to reckon with Poseidon, who cherishes a private pique because Odysseus blinded his son, the Cyclops Polyphemus. Athena helps Telemachus in Ithaca and on his travels without fear of Poseidon's anger. During the simultaneous adventures of Odysseus in Phaeacia, she helps him, but only in disguise. After all, Poseidon was her uncle and Poseidon was Odysseus' enemy until he reached Ithaca. Poseidon's last fling was to turn to stone the ship of the Phaeacians which conducted Odysseus at last to his homeland.

The gods in council took no interest in Odysseus during the first ten years of his wanderings. The moral intent of Homer is plain here too. By putting the council so late, he can permit Odysseus to wander unfriended on the fringes of the world where nymphs and monsters take the place of gods. In Books 9–12, which I call part C, we hear little or nothing of the gods except what an uninspired mortal might deduce for himself. This account of adventures that occurred many years before the opening of the *Odyssey* is put into the mouth of Odysseus himself, perhaps because Homer wished in this part of his epic to omit divine machinery. The reason why can be discovered from one or two passages where it is revealed that all the gods were angry with all the Achaeans after the sack of Troy because of the violation of temples. They were angry with Odysseus also, naturally, since he was one of the offending Achaeans. If the gods had been brought into part C, it would have appeared at once that they were against Odysseus because the hero had been bad. Since it is Odysseus himself who

relates the tale of these years of wandering, we are not surprised
that the attitude of the gods is left undefined. Thus Odysseus can
arrive in Ithaca with no disqualification for the part that he is to
play as leader of society and friend of religion. In this work Homer is dealing in black and white. He, no more than the gods,
will sponsor Odysseus in part C; the hero must perforce speak for
himself. The late date of the council of the gods also enables Homer to cite the history of Clytemnestra, who was unfaithful and
slew her husband, in contrast to the loyalty of Penelope. The example of Orestes, who avenged his father Agamemnon, is also
held up for imitation by Telemachus, who is bound to take the part
of his father. This moral contrast between the good woman Penelope and the bad woman Clytemnestra, between the wise Odysseus and the foolish Agamemnon, is strongly emphasized at the
beginning, middle, and end of the *Odyssey*.[11]

In a success story, criticism of life centers on a particular obstacle.
Some individual or group or perhaps society as a whole stands in
the way of welfare and happiness for the hero and his friends.
The possibility is not faced, as in tragedy, that the universe may
be hostile to man, or that man may have to compromise with destiny. At most, in comedy a man may need to find new resources
or a new attitude in himself before he can win happiness. In the
Odyssey a united family is the goal, and the gods at the start make
a reunion of the family their goal too. Odysseus, who has been
many years with Calypso on her island, has nothing new to learn
about life. He must merely display his qualities of craft and courage and restraint. Penelope has a more important role, for she must
create a new pattern by being more loyal to her husband than
current custom demands. Telemachus, who is just coming of age,
must develop into a man. Since the goal is clear-cut, Homer need
not show us much psychological conflict. Decisions will be concerned with means rather than ends. In Penelope's choice of an
ideal we know her decisions rather than her doubts, but the doubts
and the inner triumph are sufficiently indicated from time to time.
As a woman, she is more passive than active, so that the men and

their adventures seem more interesting at first; but she is made the emotional center of the action as she remains in the women's apartment of the palace of Odysseus at Ithaca and refuses to leave, though suitors, relatives, and even her son would prefer it. The crisis arrives when her son comes of age, so that it is no longer her duty to watch over him and protect his interests. She has no excuse for refusing to marry again except her woman's intuition, which persists in believing that her husband may be alive.

After the council of the gods, Athena goes to Ithaca to send Telemachus in search of his father, while Hermes goes to Calypso to order the release of Odysseus. At Ithaca we see the troubles of Penelope and Telemachus that are caused by the many suitors who feast daily and threaten the estate with ruin. Telemachus might order his mother to go home to her parents and take the suitors with her, but conscience forbids him to lay constraint upon a free woman. Penelope must make her own decision; he can hold out for another year. Not only the gods but the state is brought into the picture when Telemachus warns the suitors in public assembly that their violation of the rights of Odysseus as well as his own will be punished. The rest of Books 1–4 tells the story of his adventures at Pylos and Sparta as he seeks news of his father. The suitors plan to slay him on his return, thus deepening the blackness of their guilt.[12]

In Books 5–8 we see the simultaneous adventures of Odysseus on his way home and note how he pines always for his rocky homeland where men are men and for his own wife who has grown old waiting for him. This sentiment motivates his action throughout. The old theme of the shipwrecked sailor rescued by the princess may have been taken by Homer from folklore, but the moral tone which he infuses by making Nausicaä so obviously attractive as a wife and Phaeacia so luxurious as a residence is all his own. Odysseus may not accept the offer of Nausicaä's hand even out of gratitude. Homer in the end waxes satirical at the expense of the Phaeacians, who are not great athletes, but good sailors, dancers, and listeners to immoral stories about the gods.

In the third group of four books it is Odysseus' life that is threatened rather than his virtue, though he is given the chance to remain under the spell of Circe's beauty. His voyage to the land of
ghosts permits Homer to recall again the wickedness of Clytemnestra and to inform Odysseus of the virtues of his wife, but the
episodic nature of the adventures related by Odysseus is plain
enough. The episodes are carefully planned in their arrangement
and interesting in themselves, but here if anywhere Homer was
using stories that had long been current. His hero emerges from
every ordeal undaunted, but in this part of the story the force of
circumstance outweighs the moral forces. Character is less than
adventure. Homer, being as tricky as his hero, draws a veil over
his relation to the gods at this time, but his adventures are clearly
those of a man who is viewed by them with indifference, to say the
least.

In the second half of the poem, which recounts the recognitions
of Odysseus by friend and foe in Ithaca and the slaughter of the
suitors, Athena is busily at work. With her help a few righteous
fight against many wicked and triumph. Homer uses her to effect
the mutual recognition of Odysseus and Telemachus, which must
not be allowed to compete with the great recognition of husband
and wife after the slaying. Father and son are the nucleus of an
intrigue against the suitors which requires the coöperation of Penelope for its success. She must propose the competition for her
hand among the suitors that will enable Odysseus to get in position unexpectedly with his bow and shoot them down helpless
and trapped. Yet her part in the intrigue is carried out without
any recognition on her part that her missing husband is at hand.
Athena is as useful in enabling Odysseus to remain unrecognized
by his wife as in insuring his recognition by his son. Such a difference in technique, when observed, leaves no doubt that the author of the *Odyssey* was a great original genius, no matter how
much material he may have taken from others. The fact that he
used the methods of oral composition and no doubt composed for
oral delivery makes no difference. The use of a pen or a typewriter

does not suddenly make the user a master of planned storytelling, nor does the absence of these instruments prevent the inspired artist from producing a great work. To argue that, because most or even all modern oral poets are comparatively unoriginal, there can have been no Homer, is like arguing that, since there is no Shakespeare in the twentieth century, there was none in the sixteenth either.[13]

Athena is also useful in relieving Penelope and to some extent Odysseus of any criticism when their part in the tale is to cheat and deceive. Penelope's success in getting presents from the suitors by arraying herself in all her charms is due to a suggestion of Athena and receives the approval of Odysseus. It is an odd feature of the story that it should seem to be dangerous to Odysseus to be recognized by his wife, and that Athena should help him with his disguise and should make Penelope unobserving when he is recognized by the nurse Eurycleia who bathes him in his wife's presence. But it adds to our liking for the warmhearted and yearning Penelope that she should be unable to conceal her joy if she had once recognized her husband. Homer and his audience liked their women sincere and simple, incapable of carrying on an intrigue. The scenes between Penelope and Odysseus in disguise, in which he keeps his role of beggar while she pours out her heart, thus add another to Homer's scenes of temptation by good women. Odysseus must be hard and cruel until the suitors are out of the way. All his wit and self-control are taxed.[14]

The pains that Homer takes to denigrate the suitors are obvious. They are attacking the sanctity of the royal prerogative, of the family, and of private property, and the gods are unanimously against them. God, nature, and man will be in harmony as soon as a few wicked individuals are forced to cease from troubling. There are no bounds to the insolence of the suitors. They plan the murder of a host, make love to a woman in the home of her husband, disregard the rights of suppliants and beggars, and disregard the warning of a seer. They force their attentions upon a woman against her will. When Homer compares the case of

Odysseus with that of Agamemnon, the suitors play the part of Aegisthus, who slew him after seducing his wife. So, too, the suitors hope to slay Odysseus. The latter is wise, however, where Agamemnon was foolish. He has no Chryseïs whom he prefers to his wife, and he brings home no captive concubine like Cassandra. He trusts no women if he can help it and walks into no traps. This comparison and the attitude of the gods reinforce the blackening of the suitors.

There is more than morality in the *Odyssey*, however, if we investigate Homer's purpose in making Penelope the emotional center of the epic. The moral code of Homer enjoined respect for the gods and for suppliants, who were under their protection. Hosts and guests had mutual claims under the protection of Zeus. There was a standard procedure in city government which law-abiding citizens respected. Free and responsible married women were not to be coerced. Mere morality could hardly confer glory, however, in Homer. He is romantic enough to celebrate love—in the *Iliad* a love passing the love of women, and in the *Odyssey* a woman's love. Penelope is represented as a creative personality who, when all men doubt and disapprove, wins a personal success and glory by gambling against odds on the hope of regaining her husband. In Oriental fiction women die to prove their loyalty to a dead husband, as Evadne does in Euripides' *Suppliants* and as Anthea does in the *Cyropaedeia* of Xenophon. In the Confucian code of China a widow shows her loyalty by remaining unwed. There are many monuments to the virtue of such women in China. The Greeks were more practical; they did not expect such exaggerated loyalty to a dead husband, nor do women in Greek literature die in defense of their virtue. Penelope does not renounce the hope of marriage, once her son has come of age and her husband is known to be dead. In fact Odysseus himself enjoined her to marry again after his death. Hence she does not dismiss the suitors by refusing to marry. She seeks always to gain time on one pretext or another and to get certain news of Odysseus. Her willingness to believe any rumor is marked. This is an amiable weakness, a woman's whim, in the opinion of others. Penelope is isolated, but to her the love of her husband is a sacrament that she keeps inviolate in spite of reason or statistical odds. Thus Homer raises the standard of living for husband and wife and stamps with approval the assertion of a noble ideal by an individual. He is at pains to emphasize Penelope's disregard of public opinion and of prudential considerations, and to show her love as an emotional influence in her life. She acts wisely, as women are wise, for she does not underestimate the worth of sentiment, without which women are weaker than men. She acts with great propriety, never visiting the men's part of the palace except when she is veiled and attended by two handmaids. She does not, like the Spartan Helen, eat with the men. Yet the springs of feeling gush warm and melting when she is at last alone with the husband of her youth.[15]

Homer's interest in the ideal family relationship is easily forgotten when attention is focused on Odysseus. His desire to return home might seem to depend little on his personal affection for Penelope, though he states when necessary his loyalty to her above all other women or nymphs. He paints a glowing picture of married love for Nausicaä, and by so doing enlists her womanly pride and her romantic impulses as a maiden in his favor; but this may be the subtlety of a man in dire need. He convinces her by his understanding of the ideal marriage that he is personally a superior man, thus disarming her doubts of him and melting her suspicion. Later in Ithaca when Odysseus has the opportunity to spy upon his wife's behavior, she passes every test. She has the same passion for glory that inspires Homer's warriors, but holds that a woman's glory is to be loyal to her husband. The function of Athena in enabling Penelope to assist her husband's plot while apparently not recognizing him has been mentioned. It is clear that Homer has reasons for postponing the recognition by Penelope. Son is loyal to father as a matter of course, and men may be expected to plot together against foes. Penelope had nothing to lose materially by a change of husbands. Even her son had been warned in a dream not to trust his mother to look after his inter-

ests when the time should come for her to marry again. Such suspicion seems unworthy of Penelope, but it is precisely the vulgarity
of these suspicions that makes her actual conduct seem surprising
in its nobility. Thus Athena constantly interprets to Odysseus and
Penelope their mutual roles, while father and son speak freely
together.[16]

But after the slaughter of the suitors, in which Athena has assisted, the goddess tactfully withdraws and lets husband and wife
come together with no help from her except removal of his disguise and a general brightening up. Homer uses his gods with
much discretion. When he has a great scene in readiness, they set
the stage and let the actors show their motives. If Penelope had
recognized Odysseus earlier, the slaughter of the suitors must have
become the most interesting point of the story. When Euripides
puts recognition before escape, as in his *Helen, Electra,* and *Iphigeneia among the Taurians,* the women are bemeaned, and psychological interest gives way to melodramatic adventure. Homer
keeps Penelope and her emotional drama at the center of interest, first, by postponing her salvation, and secondly, by bringing
Athena and the miraculous as well as Hades back into the episodes
that follow in Book 24. Only where she is concerned do we get
a full-blooded psychological episode; in it there is even a suggestion of tragedy. Here we find sentiment intensified to the point
of passion. When Odysseus encountered Nausicaä, nothing infringed upon the delicate play of feeling on both sides. It was a disappointment when Nausicaä had to take leave of Odysseus, but her
disappointment is much less tragic than Penelope's thought of
what she had missed as the years of their separation dragged by.
There were other fish in the sea for Nausicaä.

Penelope has dreamed so long that when Eurycleia awakes her
with the words, "Odysseus is here," she cannot at first adjust herself to the reality. She is cold, then hot, but masters her excitement
before she joins the victorious Odysseus and Telemachus. Even
when Odysseus has bathed and rid himself of blood and grime,
even after he has tactfully disposed of Telemachus, who is inclined

to hurry things, she still gazes at the stranger in silence, trying to find a place for him among her memories and dreams of a far younger man. There is a similar scene in a Chinese drama written about two thousand years later, in which the wife remains coy through a protracted scene before she welcomes a long-absent husband. Here the motive is propriety, and the Chinese play apparently is chiefly concerned to show the success of the lady in concealing her feelings entirely in the interest of etiquette. There is, no doubt, some emphasis on propriety in Homer too, but he succeeds in making us feel the desperate need of Penelope to control her emotion and to yield only when she can do so without reserve. Here if anywhere we have an aesthetic of forces arranged in a psychological pattern that produces naturally a deep sympathy. There is a resolution of profound emotional stresses. The theme of wedded love is triumphant, and wedded love is made to seem the greatest of earthly bonds, as of course for a Greek woman it was.[17]

The courtesy of Odysseus in waiting patiently for his wife is underlined, for it was a tenet of Hellenism from Homer to Menander that free women must not be coerced in love. The slave woman was subject to her master, not so the wife or daughter. But at long last Odysseus shows feeling and speaks the bitter words, "Let my bed be made apart." His burst of feeling gives Penelope her cue. Yes, the marriage bed shall be brought out and made up for the stranger. With the mention of the marriage bed the years of absence fall away for both and revive the memory of union. The bed is symbolic; it was fixed in place by one leg, fashioned of an olive tree by Odysseus, but left rooted in the ground. It is not merely Odysseus' knowledge of the secret that assures Penelope of his identity; his righteous indignation discloses a passion that she recognizes. It is not subtlety but genuine feeling that rings in his voice as he denounces the man who has violated the ineradicable marriage bed, instrument and symbol of wedlock. About that bed are entwined the tender memories of early married love. Now Penelope sees in Odysseus, not the old veteran, but the stalwart youth whom she had sent to the war twenty years before. The emotions of the past well up, yet Penelope's sense of loss is keen. With a shock it comes to her that the best of marriage is gone, the joy of growing up and growing old together; but she does not dwell on this sentiment, opening rather her heart to the joy that remains. Odysseus says nothing of love or disappointment, for such expression is not the man's part in a Greek tale. His actions are eloquent enough and Homer speaks for him.

Experiment will soon show that the scene could not have been so powerful if Homer had put it anywhere else in his pattern of action. He indeed created a pattern for comedy, for later comedy always dealt with family ties and usually with mutual love of man and woman. In New Comedy the happy ending always involves a reunion of husband and wife, parent and child, brother-sister and sister-brother, or two passionate lovers. The suitors in the *Odyssey* could suppose that husband and wife had conspired against them. In fact, Homer leaves the possibility open that the wise Penelope really knew her husband from the start and only refrained from greeting him because that would have interfered with his plans. It would also have detracted from the beauty of their reunion. Homer so valued that great moment that of set purpose he sacrificed his last book to it. He had to point the moral and give the world of men its due, but he does not let what happens in that world seem very important in comparison with the happiness of a woman. As Bentley remarked, the *Iliad* was written for men, the *Odyssey* for women.[18]

Homer in the *Iliad* lets us gently down from the exaltation of a world of heroes to the considerations of daily life. When Achilles and Priam weep together, we are recalled from the romance to the reality of war. In the *Odyssey* the mood of the whole is not elevated above that of the twenty-fourth book of the *Iliad*. It is not the romance but the reality of love that is celebrated. The only decline that is possible is a decline from the devotion of intimate family life to the concerns of men apart from women—the mood of assembly and market place and battlefield. Homer glorifies this world in the *Iliad;* to do so in the *Odyssey* would be worse than to

make his ending flat, as it is. He gives us a moral and political solution and makes it final and authoritative by using Athena as *deus
ex machina,* just as she is used in the political tragedies of Athens.
For the first and only time she restrains, instead of inciting, Odysseus to action. She puts a stop to his pursuit of the kin of the suitors
after he has won a battle with the help of his father Laertes and his
son Telemachus, as well as his loyal supporters in the community.
Here Athena appears for the first time among many as the representative of political unity in Greek literature. Possibly this scene
inspired the pageant of the tyrant Peisistratus when he calmed the
fears of his fleeing opponents by sending before him in a chariot a
woman dressed and armed as Athena. She was declared to be
Athena, introducing Peisistratus as her representative, urging the
Athenians to receive him without misgiving. Presumably the Athenians recognized the theatrical aspect of this piece of propaganda,
but it was effective propaganda nevertheless. The sentiments with
which we view a patriotic pageant are not necessarily false or misleading. Certainly the Athenians approved of such representations
of Athena in their theater, if we may judge by the number of her
appearances in extant drama. Thus Homer lays down a pattern
not only for comedy, but for political tragedies that recount legendary history for purposes of propaganda—for example *Eumenides,
Ion, Andromache,* and others. In *Ion* and *Andromache,* Euripides
interwove the reunited family with his political plot. Only in New
Comedy are these strands at last separated. So long did it take to
throw off the clogging influence of Homer, who inserted the family within the framework of the state in the dull though statesmanlike ending of the *Odyssey.*[19]

Still, Homer understands perfectly the use of a *deus ex machina.*
The god must not be brought in to settle the main problem, but
only to prevent the sudden development of a new threat. Athena
intervenes only when the victory is won. To motivate this intervention Odysseus must act rashly and out of character. There is a
nodus vindice dignus, but the knot is rather arbitrarily provided by
the poet. The preceding battle bears no resemblance to the gory

struggles of the *Iliad*. It is enlivened only by the miraculous rejuvenation of the aged Laertes. Actually the miracle belittles the
battle. At any rate, it all ends with an era of good-will in which
king and state, along with morality, are supported by the goddess,
who counsels moderation. It is too early for her to recommend
democracy.[20]

Before the end, however, Homer had tied two other loose ends.
A meeting between Agamemnon in Hades and the ghosts of the
suitors is introduced, evidently to point once more the moral contrast between Penelope and Clytemnestra and to assert the power of
poetry. Bards will sing of the two women and perpetuate their
glory and shame. Thus they will bring glory or shame upon all
women. The poet's didactic purpose is evident: to teach by examples the difference between virtue and vice in wives.

The ensuing recognition scene between Odysseus and his father
Laertes is almost episodic, yet it serves to emphasize the importance
of the male line and to mark the clan as intermediate between family and state. In the means of recognition, recalling to his father an
incident that occurred when he was a small boy, Odysseus awakens
his father's memory and to some extent paves the way for his rejuvenation in battle. But there is nothing here to detain us further.
The glory has departed with Penelope. Homer displayed a world
at war in the *Iliad;* in the *Odyssey* he makes a beginning of reconstruction after the war. It is full of the gracious light of a benign
and civilizing influence. Its hero is sometimes too little concerned
about means, but his general aims are represented as noble and
good, to live on in peace and prosperity while he rules wisely and
well and gives gods and suppliants their due. It would be an
anachronism to denounce Homer as a fascist because he accepts
monarchy and even slavery. He idealizes his picture of the best
institutions that he knew, not to recommend them in preference
to some modern alternative, for such alternatives did not then exist.
He was only concerned to make men behave with due consideration of themselves and others within the frame of society as he saw
it. He was an educator, not a reformer.

II
The Tragic Pattern
of the *Iliad*

WE HAVE SEEN that the *Odyssey* satisfies Aristotle's
canon that a work of fiction should be a single organic whole. It
was well described by Alcidamas as a fair mirror of human life,
though Aristotle considered the metaphor too bold. The surge and
thunder of the *Odyssey* are indeed distant and reflected; they entertain and delight because they do not stir us too deeply. There are
dangers on the outskirts of the world, and even in the homeland
there are wicked men who make trouble; but heaven helps the
clever and brave and self-controlled who have right on their side.
The question what is right is taken for granted, and it is taken for
granted that when right prevails everyone will be happy. The universe that it depicts is comfortable and full of solid virtues; men
ask nothing better than to live out their lives in peace. The *Odyssey*
is a magic mirror that makes life seem cheerful and bright.[1]
    Longinus says that the *Iliad* was the work of Homer's youth and
the *Odyssey* of his old age. We must not forget though that the old
age was that of Homer, and that the setting sun has often an attrac-
tion that makes us welcome it after the intensity of the orb of mid-
day. Longinus' examples of sublimity in Homer are taken chiefly
from the *Iliad*. The *Iliad* is full of elemental forces. Its characters
are men of destiny who have no intention of resting quietly at
home. From the youthful Achilles to the aged Nestor they seek
glory in battle and in debate. The gods are treated with respect
some of the time when it suits Homer, especially Zeus, Apollo, and
Athena, but no one looks to the gods for salvation, except in minor

[1] For notes to chapter ii see pages 276–280.

27

difficulties. When the gods intervene in human affairs they fight among themselves and bring disaster to men as often as help. They have their prejudices and whims, which Homer does not always explain. Like the human characters, they show their humors in what they do. They press with vigor toward goals of their own. There is strife in heaven, obviously because the youthful Homer could not imagine a heaven without strife. Lust of living had not succumbed to the disease of thought or the seductions of ease.[2]

In one sense the gulf between men and gods is narrow and often bridged. The gods frequently mingle with men, even to fighting in their battles. They watch what men do with interest and may even be sufficiently shocked by their behavior to bring punishment upon them. They do not go so far, however, as to set them a good example. To quote Longinus again, Homer made his gods like men and his men like gods. Actually the gods often behave more like children, and serve as a vehicle for satire and comedy when they are not majestic or realistically treated on the human level of the *Odyssey*. Both they and their worshipers attach importance to the due performance of worship, but generous sacrifices do not guarantee divine favor with any certainty. One god may thwart another, the ruler of the gods cannot or will not go against destiny, or the same god may receive offerings from both sides to a dispute. Homer is remarkably free from superstition and magic; he is even reserved in his belief in the efficacy of religion. There is some connection between morality and religion and between religion and prosperity in the world of the *Iliad*, but not much.

There is one point in respect to which gods and men are completely severed: gods do not die and men do. Homer and his characters are obsessed by the haunting specter of death. Achilles in particular, who is half divine, resents the limitation imposed upon his life by mortality. Sarpedon uses to Glaucus the same argument as Penelope in the *Odyssey* to justify the pursuit of glory. Death cannot really be avoided; let us at least acquire fame. If there were certainty of postponing death, he would not urge his comrade to fight. In Achilles' case there is a slight variation. His goddess-mother had informed him of his fate, which depended on his own choice: he might live long or win glory, but not both. He had chosen to seek glory before Troy rather than to live ingloriously at home. There were many who felt as he did but had not his privilege of being certain of their fame. Many a lad was headstrong and went to war but won neither glory nor life. Even the shade of Achilles in Hades speaks strongly in the *Odyssey*. The humblest life on earth is better than to rule among the dead. Achilles is still rebellious in death and still interested in glory, the glory of his son Neoptolemus which Odysseus reports to him. Homer's souls, however, are notoriously fond of life; they wail for their lost strength as they leave the body. This is a point that Plato brings against Homer; he represents death as being bad for a soul. For Plato the soul is the rational man himself, and Plato is sure that death has no terrors for the rational man. In Homer the soul is not the man. In the words of *What Price Glory,* it is only a little doodle-bug inside the man that leads its own life after the man is dead. Homer's men do not fear death as much as they fear failure. They live dangerously because the real tragedy is to die without having lived nobly or gloriously. Homer himself feels the tragedy of beauty that must die. The note of pity is never long absent from his poem, and this note is his own ironical contribution. It is wholly dominant in the last book.[3]

Aristotle's statement that Homer keeps himself out of his poem is not strictly true. His characters are highly dramatic and are presented almost as objectively as Hemingway's or any modern author's, but they are also seen as living in a romantic past. The view that the gods have of them emphasizes their mortality and helplessness against fate. Homer's own comments on their mis-calculations and misapprehensions make the irony of life apparent. Prophecies and vivid anticipations of death add to the tragic mood of his characters. They face death without illusions and without subterfuge. They play the man to the end. There is inspiration in such a view of life. The essential thing in a man is his devotion to some ideal of courage or loyalty. Homer is obviously loyal to the truth that life is full of frustrations. He adjusts himself to life not by resignation or escape but by seeing in man's physical defeat his opportunity to assert his moral and spiritual independence. Homer invented tragedy, and, by communicating his vision of life through the medium of art, became a force in the lives of others. Tragedy is itself a triumph over despair, for it clears the mind of emotional weakness and enables it to pursue a rational goal. The more pity and terror there are in a picture of life, so long as the poet's vision is not distorted by pity or terror for himself, the greater the potential of his salutary shock.

The tragic sense of life is a sense of the tremendous power of ideals, a sense of something the worth of which transcends all defeat by circumstance. The best things in life are the flashes of joy and courage and insight that beckon and reward the individual, yet seem always to elude the attempt to imprison them in any institutionalized form of social security. Virtue and honesty and beauty are brightest in a setting of tragedy, and this is Homer's great discovery. He has consequently designed the *Iliad* in a pattern that emphasizes personality rather than a code of polite or moral behavior that succeeds because we think it should. There is morality and even poetic justice in the *Iliad,* but these are only a setting for the spell of tragedy. Homer transports the hearer or reader of his *Iliad* to a spiritual vantage point from which the individual is seen small and the issues of life plainly mapped. Such a vision does not remove us from the world; it gives us courage to seek the momentary bliss of high endeavor amid the suffering and cruelty of life as it is lived.

Others have presented a nobler or more rational ideal than that of any hero of Homer, yet the most intellectual or moral are precisely those who have found his simultaneous detachment and bitter struggle for the true glory an incentive to renewed dedication to their own chosen task. Witness Matthew Arnold, who says,

> Who prop, thou ask'st, in these bad days my mind?

and gives the answer: Homer, Sophocles, Epictetus.[4]

Quite recently, Simone Weil, who died in 1943 at the age of thirty-four, wrote a commentary on the *Iliad* that has the force of a trumpet call to religion. A translation was published in the monthly *Politics* and summarized in *Time* (December 17, 1945). Here Homer appears as the showman of force—force blind, unreflecting, and brutal, force that slays and enslaves the living, no less those who exercise force blindly than those who suffer from it. But there is retribution, for no one is secure in a world of violence. Nemesis operates geometrically and is the mainspring of the Greek concept of morality. Geometry in Europe is now confined to material things; for the Greeks and those who are Greeks at heart, virtue also has a geometrical quality. Men have a common lot. We are all slaves of destiny or circumstance or our own heedlessness, but we may escape the blind raging of force in ourselves by opening the inward eye, as Homer opened his own and others' eyes. He who sees life clear without illusions will realize that every human being is a fellow prisoner and sufferer. This vision of the harshness of destiny is his Gethsemane. He cannot save himself from physical suffering, but the grace of God may enable him to suffer without losing his inner integrity. He may learn to be skeptical of blind force, to oppose without hate and to pity without scorn.

Homer might say to Simone Weil as Agrippa to Paul: "At this rate it won't be long before you convert me into a Christian." Homer is, however, no preacher of one form of devotion to the exclusion of others. He is not one to preach that God is infinite and then to impose his own limitations on others in the name of God. There will not be many to find, like Bertrand Russell, a religion in tragedy, yet for some tragedy will be the most trustworthy revelation of life. They are those who find the secret of the universe in the discovery that there is no secret—at least no secret that will cure the frustration of spirit by matter and of ideals by realities.

> To think that two and two are four
> And neither five nor three,
> The heart of man has long been sore,
> And long 'tis like to be.

Homer is not systematic or consistent enough to be called a philosopher, nor subjective and enthusiastic enough to be called a religious
guide. Like Walt Whitman he believes in the institution of the
divine love of comrades, and in much more that is comforting and
beneficent besides. The poet is a channel of force, but force that
operates with the quiet conviction of beauty and goodness and
truth. Such things speak loudest to the secret worshiper.[5]

Homer's discovery of tragedy and the embodiment of his discovery in living art of exquisite beauty is comparable to the work
of Moses or Buddha or Confucius in its influence on human affairs.
The code of Moses is the law of a God of infinite power, a power
that he manifests in history. Disobedience to the code is sin that
must be expiated. Those who accept such a system will find arguments about the nature and will of God all-absorbing. Moham-
medanism also has its sacred scripture and its all-absorbing code of
law. Confucianism excludes the tragic; it is not concerned with
death, nor with life after death. Man, society, and the universe are
in harmony. Virtue is a common-sense adaptation to the routine
of life. It is so natural that anyone may have it without fanaticism
or bravado. Chinese martyrs die with serene fortitude and are com-
memorated without organized wailing or apocalyptic expectations.
Events are faithfully recorded in Chinese history for the benefit of
future statesmen, but no historian turns history into tragedy as
Thucydides does. For that, doubt must be a rival to faith; and the
Chinese, not having known the rise and fall of a civilization, had
no fundamental doubt of appearances. So too in their philosophy
the note of tragedy that animates Plato is lacking. The seen is not
sacrificed to the unseen.

Albert Schweitzer has taught us to perceive in Hindu religion
and philosophy both a life-denying and ascetic strain and a life-
asserting and ethical strain. Denial of life belongs to the old tradition of Hinduism and Buddhism. History is unimportant to such
a tradition, and life, being evil in itself, is nothing much to lose. The
acme of spiritual attainment is to become indifferent to life. The
heroes of Hindu epic and drama are above criticism, they have su-

pernatural powers and assistance, and the poet must always provide a happy ending. The effect is that of a lovely dream as compared with the enduring conflict and irremediable loss in tragedy, though art somehow makes loss bearable. In traditional Japanese tragedies the reflective element is supplied by Buddhism, or else the savage code of Bushido and vengeance is upheld. Individualism, personality, and a successful challenge to authority are not encouraged. Undoubtedly there is devotion to an ideal, but it is not a European ideal. In Europe there is an element of personal choice and insight in the great tales of devotion and loyalty. Much of this is due to the influence of Christianity, particularly when Christianity lays emphasis on the example of its founder, who rebelled against the dead letter of the law. It is impossible to separate the two strands of Greek and Christian influence. Yet Greek civilization is like the Chinese in its freedom from a sense of sin. The Greeks had, like the Japanese, rites of purification, but the purification was a genuine catharsis that removed all guilt. The Greeks glorified forethought, self-mastery, and freedom. Man's great source of weakness in Greek tragedy is ignorance of his own limitations. The limitations are ultimate and derive from the nature of things. No priest or institution can quite remove them or guarantee salvation. Man must take the consequences of his mistakes and abide the result without abasement.[6]

It must not be supposed that the *Iliad* became a tragedy because its material did not lend itself to the kind of treatment that belongs to the ethical and moral plot that we find in the *Odyssey*. The elements of the *Odyssey* are all present in the *Iliad;* they are merely overshadowed by the overwhelming interest of the tragic theme. There was war between Achaeans and Trojans, because Paris the Trojan had violated the laws of hospitality and offended his host Menelaus of Sparta by decamping with his wife Helen and much property besides. It never occurs to Homer to glorify either love that is illegal among men, or women who are irresponsible. Nor were the lovers, Paris and Helen, concerned to be honest about property; they took what they could. There can be no doubt that

Menelaus had been shamefully treated and that the offense against Zeus, guardian of the laws of hospitality, was great. Zeus would have had nothing to say if wife and property had been taken in warfare or an ordinary piratical raid. The Achaeans habitually captured women such as Briseïs and Chryseïs and made concubines of them; and certainly there was no international system of law to protect private property. Only when the rights of a host were infringed, did morality and religion rouse men and gods to the defense of justice. Agamemnon, brother of Menelaus, gathered a host including the leaders Nestor, Odysseus, the Ajaxes, Idomeneus, and Diomedes, as well as the youthful Achilles and his older friend Patroclus from the north. When the *Iliad* begins, they had been laying siege to Troy for almost ten years; for the whole city of Troy became involved in the crime of Paris when he brought Helen home and was welcomed with his ill-won treasure. His parents Priam and Hecuba, his generous brother Hector with Andromache his wife, and others, were equally threatened in the general downfall if Troy should be taken. It is taken for granted throughout the *Iliad* that Troy must inevitably fall because of the moral and religious issue involved. Still, there is enough doubt on both sides to lend interest to the struggle. In fact the poet seems to be chiefly concerned to glorify heroes. Yet he makes his sense of moral obligation clear in the words of Helen, when she points out that it is her evil destiny and that of Paris to lead an evil life that bards may sing of them and point a moral for posterity.[7]

Homer, however, is interested in more complicated problems of right and wrong. Agamemnon and Menelaus may have Zeus on their side as against the Trojans, but they are in the first book of the epic at once involved in conflict with Achilles. Agamemnon took from Achilles his concubine Briseïs. Now Achilles takes no interest in the right or wrong of the war. He fights for glory, not for justice. He is an individualist, and is not concerned to recover the property or wife of Menelaus. He is concerned to gain the honor and glory that had made him sacrifice the certainty of long life at home for the promise of glory in warfare. If one believes in social organization at all, it will be seen that Achilles cannot be countenanced. Zeus, however, does uphold Achilles against Agamemnon, not only because Thetis, the goddess-mother of Achilles, begs him to, but because Zeus is the responsible arbiter of the conflicting claims for recognition as king by divine right. Agamemnon's claim is based on descent, power, and wealth. He is a competent warrior, but unwise in council to the last degree. He foolishly insists on personal privilege when the welfare of the army is at stake, and so sacrifices his own position. He disregards the wise counsel of Nestor, is incapable of frank or generous action, and blames the gods, not his own folly, for his troubles. He acts alone from private motives of greed and gets into a blind alley from which he has to be rescued by his followers. He has the scepter of a king but the disposition of a tyrant. The sympathy of the hearer is enlisted on the side of Achilles, and Zeus's plan of forcing a surrender upon Agamemnon is carried out in Book 19 when Odysseus sees to it that the penalty is actually paid. The kingly man receives recognition from above, rather than the man who wields the scepter in unkingly fashion. This is a lesson in life, and it is made extremely lifelike. The Achilles who is glorified is a bloody man of war, but he is frank, generous, and passionate.[8]

There is equally a distinction of noble and base among the Trojans. Hector and Andromache and their infant son Astyanax form a model of family life. The marriage relationship is represented as one of courtesy and honor, and the babe fills both parents with pride and joy. If we did not see Hector taking leave of his family in Book 6, we should not be much interested in his defeat in Book 22. We are prepared to sympathize with the Trojans who watch with horror from the walls when Achilles overtakes Hector and slays him. The ransoming of Hector's body, the funeral ceremony, and the eloquent laments of Andromache, Hecuba, and Helen are the theme of the last book of the *Iliad,* and in it Homer gives Hector the victory at last over his slayer Achilles. The gods intervene in favor of the dead and require Achilles to give up the body for burial. The slain man fought for home and city and should receive the honors of war. The tragedy of the defeated absorbs us to the exclusion of any interest in the victor's triumph. Vengeance yields to pity. In the man's world where only glory counts, Achilles is superior, but if we throw defense of the home, and the tears of women and children, into the scale, the brutality of military glory is no longer preponderant. Hector is morally superior as a patriot. Achilles had left father and son defenseless at home to go to war, not in line of duty, but in pursuit of honor. Yet Homer actually upholds the military ideal through most of his poem. He undoubtedly glorifies the warrior in true Spartan fashion and recants only when the fighting is over. Hector will fight whether it means ruin for his family or not. He is tempted to sacrifice his personal honor by Andromache, who certainly is no Spartan and uses all her power as a good woman to sway her husband. She complains that his courage will slay him, and so it does, because courage goes hand in hand with honor. Tragedy is the defeat of a good man just because he is good. As soon as a hero's defects are emphasized, the tone of the plot will become moral, and we shall be able to chew the cud of poetic justice, sweet not bitter fancy.[9]

How does Homer go about making a moral hero of a man who fights for the wicked Trojans? Just as he has made Achilles dissociate himself from the righteous vengeance for Helen, so Homer is at pains to dissociate Hector from Paris. Hector scolds Paris in very bitter language and puts all the blame on him for the abduction of Helen. Pressure is put on Paris in Book 3 to fight Menelaus in person and so decide the war. It is natural that Helen, like a good Spartan, should approve of any risk that her consort takes in battle and should taunt him when he escapes death after defeat. In fact she agrees with Hector at all points. In this case the woman has an ideal of honor in spite of personal defection, and the man plays rather a woman's part. Paris, however, still prevails when it is a question of surrendering Helen to end the war. The Trojan assembly meets at the end of Book 7 to discuss the point. The victory of Paris is a moral defeat for the Trojans and spells their doom. It is not a moral defeat for Hector, because he is not present in the assembly. He had just had a grueling fight in single combat with Ajax, which is sufficient excuse for Hector. Homer's reason for the apparent lapse is, no doubt, that his tragic tale would have suffered if he had shown Hector as a party to the rape of Helen. Hector has to be insulated against our criticism. Homer could obviously have made a villain of him, as of Amphinomus in the *Odyssey*, who joined the crowd of suitors quite thoughtlessly, but heeded no warning and was slaughtered without pity.[10]

Paris and Helen, then, must point the moral, but in different ways. Paris is made a weak and womanly man at heart. Physically he can gallop to battle in shining armor, but his heart is not in the fight. He is most effective with the bow, not in hand-to-hand encounters with spear or sword. Even Odysseus makes no use of the bow at Troy; the only one who so lowers himself on the Achaean side is Teucer, and he, as his name indicates, was half Trojan. When Paris is discovered skulking at home by Hector during the battle, he is examining his collection of armor and enjoying its beauty. We are reminded of the taunt of the suitors when they see the supposed beggar Odysseus examining his old bow just before he shoots them down. They suggest that perhaps he is a collector and connoisseur of fine weapons. Paris is a living illustration of the gulf that sometimes separates aesthetics and ethics. Achilles, when he was not fighting, at least occupied himself by singing old songs full of the prowess of warriors. Paris is the favorite of Aphrodite, who was no warrior. She saves his life after his defeat by Menelaus and brings Helen to console him in daylight dalliance. Perhaps the worst trait of Paris is his frivolity and refusal to take the responsibility for what he does. His gifts are the gifts of Aphrodite and no man may refuse the gifts of the gods, so he declares. He repents for nothing and is not even stung to wrath or manliness by Helen's scorn. The real heroes in Homer have a sensitive conscience where honor is concerned. Achilles takes the responsibility when he fails in loyalty to his friend Patroclus. The weak and the half-witted blame the gods for their own troubles and credit the gods with any merit claimed by those whom they hate. Courtesy or diplomacy, of course, may require one who is friendly to blame the gods for the manifest misfortune or error of another.[11]

Helen is very different; she is made a tragic character. She does not except once lay the blame for her sin upon the gods, but we see for ourselves in Book 3 that she is a helpless victim of Aphrodite, who forces her to go to Paris though she loathes and despises him. Such resistance to divine commands is not normal in the *Iliad*. It reminds us of Aeneas in the *Aeneid* of Virgil when he is forced by divine command to leave Dido and is rebellious at heart. He, however, is rebelling against duty and would yield to temptation if left to himself. Homer makes his heroine moral, even if he has to depict Aphrodite as a devil. Helen gets neither moral satisfaction nor honor nor pleasure from her association with Paris. Her tragedy is a tragedy of fate; we may pity but not blame her. There are many in the epic who do blame her, but there were also many who cast her burden of guilt upon the gods. Homer had to rehabilitate her in the *Odyssey*. He makes Helen—but not vice—attractive. Only the intervention of Aphrodite could make such an effect possible.

Helen's loathing and contempt for Paris are in strong contrast with the mutual love and respect of Hector and Andromache, and there is no Astyanax for Paris to toss in his arms, nor can Paris pray that his son may be a better man than his father. Paris has no interest in the ultimate fate of Helen, nor she in his. They are the negation of a family and are obviously presented as foils, just as Clytemnestra is a foil to Penelope in the *Odyssey*. The contrast between right and wrong or between civilization and brute force is common not only in Greek literature but in art. We are reminded of the Vaphio cups, one of which shows the wild bull untamed, and the other the same bull domesticated and taking his place in the scheme of civilization. The Greeks, no more than the Chinese, ever doubted the value of civilization at this stage, though there were cynics who denounced it later. There is a black-figured vase that illustrates with some humor the difference between untamed nature and sacred matrimony. On one side is a satyr in a crude state of erotic excitement carrying to the woods a maiden in his arms. On the other a husband is greeting his wife with a chaste kiss; both husband and wife bear themselves with courtesy and dignity. Such contrasting pictures provide moral instruction without a conflict. A real conflict between Hector and Paris would have put Hector on the side of the Achaeans, so Homer avoids it. Actually both Hector and Paris are perfectly Greek in their family life or lack of it. If we look for the proper picture of a Trojan family with Oriental features, we find it in the domestic establishment of Priam, who had many wives and scores of sons and daughters. Zeus, too, is rather more Oriental than Greek in his family life, for he has many wives. Still, whether of Zeus or of Priam, only one wife is brought into focus. The emphatic treatment of Hera and Hecuba produces the effect of monogamy, but both seem somewhat soured by age and are shrill of voice when their advice is not asked. Old women are likely to become domestic tyrants when custom gives them complete authority in the home, so that it is considered indecent for men to intrude on their sphere. There are many realistic traits in the depiction of Zeus's home life, but for some things there are no doubt good theological reasons, as we shall see.[12]

It will be well to face here the question how far Homer's gods are independent of the author and how far he exercises control over them in the interest of fiction. There are two extremes in the estimate by critics of the function of Homer's gods. Walter Leaf maintained that they are an epiphenomenon, that the story would be the same if the gods were not brought in. In that view Aphrodite must be an impersonation of Helen's libido. That view is, I think, refuted by a consideration of the totally different effect that the presentation of Helen would produce if she were conceived as a free agent who could presumably leave Paris as soon as she found her position unsatisfactory. She might be repentant or brazen, but she could not at once loathe Paris and live with him if the way of escape were open. Alternatively, she might be presented as loving Paris and glorying in her love, but she could not be perfectly aware of the wrong she had done herself and other women and still remain with her lover. Many a bold deed in the *Iliad* is excused by the intervention of the gods. That this produces a cynical view of the divine power as acting delusively, immorally, and inconsiderately may not have occurred to Homer; it did occur to later critics. For him it was necessary, in order not to mislead his hearers.[18]

In Book 12, Hector can disregard an omen because he has just received a personal message from Zeus through Iris, in which he has been assured of continuing his victorious pursuit until the ships are reached and the sun goes down, an exact statement of what happens. So, in Book 24, Priam goes to Achilles in spite of Hecuba's protests, because Iris has similarly brought him a message from Zeus assuring him of safety and success in securing the body of Hector. In this case he appeals to Zeus for an omen from birds and is granted this confirmation. Homer has no intention of incurring criticism as encouraging men to disregard omens or common sense. If his hearers get a message from Iris in person, well and good; if not, they have no sanction to act foolishly. Elsewhere Iris takes human shape, or Zeus sends a deceptive dream, as to Agamemnon in Book 2. Athena encourages Pandarus to break the truce in Book 4 in order to put the Trojans in the wrong and to prevent their escape from destruction by making a settlement with the Achaeans. Here Homer makes treachery less hideous by linking it with the divine plan. The gods help Homer with his plot, his characterization, his morality, and with particular scenes. In Book 24 only a miracle could preserve the body of Hector after its long maltreatment by Achilles, and only the action of Thetis, Iris, and Hermes directed by the council of the gods could contrive a secret meeting between Priam and Achilles. Without their aid Homer's best scene would be ruined.

The other extreme is represented by Dietrich Mülder, who maintains that divine action in Homer is always machinery and not nature, that the gods help Homer with his composition, but thereby distort his picture of life. According to Herodotus, knowledge of the appellations, shapes, and functions of the gods, as well as their descent and relationships, appeared first in poetic form in the work of Homer and Hesiod in the ninth century. Now it is clear that a poet is pretty much obliged to present his deities in anthropomorphic roles with anthropomorphic passions if he is to give them a place in his narrative at all. The action of the gods in the *Iliad* is a product of Homer's imagination. Nevertheless he was working in this field as elsewhere with material that had to be shaped to his purpose. His gods must not be altogether unfamiliar nor too inconsistent with religious beliefs and the facts of life. It will be enough for us to see what basis in real life there is for his picture of the gods without inquiring too narrowly into origins.[14]

We note first that the gods, besides being personalized with whims and attitudes of their own, often realistically or satirically colored, spring from analysis of the three kinds of fact with which man is confronted: physical, social, and personal or temperamental. To some extent the gods are forces in nature; to some extent they are projections of the economic or political divisions of society; and to some extent they represent passions or drives in the individual.

As an element in nature Hephaestus is fire. As such he conquers water in the person of the river Scamander, when the river in a rage overflows its banks and would overwhelm Achilles. As a member of society he represents the smiths who work with fire, and he is an ideal artist. Since among those who live on a subsistence level, as in China today, the lame are forced to become smiths since they cannot earn a living at other work, the divine smith will be lame like his followers. The divine smith was a glorification of his calling and a bond of unity among those who pursued it. The story that Hephaestus was lamed when Zeus hurled him from heaven to earth is explained by the fact that it was invented to explain—the lameness of the smith-god. No doubt the familiar notion that stars which fall from heaven are rebellious angels or jinns has something to do with the tale, which is a myth. The family scene in which Hephaestus appears on Olympus, however, when he enlivens the banquet by substituting for Hebe or Ganymede as cupbearer, is presumably fiction, though I am not prepared to maintain absolutely that there may not have been somewhere, sometime, a saturnalian rite in which roles were reversed for the enhancement of mirth in this as in other respects.[15]

Apollo is lord of song, patron of bards, soothsayers, and medicine men. No doubt incantation was an important part of the treatment of disease, and the cant of soothsayers at least went as far as the reciting of prophetic verses in historic times. So far as religion is represented on Olympus, Apollo is its representative; art normally begins as an adjunct of religion, and gradually moves into the sphere of morality or sheer entertainment. As far as words and music are the medium of art, Apollo is also the representative of art; note, however, that when the medium of art is metal, it is more naturally represented by Hephaestus. In Homer, Apollo is not specifically spoken of as the patron of physicians, but he is quite clearly the god of plague, with power to stay as well as to send. It is as a slayer of men with the invisible arrows of pestilence that he is armed with the bow. Homer in Book 1 of the *Iliad* gives a vivid description of a plague that from our point of view need not be supernatural. In this case the equally vivid picture of Apollo hearing the prayer of his medicine man Chryses and swooping down from Olympus to smite the Achaeans with unseen arrows seems to us mere poetical padding, what the Greeks called *onkos*. The connection between the prayer of the medicine man and the plague would, however, probably seem natural to Homer's audience. It forms part of a pattern of belief that was independent of Homer and to that extent objective. Apollo has a sister Artemis who also bears a bow and causes the death of women by her unseen shafts. Her bow is also used, however, in hunting animals, so that she may represent the realm of wild nature. Apollo's place in nature is not very clear.

Dionysus and Demeter, who are barely mentioned in Homer, are themselves wine and grain as well as the center of religious rites and beliefs that belong to an agricultural tradition. It did not suit Homer, however, to complicate his analysis by including them.

Hermes, who is a personified boundary post, or cairn, and a tomb-stone, is patron of those who go abroad or to and from the underworld: ghosts, thieves, merchants, diplomats, and particu-larly heralds. He does the work of a herald in Book 24 of the *Iliad*, escorting Priam through the enemy lines, though he steals through instead of going openly. When Zeus wishes to communicate with men in the *Iliad*, he employs Iris, the personified rainbow, not Hermes; but Hermes alone is employed in the *Odyssey*. For orders to Achilles from the gods, Thetis, his mother, the sea nymph, does service appropriately. Presumably she began as a wraith of mist rising from the sea at eventide. She also carries the pleas of Achilles to Zeus and Hephaestus. One who looks for allegory in the *Iliad* can find it in her three missions. The first time she appears, she is summoned by her son; his prayer for the defeat of Agamemnon is answered with disastrous results for himself when his friend Pa-troclus is slain. The second time, she comes of her own accord when his cry of anguish is heard; his need of armor for doing his own work of vengeance is met when she brings him the divine panoply fashioned by Hephaestus. The third mission is the one laid upon her by the gods to inform Achilles that his shocking treatment of the corpse of Hector offends them. We have come full circle to the point where man obeys the gods instead of seeking to impose his will on them. The allegory no doubt arises more or less auto-matically from Homer's tragic and moral pattern, but he had the kind of imagination to accentuate his doctrine by such suggestive contrasts presented without comment.[16]

There are two gods in Homer who are treated with little respect, Ares, the personification of lust for battle, and Aphrodite, the per-sonification of sex relations unsanctioned by ceremony. Ares is the Thracian who fights without caring on which side he operates; nor does Aphrodite care by whose side she lies in bed. They repre-sent an element in social groupings, no doubt, as well as an element in human nature. Anything respectable or civilized in war and sex is, however, not left to them by the poet. Hera is both war goddess and patroness of marriage. In the divine family she is *mater fa-*

milias and wife of Zeus, though she does not hesitate to use the cestus of Aphrodite when she needs to influence her husband. She and Athena are perhaps both personifications of the city, which explains their interest in war. Greek cities were feminine. As city goddess Athena is even worshiped by the Trojans, just as Apollo is patron of the Achaean seer Calchas, although Apollo as a fictitious person is fighting for Troy. Hera and Athena are both inspired by an unexplained hate for Troy. In the myth, to which there is only one reference in Homer, their enmity was due to the preference of Paris for Aphrodite when the three goddesses asked him to rate their charms. The virgin Athena appears far above such interest in beauty, as Homer depicts her. She is patron of Achilles when he needs wisdom or help in battle. She shows signs of becoming the embodiment of united force and wisdom that she was later as symbol of the Greek city-state. She was also patroness of women's arts. The best of women engaged in spinning and weaving and embroidery, though the best of men were not smiths or heralds. Hence Athena, though a patroness of handiwork, is more than a cut above Hephaestus and Hermes.[17]

The great nature gods in Homer are Zeus and Poseidon and Hades, who divide air, sea, and earth among them. Hades as lord of the underworld could hardly appear on Olympus, but Poseidon plays his part in battle and is almost a sea-level Zeus. He causes seismic waves on land as well as ordinary waves at sea. Zeus is lord of the weather, wielding the thunderbolt and punishing sinners. As watcher over men in certain relationships he maintains a moral code that is more than local or political and shows a sense of responsibility that sets him apart. Since he is patron of kings, who hold their office by his favor and with his support, one who opposes a king should consider carefully whether Zeus will be against him. The dispute between Agamemnon and Achilles in Book 1 has its theological development. The former is a representative of law and order with a scepter which derives by recorded pedigree from Zeus. Achilles points out, with some corroborative detail, that Agamemnon lacks the qualities of leadership that kingship implies. He is too greedy and drunken to be a fount of honor. He is too short-sighted to lead a campaign to victory. Generosity is required in a king if he is to inspire his followers with the confidence that is needed. Homer points the contrast between the generous but irascible Achilles and the mean and stupid Agamemnon more than once. When appeal is made to Zeus, he has good reason to prefer the half-divine Achilles even though it means temporary victory for the Trojans. Thus began the European tradition that kings may not be absolute, that they too must obey the code. As the Chinese put it, the way of heaven is not unchanging; but in the Chinese system emphasis is laid on the personal and family morality of the ruler more than on the kingly qualities that are important to Zeus. Only an unconquered country like Japan could have found the criterion of legitimacy in descent, even descent from the sun goddess. Homer's king must have the qualities of leadership. Agamemnon speaks slightingly of his wife Clytemnestra, and that is another indication of his stupidity. It is his stupidity in dealing with men and affairs of state that brings about his downfall in the *Iliad*.[18]

The gods in Homer are thus in the main more than machinery. They represent to some extent the forces of nature that may aid or thwart men. They represent also forces that operate in social organization and a kind of hierarchy of classes and functions. Such forces are in general philanthropic and enable society to persist with benefits to all, but the noble or saintly individual may find himself in conflict with society. The gods also represent to some extent the forces that operate in the activity of an individual—his natural or acquired traits and skills, his good or bad luck, and the force that sets itself against him when he becomes unrealistically self-confident, that which begrudges him the complete fulfillment of his imagined bliss. The gods may on occasion warn, encourage, or guide the individual, but that is a special favor. In general, men must use technique or common sense or a conviction of rightness to decide for themselves what to do. Transgression of divine law may bring destruction, and disobedience to the command of a god

is fatal folly. Still Homer's characters are realistically treated as
men against fate. The gods, then, in Homer provide means for a
commentary on and analysis of the forces with which men have
to deal. Fate is ultimate, but the gods normally uphold and ad-
minister the decrees of fate. Individual gods are also upholders of
particular classes or individuals for whom they have a special
affinity.

Yet the gods in general may be blamed for begrudging man the
kind of happiness that they themselves enjoy and for the limitations that are imposed on man. At the same time, their anger must
not be provoked by disobedience. Thus the favor of the gods is
precarious, and death with unhappiness is the common lot. Glory
is the reward for military prowess, which in the best characters is
combined with generosity and a sensitive code of honor that includes loyalty to comrades, friends, and city. Homer also presents
an ideal picture of married love and of the love of a soldier for his
comrade. In both cases emphasis is laid on an honorable relationship which does not deny morality, though the warmth of feeling
depicted lends a passionate quality to sentiments of love and
friendship. Homer's scale of values, which is his practical philosophy, is implicit in the action of his main characters. In their great
moments his characters seem to act from inner compulsion and
without pressure or assistance from the gods. The quality of his
men is apparent in their acts, and in their personalities it is the
inner active forces which Homer reveals that make them interesting. Since we are interested in them, their tragedy is our tragedy;
and what happens to them impresses more than what they are,
though both elements are involved. No doubt this is what Aristotle
had in mind when he put plot, or action and consequences, above
character as a distinctive mark of tragedy. The heroes Hector and
Achilles are in a sense rewarded by death, for their ignoble foils,
Paris and Agamemnon, are punished by disgrace and oblivion.
They are made to seem dull and uninteresting. They have no un-
explored possibilities or possible great moments.[19]

Aristotle has something to say in the *Poetics* of double plots, but the double plot of the *Iliad* is not in his mind. He refers to stories in which there is a villain as well as a hero, so that the villain may come to grief at the same time that the hero is victorious. In a tragic plot there may be a villain who brings the hero to grief and perishes himself. Aristotle excludes the possibility of a triumphant villain, as too offensive to be portrayed. We think at once of *Othello* and of Iago as an example. In the *Iliad,* however, there are two heroes, Hector and Achilles, who meet in combat in Book 22. Achilles slays Hector, but there is no finality in his triumph, for no vengeance on Hector can bring back the dead Patroclus. Achilles' tragedy is the loss of his illusions. He had lost his honor in surviving Patroclus. That to him was worse than death, and no reconciliation of his quarrel with his fate was now possible. Whether or not the future is determined, the past is certainly irrevocable. The tragedy of Achilles was complete in Book 18 of the *Iliad* when he learned of the death of Patroclus. He might have fought beside his friend, but had not done so because he was thinking of glory and honor and would not fight before Agamemnon had apologized. His pride was his downfall, and the greater blow to his pride, when his friend was lost, was his tragedy.[20]

In this moment there was for Achilles a tragic recognition of the sort that we may call psychological. In the Aristotelian recognition scene there is a case of mistaken identity that is cleared up. Sometimes this is accompanied by a reversal of fortune when a character hitherto hated receives love, or one hitherto prosperous is brought to ruin. Aristotle does not admit of a recognition or reversal in the plot of the *Iliad,* for he classifies it as simple, and he defines the simple plot as one that has neither recognition nor reversal. The truth is that his association of tragedy with physical suffering and death, rather than with the loss of an illusion or the defeat of an ideal, blinds him to the force of psychological recognition and reversal. It is only as tragedy is universal, inextricably interwoven with life, that it affects us deeply. Men's greatest personal tragedies, for instance separation from a loved one by leprosy or death, do not lend themselves effectively to the purpose of art.

Such things are accidental, not universal. When Achilles, half god that he is, discovers that by an easily avoidable miscalculation he has sinned against his own personal code, that is universal, because sooner or later every man discovers that he is not the man he would like to be. This involves at the same time the discovery that the thing to which he attached importance at the moment of his mistake was not really so important as something else. Such shifts in perspective in the field of values are not common in Greek fiction; they must be attributed to genius in the author rather than to the rules of art. But just as in the *Odyssey* Homer uses the means available to him to concentrate on the great psychological moment that reveals the depth of Penelope's feeling, so in the *Iliad* he keeps the psychological pattern clear for both his heroes. The tragedy of Achilles does not end his career, but diverts his wrath from Agamemnon to Hector. Hector's tragedy arrives at the moment of decision, when his sense of honor requires him to stand and die outside the walls of Troy rather than be false to his promise to face Achilles. The double tragedy then leads to the climax of pity in the meeting of Priam and Achilles.[21]

Let us briefly note, then, how Homer accents certain points in his story in order to keep the moral and psychological development clear in the double tragedy of Hector and Achilles. The case of Hector is the simplest. In Book 3 he denounces the vanity and folly of Paris. In Book 6 he shows his quality by refusing all invitations to take his ease while others fight and by rejecting even the strong appeal of his wife, reinforced by the presence of his infant son. The two aspects of honor—fear of disgrace and unwillingness to lose his own self-respect—are his strongest motive, yet he sees clearly the unhappiness that his death will bring for his wife and child. He has already faced the tragic truth about life that choice is always between two evils, not between evil and good. He chooses honor, no matter what the consequences; and the difficulty of his choice is the greater because he is so keenly aware of the evil that lies in the scale of his choice. In Book 7 he fights indecisively with Ajax, and Homer thereby diverts our attention from the fact of his

absence from the assembly of the Trojans when all might have
been saved by a surrender to the Achaeans of Helen and the stolen
property. In Book 12 and again in Book 18 he is advised by Polydamas in the field to be less bold. In the first case Polydamas points
to an eagle that has had to loose its hold on a serpent and urges that
it is ominous. Hector makes the stirring reply: "One omen is best,
to fight for our fatherland," and threatens death to anyone who
slacks in the assault on the Greek camp. Homer has insulated him
against criticism by bringing him a message from Zeus, delivered
by Iris, in which he was promised success for that day alone. Contrast the second occasion, when it is no omen, but a rational deduction from the shouting of Achilles over the trench, to which Polydamas points. This time the rashness of Hector is unmistakable, for
he offers to face Achilles if the Trojans in their exposed position
are attacked on the morning of the next day. When on the next
day large numbers of the Trojans have been slaughtered, Hector
is aware of his mistake. There are three possibilities: to retire within
the walls and suffer disgrace, to supplicate the mercy of Achilles,
and to fight. The motives and the decision of Hector are made
transparently clear in a soliloquy. In the fight that ensues, Homer
treats Hector more as an object of pity than as a stalwart fighter.
Apollo helps him to flee, but no god aids him in battle; in fact,
Athena deludes and thwarts him. Whether we approve or not,
we must admit that Homer has insured his object of making
Hector's death pitiful. A hero who fights on equal terms and loses
the match is above pity. There is no justice for Hector or for those
who love him. War is certainly not glorified in such a combat.
Sheer brutality and injustice prepare us for the final scenes of
Book 24.[22]

Achilles is a more complicated character as presented by Homer.
He is a man of wrath, but also a man of equally strong love. His
wrath keeps him from battle until his love for Patroclus is brought
into play. His wrath at the slayer of Patroclus enables him to forget
in action his abasement, so that we still see him as a man of wrath
until Hector is disposed of. He has, however, lost his interest in

glory as a prime motive. It is the gods—that is, Homer—who make him relinquish his wrath against Hector. He is now left with no ruling passion that has not been thwarted. Presumably he will remain generous, honest, and irascible, but he will be no longer the demigod unreconciled to life on human terms. He had had his first experience of failure. Psychological development is confined in Greek heroes to the very young. The old in Greek story have fixed habits and an integrated view of life.[28]

Achilles in the first book of the *Iliad* appears from the start as a man who detests craft and greed. He has a high standard for kings and a sense of responsibility. Homer puts Agamemnon in the wrong by making him act alone without the approval of council or people. "He alone took her away" is the constant plaint of Achilles when he refers to his lost Briseïs. He is also angered by Agamemnon's shirking of responsibility. Agamemnon angers Apollo the plague-bringer by refusing to give up the captive Chryseïs. When Achilles calls an assembly, he is insulated from criticism, because, Homer tells us, his orders came from Athena. Similarly the suggestion comes from Thetis in Book 19. Achilles challenges the king more openly when he guarantees the seer's safety, and when the seer has demanded the surrender of Chryseïs, he openly rebukes Agamemnon for proposing to compensate himself at someone else's expense for his loss. At last the king rancorously picks Achilles himself as the man to suffer, and Achilles, if he had acted in character, would have slain him on the spot. Homer has good reason to call on a mechanical god. Except for the appearance of Athena to restrain Achilles, the story would have ended then and there. Only here does Homer require the intervention of a god in a debate; the exception illustrates his plan. Achilles obeys Athena at once and refrains from battle. In Book 9, when Agamemnon is forced to offer restitution, we see the real Achilles. He has done as Athena said, but not for the motives that she suggested, for she had pointed out how much property Agamemnon would have to pay. In Book 9, where no gods intervene, Agamemnon offers full restitution in property, but Achilles is not satisfied. He

could not bring himself to coöperate with a king who still showed
no repentance, and with comrades who had left him alone to support the common cause. Nestor knew the need of the right words
that should have accompanied the gifts. Achilles points out that
property is no compensation to a man for the sacrifice of life. Now
Thetis is brought in, not with aid or advice, but to provide her son
with knowledge of his fate.[24]

Achilles' fate was not defined in simple terms like Helen's. She
had no choice but to be a byword for adultery in after ages. Achilles' fate is of the sort that permits choice. He is offered alternatives,
each with the concomitant consequence that it entails. In a recently
published Sumerian poem the hero Gilgamesh is told:

> Enlil, the great mountain, the father of the gods
> Has destined thy fate, O Gilgamesh, for kingship;
> For eternal life he has not destined it.

The moralist will be inclined to stress the importance of choice and
to make his hero choose his own life. Plato in the vision of Er in
Republic 10 makes his souls choose their own fate. The choices of
Heracles and Paris are familiar in Greek, as is the choice of Solomon in the Old Testament. In the Greek choices the alternatives
are incompatible, so that something must be at the same time for-
gone. Achilles, to obtain glory, must sacrifice his hope of long life.
He is indignant that he should be supposed capable of caring for
possessions in comparison with honor, when he has indicated so
clearly that he values honor more than life itself. Obviously he
values it more than the punishment of Troy. In any case, his own
consort Briseïs is reft from him, and his nearest duty is to exact
vengeance on her despoiler. Of course, his claim to her as a captive
in war needed no scrutiny. We see, then, when Achilles is not held
in leash by Athena, what his real quality is, and how different he
is from the crafty Odysseus.[25]

In Book 18, when the news of Patroclus' death is brought to
Achilles, we discover that the love of glory is less for him than the
love of his comrade. In seeking glory he had lost his comrade, as his

mother had warned him that he would some day. Foreknowledge
is as unhelpful here as elsewhere in Greek literature. The emotional
turmoil in Achilles' mind is well depicted, though not in a soliloquy. Antilochus holds his hands as he lies in the dust for fear that
he will slay himself. Only the thought of vengeance on Hector
enables him to forget his woe. Thetis' prophecy that he will not
live long after Hector dies does not move him. His refusal to consider the consequences to himself is cited by Socrates to justify his
own refusal to yield to the threat of death. Plato in regard to Dion,
and Demosthenes after Chaeronea, are evidently inspired by the
same model. High ideals are important; never mind consequences.
Thus, as Dante says, love made Achilles fight again. Homer is very
careful not to let the love of Briseïs play an overt part in the plot.
To have allowed Achilles to betray any passion for her would have
spoiled Homer's clean-cut picture of Achilles as a man's man.
Briseïs was allowed only the importance of a piece of property. It
is evident that Achilles equally disregards the welfare of his son
and that of his father, for whom he later weeps in Book 24. The
psychological crisis forces Achilles to think only of Hector and
Patroclus from now on. He makes his peace with Agamemnon in
Book 19, even though the king still makes but a lame, though long-
winded, apology and craftily seeks to postpone the surrender of
the promised gifts. Achilles declares that the wrong done him was
an act of God, and shows indifference to the gifts as before. It is
Odysseus who exacts the uttermost farthing, that Agamemnon
may learn his lesson and not behave so again. Achilles' victory is
complete, as Athena had prophesied, and more complete than she
had estimated.[26]

Achilles had, to be sure, made a mistake, one that was more
galling because it might easily have been avoided; he had lost his
friend in battle because he had for once consented to craft and had
dressed Patroclus in his own armor. Homer never raises the question why, if the armor of Achilles fitted Patroclus, the armor of
Patroclus would not later fit Achilles. That would spoil the story.
The question whether his mistake was merely a miscalculation or

also a sin hardly arises in Greek. Achilles had done the wrong thing; he felt inferior because of the result. To mean well was not enough for Achilles in such a case. His repentance is lifelike, for we all regret the miscalculation that might easily have been avoided more than the besetting sin that we have to learn to live with because we cannot cure ourselves. Achilles curses strife and renounces his anger against Agamemnon, but he feels even greater anger against Hector. He is still *iratus Achilles.*

Homer subtly indicates the powerful feeling of Achilles in two places. Priam's son Lycaon makes a long plea for mercy but makes the mistake of pointing out that he is not own brother to Hector. Immediately on hearing the name of Hector, Achilles turns ruthless and slays his defenseless suppliant. Again, when Hector has been slain and the Trojans are so dazed that the city might be captured, Achilles summons the Achaeans to make an assault on the city, but suddenly checks himself as he remembers Patroclus lying unburied. Nothing can make him forget his friend; his love is stronger than death. This is psychology; Athena need not intervene. No thought of glory will ever tempt Achilles again to forget his friend.[27]

The double tragedy of Achilles and Hector is, I believe, unique in Greek literature. Elsewhere we find hero against villain or man against fate, but not hero against hero. It is only because Hector and Achilles appeal to us, each in his own way, as an ideal man that Homer can bring about the reconciliation in the last book of the *Iliad* and so enable us to see life in a different perspective. Achilles was ideal as a conqueror and warrior; on the battlefield we do not care whether a man is a good husband or a good fellow; what we need is a good fighter. Hector is ideal as a defender of the weaker side. We pity his wife and child, and in the scene of his defeat we pity *him*. Achilles is too ruthless and too inconsiderate. Hector no doubt would have liked to do to Achilles what Achilles actually does to him, but no golden rule of doing to others what we expect them to do to us is adequate here. It is not only the conduct of Achilles that is revolting, but the whole system

which he represents. No doubt there was an age when bards glorified naked force, but Homer and his audience demanded a place
for the concerns of civilized life. From the beginning of his poem
Homer had introduced from time to time a strong sense of the
sorrow of the conquered. He notes for instance, when Briseïs leads
the lament for Patroclus, that the wailing of the chorus was for
Patroclus only in outward seeming. Each of the women of the
chorus was wailing for private woes of her own.[28]

The tone of pity in Book 24 is accordingly nothing strange. The
only strange thing is to find Achilles in a mood of pity. He does
not express regret for what he has done, nor adopt a new code.
The change is not represented as psychological and must accordingly be brought about by divine intervention. When Achilles'
love for Patroclus made him renounce his wrath against Agamemnon, Homer depicted that change as psychological. In Book 24
as in Book 1, Achilles must appear out of character. If he had repented of his ruthless acts, he would have seemed somehow weak
like Orestes in the *Electra* of Euripides. Thanks to the gods, he
can be merciful without seeming less ruthless or heroic. He can
also avoid the charge that he was interested in ransom for the
sake of its value. He must not appear as a man who considers property or financial gain as important here any more than he did in
the beginning. Furthermore, by bringing in the three gods that
are required Homer has kept the interview between Priam and
Achilles intimate. He could not picture Agamemnon in such a
scene—nor can we. The moral weight of Homer's appeal to pity
is also considerably reinforced by the unanimous intervention of
the council of gods. The *Iliad* maintains its unity to the end and
prepares the way for the *Odyssey*.[29]

Just as we find Homer in the Odyssey making his last book flat
in order not to let interest in battle overshadow the emphasis on
Penelope and her psychology, so in the *Iliad* he has deliberately
removed all satisfaction from the victory of Achilles over Hector
in order to prepare us for the great scene of the last book in which
Priam and Achilles weep together. Priam weeps for his son, and

Achilles for the father whom he had deserted in his old age. Priam forces himself to kiss the hand that slew Hector; and Achilles yields for ransom the body of the man who slew Patroclus. Thus Homer made strong the sense of common humanity and made weak the lust to kill merely because killing and destruction are glorious. The *Iliad* preaches glory, loyalty to a loved one, and, last of all, pity; but the greatest of these is pity.

III
The Social Consciousness
of Aeschylus

THERE IS a gap of at least two centuries between
Homer and Aeschylus. With Aeschylus we are within the frame
of recorded history. He helped to make history at Marathon, as
he boasted in his epitaph; and his account of the struggle at Salamis
in his *Persians* is our most trustworthy historical source for the battle that turned the tide against Xerxes in 480 B.C. He did not boast
of his tragedies, of which there were at least sixty, for he had dedicated them to time. They continued to be performed by special
regulation at Athens after his death. Actually he was, more than
any one man after Homer, the inventor of tragedy, since he first
gave the actors more to say than the chorus and increased their
number. The grandeur of story and diction that Aristotle also requires for tragedy can be seen in his seven extant plays.

The influence of Homer on tragedy is often underestimated. The
appearance of gods, whether at beginning or end, or as actors in
a play, needs no other explanation than Homer's use of the gods
as symbols or as machinery. Even the choruses in tragedy have
their counterparts in Homer. Consider what Aeschylus has done
in recasting the story of Achilles from the *Iliad*. In the three plays
of his trilogy he used choruses of Myrmidons, Nereids, and Phrygi-
ans, that is, Trojans. The Myrmidons do not speak, but are described collectively, in Homer. Aeschylus had only to make them
vocal and to let them be present when the death of Patroclus was
reported. So with the Nereids; they accompany Thetis as a wailing chorus when she goes to help her son. They have no words,
though their names are given. Aeschylus presumably kept them

on the scene until Hector was slain. The Trojans do not appear at all in the scene of the ransoming of Hector's body in the last book of the *Iliad;* they mourn for the dead when the body is brought home to Troy. Aeschylus merely made them participate in the scene of supplication as well as in the mourning, as far as we can guess. Aeschylus is said to have declared that his tragedies were large cuts taken from Homer's mighty dinners. It will be seen that his Achillean trilogy must have omitted approximately the first half of the *Iliad,* presumably taking the quarrel with Agamemnon for granted and concentrating on the crises of Achilles' emotional experience. It is clear that even the three plays of a trilogy could present only concentrated moments and cross sections of the *Iliad.* The Homeric background of heroic myth and Homer's accounts of the gods are a presupposition of all tragedy, though the dramatists used much material that ranged beyond the generations with which Homer dealt. Their material might come from any source, but tragedies were always comparable to cross sections or episodes of heroic story as compared with the whole view of man and god that Homer provided in his epics. He was a purveyor of God's plenty. Still, the total volume of Aeschylus' ninety plays must have far exceeded that of *Iliad* and *Odyssey* combined. Even if we assume that a quarter of them were satyr dramas and hence hardly serious enough to be considered in an estimate of his contribution to great literature, there is enough in what remains to make us cautious in gauging the variety and breadth of his achievement. The seven plays that we have are enough to indicate his main interests, something of his development, and the extraordinary power of his imagination.

In Aeschylus there is an immediacy of emotional appeal and moral tension that the epic hardly equals in its most intense moments. Aeschylus is not detached and does not look at life ironically. The issues that are fought out in his dramas are at the heart of moral and political life, and he mingles this essential realism with strange gods and embodiments of mysterious forces in such a way that, if we do not appreciate their allegorical and symbolic significance, we may miss the terrific impact of his creative power. He seems to go deeper than Homer because he emphasizes forces that operate below the surface in human life. He does not go quite so far as the Sanskrit drama of Bhasa in which the anger of a living person appears embodied on the stage and executes vengeance. The belief that an emotion or fleeting wish may be irrevocable and have fatal consequences still persists in modern Japan and no doubt elsewhere within the orbit of Hindu influence. The spoken curse that operates during the lifetime of the speaker appears in the *Iliad* in the story of Phoenix, but Homer does not admit such motives in the history of his main characters. Seers and oracles must be used as sources of information, but even they are disregarded by Homer's leading characters. Occult forces become important in Homer only when they receive the sanction of the gods. The gods are not disregarded by his heroes. Even the rights of the dead Hector are upheld by the Olympians. Aeschylus represents the anger or the blood or the curse of a dead man as having in itself a power to work its will by occult influence on the living. In this Aeschylus does not go much beyond the conceptions that are embodied in the legislation of Athens, and in the *Laws* of Plato for that matter. Magical practices and curses were negligible to Plato and Aeschylus both; the violation of some principle of duty or conscience, however, might bring doom the more surely because of the curse or wrath or unavenged blood of the dead victim. The occult forces in Aeschylus are somehow instruments of justice.[1]

Aeschylus differs from Homer in his more serious attitude toward the gods and in his purely nonmechanical use of them. In his *Suppliants* the women who seek a refuge appeal to the gods, but the gods are not seen as actors in the play to insure the success of the suppliant as they are when Priam goes as suppliant to Achilles. The *Persians* tells the story of the humiliation of a great king, but we do not see Zeus in person nodding assent to an appeal against him. Human characters interpret the attitude of the gods and no doubt speak the poet's mind, but the effect is much

[1] For notes to chapter iii see pages 281–284.

more religious than if the gods were brought upon the stage. In the *Seven against Thebes* we find a doomed hero defending his city like Hector, but the god who dooms him works unseen. In the *Prometheus* the gods are used as counterparts of human types, but they are used for propaganda against tyranny and against stupidity, not for entertainment. In the *Eumenides* Apollo and Athena represent institutions which are active and to some extent competing forces in human life, religion which deals with sin, and the state which deals more successfully with crime. Aeschylus' slices of life give us Homeric situations slightly changed but much more energetically presented, perhaps partly because in drama we apprehend conflicts directly, but also because Aeschylus was interested in the establishment and maintenance of a particular way of life in a particular setting. He was not merely an educator, but a propagandist in the best sense of the word. He displays a missionary fervor for civilization, Hellenism, and the Athenian democracy. His pictures of the past are designed to reinforce his interpretation of the present and his dynamic interest in the wave of the future. It may or may not be possible to discover from his account exactly what happened in the early development of Greece, or even what conflicting theories were at work; we *can* discover what Aeschylus considered important in his own day and why.

In Homer it is the poet, not the characters, who knows what the gods on Olympus are planning. In Aeschylus we are mostly dependent for our view of the gods on statements made by individual characters or by the chorus in its odes. Since the chorus itself takes part in the action as a character, or even a group of characters, we must be wary of supposing at any time that they are not speaking in character, but as ideal observers or as a mouthpiece of the poet. Undoubtedly Aeschylus used the chorus to express his own philosophy or theology, but he is not in the position of Pindar, whose singers were not participants in a drama. Aeschylus, his actors, and his chorus were, when performing a tragedy, taking part in a religious exercise, for tragedy was performed for the honor and pleasure of Dionysus. We need not doubt that the tragic chorus derives from a religious dance of ecstatic worshipers of the wine god. It might be supposed to represent Nietzsche's Dionysiac as opposed to the Apollonian element in life and art. The worship of Dionysus celebrated the renewal of life and was for the worshiper a source of new life and strength. As a matter of fact, however, Aeschylus does not so much as mention Dionysus in his extant plays, and the one fragment that refers to him comes from a trilogy the subject of which was the triumph of Dionysus. Aeschylus is far less Dionysiac than Homer if we look for mention of Dionysus in his choral odes.

Aeschylus makes bold use of spectacular devices to produce his effects. He was concerned to invent new measures for the dance and is said to have instructed the chorus himself. Even the chief actor's part in the *Seven against Thebes* is said to have been danced. When one considers that Oriental drama, particularly the Chinese, is largely music and dancing, and that in many scenes spoken words are either absent or quite unimportant, it is clear enough that we no longer have the visual material that is essential to the understanding of many scenes of Aeschylus; nor can we form any notion of the effect produced by his musical accompaniments. We can see that he was fond of striking effects and note also his fondness for Oriental or barbaric costumes and gestures. In the *Choephoroe* there is one chorus whose words render the sound of the beating of breasts in an Oriental lament; translators commonly neglect this element so marked in the original.[2]

The sense of worship is strong in many odes. Aristophanes represents Aeschylus in the *Frogs* as deriving his inspiration from Demeter, whose mysteries were celebrated at Eleusis, the native place of Aeschylus. There was more solemnity in the rites of Demeter than in those of Dionysus. Even a slave had human rights under her protection. Dionysus is a god who rules men from within and stirs them to orgies of emotion from which they emerge somehow saved or purified. If Aeschylus is a trustworthy witness to the worship of Demeter, it was thoughtful as well as emotional, and might indeed enlarge the springs of action that flow in any man. The

religious experience of a mystic after the order of Aeschylus gives
him a sense of life, not as something merely to be felt or understood, but as something to be expressed in action and in the exaltation that comes with devoted endeavor, not merely from disconnected contemplation, whether intellectual or visceral.

To participate, then, in a drama of Aeschylus is to be conscious
of a struggle between cosmic forces of good and evil. In this struggle the individual may be battlefield or combatant. The struggle
may be seen as a conflict of natural forces emerging through eons
of development into the light of the present. In this case the human characters can only be sufferers, not really active or decisive.
In other cases human individuals make decisions either with forethought or through faith and devotion to a higher principle. There
is no cleavage between man and nature or between man and society. Salvation is identical with civilization. The forces of nature
and the moral forces within man work together to establish a reign
of law and order in which God, man, and nature are equally triumphant. The theme is atonement, if by atonement we mean that
forces once in conflict are now at one. Naturally there are scenes
in Aeschylus that belong rather to mythology and entertainment
than to the exposition of his dynamic view of life; but it is probably no accident that the seven extant dramas fit into a pattern that
is ethical like that of the *Odyssey* rather than tragic like that of
the *Iliad*. The emphasis in Aeschylus, however, is on institutions,
particularly the Greek city and Athenian democracy, rather than
on the success of individual or family. The individual who fails
either deserves to fail or achieves essential success by producing
through his suffering a new security for others. Thus there is no
ultimate frustration; nor is mere glory the reward of heroes doomed
to death, as in Homer. There is much suffering in Aeschylus; but
men learn by suffering, and that is all that matters.

The imagination of Aeschylus ran riot like that of Pindar in his
own time or that of Plato later. He achieves a dramatic consistency
that goes beyond the brief or disconnected bursts of flame in Pindar, but his towers of tragedy lack the logical foundation that gives

stability to the inspiration of Plato. All these writers were something of a mystery to the Greek critics. These felt the power in their work, but worried over their lack of patterned self-control, much as Shakespeare's excesses disturbed the critics until Shakespeare himself was made the pattern of excellence and his errors became canonized. So, too, Walt Whitman is now felt to be justified by his works in spite of the absurdity of them when tested by the canons of common sense. Aeschylus was well appreciated by his own generation between 484, when he won his first victory, and his death in 456. Sophocles challenged him in his own vein and won in 468, but Aeschylus went on to produce his greatest work and win more victories later.

Aristophanes in the *Frogs* gives Aeschylus the victory over Euripides, but implies that Sophocles might have challenged his great rival successfully. The test by which Aeschylus wins is the test of weight determined by the scales. Euripides accuses Aeschylean tragedy of suffering from tumor or tumidity. He complains that Aeschylean tragedy was swollen. It so happens that Greek has a word *onkos* that means, like our 'mass,' either weight or bulk, and is also used as a medical term for tumor. The word is particularly appropriate to describe the majesty of Aeschylus, for it can be turned against him by those who agree with Euripides in the *Frogs* that Aeschylus was not really weighty, but unhealthily swollen. Aristophanes is consequently quite logical in letting Dionysus apply the test of the scales to see whether the bulk of Aeschylus represents real weight or mere bombast.

From Plutarch we know that Sophocles also spoke of the *onkos* of Aeschylus in terms which suggest that it was something puerile. I translate: ". . . Sophocles said that, having played enough (διαπεπαιχώς) with the grandiosity of Aeschylus, then with the harshness and artifice of his own style of composition, he was now making a shift to a third kind of diction, which is the most ethical and the best. . . ." It is the word 'played' that conveys the derogatory sense of the word *onkos* in Sophocles' statement as quoted. The author of the treatise *On the Sublime,* whom it is convenient to call Longinus, uses the same word to point a contrast between childish imitation of grandeur and genuine Dionysiac power in art. Of certain bombastic orators he says that "when they think that they have the divine afflatus, they are not dancing the bacchic dance but playing," i.e., indulging in puerility (οὐ βακχεύουσι ἀλλὰ παίζουσι). Thus for Longinus, as probably for Sophocles, the word onkos implies artistic imposture rather than imposing artistry. Tumidity or turgidity in later criticism is the vice of the grand style. Horace lists the vices of the three styles: Brevis esse laboro, obscurus fio; sectantem levia nervi deficiunt animique; professus grandia turget. "Trying to be concise I find myself obscure. The partisan of smoothness lacks sinews and spirit. The self-styled exponent of the grand style is inflated." Longinus, when he denounces tumidity as a false sublime, gives an example from Aeschylus, in which Aeschylus represents the north wind as blustering exuberantly with a shocking mixture of metaphors. No doubt Aeschylus could have defended this as exactly the kind of language for Boreas to use. You mustn't make whales speak like little fishes. The remarkable thing, though, is that Aeschylus, who seems truly sublime to us, and who, Plutarch says, was full of Dionysiac power, should not have impressed Longinus. Shakespeare and the Romantic Movement have taught us to regard poetry very differently from the ancient critics. Chamaeleon asserted that Aeschylus wrote his tragedies, like any Chinese poet, under the influence of wine.[3]

Sophocles is said to have brought against Aeschylus the reproach that, though he was right in what he did as a poet, he did not know what he was doing. Socrates, of course, in Plato's *Apology* brings the same charge against poets and politicians too. The authenticity of Sophocles' remark is, however, confirmed by what seems to be an echo of it in Aristotle's *Poetics*. The plots suitable for tragic presentation, he says, were discovered by accident. At first poets disregarded the quality of the stories that they dramatized, but later they concentrated on men who inflicted or suffered terrible disasters. Modern critics would probably prefer the conflicts of principle that appear in Aeschylus to the blood and ruin that suits

Aristotle. Aristotle classes the *Prometheus* of Aeschylus and the *Phorcides* with scenes in Hades as the lowest form of tragedy, producing neither pity nor terror nor concern for and satisfaction in social welfare. Unfortunately, the word which he uses to define the quality of this kind of tragedy must be guessed from traces in the text. The suggestion of Bywater, *opsis* 'spectacle,' has been frequently accepted, but is it likely that Aristotle was thinking of the *Prometheus* as seen rather than as read? Even as read it is far from sober history. In any case, he is discussing plot, not diction or spectacle. I suspect that Aristotle, like Sophocles, felt that such grandiosity of plot as well as spectacle belonged to the primitive stage of tragedy. I should read *onkos,* which is in fact as probable paleographically as any other word that has been suggested. It means anything from majesty or grandeur to bombast and inflation. Perhaps 'grandiosity' is the most neutral word in English to express greatness that need not be, but may be, pure pretense. At any rate Aristotle nowhere hints that he was impressed by the grandeur of Aeschylus, though he would presumably have agreed with Aristophanes that the Aeschylean massiveness had some weight as well as tumidity. No one will deny the grandiosity of Aeschylus' diction and spectacle. That he could also be grandiose in plot or subject matter could not be better illustrated than by the *Prometheus,* if we look on it as an exercise in theology and philosophy. Plato seems to have considered the Prometheus trilogy a study in the association of wisdom and power. He was a kindred spirit to Aeschylus. Still, the presentation of such a theme with gods as chief actors is grandiose in itself.[4]

Of the seven plays that we have, one, the *Persians,* which is an interpretation of history at most eight years old, may be considered as complete in itself without reference to the other plays that were produced with it. Three plays make up the trilogy of Orestes, produced as Aeschylus was nearing the end of his seventy years of life. The *Prometheus Bound,* which cannot be much earlier, is the first play of a Prometheus trilogy; this can be reconstructed in vague outline with the help of fragments and imaginative extrapolation. The *Suppliants* is the first play of a much earlier trilogy, which can also be reconstructed, but with even less certainty. The *Seven against Thebes* is the third play of a trilogy that told the story of three generations doomed to death by an evil destiny. We know the story of Laïus and Oedipus that preceded the *Seven*, but do not know at all how Aeschylus treated it. Thus we have a clue to one early trilogy, and to three that were produced after Sophocles' victory of 468. The date of the Prometheus trilogy is, however, not attested in our records. We know that the *Persians* was produced in 472, almost certainly with Pericles as choregus or producer, the *Seven* in 467, and the *Oresteia* in 458. Aeschylus lived about three years more, before he met his death in Sicily.

It is clear that in the one case where we have a complete trilogy it must be treated as a unit, though each play within the trilogy with its distinct chorus will also form a subordinate unit. In the one case of the *Seven* where we have the isolated last play of a trilogy, we may profit by comparing it with the conclusion of the Orestes trilogy in the *Eumenides*. In the two cases *Prometheus* and *Suppliants*, where we have an isolated first play, we must interpret the poet's intention largely by what we can deduce from the scanty fragments and from our knowledge of the one complete trilogy that is extant. We shall also have to take into account the developing possibilities of dramatic technique as well as the changing moods of popular interest and of political trends. It must be remembered that we are intentionally limiting our observation to the depiction of forces as operating in nature and within man. Much that is thoughtful, informative, or entertaining will receive scant mention here, or none at all. The state or its institutions are conspicuous in the main theme or outcome of every work of Aeschylus. He speaks with the eloquence of statesmanship; it remained for later poets to use the more partial methods of the law courts. Even in a trial scene Aeschylus deals with constitutional and public, not private, litigation. In the Danaid trilogy marriage was probably established as an institution in a political frame; in *Persians* and the *Seven* a civilized city is saved from external attack; the

Prometheus deals with tyranny and the *Oresteia* with the substitution of trial by jury for private vengeance in a case of murder.

Let us begin with the *Suppliants,* which is proved early by several features. The chorus enter without any preceding prologue; there is neither monologue nor dialogue before they appear. This happens elsewhere only in the *Persians.* The chorus are not only concerned in the action; they play a leading part. The daughters of Danaus, fifty of them, are more important than their father, who might almost have been omitted. Such importance of the chorus is found elsewhere only in the *Eumenides.* The choral odes also take up a larger part of the drama than in any other Greek tragedy. There is only one short scene that requires two actors. Actually there are three forces in the action—the chorus asking for protection, the king who protects them, and the aggressive herald of the Egyptians who attacks them. This is the only chorus of fifty that appears in tragedy. Aeschylus was content with twelve in the *Agamemnon.*

The action is highly concentrated in one moment, which is presented visually and by anticipation in the emotion expressed by the chorus. The fifty Danaids at the beginning seek sanctuary at Argos, having been pursued across the sea by their fifty male cousins, sons of Aegyptus. The king, Pelasgus, is finally persuaded to give them protection when he discovers that they are of Greek descent, that they are unwilling to marry their cousins, and that they are prepared to invoke the anger of the gods against him by hanging themselves from the shrines. He sends their father Danaus to make an appeal to the assembly on their behalf. Danaus returns with news of his success, but soon sees that his pursuers are landing. He goes to notify the king, who had already left the scene. Thus the girls are alone when the herald of the Egyptians arrives and threatens them with violence and death if they will not surrender to their rough wooers. The king arrives just in time to save them from the herald, and they gratefully withdraw to the city. The king has been placed between two forces and has had to make a difficult decision on the political level, for the fate of his people as well as his own is involved. No interest is taken in the psychology of wooers or wooed. They are counterparts of satyr and nymph in the depiction of rape that is found on the vase whose painter contrasted lawless love with lawful matrimony. There is no obvious reason why the girls should not have married their cousins, and it is useless to seek one. Aeschylus is satisfied to show us a violent attack on women by men who, though Greek by descent, have most un-Greek manners. The protection of suppliants is a favorite theme of patriotic Athenian orators as well as dramatists. In later plays of the sort the Athenians are rather more easily persuaded to receive the suppliants and are more easily victorious over the villains. The theme of a detested marriage was also in later drama left to comedy and to the burlesque *Helen* of Euripides.[5]

The very simple plot of the *Suppliants* has a beginning, a middle, and an end. From the point of view of Pelasgus there is an unexpected and alarming situation; he makes a difficult decision; his action is temporarily successful. If a god from the machine had been brought in to stop further fighting, the play would be complete as a moral and political unity. Aeschylus, however, gives successive slices of history in the three plays of the trilogy. Presumably the second play of the trilogy was the *Egyptians* and recounted the victory of the wooers with defeat of Pelasgus and the forced marriage of the Danaids. From the *Danaids,* which must have completed the trilogy, we have fragments which indicate that it began with the disclosure that in the marriage bed forty-nine conspiring Danaids had slain their husbands, and contained a defense of the fiftieth by Aphrodite. One of the Danaids, Hypermnestra, magnificently false, had betrayed the plot to dispose of the Egyptians by accepting Lynceus as husband and lover. We may suppose that there was a trial in which the loving couple were defended by Aphrodite, goddess of love, before the bar of Hera, goddess of matrimony. The plea that love is a higher power even than a father in deciding a girl's choice is made by Medea in a Latin play. At any rate the union of Lynceus and Hypermnestra must have received some final sanction, for they became the ancestors of a line of Argive kings.[6]

If this vague sketch is at all correct, we see that Aeschylus provides a triptych on love and marriage in place of the Homeric diptych that contrasts Hector and Andromache with Paris and Helen, and of the contrasting scenes of satyr and citizen taking a mate on the black-figured vase. Aeschylus shows us violence on both sides, the forced marriage and private vengeance for it, in contrast to the final reconciliation, which is not only a reconciliation of two individuals but the reconciliation of a force of nature, sex, with the institutions of a civilized community. Lynceus and Hypermnestra must also have been contrasted with their unreconciled brothers and sisters. It is idle to speculate whether Lynceus was represented as repentant. At any rate he is first a ravisher and later a husband, just like the heroes of New Comedy. The scene in which Aphrodite appeared was no doubt grandiose enough, but it was no empty show; it was propaganda for the freedom of women to choose, whether to reject or to elect a mate. Normally, daughters accepted in first marriage the man chosen by their fathers, but were then free to remain with that husband in spite of opposition from their own kin, just as Penelope the widow was not coerced by parents or son. Aeschylus' glorification of women and marriage is very much in the tradition of the *Odyssey* and must be classed with it as having an ethical plot. It is not tragic in the Aristotelian sense.

Let us consider now the two plays in which Aeschylus depicts the defense of a Greek city against the forces of barbarism. In the *Persians* the city is Athens, the attack was historical, the scene is laid at a distance, and the attacker is ridiculed and belittled after his defeat, for the pleasure of the Athenian audience. In the *Seven* the city is Thebes, the attack is brought by one of her own citizens, and the scene is within the beleaguered city, whose danger is emphasized in the most vivid way. Her defender is glorified, and his death is tragic in one sense, since he is slain, but his tragedy does not involve frustration since he succeeds in saving his city.

The *Seven,* which shows us the side of the defense and glorifies the self-devotion of the patriot, is much more effective than the *Persians,* which shows us the humiliation of a surviving attacker. The belittling of unsuccessful villains and impostors is matter for comedy; their personal problems cannot be taken seriously. But Pindar also in his odes of triumph for athletic victories draws a picture of the defeated competitor skulking to his home that accords ill with modern sportsmanship. The defeated lost all else and honor too.

In the *Persians,* then, Aeschylus tramples on Persian pride with no less pride himself. The scene is laid at the gates of Susa; the dramatic date is seven years before the date of first production. The chorus of Persian elders enter and relate the magnitude of the armament that has been hurled against Hellas. They hope for good news of the campaign of 480 B.C. Atossa, mother of the Persian king and commander, Xerxes, enters with great pomp and relates an ominous dream, but points out that her personal concern is for her son, who will still be king in spite of any disaster that he may cause. The chorus tell her of the resources of Athens, her silver mine, her men who fight hand to hand in heavy armor, her democracy that allows no man to call himself master of others. A messenger arrives with news of the Greek victory at Salamis and the disastrous flight of the army, relieved only by the escape of Xerxes. Atossa goes to sacrifice and returns without pomp to pour offerings to the spirit of Xerxes' father Darius while the chorus summon him to appear. The ghost of Darius is a prophet and a moralist. He is not very consistent, since he must ask about the past disaster before he can foretell the future defeat at Plataea.

With one accord the Persians blame Xerxes for their disaster, except that Atossa blames the advisers who urged him to show his manhood by leading the expedition. She would have kept Xerxes a spoiled child all his days. The intent to ridicule the Persian is clear enough here. The ghost of Darius blames his son for doing just the things that the historical Darius had also done. Zeus, Poseidon, and Athena are mentioned as the gods who brought dis-

aster on the Persians. Poseidon was offended by the bridging of
the Hellespont. Zeus loves to smite the man who is too prosperous.
Athena fights for her city Athens, and the other gods join her.
The difficulty of supply in mountainous Greece and the ruse of
Themistocles by which Xerxes was persuaded to attack the Greeks
in the fatal strait of Salamis are also mentioned, though no Greek
is cited by name. God, man, and nature all get credit for victory.
There is much pride in the Greek achievement, as well there might
be. There is also much confidence in the power of the gods that
assisted the Greeks. The rashness and folly of Xerxes and his gulli-
bility are also recognized. In Atossa we see the queen of the harem
who corrupts the son of a mighty father. Plato was later to tell the
same tale of the fatal influence of women on their royal sons.[7]

Xerxes himself we see only in the moment of disaster and repentance. The unsympathetic Athenians must have found him
comic, like the eunuch of Euripides' *Orestes*. Wailing for dead
heroes is common in tragedy, and Plato denounced it. The man
who bewails his own misfortunes and folly, however, is not depicted as a hero. Creon in Sophocles' *Antigone* and Orestes in Euripides' *Electra* will illustrate the point. The *Persians* is highly
moral in tone and not tragic at all for the Athenian audience. It
could interest only an audience that was sympathetic with the
Athenians and antipathetic to Xerxes. The *Persians* is, in fact, just
the reverse of a tragedy, for the audience, far from feeling frustration, pity, or terror, were given the best possible conceit of themselves. Even their gods were superior. The victory of the Greeks
was a triumph of civilization, of Europe over Asia, of freedom over
despotism, of courage over material odds. Thus Aeschylus magni-
fied the Greek cause and did his part to make the Greek spirit
a lasting force in European politics. He sings a paean for men whose
faith worked miracles and for whom miracles strengthened faith.[8]

In the *Seven* we see a threatened city from within; we are not
studying the effect of the news of defeat on a foeman's distant
population, but observing the response of the inhabitants of the
threatened city to the imminent danger of destruction. Aeschylus

strains the situation to make it seem that Thebes is a Greek city threatened by barbarians. The leader of the seven attackers is Polyneices, a Theban exile, who is returning with a host to destroy his homeland. Eteocles, his brother, is the defending hero. The chorus of panic-stricken women serve as a foil to him. There are no other actors but scouts and messengers, unless we count the sisters Antigone and Ismene who lead the mourning for their dead brothers in the final funeral procession. Thus we have a very simple arrangement of three forces: the attackers, who are heard but not seen; the city to be defended, represented by the chorus, who appeal to the pity of the audience; and Eteocles, who must decide. From his point of view we have the simple plot of situation, decision, and consequence. It is odd that Aeschylus takes no account of the relations of the two brothers Eteocles and Polyneices before the resort to war. Polyneices claimed that justice was on his side, but the seer Amphiaraus denounces him for attacking the city that was his mother, regardless of the justice of his cause. Amphiaraus, like Arjuna in the *Bhagavadgita,* sees the folly of the war but carries out his duty as a soldier nevertheless. There is a kind of inhuman fatality about the whole affair that baffles thought. The *Seven* is a drama brimful of Ares, and Ares was not a thinker. Aristophanes noted, nevertheless, that Aeschylus' fighting generation accomplished more than their descendants, who learned from Euripides to question everything.[9]

Those who wish may suppose that the hostility of Apollo to the house of Laïus accounts for everything. At any rate Eteocles does not doubt that he personally is hated by the gods. If the enmity of the gods derives from his grandfather, the guilt does not rest upon him. In any case his father Oedipus had cursed his two sons. They were to divide their kingdom by the sword. Eteocles is convinced of the efficacy of the curse, just as Hector in the *Iliad* knows that his cause is hopeless. Aeschylus does not say why Oedipus cursed his sons. In other sources he was offended by the portion of sacrificial meat that was offered to him. There is a report of a tribe in central Asia who brought death to their old men by feeding them on certain portions of meat exclusively. Possibly in the original tale Oedipus had excellent reason to curse his sons. Eteocles thus is limited in his choice of ends, but he still has a choice, whether to die like a hero and patriot or to withdraw from the struggle. Actually the determination to save his city is apparent in all his acts. The fact that if he slays his brother no purification will be possible does not move him. No matter what the cost, he will fight and slay. If he too is slain, as actually happens, blood will be expiated by blood.[10]

The chorus are saved in spite of themselves. They do their best by spreading panic to lose the war until Eteocles reduces them to order. They do their best, like Andromache in the *Iliad,* to keep their hero from fighting. They point out the soft life that Eteocles might lead; they believe that Apollo might be bribed or persuaded to relent; they see only frenzy in the behavior of the king. They have no understanding of the heroic compulsion to fight that is illustrated equally in the case of the good Amphiaraus. Aeschylus uses them as a foil to throw into relief the patriotic self-devotion of Eteocles, the man under a curse, hated by the gods. No better picture could be presented of the reasons why men fight. Aeschylus does not settle the problem for *us.* We may see in Eteocles either a hero or a madman; in his death either a tragedy or the greatest success of all, self-mastery in the service of an ideal. Sophocles produced some of his greatest tragedies when he took as heroes other members of the same family who went to self-sought destruction. He certainly approved of Antigone; Oedipus he makes more a sufferer than a sinner and leads him to a peaceful end at last. The family likeness is remarkable.

It is not likely that we should have much greater insight into the *Seven* even if the *Laïus* and *Oedipus* were extant. We know from the *Seven* that Laïus had been warned by Apollo's oracle to die childless and save his city. The impression that we get from the *Seven* is that Eteocles was doing just that. Of course, history gave Eteocles a son, but any Greek poet was allowed to remake myth, or at least had the skill to misrepresent the myth convinc-

ingly. The introduction of a son of Eteocles would spoil the drama
in the same way as the presence of Hector in a Trojan assembly
would mar the pattern of the *Iliad*. The poet is not nodding when
he keeps his hearers awake by his intentional oversights. Aeschylus believed that the sins of the fathers might be visited upon the
sons; he did not in the end believe that the gods were jealous of
prosperity. It is quite possible that Laïus was represented as sin-
ning by his unbridled love for Chrysippus, son of Pelops, but we
do not know. At any rate Aeschylus has made a great patriotic play
of the *Seven* and ends the story with a double slaughter that is also
a double expiation.

It is possible that there is more propaganda in the play than meets
the eye at first sight. It was presented at a moment when Themistocles had been punished by banishment for treason to Greece and
had been established in power on the border of the Persian empire or had at least sought refuge in Persia. It was rumored that
he would lead a new Persian invasion. His likeness to Polyneices
is obvious. Plutarch tells us that the audience, when the *Seven* was
produced, recognized Aristeides in the description of Amphiaraus
as one who chose to *be,* not to be thought, honest. Certainly Aristeides must often have fought bravely for Athens when he could
not altogether approve of the policies of her leaders. Amphiaraus'
denunciation of the man who attacks his own city even justly
would well express the case of Aristeides, who had coöperated with
Themistocles but must now oppose him. Whom does Eteocles
represent? I suggest that even if he were not recognized as a mask
for Pericles, the picture that Aeschylus gives of a man under a curse
who saves his city in a fight that requires him to disregard the
closest personal ties was good propaganda for Pericles, who at this
point was just beginning his rivalry with Cimon. The curse of
the Alcmaeonidae, which rested on Pericles, was no doubt urged
against him by some in Athens as well as by Spartan ambassadors.
Others may have suspected him because of his political association with Themistocles. He had been producer when Aeschylus'
Persians was put on in 472. His rival Cimon had led the board

of generals when they were asked to act as jury and awarded the prize to Sophocles in 468, just the year before the *Seven* appeared. Aeschylus was not above the battle either in the literary, the military, or the political sense. Circumstantial evidence points almost glaringly to the *Seven* as a manifesto for Pericles and Aeschylus with him in opposition to their old leader Themistocles, and also to the new political influence of Cimon. It was about five years later that Cimon was ostracized and Pericles became supreme.[11]

From the *Seven*, which was the last play in a trilogy, we come to the *Prometheus Bound*, which was presumably a first play. We have moved from earth to heaven and from unquestioning devotion to country to an equally unexplained devotion to the creative spirit of progress that lives in wisdom and is the opponent of blind force. Plato saw in the heavens a kingdom of reason to which the philosopher owes allegiance and for which he lives and dies rather than for any mortal state. In Aeschylus' *Prometheus* the hero is a fighter for freedom from the arbitrary rule of Zeus conceived as a tyrant. Prometheus is an allegorical figure. He represents the fire within man, the subtle essence of thought that enables him to use fire and other inventions and to discover his own way of salvation from the miseries of savage life. He is the spirit of progress, political as well as scientific, and in him we also see the wise man confronted by political anarchy or tyranny. Zeus the tyrant has used the scientist to win the battle for power, but disregards the one wise man when the battle is won. Wisdom would save man, but brute force would let him perish. Modern science has the same problem of adjustment to political power. The allegory is not forced. The minor characters of the conflict are just the sort of individuals or types that Aeschylus must have seen active in Sicily when he visited the tyrants there. He was interested in many things besides the volcanic activity of Sicilian Aetna that is described in the play. The gods of the *Prometheus* are even more human than Homer's; it is Aeschylus' most realistic sketch of political life and conflict.[12]

As usual, Aeschylus does not explain the motives of his characters, but concentrates on the situation. Zeus had won a victory over his father and the Titans with the help of Prometheus (i.e., Forethought). Then Zeus would have let man die, but Prometheus stole the fire of Hephaestus and gave it to man. It was Prometheus who taught man all arts, including divination, that are necessary to civilization. Zeus, however, will not tolerate insubordination and condemns Prometheus to be riveted to a crag at the point where Caucasus reaches the eastern ocean. Probably Aeschylus supposed that the Caspian Sea was a bay of the ocean. During the whole play the gigantic figure of Prometheus dominates the scene. Only an earthquake can remove him at the end. It is an impressive symbol of the patient persistence through agony of the intelligence that brings salvation to men and to gods. In the prologue Prometheus is silent while he is clamped to his crag by Violence and Power, under the direction of Hephaestus. Hephaestus is an unwilling servant of the tyrant, but is forced by the ruthless and scurrilous jibes of Kratos (Power) to carry out his mission. In general, the lower the character, the more realistically Aeschylus depicts him. Of course Hephaestus is both a divine person and the fire that saves man or that may be used by brutal power against him. Zeus the overlord represents the universe set free from the devastating forces in nature but not yet governed by wisdom in social and political relations. His spirit is embodied in every dictator who would suppress freedom of thought. It is interesting to note that Aeschylus ends his trilogy happily with the establishment of civilization. Shelley's revolutionary *Prometheus Unbound* has a happy ending that is just the opposite, for it involves the overthrow of civilization as well as of Zeus.

When Prometheus is left alone, he bewails his fate, which, though foreseen, is worse than he expected, and calls upon earth, sea, and sun to bear witness to his suffering. He is visited by two kinds of sympathizers. First are the chorus of Oceanids, daughters of Ocean, who comfort him but are shocked by his ranting against Zeus and his threat that Zeus too will be overthrown if he does not come to terms. But though they disapprove of strife, in the end they are swept from the scene by the same crashing blow that involves Prometheus. The other sympathizer, their father Oceanus, is a wise Polonius, the appeaser who is sure that he can reconcile the quarrel but who will never be bold enough to endanger his own dignified ease. His proposal to arbitrate is in effect a betrayal of the cause for which Prometheus is suffering. The latter rails at him and sends him scurrying home in terror for himself. Prometheus has met a situation with a decision. Although physically helpless he is active mentally and knows that he will win in the end.

His next visitor is the one mortal in the play, the maiden Io, who was sought in love by Zeus and transformed into a heifer by Hera. She is driven over land and sea by a pursuing gadfly just as Orestes is pursued through many lands by the Furies in the *Eumenides*. Aeschylus is fond of introducing travelogues into his plays, full of strange names and even stranger etymologies. Io presents a contrast to the god. She is a suffering mortal who neither understands the present nor can guess the future. Prometheus had followed his own bent knowing that he would suffer. Io was innocent and yet condemned. Still, her union with Zeus would ultimately lead to the birth of Heracles, who was half-divine, and would release Prometheus. The problem of suffering is greatly enriched by her presence. There is a suggestion of a divine love going out to mortals that brings blessing after long and arduous birth pangs. We need not suppose, however, that Zeus has a plan. Arbitrary power working blindly will defeat itself. The uninstructed will thwarts itself automatically. Zeus becomes a savior in spite of himself. After Io's departure comes one more chance for Prometheus to weaken. The herald of Zeus, Hermes, appears and like a saucy lackey orders Prometheus to cease from threatening or take even worse consequences. Prometheus is the kind of tragic character who accepts his doom knowingly but not submissively. His spirited replies to some extent justify the tyrant who punishes him; in any case there would be no drama if Prometheus were not a stout fighter. The play ends when Prometheus, crag and all, and the chorus as well, are swept down to Tartarus.

In the sequel, Prometheus was brought back to the light and was released by Heracles. In the end there was no doubt a reconciliation between Zeus and Prometheus, who symbolize power and thought, will and reason, or the might and right whose union, according to Solon, is the goal of the statesman. The trilogy probably ended with the founding of a rite that celebrated the bringing of fire by Prometheus and glorified the fire-god Hephaestus. The rite, of course, was nothing new to the Athenians, but the grandiosity of Aeschylus' interpretation of it was a new force not only in Athenian life but in all life of the spirit.[13]

The theme of a crucified savior appears not only in this play, but in the Christian gospels and in a Japanese drama that shows Buddhist influence. The differences are considerable. The Greek poet may blacken the character of Zeus as he pleases. For him it is a god that must be reconciled to men. If in the end Zeus becomes wise, not only Prometheus, but man, may loyally accept his rule, which is the rule of reason. For Christian theology the problem of atonement is more difficult, for man must be saved, not from God, but from man's mistaken conception of God as a power to be feared. It is men who must learn a new wisdom. Their salvation is not external, but internal; they are saved from sin—moral, not intellectual, error.

The sense of sin is almost as foreign to the Greek as it is to the Japanese. In the Japanese story *The Ghost of Sakura* there is no god who is crucified for all mankind, but a man who intervenes to save his fellow farmers from cruel oppression by an overlord. They are saved, but the leader, Sogoro, is condemned to crucifixion. Later his ghost takes revenge upon the wicked overlord. The terror of the play is ghostly; its pity is for victims of concrete wrongs. The most notable difference in the Japanese play is that no rule of reason, justice, or mercy is established. The powers that be are not defeated in the imagination of the author. Sogoro saved a few peasants. His ghost won him a shrine and semidivine honors, but we miss any criticism of a political system that permits overlords to do as they please. Aeschylus' play is an attack on the very principle of tyranny,

and the Christian story asserts the existence of a spiritual kingdom
that is stronger than all earthly tyrants. The tale of Prometheus
is not an ordinary story of success or failure, because his strength is
quite superhuman and mythical. He knows the secret that will
overthrow Zeus unless Zeus avoids marriage with Thetis and the
begetting of a son greater than himself. But the corresponding
human situations come readily to mind; there is nothing mythical
about the conflict between tyrant and philanthropist, which happens every day on countless battlefields. For Aristotle the play has
only its grandeur to make it qualify as tragedy, since it shows
neither virtue rewarded nor greatness frustrated. Plato, who knew
that there is a realm beyond realism that can be expressed only in
myth, could appreciate the sublimity of Aeschylus. One wonders
what Aristotle would have found to say about Dante.[14]

We come now to the last three plays of Aeschylus, which compose the *Oresteia,* the trilogy that describes the rescue of Orestes
by Apollo and Athena. Aeschylus is again dealing with a universal
problem and contrasting savagery with civilization. This time the
problem is murder and the civilized institution that deals with it
is the court of the Areopagus in Athens. In the first play of the
trilogy, the *Agamemnon,* in which Agamemnon is murdered by
his wife Clytemnestra, Orestes does not take part. He is perhaps ten
or twelve years old and has been sent abroad by his sister for safety.
Clytemnestra explains his absence as she explains the absence of
tears from her own eyes. Both were signs of her disloyalty to the
family. The prophetess Cassandra, before she goes to her death
with Agamemnon, foresees that he will be avenged by Orestes. In
the second play, the *Choephoroe,* Orestes executes vengeance on
his mother Clytemnestra by the command of Apollo. In the third
play, the *Eumenides,* Orestes seeks help from Apollo and after
years of tormented wandering finds it in Athens, where Athena
persuades the pursuing Furies to cease their hostile function and
become kindly powers. Besides the personal salvation of Orestes,
his family are freed from the curse of mutual murder; mankind is
freed from superstitious terror of the Furies, and society is freed

from the blind operation of a code of private vengeance for murder. There are to be no more lynchings. Orestes is somewhat like Io in that he is an innocent sufferer, being careful always to obey Apollo. It is through his suffering that redemption and a better system are brought about. He is not so strong a character as Eteocles, with whom the family curse likewise comes to an end. Eteocles has Apollo against him and must save himself. The introduction of gods in the *Eumenides* inevitably results in a belittling of the human hero.

Orestes makes his only decision in the central play, the *Choephoroe*. The first play, the *Agamemnon*, shows the bloody tradition that Orestes must put right. In the *Eumenides* his earlier decision is crowned with success. The *Choephoroe*, if shorn of its introduction and its sequel, provides a plot either for a success story in itself, as we see in Sophocles' *Electra*, or for a tragedy of pity, as we see in Euripides' *Electra*. The *Eumenides* in itself is, like the *Suppliants,* a political play of supplication and deliverance. The *Agamemnon* is much more like the simple story of personal revenge that we find in Euripides' *Medea* than it is like any other play of Aeschylus. If tragedy by definition is to be a tale of blood or suffering, it must deal with those who inflict suffering upon themselves or with those who have enemies. The enemy may be a god who works openly or subtly, or some man or woman who uses intrigue or violence. Aeschylus has hitherto been interested in the principles involved in a conflict more than in psychology or intrigue or surprise. Only when a principle operated through the devotion of a human character to it would he be interested in motives. In the *Prometheus* we find for the first time a large number of characters beautifully contrasted and consistent. They illustrate but do not determine the action.

In the *Agamemnon* we have again six clearly drawn characters besides the chorus, and we have also a situation that develops as one character after another appears. The unusually long play falls into three almost equal parts. In the first the sentinel describes the signal fire that reports the fall of Troy, while the departure of the expedition for Troy is recalled by the chorus, and Clytemnestra gives vivid descriptions of the system of telegraphs and of the scene in captured Troy. In the second a herald brings news of the arrival in Argos of Agamemnon, and tells of the war from the point of view of the soldiers who fought, and of the storm that allowed only one ship to reach home unscathed. Agamemnon's entrance leads to a scene of decision. The audience, knowing the story, do not require to be told that Clytemnestra will slay her husband. They hear her long professions of loyalty, which include one simile taken from Homer's account of the joy of Penelope at seeing her husband, and the debate whether Agamemnon is to walk on a red carpet in Oriental splendor. The debate keeps his mind on unimportant things, and shows that he lacks the insight of a sober and wise leader. His fate is decided when he enters the palace. In the third part of the play the hidden horror of the situation is at last revealed.

Cassandra is an innocent victim, who nevertheless by her presence shows again Agamemnon's disregard of right. He had slain Iphigeneia and lost the love of Clytemnestra. To bring Cassandra home as a concubine was an open insult to his wife. Cassandra, guided by her foe, Apollo, devotes herself to death and laments her own fate in a scene that prolongs the suspense of Agamemnon's fate. Her prophecy of doom is soon succeeded by doom itself. The eccyclema, a device for showing interiors, reveals the deaths of Agamemnon and Cassandra, while Clytemnestra in a new mask reveals her own duplicity. Gradually she grows more feminine and answers the threats of the audience by an appeal to Aegisthus, who enters opportunely with armed men and suppresses the loyal chorus.

The passion of Clytemnestra is but a means to an end, the establishment of Aegisthus upon the throne. This would be a terrible anticlimax if another play were not to follow, as well as a violation of Aristotle's dictum that a villain must not be left triumphant. In any case, it is characteristic of Aeschylus not to make a woman's revenge his central theme, as Euripides did in his

Medea. The final revelation of the play is that Clytemnestra herself was but a pawn in the man's world of war and politics. Cassandra is another pawn, who fails to save her king.

The *Agamemnon* is remarkable as the one tale of plotted vengeance on the Greek stage that does not show the plotters at work. Nor has it a recognition scene to make reversal more moving. Just because the story was so well known, Aeschylus could provide surprises and not lose the effect of impending doom. He can also avoid painting the moral tones in black and white. Agamemnon is in the wrong, but justice no more justifies Clytemnestra in slaying her husband than it justified Polyneices' attack on his own city. She brought ruin to the family and slavery to the city. The tangled skein of justice must be unraveled by a stronger hand. So, too, Aeschylus presents two attitudes toward the Trojan war in his choral odes. The crime of Paris was punished when Troy fell, and the Aeschylean chorus see the righteous hand of Zeus at work. At the same time they resent the war which condemns so many good men to die for a bad woman. They see in the sacrifice by Agamemnon of his daughter Iphigeneia to get a favorable wind an act of frenzy that must in turn bring retribution. Justice demanded the punishment of Paris, but it did not justify new crimes. Aeschylus likes to confront his heroes with impossible decisions—with situations where any choice involves disaster to something precious. Thus he makes of life a mystery and shows evil leading somehow to good. The greater the terror and frustration of life as seen in the first play of a trilogy, the greater will be the lesson of atonement as preached in his third play.

The *Choephoroe* presents a much simpler situation, for besides the blood of Agamemnon which cries out for vengeance there is the express injunction of Apollo the lord of Delphi, who prescribes purifications for murder: he has ordered Orestes to avenge his father by slaying his mother, or suffer, for not doing so, a terrible fate.

We may note in passing that the introduction of a god to give sanction to the occult influence and to strengthen other forces that coöperate to produce a single result is thoroughly Greek for this period. In the *Persians,* economic, military, and political causes are cited, while individual skill or courage as well as material conditions and shifts of weather have an effect too. Yet gods are also brought in with their different reasons for opposing the Persians, in addition to the general indictment of pride and insolence that is brought against the defeated nation. We may also note that Apollo represents a social force that operated in real life—the influence of Delphi. Delphi prescribed solutions for all sorts of problems that were brought to it and might thus determine the success or failure of individuals or states. This was more than prediction of the future, it was intervention, and Apollo intervenes in favor of Agamemnon. In real life there was naturally a strong tendency to use Delphi for private ends and to put to the god only such questions as might implicate him in one's own undertaking without giving him any power of decision. One might ask him how to go about an enterprise instead of asking whether the enterprise would succeed. Apollo is not taken seriously in drama as an active power in human life after this play. In fact, in Atossa's dream in the *Persians,* Phoebus Apollo failed to protect the Persian eagle from the Greek falcon, a patent reference to the pro-Persian stand of Delphi in the great war. In general, in Greek fiction, Apollo is likely to appear as a destroyer. He was a plague demon and had something of the vindictive, enigmatic quality of the seers whose patron he was. His power to save is not comparable in drama to that of Zeus and Athena.

The action of the *Choephoroe* is concise and concentrated. All the characters are on one side or the other. Orestes, Pylades, Electra, the chorus of captive women from Troy, and the old nurse of Orestes—all work together to further the plot against Aegisthus and Clytemnestra. Orestes and Pylades were brought in at the start. A warning dream notified Clytemnestra of the danger, and she attempted to appease her dead husband's wrath by sending libations to his tomb. The chorus advise Electra to use the libations against the queen, thus turning her act against her in ironical fashion. Orestes is recognized and joins Electra and the chorus in an invocation of the spirit of the slain. A plot is quickly laid in presence of the audience and of course the chorus too. Clytemnestra is deceived by Orestes pretending to bring news of his own death. The old nurse, who is sent to summon Aegisthus, is an interesting character, but she is also an essential factor in the action, for the chorus persuade her not to warn Aegisthus to come with a bodyguard. This distribution of the action to include humble characters, who help without being principals in the plot and more or less by accident, brings us nearer to a realistic divorcement of action from the plan of any one character or group of characters. The interventions of chorus and nurse are unplanned but natural. Still, we are a long way from the ironical situation in which the action is furthered by characters who would do just the opposite if they could. The nurse and the chorus have no detached motives to divide their loyalty to Orestes. The plot of the play is precisely the plot of Orestes as shared in imagination by the audience.[15]

Aegisthus when he arrives is soon dispatched, and Clytemnestra appears from the women's quarters to defend herself. Here action is suspended for a moment to introduce a scene of decision that is completely unrealistic and stiff with formalism but for that very reason highly effective. Orestes stands with drawn sword before the bared breast of his mother and debates whether he shall slay her to avenge his father. Behind him is Pylades, who speaks but once in the play. Pylades delivers the word of Apollo that Orestes must strike. He does so, but there is no triumphant ending, for Orestes is at once hounded from the scene by the avenging Furies, who seek blood for blood. Aeschylus has centered attention on the difficulty of Orestes' problem. The dire punishment with which Apollo threatened him if he did not slay his mother was worse than the actual evils brought on him by the Furies. The embodiment, however, on the stage of the forces that operate on both sides reduces him to the dimensions of a puppet in a dream world.

The skill with which Aeschylus gradually prepares us for the actual appearance of the Erinyes, or Furies, as chorus and actor in the *Eumenides* is notable. Cassandra can see fiends haunting the palace in the *Agamemnon,* and Clytemnestra welcomes the suggestion that she was possessed by an evil spirit when she murdered her husband, but the audience see nothing. In the *Choephoroe* the active forces—the dead Agamemnon and Apollo's command versus the fear of the Erinyes—are so emphasized that in the final play of the trilogy we are ready to step into the world of allegory. We have left the psychological world of the *Agamemnon* for a realm of moral and political insight which will rather startlingly bridge the gap between the heroic world of Orestes and the religious and political problems of Aeschylus' own day. His gods are made sufficiently human in detail, but even in their superhuman character they are equally man-made and serve to guide the Athenian citizen to right thinking about Delphi and the Areopagus. Yet the injunction of Athena to her citizens, "Neither anarchy nor despotism," is vague enough not to have offended anyone. She does not, like the trumped-up Athena of Peisistratus, support any individual or measure.

Aeschylus' history, as well as his gods, is largely a product of the imagination intended to influence men for their good. The first thing that is impressed upon us in the *Eumenides* is that even the sacred shrine of Apollo is not a defense against avenging Furies. Just as the Persian eagle was attacked at Apollo's altar, so Orestes is still haunted after Apollo has purified him. It is the priestess at Delphi who in terror informs the audience of the presence of fiends in Apollo's temple. Then we see the Furies sleeping while Apollo dispatches Orestes on his long journey to Athens under protection of Hermes. The ghost of Clytemnestra awakes the Furies and they are off in hot pursuit. After a long gap in space and time Orestes seeks sanctuary again, this time at the shrine of Athena. The lesson could not be plainer that no religious organization can be final arbiter of criminal matters. Athena organizes a body of Athenians to serve as a jury while she acts as judge in the trial of Orestes. The Erinyes prosecute while Apollo defends. The jury are evenly divided, so that Athena casts the deciding vote. Orestes is acquitted, but there is more business to follow. The Erinyes must be induced to give up their function of punishment for murder. In other words, men must learn to deal rationally with crime in the interest of society, not to leave the murderer to be dealt with by kinsmen or, where the murderer is himself next of kin, only by imaginary powers of vengeance. Apollo had already recognized the superiority of Athena, the state. The Erinyes are less civilized, and only the patient persistence of Athena's moral suasion induces them to become Eumenides, kindly powers, instead of the avenging fiends that they have been. They are led from the scene after songs of blessing by a procession of Athenian citizens. Orestes had already promised his blessing upon the people and his protection from invasion by Argives for all future time.

Scenes of conversion are rare in Greek fiction. The contrast of good and bad is usually presented in different characters. It is not likely that Aeschylus showed a character converted to a higher moral standard of living, though he declares that the principle, "Suffering teaches," is an ordinance of Zeus. He expects men to learn by their own suffering, but in his plays gives them instruction in terms of the suffering of others. Yet he celebrates the progress of mankind in his allegories. The Zeus of the *Prometheus* must have been a convertible god, one who himself learned by suffering. There is no doubt that the Erinyes, who are utterly barbaric in their association with mutilation and torture, are converted by Athena into Eumenides. Their conversion entails the elimination of barbarities from the law for citizens. It is characteristic of the period that slaves did not count. They continued to be tortured when occasion arose. Aeschylus has also disregarded the fact that in Athenian criminal law purification did not precede the action of the court, but followed it. He has put the cart before the horse in the case of Orestes for his own dramatic reasons. Apollo must do his part first if his subordinate position is to be emphasized. Yet conflict is avoided between Apollo and Athena by the device of putting punishment for crime into the hands of the elemental Erinyes. We know how the Athenians dealt with murder. In

Homer, murder concerned only the kin of the murdered man, who might or might not take compensation in a settlement.[16]

In classical Greece unavenged murder was a source of pollution and might bring plagues upon the community. Hence the next of kin of a man who might have been murdered was obliged to prosecute the suspected murderer and might himself be prosecuted and put to death for impiety if he did not take steps to rid the community of pollution. It was the courts that decided the degree of guilt and the punishment or purification required. The purification itself was a religious ceremony and subject to the control of authorities at Delphi. The stain of guilt might be shifted to inanimate objects or to a person or persons unknown. Athena in the play is thoroughly democratic and is prepared to accept the verdict of an Athenian jury. The gods of Aeschylus follow the election returns. If there is a religious mystery for him, it is not embodied in the bright figures of the Olympians, who are either functional or fictional for him as for Homer. As far as they are fictional, they produce a lively satirical effect, as in the trial scene of the *Eumenides*. As far as they are functional, it is Aeschylus' interpretation of the needs of civilized man that largely prescribes their functions. He is no blind upholder of tradition. He reshapes the past in the present for the sake of the future. He is the opposite of Hesiod, who pictured the past as a golden age. For Aeschylus even the heroic age was but a prelude to the era of civilization and he finds in the past a hell to frighten the bad citizen. His heroes may have the Satanic character of Eteocles or Prometheus; they may be suffering servants like Io and Orestes. In either case the results are good for mankind and illustrate a struggle that still goes on in the lifetime of Aeschylus.

The great operas of Richard Wagner owe much to Greek tragedy and particularly to Aeschylus, but they are far removed from the moral and political realism that we find in Aeschylus. No doubt, dragons and valkyries and magic swans correspond to much that must be classed as imaginative grandeur in the plays of Aeschylus, but the Greek poet was also interested in the contemporary world and its problems. He is concerned to strengthen institutions and to present examples of devotion to rational progress. He has fixed his gaze on Athens and his heart is full of love for her. The world of his plays is often a dream world full of impossible adventures that still have power to stir strange deeps of feeling and to produce an awful awareness of the responsibility of the individual. The result is a sense of achievement and of the importance of wisdom and courage if civilized life is to be established and maintained. For him the city is all-inclusive. Only in the case of Agamemnon does he question the claims of power and appeal to pity against the conqueror. Agamemnon, be it noted, represents not the state but the man who yields to the temptation to pursue Oriental goals of limitless rule and self-glorification. Aeschylus calls up horrors, legendary or typical, to illustrate the evils of unbalanced impulse and to inspire devotion to the principles of reason and moderation. The state that he loved was no aggressive, merciless imperialism, nor would the *Agamemnon* give sanction to such a state. The ethical side of Aeschylus is so strongly affirmative and optimistic that we cannot expect to find in him any interest in the theme of frustration as we saw it in the *Iliad*. Aeschylus is content to be constructive as a man. He is not, like Homer, preoccupied with the theme of death, nor does he care much about glory. He is a poet of action that leads to concrete results. The grandeur of his conception of life makes the disappointment or death of the individual seem unimportant, however keenly it is felt. The horrors of mental darkness and the fears of those that walk in darkness fade in the light of the great salvation that he sees firmly established in Greece and in democratic Athens.[17]

IV
Sophoclean Tragedy

THE EXTANT tragedies of Sophocles, like those of
Aeschylus, are seven in number. It is generally agreed that *Ajax*
and *Antigone* were produced before he was fifty-five years old,
that *Oedipus Tyrannus* and *Trachiniae* followed before he was
seventy, and that the last three plays appeared in the ten years
before he died at ninety in 406 B.C. Shakespeare and Menander died
at fifty-two. We may be grateful that the Greek tragedians lived
much longer to complete the great works that are extant. Sophocles
won his first victory at the age of twenty-seven, and we can only
guess what kind of work he produced in the next twenty years.
The earliest extant dramas, the *Ajax* and the *Antigone,* are tragedies of personal devotion to an ideal, set in a frame of political
morality. This is essentially an Aeschylean tactic, though Sophocles' technique is necessarily modified to accord with his practice
of writing, no longer trilogies such as Aeschylus wrote, but dramas
complete in themselves. In these two plays he introduces seers and
oracles and explains disaster by the anger of the gods. He never
uses curses as a motivation, as Aeschylus did, and employs the
dream only when in the *Electra* he is adapting the *Choephoroe* of
Aeschylus.

In the *Trachiniae* and *Oedipus Tyrannus* he disregards any
moral except the moral that human life is uncertain. The gods are
not brought in, and character and psychology are made to explain
the action. In both plays a skillfully arranged disaster is produced
by individual actions directed to quite other ends. There is thus a
plot in the play that is not the plot of any one character, but the
plot of the author against his characters. The tragedy is one of
frustration by circumstance, and no other effect is allowed to inter-

88

fere with emphasis on the theme of paradox. The action must con-
vince and surprise at the same time. The result is to produce a
strong sense of injustice. Life seems to have set a trap for characters
who do not deserve it, but since the gods are not brought into the
action it cannot be said that they are hostile. At any rate they do
not save. Sophocles no longer shows us gods, but leaves them in
place behind a curtain. Euripides will later draw back the curtain
again and show us that there never were any gods there. The gods
were evidently man-made even in Aeschylus, but they were not
made by and for the theater, as they came to be later.[1]

In the last three plays of Sophocles, character is the key to destiny. Heroic patience is rewarded with a happy ending; the oracles
that are brought in operate through human belief in them. The
sympathy of the spectator is strongly enlisted on the right side by
the appealing presentation of characters who sacrifice everything
to do what is right. Plutarch compares with the development of
Sophoclean tragedy the progress in virtue of students of philosophy. When they pass from the ostentatious and artificial to the kind
of discourse that involves sympathetic and passionate feeling, they
begin to make genuine and unfeigned progress. Plutarch's words
for feeling are *éthos* and *pathos*. The distinction between the two
was made by rhetoricians. The effect of *éthos*, 'homeliness,' is
found when a client is depicted as essentially a good fellow. He is
seen in the ordinary activities of life so vividly depicted that the
juryman cannot help liking him and putting himself in his place.
The effect of *pathos*, 'intensity,' is to rouse the indignation or fury
of the judges and so to sweep away all consideration of caution or
delay. One kind of feeling is reflective and apparently calm; the
other is impassioned and irresistible.

Plutarch cites a statement of Sophocles that divides his career
into three stages, one of Aeschylean *onkos* or grandiosity, one of
harshness and artificiality in construction, and a third kind of style
that is most ethical and best. Unfortunately, Plutarch or someone
else has garbled the quotation by interpretation, so that we do not

[1] For notes to chapter iv see pages 285–292.

know whether the grandiosity is of style, construction, or spectacle, or all three at once, or whether the change from harshness and artificiality of construction to a new kind of diction also involved changes in construction. The words "most ethical and best" at least suggest that Sophocles, whatever Plutarch may have thought he meant, was really talking about plots, for Aristotle introduces an argument into the *Poetics* against the view that a complex ethical plot is better than a complex tragic plot. He may have had Sophocles' statement in mind. The harshness of Sophocles' construction was the opposite, no doubt, of the construction that would please the spectators, as Aristotle reports that the ethical plot with happy ending did. I should assume then that harsh or bitter is the opposite of sweet and pleasant and means simply what Aristotle means by tragic, a tale of suffering or death with unhappy ending. Aristotle cites the *Ajax* as an example of the simple tragic play, and the *Oedipus Tyrannus* as a complex tragic play. Since the plot of the *Oedipus* has always been admired for its diabolical ingenuity, it is hard to believe that it is not what Sophocles had in mind when he spoke of his own harsh and ingenious or artificial construction. As far as *êthos* in the sense of character study or psychology is concerned, there is plenty of that in the *Oedipus Tyrannus,* more in fact than in any other play of Sophocles. The plot, however, is tragic in the strongest sense, since it seems to show life as fundamentally treacherous, ingeniously defeating our best efforts to achieve security. The *Oedipus at Colonus* is in a way a recantation on the part of Sophocles.[2]

There are other uncertainties in the language of the statement that Plutarch attributes to Sophocles. He is made to say that he had finished playing with, or had artistically perfected, or had served an apprenticeship to, or had done his duty as a dramatic artist by, the Aeschylean pomp and his own harshness and artifice. The Greek is literally 'having played through.' The word for 'play' might suggest immaturity, or lack of seriousness, or merely work in connection with festal matters, the artist's consecration, playing the game as an artist. But in Longinus it is used for the puerility that apes the grand manner. The word 'through' may suggest either being finished with a thing or bringing it to perfection. Certainly no statement of Sophocles himself could prove that he did not later revert to an earlier manner that he once supposed himself finished with. The grandeur and pomp of the *Oedipus at Colonus* are as nearly Aeschylean as anything we have of Sophocles. In fact when Sophocles said that he was shifting to a third style—or perhaps shifting a third time, if we suppose that his own harsh and artificial construction is meant to include two stages, one harsh, the other artificial—he need not have meant that he had quite abandoned the styles that he had perfected earlier. He may have meant: "I have attained mastery in two kinds of drama; from now on I shift on occasion to a third kind." I have no desire to maintain the thesis that the three groups into which the seven extant plays of Sophocles fall are perfect illustrations of the three stages referred to in his statement. There is too much uncertainty for that. It will be better simply to discuss the plays without prepossessions, recognizing that the apparent changes in Sophocles may be largely illusory and due to our loss of the great bulk of his work.[3]

In the earliest play that we have, the *Ajax*, Sophocles has been at pains to introduce an extraneous moral pointed by the goddess Athena in person. According to the story, the arms of Achilles after his death had been offered in competition to the best of the Achaeans. By sharp practice they were awarded to Odysseus. Ajax resented this and planned to slay the Achaean chiefs. He did not succeed, solely because Athena, chastening his pride, sent upon him a delusion which led to his slaughtering the herds of cattle and sheep instead. The play opens with a demonstration of the pride and ferocity of Ajax and the power of the gods to humble the proud. It should be noted that the pride, stubbornness, and unrestrained wrath of Ajax against Agamemnon and Odysseus are all his own. He is an Achilles who goes too far and challenges the gods as well as men who thwart him. In Book 1 of the *Iliad*, Achilles had been on the point of slaying Agamemnon when Athena checked him. He at once shifted his policy to conform to her orders.

Ajax, so the seer is reported as stating, had once declared that a brave man should stand alone without divine assistance, and had in battle refused the partnership of Athena herself. Seers, be it noted, never operate in drama on a high moral plane; they are purveyors of superstition. Athena herself as drawn by the poet represents the principle of moderation, particularly in the treatment of a fallen foe. Odysseus watches in terror while Athena keeps him concealed from the mad Ajax. Ajax has bound a ram and is flogging it savagely in the delusion that he is punishing Odysseus. When Athena makes a plea for pity to the foe, Ajax refuses to heed her and addresses her in tones of self-assertion. Odysseus takes to heart the lesson that man's pride is baseless. The gods may humble the strong or the wealthy in a day. The wise man will recognize that he is one with other men and will pity them in misfortune. In this view the gods represent the uncertainty of human life, and he who fears them will heed the plea of humanity.

The introduction of Athena has also the effect to some extent of glorifying Ajax. Only a god could have overpowered him. Odysseus is afraid of him, and it is clear enough that Agamemnon and Menelaus would have been slain if Athena had not intervened. Their attitude to him when they appear after his death is that of foolish tyrants who prate of justice and are puffed with pride because a foe has succumbed to the vengeance of the gods. There is, however, good sense in Agamemnon's plea that men like Odysseus must be preferred to men of mere physical prowess if states are to be established and maintained. Teucer, however, denies that Ajax owed allegiance to Agamemnon, which is equivalent to denying the latter's right to command. Thus the problem of political morality is raised in an ambiguous way. If Agamemnon represents political justice, those who oppose him are rebels. The Greeks, however, never admitted the claim of one city to rule other cities. When a ruler extended his claims beyond his own city, he became an imperialist and was at once suspected of tyranny. It is true that Athena and Odysseus are on the side of Agamemnon, but this tends to compromise their position, for he has been unjust in the view of Ajax and Teucer, and is seen in the play as an ungenerous commander. Presumably it was the opinion of Sophocles that public injustice would not justify private retaliation. A state is like a parent and should receive deference even when it acts unreasonably. Ajax is like Polyneices in the *Seven against Thebes,* who was rebuked by Amphiaraus for seeking to avenge himself against his motherland.[4]

There is also a conflict of conceptions in the play, for Ajax and Teucer would deny the existence of any but personal obligations in the case. Sophocles makes sure that our sympathy will be with Ajax as a warrior of great pride and independence, but he also lets us see that such proud tempers must be curbed in the interest of society. In the *Iliad,* Book 24, Achilles is taught by the gods to pity the defeated. It is precisely the same lesson that Ajax refuses to learn in Sophocles and that Odysseus does learn. Ajax is a mad Achilles even before Athena intervenes. He is a tragic hero, more courageous than most men, but guilty of pride and inhumanity, for which he is laid low. Sophocles might have pointed his moral without introducing Athena, but he would then have had to make Ajax a less sympathetic character and to allow Agamemnon to achieve success. Agamemnon is much too successful as it is, for when he grants permission for the burial of Ajax rather as a favor to Odysseus than as the right of the dead man, he seems to have learned nothing, and still to be enjoying the fruits of chicanery. Sophocles is giving us only a slice of the epic and cannot show in this play the vengeance of the gods upon Agamemnon. It is Odysseus who wins a moral victory over both Ajax and Agamemnon, for he alone accepts the divine principle of moderation in success, triumph without undue exultation.

It is no doubt impossible to write a great tragedy that will not convey a profound moral to the thoughtful, but artistically it is difficult to present a tragic character in a frame of social or political morality, as Sophocles does in *Ajax* and *Antigone.* If the *Ajax* is a moral play, Odysseus must be the hero; if it is a tragedy, as it mainly is, Ajax must be glorified. There are comparable examples to show that a good tragedy can be written about a man who is too proud to succeed in politics; witness *Coriolanus* and the Japanese *Lord Dewa*, which are purely psychological in their motivation, like the later plays of Sophocles himself.[5]

There is another difficulty about the introduction of Athena into the play. Either the gods are moral rulers of the universe or they are merely a personification of vicissitude. Herodotus frequently illustrates the jealousy of the gods, who bring misfortune on the prosperous man solely because he is too prosperous—just the technique of tyrants in maintaining their sway. The notion that a chance remark may provoke the enmity of higher powers is widespread in the world, but does not argue a belief in the benevolence of such spirits. Psychologically, of course, the man who oversteps the bounds of proper speech may be expected to overstep other bounds too and so to come ultimately to grief. But the gods cannot at the same time behave with petty malice and spite and exercise a good moral influence. Athena in the *Ajax* is mainly designed to frighten the audience into good behavior rather than to lead them to virtue through understanding and through confidence in the moral forces of the universe.

It is the attempt to combine the tragedy of Ajax with the moral principle which is involved in permitting him to be honorably buried that makes the drama a historic rather than a philosophic unit. That the question of burying the dead may be good material for drama was proved by Sophocles in the *Antigone*. In the *Ajax* Odysseus' victory is too easily won to be dramatic. Sophocles wrote one of his most impressive plays about the burial of Oedipus, but he did not combine the theme in one play with the downfall of Oedipus. Disaster and rehabilitation are both good subjects for drama, but they must not be treated simultaneously in a story about the same character, or the drama is likely to degenerate into a mere pageant. The *Heracles* of Euripides is exceptional.

When Sophocles is dealing with the personal tragedy of Ajax, he makes his strongest dramatic impression by psychological means. Tecmessa, the captive concubine of Ajax, imparts to the chorus of Salaminian sailors her grief and fears. Ajax had come to his senses amid the carnage that he had created and had forced Tecmessa to tell him the truth, that he had betrayed his hostility to the Achaean host by attempting to slaughter them, yet had in his madness only succeeded in making a laughingstock of himself by his attack on the herds. Soon we see Ajax himself for the first time reduced to lamentation, which he hitherto had scorned as unworthy of a hero. He will later practice deception, which before his fall he would equally have scorned in conversation with friends. He has thought of himself as the spotless hero, whom nothing could dishonor. His tragedy is as close as possible to that of Achilles in the *Iliad*. It is the tragedy of the tarnished ideal, which nothing can ever set right. A hero once dishonored is always dishonored. Achilles lived for vengeance after his disillusionment, but Ajax has no vengeance to hope for, since the goddess is his foe and has proved her power.

The logic of the situation is clear and he resolves to die, but he will die alone as he has lived. Before he goes he takes leave of wife and child, and here Sophocles presents us with a contrast to Hector's leavetaking in Book 6 of the *Iliad*. Ajax shows no tenderness for Tecmessa, but rejects arguments and blandishments alike in curt rebuke. Women have no place in the hero's calculations. Hector's son had shown fear. Ajax's son must not do so. His pride appears even in his prayer for his son. Hector had prayed that his son might be a better man than his father. Ajax prays that his son may be like him, but luckier. We could have no better evidence of the unrepentant pride of Ajax. He was bound to be crushed sometime by forces that he could never estimate. He commends his wife and son to the care of his half brother Teucer. When he has persuaded the chorus that he hopes to make his peace with the gods and is going to the shore to bury his sword instead of slaying himself, he departs alone.[6]

As soon as Ajax goes, a messenger arrives with news that the seer Calchas declares that Athena's hate will not vex Ajax after that day. Teucer has ordered that Ajax is to be watched. Tecmessa

is stung to think that Ajax must have deceived her in pretending to
be reconciled to life, but she and the chorus go in search of him.
This clears the stage for Ajax to enter and commit suicide. He
curses Agamemnon, Menelaus, and the whole Achaean host as he
dies. This curse serves merely to indicate the character of the desperate hero, who is born to hate rather than to love. The curse is
not part of the action of the drama. Indeed, if the dead man's curse
were to be taken seriously, he would have to be placated by honors
after death, as usually happens in Japanese stories of injustice, or
else it could hardly be assumed that death puts an end to enmity.

Teucer acted in the spirit of Ajax when he refused to invite Odysseus, even after his friendly intervention, to attend the funeral of
Ajax. Teucer, being alive, might be reconciled to Odysseus, but
the wrath of the dead continues to work. We find the same view
in Plato's *Laws*, nearly a century later. The seer's statements about
Athena's wrath turn out to mean in the end merely that Athena
would not hate Ajax after death. Oracles in drama are always fulfilled but never helpful. They are precursors of tragedy and are
used to set action going. The attempt to avert the disaster of which
an oracle or seer's prediction gives warning, is either itself disastrous, or adds to frustration by illustrating the futility of human
endeavor. Athena had already done her work. Watched or not,
Ajax could not live in dishonor. He had bent to lament and deceive,
but the very bending made life intolerable. It is his tragedy that his
code of honor forces the weaklings to combine against him. Like
the Japanese warrior, he hopes to take vengeance as a spirit by
projecting his wrathful curse at the moment of death. The ration-
alists retaliate by refusing to take the dead man seriously, or his
code either. They worship Athena, goddess of wisdom and power
both.[7]

Laments by Tecmessa and Teucer are followed by the threat of
Menelaus that he will prevent the burial of Ajax. When he is beaten
in the war of words, Tecmessa goes to fetch the son of Ajax, and
on her return the body of Ajax and his armor are guarded by the
helpless wife and child as symbols of the dead man's interest. Aga-

memnon now appears and belittles the dead man. In the name of
law and justice he does less than justice to Ajax. Actually, treason
as gross as Ajax's is not usually condoned. Themistocles was not
buried in his native land, and Phocion's remains were preserved
secretly by his wife. Benedict Arnold is honored by an empty niche
in the battle monument at Saratoga, and, at the spot where he was
wounded in the battle, by a stone that commemorates his military
glory. But even suicides are buried nowadays, though they may not
always be accorded Christian burial. It is Odysseus who argues in
the end for justice to the dead man and for recognition of his
proved worth as a warrior. Agamemnon would separate politics
from piety, but is willing to grant permission for the burial solely
as a personal favor to Odysseus. That is obviously good politics. It
is also good policy for Odysseus to pity Ajax, since he himself will
need burial some day. Agamemnon can appreciate the golden rule
when it is stated in a way to show that all parties derive private
advantage from it. The chorus recognize the wisdom or cleverness
of Odysseus, Teucer accepts his friendship, but not his presence at
the funeral. The chorus end the play with the statement that no
man can foretell the future.[8]
    Sophocles has kept his characters remarkably consistent. His
Agamemnon is like Homer's and Aeschylus's, being concerned to
rule at all costs. Odysseus used the same kind of argument to
persuade him to do the right thing that Clytemnestra had used to
inveigle him. Menelaus, like his brother, would not permit kindness to a foe; as Achilles says in Book 24 of the *Iliad,* the Atridae
would not have shown mercy to Priam if they had known of his
presence in the camp. Odysseus is consistently crafty. He shows
fear in the first scene and is so tactful in dealing with Agamemnon
at the end that his moral victory lacks luster. He does the right
thing, but not very obviously for the right reason. Athena's ad-
monition is a sufficient explanation of his conduct, but his moral
stature shrinks when we compare him with Antigone. He is as
flexible as Ajax is inflexible. Of course Odysseus is right about piety
and about policy too, but he is rather contrasted with Ajax than

glorified. If Ajax suffered injustice and Odysseus profited by it, there is something cynical in the award to him of final honors in ethics as well. It was Ajax with whom Socrates hoped to converse in Hades as a fellow victim of injustice. Pindar tells us that Homer beguiled men into thinking too highly of Odysseus. He himself preferred Ajax as a hero. It is clear that Sophocles has fallen between two stools. The burial that Ajax gains, being a gift of Odysseus, would not have helped him to lie easy. Historically, he had to be buried and to be glorified as a hero. Philosophically, a man of his type will not fit into a political framework. Sophocles finds a political niche for the prophet of personal honor by building the tomb of the man whom politics had rejected. The grave makes strange contrasts between the life of a man and his honor after death, whether in Judaea or Japan. Otherwise Sophocles does more than justice to Ajax by giving him all the best lines and by showing him surrounded by the love and affection that he himself apparently accorded to no one. The death of Ajax is most moving, as is the defeat of any strong or obstinate character who goes down with flag flying, but he is not really vindicated or appeased in the sequel. In the *Odyssey*, Book 11, he does not accept the apology of Odysseus, and Sophocles does not contradict Homer.[9]

The *Antigone* amounts almost to a recantation or retreatment by Sophocles of the theme that he had treated in the *Ajax*, the claim of the dead to respect and the tendency of politics to disregard pious feelings and unwritten laws. He still brings in the intervention of the gods, not explicitly, but by the implication of his plot. As Athena avenged herself on Ajax, so Hades strikes back at Creon. Poetic justice is a little too mechanical. If such divine intervention is an element of Aeschylean *onkos*, we see the last of it, as far as Sophocles is concerned, in this play. The element of harshness is present in character and fate. Antigone has her father's savage temper; she is as willing to die for honor as Ajax, but she has the advantage over him that, when she defies the tyrant in order to bury her brother, she is doing right. Hence she can win a moral victory over Creon and be glorified unequivocally. Sophocles is completely successful in combining tragedy with a political and moral framework; his construction is becoming ingenious. Still, the difficulty remains that first-rate tragedy is so moving that the moral lesson that Creon learns after the death of Antigone is a dramatic anticlimax. It is interesting to compare the speed with which Sophocles finishes off the much later *Electra*. The later heroine is also more complicated than Antigone psychologically, equally stubborn but less easily dismayed. Both are sisters in love with a brother and capable of scorning a sister who is less virile.

The *Antigone* has appeared in many modern versions as a drama of conflict, the conflict between the obligations of religious or personal feeling and the obligations of political responsibility. In Sophocles there is a conflict between two obstinate characters, Creon, the king, who refuses burial to the traitor Polyneices, his nephew, and Antigone, who persists in giving her brother such burial as she can in spite of Creon's decree. She appears in the prologue already prepared to do the deed. She puts the obligation on the plane of honor and adopts an attitude as uncompromising as any exhibited by Ajax or Achilles, but with the moral advantage that she herself represents a higher morality—not a personal code, but religious duty as embodied in unwritten law. Pericles is said himself to have emphasized the importance of unwritten law, when he admonished the Athenians to enforce not only the written laws against impiety but also the unwritten laws that were expounded by the Eumolpidae. These laws none had yet received authority to repeal nor had ventured to gainsay, nor was their author known. Respect for these laws would encourage a belief that not only men but gods punish impiety. Antigone names Zeus as the author of the unwritten laws to which she appeals, and Tiresias threatens Creon with vengeance springing from the wrath both of the Olympians and of the gods below.[10]

It was not until nearly forty years after the production of the *Antigone* that the Athenian democracy definitely canceled the political validity of unwritten law. This was the time of which Plato says that laws and customs were changing at an increasing rate that made him giddy. One priestess had the courage to refuse to curse Alcibiades when he was exiled, on the ground that she was a priestess for blessing, not for cursing; and at all times women have mourned and buried their loved ones without regard to political axioms. The wife of Phocion is a case in point. Antigone, however, went further than mere burial; she defied her uncle the tyrant, expounded her views in lofty tones, vigorously and emphatically expressed her scorn for him, and left him no opening for mercy if he was to save his face.[11]

Creon illustrates the remark of Agamemnon in the *Ajax* (v. 1350) that it is not easy for a monarch to be pious. He scoffs at superstition, but at the same time disregards the moral forces that hold society together. He represents the school of thought of which Machiavelli the Italian, Kautilya the Hindu, and Lord Shang the Chinese, are advocates. It holds that the prince makes the law and that men not only may but should obey him regardless of morals or conscience. Democracies may of course be quite as arbitrary as tyrants, unless freedom of thought and speech is included in the definition of democracy. Creon's political creed does not prevent his masquerading as the state, but no Athenian would have accepted his undemocratic principles. When he accuses the seer of taking bribes, he is behaving like the traditional tyrant. He also behaves like Agamemnon when he shows no sense of the sanctity of family ties. This comes out strongly in his scene with Haemon, his son, who conceals his love for Antigone but loathes with all the impatience of youth his father's ungenerous insistence on foolish consistency and face saving. Creon is, however, not a rugged villain. In dealing with Ismene, who was an accessory before the fact, he pardons her by an afterthought. She is too womanly to be dangerous. The seer, too, frightens him by prediction of disaster. Actually, he is superstitious at bottom and can feel the want of family ties when they are severed. He is a foolish villain who is surprised and alarmed by the results of the policy that he had supposed was clever and expedient. When the chorus fail to back him against the seer, he is completely deflated. He is essentially the same as he is in two other plays of Sophocles, *Oedipus Tyrannus* and *Oedipus at Colonus,* a man concerned about protocol, cherishing petty ambitions, and devoid of generous sympathy.[12]

It is not only the womanly Ismene who throws into relief the noble courage and high thoughts of Antigone. The guard who arrests her when she performs the rite of burial a second time is a perfect example of the citizen who is ruled only by fear, not by conscience. It is a commonplace in Greek, made much of by Plato and others, that slaves must be governed by fear, but free men by their conscience and their sense of respect for the rights and feelings of others, their *aidôs.* Creon's methods would reduce all to the slavish level of the guard, who considers it important only to avoid punishment and is as evasive as Antigone is bold. Here alone Sophocles depicts with such care a low character in tragedy. He evidently wants all to see what a tyrant's henchman is like, and what kind of men are produced by a state whose mainspring is fear. There is nothing furtive about Antigone; she acts on principle. She is not interested in technicalities, whether her brother has had his due with one ritual burial, or whether the removal of the earth that she has cast upon his corpse can unbury him again, as Creon assumes. Her attitude persists, and with it her continued disobedience. She wins glory by excess of loyalty, as Penelope did, but her reward is death. This is a kind of tragedy of which Aristotle conveys no conception in his criticism, the tragedy of a willing martyr who makes no mistake but goes serenely on the way that leads to certain death. There are many scenes of patriotic self-devotion in Greek tragedy, but only Antigone dies so clear-sightedly and in such isolation. It is instructive to compare her tragedy with that of Socrates, which it greatly resembles, no doubt because Plato, who wrote the *Apology,* had meditated on the *Antigone.*[13]

Socrates, like Antigone, refuses to be moved from his course by the threat of death. Like her he rationalizes, explaining that death is for him a happier fate than life. Like her he provokes by his defiance the angry vengeance of his judges. Like her he claims to be serving a power that is above the state; he would save the state in spite of itself. So Antigone represents forces without which a good state cannot be realized. Socrates differs only in that he does not lament his own death. Both Antigone and Socrates no doubt brought their doom upon themselves, but they were guilty neither of intellectual nor of moral error. It was their virtue that doomed them. Aristotle has little excuse for not recognizing this type of tragedy, unless perhaps that it hardly occurs elsewhere in Greek except in episodes. It is true that Antigone is unnecessarily insulting both to Creon and to Ismene, but that is part of her loyalty to her ideal. She will not see it profaned by a lip service that is not whole-hearted, and she will not accept overtures of friendship or kindness from a man who denies that ideal. Her glory is not in surviving or in converting her foes; she must be herself. Her noble conception would be ill served by a humble attitude. A high calling invests the individual with an authority that seems insolent to the skeptic, but there are times when not to assert a principle is to desert it. To hold that Antigone would have been more admirable if she had let Ismene and Creon dodge the issue is to set our sights too low. Antigone is magnificent. Still, as A. A. Milne has pointed out, it is a mistake for a dramatist to make a character who is killed off early in a play so interesting that the rest of the play is inevitably dull by comparison.[14]

It would be, however, un-Greek not to play with a theme on different levels. The example of Plato and the orators is convincing of the fact that fallacies and irrelevancies in an argument are not excluded by any Greek code of logic or taste. Once a plea that is convincing on the highest level is finished, the Greek author is likely to get down to the trivialities and personalities that are so much more effective in persuading some juries than pure logic or idealism. Antigone presents a sophistical argument for devotion to a brother that to the modern ear strikes a false note. Perhaps it is good psychology to make her lose her grip on realities at this moment, but it is not good drama to make such a heroine suddenly pitiful. Appeals to pity are, however, part of the essential armory of Greek tragedy even in the case of men. Antigone differs from Ajax in that she laments in public and in that the chorus show her no sympathy. Their attitude is that of the Chinese emperor who rewarded an honest censor by promoting him to high rank and ordering his death in one sentence. So in that favorite Japanese drama, *The Soga Revenge,* the heroes, when they have defied the authorities in order to avenge a father, are made happy by being allowed to commit seppuku with special marks of distinction. The chorus congratulate Antigone on the special honor of being immured in a tomb like Niobe. In Greek drama this sort of thing is recognized as a mockery.[15]

It is like Creon to immure Antigone in a tomb with a little food so that her death will not be a pollution. He really is superstitious. That is a fate that lies in wait for the cleverly irreligious. It is like Antigone to thwart his calculations by hanging herself. She does not curse him audibly, but such a suicide was a curse in itself. Haemon, who loves her and has pleaded with his father for her life, tears open the tomb and finds her dead. About this time Creon has decided to yield, ignorant of the doom that is already enfolding him. The seer Tiresias frightens him too late. He hastens to bury Polyneices more adequately than Antigone had done. Since he has been conspicuously lacking in insight up to this point, we need not be surprised that he does not first unbury Antigone. He probably feels that a little time in the tomb would be good for her before she discovers that he had been forced to pardon her. His is a case, not of repentance with new understanding of life, but of regret without reform. He is punished without being enlightened, like Xerxes. There is poetic justice in his suffering. He has abolished family feeling, and his family turns against him. He had mocked Antigone's love for her brother. Now Haemon, his son, spits in his face and tries to kill him, then turns his sword on himself. When he returns home with the body, he is met by news that his wife, already grieving over the loss of another son, has cursed her husband and stabbed herself. Creon would be glad to die himself in his abasement. The chorus comfort him by speaking of fate, but point a moral for the audience. Impiety is punished by the gods.[16]

Thus if we turn our attention from Antigone herself, the moral structure of the play becomes evident. To be sure, the moral plot in Aristotle's usage involves the triumph of a hero, and no one triumphs in this play except the gods. Yet the death or fate worse than death of a man of sin has the same effect as the triumph of a good man. At any rate, we have here a type of tragedy in which a great political or moral error causes the ruin of a king or other hero. If Creon had been depicted as a great character, the effect would have been mixed; he might have been represented as clever but dishonest, like Odysseus, or courageous and brutal, like Ajax. The effect would still be highly tragic. Instead, we find ourselves on the lower level of ordinary life, with its interest in minor characters regardless of great issues; and this is bound to happen as soon as the hero is made foolish or weak. Creon seems to be honest and well-intentioned, but his virtues are not enough for a king. Rule shows the quality of a man. Creon appears smaller when he is in office.

Still, there is a melodramatic contrast between the scene after the first chorus, when he promulgates his edict amid general acquiescence, and the last scene, when he bewails his folly and his fate. He had suffered a psychological overthrow from the moment when the seer Tiresias had inspired fear in him. He had bullied the guard, Antigone, Ismene, Haemon, and even Tiresias, with increasing ruthlessness. His greatness was in external trappings. Antigone seems at first a ridiculously puny opponent, a mere woman. But the circle of sympathy spreads wider and wider until the chorus too turn against the king. From this moment calamities come crashing on his head. Yet there is something mechanical in the effect. We have seen a little of Haemon, but nothing at all of the queen, Eurydice. They are but instruments of vengeance. Furthermore, there has been no indication that Creon was the kind of man who values family ties. His punishment is of a sort that could be appreciated more by others than by himself. He has sacrificed piety for politics; he has still a political future at the end of the play. He will not grieve overmuch in the sequel. Though the poetic justice of the ending is clear, since Haemon's impious attack on his father is the reward of impiety, it taxes our credulity to see events moving so fast to execute poetic justice. We must remember that disrespect for parents is also impiety in Greek. Plato is content to assure the criminal that he will live again to suffer in another life what he has done wrong in this. Sophocles brings retribution in kind on the same day. This is not the way things happen in real life—at least not often—and hence the imposing machinery seems artificial. False grandiosity is *onkos,* and Sophocles never indulged in it again, as far as we know.[17]

In the next two plays, the *Trachiniae* and *Oedipus Tyrannus,* the downfall of a great man is once more related in a way to recall the fate of Creon, but interest is concentrated on the downfall. The fatal instruments are still the man's own wife, but the wife loves and would save her husband. Thus we get the interesting situation in which a hero falls through obscure causes that operate without the will to harm of any living creature. Perhaps such things are the work of the gods, as Teucer believes; the chorus says at the end of the *Trachiniae* that they are Zeus. They seem meaningless and absurd and depress the intelligence that fails to avert them. They increase man's sense of insecurity, but not his sense of responsibility. If in a tragic plot a man dies with no one plotting, surely life itself or the gods, if they regulate life, have plotted against him. The plot, of course, is that of the author of the play, but if he depicts his characters convincingly the impact will be impressive and much more tragic than if the effect were commensurate with the cause. It is when justice is not done that Aristotle finds a truly tragic plot, and Sophocles is particularly concerned to leave justice out of these two plays and to emphasize the paradox that the race is not to the swift nor the battle to the strong. Time and chance happeneth to them all.

The plot of the *Trachiniae* is of course the plot of the dead centaur Nessus, but his plot succeeds because he has long been forgotten. That the mighty Heracles should be slain by a woman would be paradoxical even if there had been no Nessus. Women in Athens were quite capable of slaying their husbands with love potions, as we know from a speech of Antiphon. Sophocles was interested in the irony of good intentions that backfire. He includes in his play only the good intentions. Nessus appears as an afterthought. The story is that the centaur Nessus ferried people across a river, but that when he took the wife of Heracles, Deianeira, on his back, he made off with her, since Heracles was on the other bank. The poisoned arrow of Heracles, however, could still reach him and slay. As he died, he recommended a phial of his blood to Deianeira as a love potion. The blood must not be exposed to the sun, and should be used to steep some garment that Heracles wore next his skin.

The *Trachiniae* tells how the lady used the potion and found that it was a poison and that she had killed her husband instead of curing him. An oracle warns her that a certain day is critical for him. She sends her son Hyllus to get news of his father, like Telemachus in the *Odyssey*. News soon comes that Heracles has won a victory. His squire Lichas comes bringing captive women to deliver to the care of Deianeira. She pities them, particularly one fair princess, whose name Lichas professes not to know. When he is gone, a villager reports to Deianeira that the princess is Iole and that Heracles will make her his bride and expects her to share the house with the first wife. No Greek woman tolerates such a position in fiction. Deianeira convicts Lichas of lying, pretends to be indifferent, and sends to Heracles a special robe steeped in the centaur's blood. She holds that dark works, if kept dark, need do no harm. Soon, however, she has misgivings. Perhaps she was rash to trust the centaur. Hyllus now returns with news of his father. Heracles had put on the robe and was soon distraught with pain and frenzy. Deianeira does not reply to her son's reproaches and curses, but goes in and stabs herself. Hyllus is repentant too late, but enters again with the dying Heracles, who laments and points out his strange fate—to die by a woman's hand, after all the battles he had won. He learns the truth that, even more strangely, the oracle, which had foretold that a dead person would kill him, was to be fulfilled. He orders Hyllus to construct a pyre for him on Mount Oeta and, before he goes on his way to die, compels his son to agree to marry Iole.[18]

There is one moral that Sophocles does make explicit, the moral that good intentions are not enough. Deianeira also points a moral when she repents of the deceit that she practiced on Lichas and Heracles by secretly smearing the robe. She had herself just rebuked Lichas for his own deception in the matter of Iole. The extreme gentleness and humility of Deianeira contrast with the dire effect of her good intentions and modest intrigue. Her self-effacement also enables Heracles to hold the stage by proxy during the greater part of the play before he appears in person. The fact that the chorus abet Deianeira excuses her to some extent. Sophocles has created a husband-slayer who is just the opposite of Clytemnestra, and a jealous wife who is as gentle as Medea is ferocious. His fatal woman is no champion of women's rights, but recalls Euripides' *Alcestis,* who died for her husband.

Sophocles makes up, however, for his tender portrait of a murderess by his failure to emphasize the sins of her husband. He does this by omitting all psychology or morality from his portrait and building him all of history and rhetoric. Thus we get morality this time framed in a story of death that is not moralized at all. The opportunity for a moral is clear enough. No wife could be more neglected by her husband. She saw him only at long intervals and he had loves galore. But he is blamed by no one in the play, and, far from repenting, shows not the slightest concern for the fate of his wife. What happens to him is no more than poetic justice, but Sophocles is careful to neglect this aspect of the matter. In fact, he makes more protests against the cruelty of the gods in this play than elsewhere. There was an easy answer, that Heracles was on his way to immortality. Possibly Sophocles trusted his audience to supply that answer. In that case, however, they might also see how badly Heracles behaved when he sacked a city for love

of Iole. He is, however, no worse than Ajax, who won Tecmessa
in the same way. If the Greek poets had not accepted such acts as
natural in a hero, they could hardly have used the old material.
It is not until we come to the comedies of Menander that we find
men repenting of wrongs done to a woman. The women of tragedy
are inevitably meek or wicked in dealing with their mates. It is
not merely heroes in Greek tragedy who do violence to women.
The gods were equally bad. They are rebuked by Euripides, but
no one rebukes the heroes. In the case of Heracles, moreover, absolutely nothing is done to make him seem a great character or
to present him in a favorable light, or even to make him sympathetic. Sophocles himself considered love a tyrannical master, as
we know from Plato. Love destroyed Haemon in the *Antigone;*
so it destroys Heracles. It even made him unheroic and unlovely.
Even in comedy love is not always glorified, but there it may produce desirable results. The greatness of Heracles could be taken
for granted in addressing a Greek audience. His weakness with
women and his violence are made very apparent in the play.

Ajax and Antigone were defeated by the structure of the state
with which they had to deal. Heracles is defeated by something
in the structure of the universe. We are dealing with inscrutable
destiny and the irony of fate. It no longer helps to believe in gods
if the ways of gods are entirely unpredictable. It is worse if the
gods are jealous of all greatness. Ajax the warrior, Antigone the
embodiment of piety, and Heracles the scourge of monsters, are
alike brought low. In *Oedipus Tyrannus,* Sophocles shows the fall
of a man of action who is also an intellectual. He is as nearly as
possible the opposite of Creon in the *Antigone,* but the contrast
between his greatness and his decline is much the same. He does
not scoff at pollution or disobey oracles; he is a successful king
and honest in pursuit of the welfare of the city. He is great enough
to be a tragic figure, and for the first time Sophocles concentrates
his interest on the psychology as well as the fate of his main character. He so complicates the issue that the attempt to find a profound moral tells us more about the critic than about Sophocles.

The poet seems to be certain only that there is no certainty. He offers no formula for salvation.

The plot of the *Oedipus* is particularly ingenious in that there are no obviously malicious characters. There is a suspected intrigue, but no evidence to prove it. There is none of the rhetorical persuasiveness of the character who uses speech to conceal his purpose. Even Ajax and Deianeira are guilty of deception. Hence their language is for the moment not capable of revealing character, for it must picture them as what they are not, or the hearer in the play will not be deceived. Character is presented with dramatic directness in the *Oedipus;* all statements may be taken at face value. Yet there are successive revelations of character in successive episodes, and so accurately are character and personality intertwined that the weaknesses and fears that are revealed in Oedipus seem to have determined his destiny from the start. Sophocles was forced to probe unusual depths in order to make the self-blinding of Oedipus plausible. He has turned physical horror into psychological. The effect is just the reverse of mechanical. The two oracles about Oedipus that are fulfilled are not public factors, but private memories of ancient bereavement. A man's past is certainly part of his inexorable destiny, and Oedipus' fate cannot be averted now. The revelation of his past might conceivably have been averted. Since Oedipus is the kind of man who must know himself at any cost, he seems, like Antigone and Eteocles, to be bent on his own destruction. No one else is eager to damage him by information. He is the detective who detects himself.

The oracle, it is true, might seem to have contrived his ruin by its three declarations. His father Laïus was told that his son would slay him and marry his own mother Jocasta. This led to the exposure of the infant Oedipus to die. Oedipus was given the same information about himself as a youth. The news sent him frightened away from Corinth, the home of his royal foster parents, toward Thebes, where the oracle was fulfilled. After many years came the plague, in which men died by the invisible arrows of Apollo, and from Apollo at Delphi came the oracle that to stop the plague the murderer of Laïus must be punished. Yet in all this the oracle is not an active agent. It does not order Laïus or Oedipus to do what they did, as it ordered Orestes to slay his mother in the play of Aeschylus. It merely provides accurate information of the future. The information, to be sure, produces it own fulfillment, when men seek to evade the catastrophe, but is not that the fault of their unenlightened superstition? The oracle would have no effect if there were no believers. Those who resort to Apollo perish by Apollo. The oracle was even helpful in staying the plague, for we hear no more of that, once Oedipus has pronounced his awful curse on the unknown murderer. Too many characters cooperate in the development of the action for it to seem unplanned. Who but the god could plan it?

For this is a play of unplanned action. The actions of numerous individuals are well motivated by circumstance and character. They are disconnected in their causes but convergent in their effect. We have seen how Aeschylus in the *Choephoroe* introduces independent action by humble characters to further the plot. Their action, however, is sympathetic successful action, consciously directed toward an end that is achieved. In the *Oedipus,* action is taken in ignorance and its purpose is self-defeating. We have, then, a case of unconscious coöperation, acts convergent toward an unplanned, undesired result. There was a concatenation of action in the tragedy of Creon in the *Antigone* that was quite different. The successive suicides of Antigone, Haemon, and Eurydice form a chain of cause and effect, the final effect being the tragic suffering of Creon that is seen only at the end. In the case of Oedipus the concatenation is psychological. We see his successive moods of curiosity, hope, and despair, and can share with him the progress of his downfall. Since the action is autonomous, that is, not governed by human calculation, an effect is produced as if an external force were working, whether divine providence or pure chance or some hostile god. Aeschylus would invoke a curse or a demon. Sophocles produces more doubt by not doing so. If the results were happy, or if they produced an effect of poetic justice, they would promote

cheerfulness and optimism. Since all good intentions are frustrated
in the *Oedipus*, the effect is either to promote pessimism and ir-
responsibility or to set men searching for flaws in the plot or for
justification of the result.

There is no prolonged discordant action in the plot. What there
is arises from Oedipus' search for a villain. He finds one in the
seer and another later in Creon. His detective zeal makes him angry
at concealment, and the seer tells the truth. Not at all appalled,
Oedipus joins Creon with Tiresias in his indictment. There is no
evidence in the play that Creon was not a plotter, but if Creon
was innocent, there is poetic justice in the turning of the tables
against Oedipus at the end. Creon is an Odysseus rather than an
Ajax; he is fluent with arguments and offended rather than angered even when he is threatened with death. He does not reproach
Oedipus after his blinding, but pointedly uses the trick of *prae-
teritio*, for to say that he does not reproach Oedipus is to make it
plain that he could. Nor does he propose to allow the fallen king
any liberty of action. The appeal to Delphi was a useful means of
coercion in Greek politics. But Sophocles carefully refrains from
emphasizing the theme of poetic justice. Oedipus must have our
sympathy, not Creon, and there must be no successful villain—a
possibility that Aristotle rejects as abominable. Yet the fall of Oedipus is no tragedy for Creon, as it is for Jocasta, the old shepherd,
and the chorus.

Let us see how Sophocles produces his complicated and riddling
effect. In the prologue the king is seen in all his majesty, confident
of his power to aid the people, who are suffering from plague and
blight. Thus the theme with which the play ends is emphasized
at the beginning. Count no man happy. The greatest prosperity
may be ended in one day. This is the outer frame of the play, which
is melodramatic with emphasis on the external vicissitudes of life.
Oedipus has already acted by sending the queen's brother Creon
to Delphi. Creon returns crowned with laurel, since the oracle is
helpful. To end the plague the murderers of Laïus must be punished. Oedipus has no suspicion that he is himself the murderer,

for all reports speak of murderers. The one man who escaped had preferred a vague statement. Oedipus was king when he returned, and how should a slave accuse a king? In the next scene Oedipus takes proper measures against the unknown criminal by banishing him with a curse. Plato threatened murderers who did not confess with the fate of being cast out unburied if they were caught, but Oedipus can hardly go so far in this play.

The next step is to consult the seer Tiresias, as the chorus suggest. Again Oedipus had forestalled them, acting on a previous suggestion of Creon. Seers in Greek drama are almost as unaccountable and touchy as the holy man in Hindu stories, whose almost unprovoked curse may force a goddess to dwell on earth or prevent a king from recognizing his beloved wife. Tiresias produces no such effect; he heightens mystery and disturbs the chorus. He knows that Oedipus is the murderer of Laïus, but prefers to keep the secret to himself. He had not come to make that disclosure; but when Oedipus denounces him with anger, he with no less anger denounces Oedipus as the murderer and worse, for he will discover his identity and his pollution that very day. Oedipus scents a plot concocted between the seer and Creon to place the latter on the throne by accusing Oedipus of murder. There is irony when he twits the seer with blindness, and poetic justice when he himself is later blinded. Only once does Oedipus strangely pause in his wrath, when he catches a reference by the seer to his parents. Thus he betrays his hidden secret and the gnawing inferiority that derives from the doubt that had been cast on his birth. This technique for disclosing a ruling passion is a new application of Homer's method with Achilles. We shall not be surprised later to find that Oedipus is more troubled by doubt of his parentage than by any other calculation.[19]

In the next scene Creon appears in order to purge himself. This time the anger of Oedipus does not rise gradually; it bursts at once. It is clear that he does not like Creon, the comfortable serene highness who is satisfied to enjoy the honors and emoluments of a queen's brother without any of the responsibilities or obligations of office. One is reminded of the Chinese saying that there are two plagues of government, eunuchs and wife's relatives. Creon's horizon is limited to his personal interest. His calm sense of security as he claims special privilege and defends himself is more than the self-made Oedipus could bear. Here we have one of Sophocles' best-portrayed contrasts of character. Creon is always assured, but Oedipus becomes a creature of uncontrolled passion when by quick wit he reaches a conclusion that is not immediately concurred in. His anger is as quick as his wit. Jocasta arrives in time to calm him. Creon is let off and goes away grumbling that Oedipus has grown strange, which puts Creon on a level with the multitude. The correct interpretation of this line is important for an understanding of Creon. He is a born aristocrat. He is all for secrecy and privilege in government.[20]

Oedipus has also obviously been behaving like a tyrant. The plague, the suggestion to consult the seer, the seer's accusation of the king as responsible for the plague, the king's anger at the seer and at the man who proposed consulting him—all these are exactly the matter of the *Iliad's* first book, whereby Agamemnon was stamped as a bad king doomed to destruction. Creon was accused of tampering with oracles and seers to gain power. Oedipus had denied a trial to Creon, and had granted free speech to the seer only because he could not suppress the independence of the servant of Apollo. Such behavior shows a disregard for sacred things like that of Creon in the *Antigone*. A plain sign of the god's power is needed if worship is not to cease altogether. In these scenes, then, Oedipus betrays faults of character that haunted him all his life. He took little things too seriously, fell into a temper, and acted rashly. His intellectual pride is manifest. When his political position is threatened, he tries to deal rationally with the claims of oracles and seers.[21]

When Creon is gone, Jocasta questions Oedipus and there is an intimate mutual confession of repressed anxiety and doubt that is not paralleled elsewhere in Greek tragedy. Jocasta tells the story of the oracle that had come to Laïus and of her babe cast out to die in order to avert fulfillment, then of the death of Laïus at a place "where three ways meet." As she speaks on, Oedipus hears nothing more. He had slain a man where three ways meet. Up to this point he had triumphed over obstacles with a high hand, but he cannot face his knowledge of the curse that he had put upon the murderer. He is soon convinced that he really is the murderer, and reveals his past history. He has two hidden shames. First, he was called a bastard by a companion and could get no comfort from his adoptive parents' assurances. Next, he went to Delphi to consult the oracle, but was branded there as a man doomed to commit incest with his mother and to become a patricide. To avoid this doom he fled from his supposed parents, met and slew Laïus, and, by reading the riddle of the Sphinx, became king of Thebes and husband of the queen. The restless insecurity of Oedipus, once doubt was cast on his birth, and his horror at the very possibility of incest and parricide, are well brought out. But those matters are not immediately pressing. It is a terrible but minor threat that must be faced, the curse on Laïus' murderer. The slave who had escaped is the last hope. If it was murderers in the plural who slew the king, then Oedipus is acquitted. The contrast between the eagerness of Oedipus to know and Jocasta's willingness to be satisfied with less than certainty is well brought out. She would go on living on any terms, but for Oedipus truth is a passion. Jocasta is sure that oracles do not matter; at least, Laïus was not slain by his son.

The chorus are not shocked at her attitude, nor were the Athenians. Plutarch tells us in his life of Demosthenes that Demosthenes before Chaeronea suspected the Pythia of complicity with Philip of Macedon and urged Thebans and Athenians to disregard oracles and omens as had Epaminondas and Pericles. Those leaders used their reason and considered oracles as but pretexts for cowardice. Certainly the Athenians, when the *Oedipus Tyrannus* was produced, either had begun the Peloponnesian war, in spite of the opposition of Delphi, or were about to begin it. They also followed Pericles in spite of the supposed Cylonian curse that was upon him. If we knew the date of the *Oedipus,* we could judge whether it was intended to affect the political fortunes of Pericles. It seems to be a warning that oracles may come true, but at the same time the rationalist might reflect that it was the very attempt to profit by the oracle that brought destruction. By no possible combination of circumstances could the oracle have proved helpful. Faith is all very well, but if faith does not save, who would recommend it? The chorus propose to be guided by the evidence, but they personally prefer to be pious and humble.[22]

The next scene shows us Jocasta praying to Apollo for help because Oedipus is so overwhelmed by his superstitious fear of curse and oracle. Prayers that are not answered are of course a commonplace in Greek fiction. Ironically enough, a messenger from Corinth arrives and seems at first to bring deliverance. The king of Corinth is dead, the foster father of Oedipus whom he feared he might slay. This is joyful news since it relieves Oedipus of his fears. He and Jocasta are elated at the apparent proof that oracles are fallible, until the messenger reveals that Oedipus was a foundling from Theban territory. Jocasta sees the truth at once and, failing to stop the investigation, goes out quietly to hang herself. Oedipus is too intent on solving the secret of his birth to notice her despair. He thinks that her pride is hurt. His enmity to Creon was no doubt based on a similar antipathy to the proud and secure. The chorus are joyful to think that Oedipus is really a Theban. Thus the action seems to vacillate as gloom is lightened for the moment. Sophocles has similar joyful choruses in Ajax and Antigone, for his choruses are not so much ideal observers as interested observers, if not actors, in the drama.

When the Theban shepherd arrives, it is soon evident that Oedipus is really the son of Laïus and Jocasta and that the oracles are all fulfilled. When Oedipus faced merely the prospect of finding that he had cursed himself, he saw in his fate the work of a cruel demon. There is something daemonic in the fury with which he extracts the secret of his birth from the unwilling shepherd, but there is also something of the glory of self-devotion. His unwillingness to lead a life based on shame has its noble side, and there is much of Antigone and Eteocles in him. Without this aspect of devotion to honesty and intellectual sincerity, his tragedy would lack the element of greatness. At the end he accepts his fate without evasion. He names Apollo as his enemy, but is full of shame and horror of himself. He justifies his action in putting out his own eyes with the same kind of rationalizing argument that Antigone had used to justify dying for a brother's burial. He abases himself to Creon and takes leave of his children, for Creon will not let him keep them with him. Oedipus is no longer a free agent. The chorus end the play with the familiar moral: count no man happy until his life is over.

The *Oedipus Tyrannus* is for Aristotle the model drama. Since it is unique in the history of fiction, it has evidently never served as a model for later playwrights dealing with other characters. The circumstances of the hero are too unusual to lend themselves to imitation without copying. It has also proved impossible to improve on the *Oedipus* of Sophocles; his introduction of the characters and the psychology that are required to make the plot plausible, is better than the best efforts of later poets who have reconstructed the play. The unique element in the plot is the man who recognizes himself. There is peripety in the *Trachiniae* when Deianeira realizes that her effort to save herself means ruin, since she has slain, not regained, her husband. She has made a mistake about the effect of an action. In the recognition scene there is usually a mistake about the identity of some person. The *Oedipus* obviously has a case of mistaken identity as the *Trachiniae* does not. It is not, however, very often that an adult does not know his own identity. Usually if a man's identity is unknown, that is because he is keeping it secret as part of a plot, like Odysseus in the *Odyssey*. There may, of course, be unplanned happy disclosures of identity, as in the *Iphigeneia in Tauris* of Euripides. Since Aristotle strongly approves this recognition scene as well as the plot of the *Oedipus,* he seems to have had a predilection for the recognition that surprises everyone or nearly everyone. It is only the old shepherd in the *Oedipus* who can be said to have plotted to keep the identity of Oedipus a secret, and even he could have identified him only as the murderer of Laïus. The seer, to be sure, also knew the truth, but his motives are incalculable.

The knowledge of his identity need not have been so fatal to the hero if others had not felt strongly about incest. It is said that when some Macedonians saw this play they were surprised that incest should cause so much commotion. They may have practiced it and found that no harm came of it. In fact, it would be possible to turn the story of Oedipus into an attack on social prejudice, and it is easy to imagine Euripides treating it in that way, since we know that he was prepared to justify the love of Pasiphaë for the bovine begetter of the Minotaur. Sophocles has done just the opposite, and has created an unreasoning atmosphere of terror in the presence of sin, regardless of good intentions. Oedipus in this play is as incapable of justifying himself as is Phaedra in the *Hippolytus* of Euripides of justifying herself. In the *Oedipus at Colonus* we find that after a lapse of years he could see himself objectively and calmly, and defend his own innocence. Just so in the *Oedipus Tyrannus* he can see after a lapse of years that he had taken the matter of his birth too seriously; yet in the heat of discovery he still feels the old suicidal urge to know the truth, break forth what will. He is not an integrated character, being at the mercy of old fears, of social sanctions, and of a sense of inferiority.[23]

The invitation of Apollo at Delphi was KNOW THYSELF; Sophocles has shown us a man for whom to know himself was tragic despair and self-mutilation. He cannot bear to live with his new identity. I have seen a motion picture with such a climax. It represented a Nazi youth who was persecuting Jews with loathing of his victims. His father in the end, to restrain him, disclosed to him the fact that he himself was one-fourth Jewish. At once he lost position, the love of his bride, and his hope of happiness. He could not live with himself. In his case there was poetic justice, but Oedipus had not traded on his birth—at least not as far as we know. Sophocles has succeeded in making the fate of Oedipus a moral enigma. He had in all innocence made the mistake of marrying his mother after slaying his father, but no civilized court would have punished him. He does have moral faults, however, that make him dangerous to others, and psychological weaknesses that make him dangerous to himself.

There are at least five ingredients in the play, and their combination produces a dramatic punch of unusual strength. Sophocles leaves the choice open to us how we shall explain the irony of fate that makes every act of Oedipus contribute to self-destruction and that shows the man who apparently is a brilliant success suddenly become the most miserable of men. As first of these ingredients we find that, from the point of view of Oedipus, Apollo in his inscrutable providence has doomed Oedipus from before his birth. No one defends Apollo. Oedipus had not offended by disbelief. Even Jocasta merely supposed that oracles might be manipulated. They were given through human agents. Secondly, from the point of view of Creon and Tiresias, Oedipus, in his tyrannical haste to act without investigation, had condemned himself morally. He was guilty of rashness and misapprehension. He was not a good king, for a good king looks before and after. Thirdly, Oedipus was guilty of the ignorance that thinks itself knowledge. He assumed that he knew the meaning of an oracle when he did not. Since the Greeks classed wisdom as a virtue, the intellectual error of Oedipus was sin. He did not know himself. Fourthly, Oedipus has the psychological weakness of being too easily upset by imaginary evils. He learned to be proud of his possible base birth, but ignorance of his birth still seemed to him an intolerable evil, and he was self-assertive in the presence of those who were secure in the position to which they were born. The mere thought that he might slay his father or marry his mother was as terrible to him as if he had committed the acts. It is Jocasta who points out that men frequently dream of intercourse with their mothers. Oedipus apparently has had no such dreams. He did not know his mother's identity. He suffers from lack of self-control. He fears more than he should. This is a vicious handicap in his constitution. Possibly Oedipus could not help it, but the more inevitable his

fate, the more surely is our ideal of happiness as the birthright
of every man frustrated. Fifthly, we may regard the play as a glorification of the spirit of man, who devotes himself to knowledge
regardless of the catastrophic effect on his own life. This would
be Jocasta's judgment of Oedipus, no doubt. To be sure, Oedipus
did not know the worst that could happen as a result of his research,
but that is equally true of men who invent the airplane, discover
a formula for converting mass into energy, or create philosophies
that put passion above thought.

The play thus produces a probing spectacle of life at five different
levels. First, the melodramatic superficial aspect depicts the collapse
of a once strong man. Whether he is defeated by fate or accident
or by a divine plan makes no difference. Just below the surface
operates intelligence in a vain attempt to solve the problem of happiness. On the third level personality begins to emerge as we discover the rash temper that precipitates crisis after crisis. Deeper
still lurks the terror and insecurity of a tormented fugitive from
himself. Then at the core, fifth and last, we find the mainspring, the
self-assertion defying fate of a soul hot for certainty. The stereo-
scopic effect is almost without parallel in literature.

In this possibility of multiple interpretation we find a new element that is almost entirely Sophoclean and is wholly lifelike. To
be sure, Homer makes his characters take two views of Helen;
some considered her a victim of the goddess, others thought her
a bad woman. He also assigns more free will to one character than
to another, but he has no character whose fate is as enigmatic as
that of Oedipus. Homer's Achilles is nevertheless to some extent
the model for Oedipus. Just as Achilles is wholly intent on the
political situation until he feels his guilt as accessory to the death
of Patroclus, so Oedipus has no doubt of his ability to deal with
his royal problems, until the sense of personal guilt unmans him.
In the case of Oedipus there is a deeper chasm of guilt—parricide
and incest—that casts him to a lower circle of the pit. It is the succession of shocks that makes his utter overthrow credible. Achilles
made one mistake and could still take action to redress it. Yet in

both cases we may note the moment of development when the whole plot turns on a psychological pivot, when the hero sees himself in a new light. The plot of Sophocles is the more philosophical because it introduces more of the appearance of design. Unfortunately, life in this particular design seems to be cruel and unjust. This is the essence of tragedy.

The only weakness of the play is that, though Oedipus' fate is cruel, it is also unusual. Sophocles never made things happen that way again. He had reached the logical culmination of his own contribution to tragedy—harshness and artful construction. In his later plays he may be equally artful, but he provides a happy ending, and that makes all the difference. The jury awarded only second prize to Sophocles when he produced the *Oedipus*. It was too tragic a play to please. As a tragedy it could not be surpassed by a play on the Greek model. It is lifelike in two ways: in the psychological treatment of the forces at work within Oedipus, and in its objective treatment of the external forces at work. So many possible answers are suggested to our questions that we find no final solution any more than we do when life itself ill-treats us. The only way to understand the play is to find in it a confession that we do not understand life.

Before we take up the remaining dramas of Sophocles it will be necessary to see what Euripides was doing in the meantime, for the development of new fashions is more apparent in his work than in that of Sophocles. In any case, we have no more Sophoclean plays with tragic plot. Much as Aristotle preferred Sophoclean tragedy to Euripidean, he had to admit that Euripides is the most tragic of the poets; in fact, his work is strikingly original in the next generation, while Sophocles continues to write plays that will supply models of character and stimulate the hearer to decisive action. Acceptance of life even at its worst is their strong characteristic. Only in the *Trachiniae* and *Oedipus* is the note of pessimism strong. Perhaps such plays belong to an age in which optimism is at its height in real life. The audience could be trusted to react strongly with thoughts of their own. Such plays may ultimately aid faith by the test to which they subject it, but for the moment at least they weaken the springs of action while the mind ponders. It seems not unlikely that Sophocles had known a year that rocked and reeled beneath him, and that the force of the *Oedipus* springs from his own doubt; but it is useless to speculate. The result, in any case, was more faith.

V
Euripidean Tragedy

It is not easy to classify the sixteen plays of Euripides that were produced as tragedies. Of the other three preserved as his the *Rhesus* seems clearly to belong to some writer of a later age and must therefore be considered separately. The *Cyclops* is a satyr drama and hence is irrelevant to our purpose. The *Alcestis*, which took the place of a satyr drama in 438 B.C., is much the earliest of the extant plays. Euripides was born probably in 484 B.C. He was first allowed to produce a play, *The Daughters of Pelias*, in 455. The plays that we now possess appeared in the last quarter century of his life, from *Medea* (431) to *Bacchae* (405), which came out after his death in the preceding year, and *Iphigeneia at Aulis* (401), which was performed even later.

I shall consider first seven tragedies of Euripides that show development. *Medea* and *Hippolytus* (428) are roughly contemporary with the *Oedipus Tyrannus* and have the same regard for unity of plot and a similar interweaving of character with action. *Hercules Furens* (*ca.* 424) and *Hecuba* (*ca.* 426) are plays in which reason and rhetoric are appealed to in an attempt to deal with the anomalies of fortune. They show a certain faith in political and legal institutions that tempers tragedy with morality. In the *Trojan Women* (415), the *Electra* (413), and the *Bacchae* (405) tragedy has shifted to a new basis. It has taken on a tone of universal pity that undermines any faith or satisfaction in success. The power of pity intervenes against revenge and tends to paralyze all human endeavor.

The specifically political plays must be considered together: *Ion, Andromache, Suppliants,* and *Heracleidae* of Euripides, with the *Oedipus at Colonus* of Sophocles. Two adventurous and happy plays, the *Iphigeneia in Tauris* of Euripides and the *Electra* of Sophocles, belong with them as serious stories of moral success. The remaining plays will also be grouped together because in one way or another they illustrate the decline of tragedy to the level of entertainment or introduce tendencies that become dominant in New Comedy. Sophocles' *Philoctetes* and Euripides' *Alcestis* show a character converted to right conduct by noble example. Euripides' *Helen* (412) and *Orestes* (408) illustrate the comic possibilities of burlesque tragedy. *Phoenissae* (409) and *Iphigeneia at Aulis* (401) display a disintegration of tragedy into diversified scenes of little profundity that offer opportunities to versatile actors. The *Rhesus,* which is much later, shows how tragedy became in the end an art divorced from religion and dedicated to the pleasure of a refined audience. Its lively and varied action is far removed from the concentrated power of *Prometheus, Oedipus,* or *Medea.*

Euripides makes frequent excursions into one never-never land or another, even in his tragedies. Gods and miracles produce, wherever they appear in a play, a kind of magic that disconnects us from sorrows of our own. Such a play is never a problem play except perhaps for the critic. Stageland lies in a province of dreamland. Its people are uninhibited in virtue as in vice. On the same day that Euripides exhibited the virtuous Alcestis he also exhibited Pasiphaë in love with a bull, and made his characters exercise much serious wit in analysis of her aberration and its complications. He dealt rhetorically with a new world of ideas, where anything could be discussed pro and con. Such a topsy-turvy world is exciting enough when we are not required to live in it personally.

Besides gods and miracles and the cool detachment of clever rhetoric, Euripides has other tricks for turning life inside out without committing himself to a program of immorality. But the practice of detached cleverness is easily learned, and with it comes the habit of acting first and thinking afterward of a good plea in extenuation. Euripides also liked to produce paradoxical effects, to show the base as noble and the noble as base, and by a clever arrangement of scenes to suggest the inconsequence or futility of life.

Reason in his plays has little control of decisions. It is the slave of the passions and is often used for base ends. Plots succeed in Euripides as they do not in Sophocles except for the *Electra*. His characters also lack the integrity that abounds in the earlier poet. They may be drawn from life with good dramatic or rhetorical *êthos*, but they lack the moral and psychological *êthos* that results from rational control of impulse. Only in political plays when Athenian rulers not earlier than Theseus are depicted does Euripides show wholly resolute and responsible men. His Theseus is statesmanlike, but his Spartans and Thebans talk like lawyers, not like statesmen.

Yet Euripides' plays were a criticism of life. By pretending not to be serious he might catch men off their guard, as Bernard Shaw has done. The plea for recognition of virtue even in a slave that was found in the *Alexander* was a criticism of current morality. Thus, though Euripides seldom strengthened the hold of good habits, he often weakened the hold of bad habits. In the end he taught men to weep for their fate, to see greatness in the small and smallness in the great, to mingle laughter with tears, approval with disapproval, and to expect little of life. In the course of his art he reduced passion and grief to pure entertainment, and produced a kind of action that was unconcerned about morals, but rather filled the stage with the excitement that results when no one stops to think, or even to argue with any but rhetorical logic. Traits of character were still depicted, but no men and women of character. The poet had abdicated in favor of the actor.[1]

The greatest tragedies of Euripides are neatly spaced, first *Medea* (431) and *Hippolytus* (428), which bear comparison with Aeschylus and Sophocles, then the *Trojan Women* (415), a purely Euripidean masterpiece that looks forward to Virgil, and last the *Bacchae* (405), a tragedy that carries us into a world of strange and terrible beauty that is at war with realities. *Heracleidae* and *Suppliants* are patriotic pageants. *Ion* and *Andromache* are political fiction embroidered with domestic crisis as entertaining propaganda. Ill-used mothers gain thrones for sons saved from death.

[1] For notes to chapter v see pages 292–298.

The *Heracles* is a play in which a great man falls and is raised again by friendship and humanity. It has a serious moral with patriotic overtones. *Hecuba* is a more or less moral tale of crime and punishment, interesting as a contrast to the *Trojan Women*. In the latter play weakness is innocent, not vindictive; its only weapon is pity. Charged with real feeling, the drama might be a stimulant to thought and action. It is probably the most tragic of all Greek plays. Its contemporary, *Iphigeneia in Tauris,* is a play of grief, recognition, and intrigue crowned by success. The *Electra* turns the story of a successful plot into a tragedy by judicious use of debate and lament. The *Helen* shows tragedy sinking to the level of burlesque. A virtuous Helen saves her husband and is saved by him as the barbarian foots the bill. *Orestes* and *Phoenissae* are pure entertainment except for a political debate in the latter play. *Iphigeneia at Aulis* has the liveliness and suspense of the *Ion,* but gives a much more natural picture of human relations, since no god intervenes until the end.

It is hard to say when we pass from the tragedies of Sophocles to the *Medea* and the *Hippolytus* of Euripides just what the difference is. Aristophanes felt strongly about it, so the difference must have been quite apparent to contemporaries. In both plays a woman in love is a destructive force, but so are Clytemnestra and Deianeira. The answer is partly that Clytemnestra was punished in the next play and that Deianeira did not mean any harm, but that is not all of it. Euripides has omitted from his characters a certain stately majesty that removes tragedy from ordinary life. Medea and Phaedra feel strongly and act with abandon when their honor is touched. They claim a man's right to vengeance when they are lovesick. Love is a reason but not an excuse in Sophocles. In Euripides it becomes an excuse and finds means to destroy where it cannot have satisfaction. Manly passion for glory had been respectable in the case of Ajax. Other passions get a hearing from Euripides. He shows men as they are, not, like Sophocles, as they ought to be. Yet it is not so much a question of bringing bad characters on the stage, for Sophocles had done that, as of the variety of interests that appear in Euripides and the frankness with which Euripidean characters disregard inhibitions. Characters in comedy are so careless of propriety that they become ridiculous; in Euripides, character is not drawn on so low a scale as that except in the *Orestes,* but it approaches the level of realism that we find in New Comedy. The Sophoclean tyrant will allege reasons of state for his actions. The Euripidean villain admits that he is out for all he can get, and he does not think any the worse of himself for that.[2]

Clytemnestra had at least pretended to be a good wife in spite of provocation, and her plot had to be kept secret, since the chorus would not favor her. Medea intrigues successfully against Jason and gloats over her revenge on him. She is saved from punishment by a final revelation that she has superhuman assistance. She would be the triumphant villain that Aristotle excludes except for her transformation into something like an avenging deity. We find the same otherworldly vengeance in *Hippolytus* and *Bacchae.* When a seeming human foe turns out to have supernatural backing, disaster is complete, because there is no appeal from the divine verdict, even when it is unjust. Jason in the *Medea* is very like Creon in the *Antigone.* He has the same political impatience with one who insists on maintaining family ties as sacred, and is punished in the same way by losing all his family. But Medea turns out in the end to be no Antigone. She had deserted her family for Jason. Hence there is some justice in her plight, particularly if we remember that she had killed her own brother to cover her escape. She is a force that disguises itself in order to succeed, but that does not apologize.

Preoccupation with death and suffering is a fundamental feature of Greek tragedy. Homer had found in glory one answer to death and in humanity and civilization another. In the Semitic story of Gilgamesh the search for an antidote to death is the main theme. There is some resentment against the gods when the search is unsuccessful. The gods are thought of as grudging, just as they are in much Greek literature. Preoccupation with death is in the background of Homer's poetry. It is no longer possible with him to hope for an antidote, but the wish to escape is still present, as well as a certain resentment that beauty and strength and virtue must die. The lesson that mortals must not behave as if they were gods is always at hand. Tragedy takes a savage delight in showing the insecurity of the strongest bulwarks of life. Those stories, as Aristotle says, in which the nearest ties of love and kinship are broken, became its favorite material. The self-destruction of Ajax and Oedipus perhaps strikes nearest home, if we adopt the view that a man is his own best friend, but the voluntary element in self-destruction makes it less shocking at the same time, and suicide, like natural death, might be enacted on the Greek stage.[3]

In the *Medea* we have the mother who slays her own children intentionally, an act sufficiently horrible, and difficult to make plausible. In Maxwell Anderson's *Wingless Victory* the mother slays her children in mercy, because she cannot bear to think of their fate. Medea has the same thought, but Euripides puts more emphasis on the motive of revenge. Tragedy deals with the more barbaric and self-assertive emotions in general. At the beginning of the play we learn from Medea's nurse and the children's tutor that Medea is in a mood to slay her offspring because their father Jason has won a new bride, the daughter of Creon, king of Corinth, whom he is soon to marry. This touches Medea's honor, for her code was that of the Greek wife who permitted no rival in the same house or with the same privilege of bringing up children. This method of foreshadowing disaster by human agents is in one way more effective than the use of an oracle, but it is less ambiguous and forestalls surprise. Nurses in a Greek play are usually inciters to crime, for the poet normally wishes to make his heroine attractive and to show her as yielding only with reluctance to evil suggestions. Medea, on the contrary, is to be made as self-sufficient in evil as possible. Her all but deification at the end will remove her from the ordinary criticism as well as punishment of bad women. Yet Medea must at the same time win some sympathy. This is insured by the very violence of her expression of feeling, her sense of injustice, and the cleverness of the intrigue by which she deceives successively the chorus of women, Creon, Jason, and the Athenian king Aegeus with whom she secures a refuge.

Since Medea must plot and deceive, the character that she displays will be feigned, like that of Clytemnestra. The *êthos* in her speeches will be rhetorical, not psychological, and certainly not ethical, for her self-restraint is directed toward the gratification of her passions, not their suppression or regulation. Consequently there must also be scenes in which she appears unveiled, though such self-revelation in the presence of the chorus might be expected to defeat her plot. Euripides' chorus, once they are won over, cease to behave like actors and become singers only. The fooling of the chorus is beautifully done and has often deceived readers of the play as well. Medea generalizes in terms that are intentionally obscure but produce a vague effect of mystery and grandiloquence. Then she suddenly presents herself as a suffering woman and voices a general complaint about the unfairness that women suffer in matrimonial relations. This brings her into the same category as the chorus, though they are Greek women, not barbarians; and they prepare to abet her vengeance on the man who would violate his oath and her monogamous rights. There is irony in her complaint that she has no family to take her part when we reflect that she had alienated her family by her aid to the invader, going even so far as to slay her brother to assist Jason. She is in the same position as the man on trial for slaying his father and mother who pleaded for mercy on the ground that he was an orphan. On the other hand her crimes might be taken as evidence of her great love for her hero. Her appeal for justice, however, is strongest when she points to the violation of his oath to cherish her if she should help him.

Euripides is at some pains to get Aegeus the Athenian, with whom Medea is said to have sought refuge, into the story. It is probable that a less sophisticated age would have been content to bring Aegeus in at the end and let him lead Medea from the scene as a suppliant whose part he takes. His role is that of Ae-

gisthus in the *Agamemnon;* he provides needed support for the
criminal. Euripides prefers to make Medea herself rather than
Aegeus the god from the machine. In this way Aegeus promises
the lady a refuge and binds himself by an oath before he knows
with what crime upon her head she will arrive. He becomes a
victim rather than an accomplice. Of course, Medea's sudden godlike powers at the end make Aegeus unnecessary for her purpose,
but it might be supposed that she had not herself expected such
divine assistance as a chariot drawn by dragons. At any rate, it
is a convention in Greek tragedy that the play is over when the
gods intervene. Medea is represented as being in doubt after her
scene with Creon. He has banished her and her sons but has foolishly yielded to allow her one day of grace. This she will use for
vengeance, prepared, if necessary, to sacrifice her own life. If, however, she can find a place of refuge, she will use craft and herself escape. Jason offers her money and help, but she will have
none of him or his friends. She is as hot as he is cool, and rejects
the argument that he has sought only her good. She was entitled
to be consulted before he acted. This again is good Greek doctrine,
for any man who won his wife's consent had the right at Athens
to give her to another and take a new wife himself. The Athenian
Aegeus solves her problem. There is something lifelike in the solution of Medea's problem by a chance arrival. Since she was prepared to act according to circumstances, there is nothing forced
in arranging a circumstance to produce this result rather than that.
No doubt the Athenians liked to see their kings on the stage and
to hear choruses in praise of Athens. Aegeus is not necessary to
Medea's vengeance, but Euripides could not easily leave him out,
once he had got into the story. Euripides is satisfied to make the
intervention of Aegeus as inoffensive as possible. With Aristotle,
Aegeus is a byword for the character who arrives unexpectedly
and opportunely, but if there were no chance arrivals in life the
resourceful heroine would have fewer opportunities to exercise
her charm.[4]

Having gained Aegeus and dismissed him, Medea employs her

art on Jason. She begs that the children may stay with him instead of going into exile, just the object that he would have liked to gain. He offers to introduce the children and their gifts to the bride. When he prays for long life for them, Medea betrays her feelings by weeping at the thought that, if they succeed, she must slay them. When they return, having won remission of banishment, Medea seems again to be undecided. There is a battle within her between two emotions, love of children and anger at Jason. This psychological battle is remarkably like the decision of Orestes to slay his mother in the *Choephoroe,* but Euripides dispenses with the external manifestation of the conflicting motives. Medea is alone with her children. She does not arrive at a decision by thoughtful consideration of ends and means, but by rapid oscillation until the scales incline for death. This is excellent material for a clever actor, since it combines in one scene the same opposition of two moods that had appeared before in the contrast between the furious anger of Medea against Jason and her subservient wheedling when it suited her purpose. The effect, however, is artificial and lends itself to parody. In later works the vacillating character is given more time for a change of mood. The contrast of moods in Medea, however, serves a special purpose in making her a more sympathetic character. She seems wholly lacking in responsible control; and we see that Jason is right when he remarks at the end that he made his initial error when he accepted the kind of aid that she could give and bound up his life with hers. It is useless to blame Medea; and she is even pitiable, for she, no less than Jason, has lost her children. He might be expected to be more concerned about his new bride, destroyed by the gifts that she received from the boys. At any rate, the calculating Jason has miscalculated.

If we compare the *Medea* with Maxwell Anderson's *Wingless Victory,* which is an adaptation of the plot, we note how the modern writer has shifted the theme from conflict between man and wife to the defeat of ideal love by adverse conditions. Euripides does not make society responsible for the isolation of Medea. In fact, he shows her aided against her husband by the women of Corinth. Nor is tragedy allowed to treat of love except as a destructive force. We see nothing of Medea's love except its effects, and before the play begins it has turned to hate. Thus the play is one of personal conflict assuming various aspects as the intrigue and revelation of character proceed. There is of course the contrast between man's world and its concerns and woman's preoccupation with her own intimate feelings; there is the conflict of the apparently helpless deserted creature against the king and his cohorts; and above all we are reminded in the end of the difference between Greek and barbarian. There is no singleness of mind, however, like that of Antigone, to give consistency to any one issue. The Athenians could hardly award the *Medea* more than the third prize which they did award, if they had any regard for consistent support of principles. Its perspective is too ingenious. But the *Medea* has a virtue that we found in *Oedipus,* in that psychological horror is more important than physical. We have seen what human beings are capable of when driven by the furies of terror or jealousy. Medea's triumph does not remove her dissatisfaction with life. As she taunts Jason at the end and refuses him the privilege of burying his children, she is godlike in power; she is also like a Greek god in malice and vindictiveness. As a woman she is tragic. Pity for weakness and folly begins already to make itself felt as the ultimate residuum of a Euripidean play.

The *Hippolytus,* produced three years after the *Medea,* is in strong contrast with it, though we have again a man who is ruined by a passionate woman. There is, however, idealism in the play, for Hippolytus is in love with the goddess Artemis. Since she is a virgin goddess, his relation to her is a romantic mysticism that combines love of nature and solitude with the strong joy of athletic pursuits. Plato in the *Laws* tells of athletes who avoided all sexual experience for the sake of athletic success. To Hippolytus, victory in all games is the height of happiness. To his father, Hippolytus appears to be a bookish prude and a devotee of Orphic rites. By bringing the goddess Artemis on the scene before the death of Hippolytus, Euripides strengthens the impression of genuineness in his hero's romantic devotion to Artemis. He appears as a martyr, half religious and half in love. Artemis cannot help him, but must go before he dies. She does assure him of a continuing ritual in his honor. Artemis will avenge him on Aphrodite by slaying her favorite Adonis. The relation between Aphrodite and Adonis will naturally be very different from that between the chaste Artemis and her chaste lover. Except for his relationship to Artemis, Hippolytus would provide a moral theme rather than a tragedy; his love for the goddess gives him warmth and makes him the representative of something greater than himself that is not altogether negative. He is a forerunner of Saint Hippolytus, who died for his Christian faith.[5]

Euripides foreshadows the fate of the hero in the opening. Aphrodite in a set prologue announces that she will punish him for scorning marriage and preferring Artemis alone. Phaedra, his stepmother, is in love with him, and his father Theseus will discover it, will curse Hippolytus, and so will bring death to him, since Poseidon has promised to honor three prayers of Theseus. Phaedra too must die though innocent. The goddess does not value mortal pain when set against her triumph. Hippolytus and his chorus of huntsmen then enter and worship Artemis at her shrine. There is also on the stage a shrine of Aphrodite that Hippolytus neglects, even when a loyal servant begs him not to offend the goddess. The two goddesses represent two ideals of life. Hippolytus is the son of Theseus' Amazon queen. The Amazons were a race of women who lived without men, as far as possible. Thus Phaedra and Hippolytus may not be blamed for their disaster, for each is in a different way the victim of a goddess. Phaedra's innocence is further underlined when we see her sick to death of love and only after long persuasion betraying her secret to her old nurse. The nurse has this time the role of tempter, but Phaedra will die rather than stain her honor. The nurse, however, hopes to save her life by informing Hippolytus. Her good intentions produce the opposite result, for Hippolytus is so outraged that he denounces the innocent

Phaedra and forces her to die—or live humiliated. He is guilty of misunderstanding and rashness, just the faults of Oedipus and of the heroes of New Comedy. When Phaedra hangs herself leaving a note that accuses Hippolytus of violating her, Theseus believes the dead woman rather than his son and prays to Poseidon to destroy him. The miracle occurs and Hippolytus is mangled by his own runaway horses. Artemis appears in order to inform Theseus of his son's innocence. Hippolytus at her bidding forgives his father before he dies. Artemis blames Theseus for slaying his son, though by his own act he had only banished him. It was Poseidon who in answer to Theseus' prayer caused his death.[6]

Theseus had been guilty of misunderstanding and rashness, so that on a purely human level poetic justice was done to Hippolytus. He received the same measure of justice that he gave. Phaedra's name is cleared, but the end of the play is a tribute to the piety of Hippolytus, who had been guided by Artemis and had remained loyal to his father throughout. The play received first prize, no doubt for its emphasis on the virtuous hero and his heed of honor. There are no bad characters in the play, for even the nurse has the best of intentions. To each of the three principals a god is assigned to take the blame for any aberrations. Phaedra is reduced to a secondary role. Circumstances are to blame as in the *Oedipus,* but Euripides specifically introduces a vindictive goddess; Sophocles had left the activity of Apollo to be inferred or not at the hearer's pleasure. Misunderstanding and rashness are punished in the *Hippolytus* as in the *Oedipus* when they recoil upon the guilty man, but the punishment of the hero seems excessive. Theseus wins absolution for his own rashness by repentance, and in any case Poseidon was more to blame than Artemis admitted. Euripides has inculcated piety while making the gods seem indifferent to the fate of men or even to their deserts. Still, Artemis is grieved at the death of her worshiper and gives what consolation she can. At any rate, her worship is represented as a force for good in human life and something to be valued for its own sake. This is a drama of frustrated ideals rather than of conflict like the *Medea.* There is no conflict between human characters, for all are essentially at one in appreciating the way of Artemis. No one ever glorified love less than Euripides does in this play. Aphrodite serves as scapegoat, just as she did in the *Iliad*. Thanks to her, Phaedra appears, like Hippolytus, as a martyr to chastity, and Euripides recants his first evil interpretation of her story that had so shocked the Athenians. The line of Hippolytus, "My tongue hath sworn; no oath is on my soul," was remembered against Euripides by Aristophanes, but actually all oaths are kept in the play to the letter. Hippolytus is glorified as an innocent victim.

In the next two tragedies, the *Mad Heracles* and *Hecuba,* Euripides is concerned to represent the vicissitudes of human life and to see what remedy for disaster man has in his own power. They have tragic moments, but illustrate a belief in the power of reason, justice, and enlightenment that is Aeschylean. Aeschylus would, however, have kept some superstitious elements and would have made the gods his spokesmen of enlightenment. In these plays of Euripides the gods represent only the blind forces with which men contend. He introduces Theseus at the end of the *Heracles* as the representative of enlightenment and in the *Hecuba* shows debate and decision as a roughly effective instrument of justice. The *Heracles* in the end follows the model of political plays. Theseus' kindness to Heracles prepares us for his greater part in the *Oedipus at Colonus* of Sophocles. It is characteristic of political plays to be episodic, and the *Heracles* at first sight breaks into three quite different parts. Euripides is, however, experimenting with the effect that can be produced by contrasts. He is concerned more with an arrangement of moods in the mind of the hearer than with the presentation of a pattern of action either planned or unplanned. He will treat as a problem the most fatal disaster that can happen to a man in the very moment of success. To make the problem difficult the disaster must be as senseless and undeserved as that of Oedipus, but some kind of victory must be snatched from defeat.

Thus the *Heracles* is not a play of opposing forces that persist through an action, but a play of forces introduced successively to illustrate the uncertainty and complication of life. First we have the moral pattern of persecution and deliverance. The family of Heracles huddle about an altar, where they have taken refuge to escape from the upstart Lycus, who is tyrant in Thebes for the moment. Lycus jeers at the absent Heracles and is answered by his aged father Amphitryon. There is a debate about the use of the bow as unworthy of a hero that fits the situation after the Athenian victory at Pylos in 425 B.C., for that was won by bowmen. The tension becomes acute when Lycus threatens to build a fire that will roast the suppliants if they do not leave the altar. Heracles, of course, returns in the nick of time and shows himself not merely a mighty savior but a tender father. Lycus is lured into the palace and is slain. This is obviously a good place for the story to stop, but Euripides is interested in a trilogy, or at least a triptych, in one play. Suddenly, Madness personified appears, escorted by Iris and obeying the orders of Hera. Madness enters the palace to attack Heracles, and the chorus describe what happens within. Heracles mistakes his wife and children for enemies and slays precisely those dear ones whom he had a moment before saved from the tyrant Lycus. The harsh blow struck by Hera or circumstance receives no moral justification or palliation. Life can strike such blows, and man must be ready for them. The *Ajax* of Sophocles had committed suicide when Athena prevented him from slaying his enemies. Heracles is in a worse plight, for he has slain his friends. Nor has he personally done anything to provoke Hera or to cause his disaster. Euripides has, unlike Sophocles, presented Heracles without a fault, and the effect is, as Aristotle warns us, abominable. The goddess has done her worst. Hera's cruelty, however, provides man's opportunity.[7]

Before Heracles recovers his senses, he is exhibited sleeping and bound, like a moored ship, among his victims. Old Amphitryon laments, fears further violence, if Heracles wakes, and cautions the chorus to let him sleep. Euripides repeats this scene in the *Orestes;* in the *Bacchae* he greatly improves on the ensuing recognition scene in which the madman, coming to himself, discovers what he has done. He resolves on suicide, since he is so polluted with blood that no one will receive him. He veils his head to save his friend from pollution, as soon as he sees Theseus approaching. It now appears that friendship is stronger than the enmity of gods. Heracles boldly asserts his independence of divine favor or hatred and is not punished. Theseus says that friendship is an antidote to pollution, and promises to purify Heracles in Athens and grant him honors and precincts there. Heracles had once saved him, and he will now save Heracles. The enmity of the gods makes the need greater, and friends should help precisely in time of need. Theseus points out that the gods themselves consent to live, though according to the myths they have been guilty of all kinds of crimes. Heracles will have none of this argument. He does not believe such stories of the gods. Yet he is convinced that there is still work for him to do in the world and resolves to live for philanthropy. No one in the play expresses any doubt that Hera has shown hate for Heracles because of her jealousy of his mother, who conceived him in the arms of Zeus. Yet Heracles is doubtful of the very identity of Zeus and considers Amphitryon his real father. The hero himself repudiates all connection with gods and cares only for the fame that he gains by his labors on behalf of men. Thus Euripides proclaims an age of reason when philanthropy and friendship will replace the old fear of gods and the old struggle to gain their favor or to avoid offending them. There are parts of China where a drowning man is left to die for fear that the river spirit will be offended if a victim is snatched from it. Euripides would rescue even the madman. By accepting the enmity of Hera as an axiom he makes the lesson stronger, but by casting doubt on other stories of the gods he makes it certain that no auditor will take Hera very seriously. Madness is a fact that must be dealt with; why complicate the problem by superstition?

The patriotic presentation of Theseus as an ideal friend and representative of enlightenment would justify classing this as a political play, except for the wider interest in man's fate that is clearly present. Certainly it is not so much a tragedy as a problem play. Since, however, a solution is provided for the problem, it ranks with the ethical plays of Aeschylus. In fact it is three plays in one, having parts that are ethical, tragic, and rational. Its lesson is that brute success is not enough. Men must have courage also to meet every kind of disaster. Failure requires more courage than success. Heracles, saving his children, compares them to boats in tow. As he leaves with backward glances at the end, propped and propelled by Theseus, he is himself a disabled wreck that must be towed. Thus Euripides preaches courage and mutual aid instead of the paralyzing pity and fear of conventional tragedy. The *Heracles* has not usually been rated high among the dramas of Euripides, in spite of its bold and timely message. Euripides did not again offend by mixing such a moral with a tragic plot. No doubt mere rational solution of problems is dull in the theater, as compared with the excitement of conflict or despair. The *Mad Heracles* is a Greek version of the parable of the good Samaritan, with obvious differences. It does not preach universal neighborliness or love of enemies.

Though the *Hecuba* is sometimes played even now, it is difficult to discover in what its appeal lies. There are two ghosts. Achilles demands the death of a Trojan captive, Polyxena, in honor of his tomb. Polydorus, her brother, son of Priam and Hecuba, appears to the audience in the prologue and to Hecuba in a dream to tell how he was slain by the Thracian Polymestor. When Troy fell, the Thracian disregarded the most sacred obligations to protect the boy, and murdered him to get possession of the Trojan treasure that came with him for safekeeping. The ghost of Polydorus naturally seeks vengeance. Thus the play has two parts. The slaying of Polyxena is necessary to the vengeance of Polydorus, for only when water is sought to wash her body will the remains of her brother be found on the beach and confirm Hecuba's dream. Agamemnon, the conqueror of Troy, is a key figure, for he is represented as willing to aid Hecuba because he is in love with her daughter Cassandra. In his contest with the ghostly Achilles the king is defeated, for the army votes to sacrifice Polyxena. The Athenian heroes point out that honor demands that men be preferred to women, the strength of Achilles to the weakness of Agamemnon for Cassandra.

It is expediency, however, as advocated by Odysseus, that carries the day against Agamemnon. He argues that if heroes are not honored, no one will want to fight in future. Thus policy rules out pity. Odysseus has an opportunity to repeat his speech on stage when he comes to take Polyxena from her mother Hecuba. Hecuba has appealed to pity, but Odysseus is as eloquent as she. Polyxena refuses to struggle, recognizing death as preferable to slavery. Her noble voluntary death is reported by Talthybius, the herald. She has won a victory by yielding and is honored by the foe. The spirit of Achilles has triumphed and pervades this part of the play. Nowhere else in Greek literature do we find an ideal so close to the Japanese admiration for the concubine of Yoshitsune, who with perfect grace and propriety danced in the presence of his enemies, and defiantly prayed for her husband though she knew that the son with whom she was pregnant would be slain at birth. The propriety of Polyxena's acceptance of her own death is mixed with expediency in the usual Greek way. No Greek rhetorician could avoid including the topics that relate to advantage as well as the theme of honor in a deliberative speech. Yet the effect is to glorify a savage code and to make it seem genuinely Greek. Rhetoric merely finds new arguments to support the old ideals.[8]

In the second half of the play we come down to earth and see justice inflicted on the greedy barbarian. Athens in the year 429 had had some experience with a Thracian ally. Sitalces had plundered the territory of Greek cities that were in rebellion against Athens. No doubt the Thracians had been guilty of atrocities that might arouse qualms in the stomach of an ally who brought them in. At any rate, Euripides' picture of the false and greedy Thracian and his exemplary punishment would serve excellently as anti-Thracian propaganda, especially if it were necessary to counter any Thracian demand for assistance in return. The Thracian at the end is as abject as Xerxes in the *Persians*. In this episode, then, we see the fall of a successful villain in contrast with the honor

that Polyxena won for herself even in defeat. The army still consider the Thracian their friend, since he slew a Trojan, but Agamemnon will assist Hecuba in avenging herself if she can do so
without seeming to involve him. This she does by persuading
Polymestor that she can disclose to him the secret of another treasure. The Trojan women overpower him when he comes alone to
her tent, kill his sons before his eyes, and blind him. When Agamemnon sits in judgment on the act of Hecuba, it is easy for her
rhetoric to win the decision over the Thracian. Agamemnon orders
him to be marooned on a desert island, but he prophesies the doom
of his tormentors before he goes. He is made as ridiculous and
futile as possible.

Polyxena and Polydorus are buried in one grave. Thus Euripides
adds another artificial tie to hold the two parts of his play together.
There is a theme that runs through the whole play, the question
of divine rule, the supremacy of law and justice, and the part played
by rhetoric in furthering the ends of life. In the first part there is
much talk of honor, which ends in the defeat of Hecuba and the
loss of Polyxena. In the second part Hecuba discards all the ap-
paratus of justice, uses eloquence and cunning for private ends
stealthily, and succeeds. She is a barbarian dealing with a barbarian, and somehow the savage code of vengeance, unencumbered
by legal quibbles, brings clearly to view an aspect of life that is
decently concealed in civilized practice. Euripides has reversed the
usual order and given us a picture of the crimes of civilization before he shows us barbarism. Yet Hecuba's vengeance is justified
in an informal debate, and the spectators have the satisfaction of
repudiating the crimes of greed to compensate for the approval that
they have given to the sacrifice of Polyxena, which was perpetrated
in the name of honor. Euripides is depicting men as they are. His
Agamemnon is not moved by Hecuba's plea for justice; only when
she urges the low motive of his love for Cassandra does he help
her. Still, the play is not altogether unpleasant. The young victim
wins respect and tears; the old Hecuba wins revenge. The clear
contrast has its interest, and the final result is disquieting. The play

seems to be an exhibition of the value of cleverness and eloquence, but it leaves us mourning the lack of a surer guide to bring beauty and peace. Yet the *Hecuba* may have been very good theater when it had topical interest as well.

The chief interest of the *Hecuba* is in the contrast that it supplies for an appreciation of the *Trojan Women,* Euripides' tragic masterpiece. The *Hecuba* leaves us intellectually dissatisfied; the *Trojan Women* is addressed to the emotions and leaves us with a burning sense of wrong. The appeal to pity is so strong that it cannot be dismissed as merely sentimental. There is no division, as in Virgil's *Aeneid,* between emotion and duty. Nothing is said about duty, and the gods are ready to punish the strong. In the *Hecuba,* honor was still a consideration and gave the victors a specious glamour. In the *Trojan Women* honor does not help. It is precisely the best and finest things in life that are trampled on. The Greek conquerors of Troy deal with the Trojans just as Athenians were dealing with the conquered Melians in the year 415, when the *Trojan Women* was presented. Thus the play has a topical interest that can hardly be denied, since we know its relation to the history of the time as reported by Thucydides. He, too, has devoted much space to an exposition of the shameless motives that led the Athenians to slaughter the men of Melos and sell their wives into slavery. The Athenians no longer honored justice or decency with their lips, and Euripides has created his victors in their image. The structure of the play is ingeniously designed to rouse the utmost pity and yet to close all roads to emotional satisfaction in the play. By omitting to supply the thought and action that strong emotion demands, Euripides is pressing the audience to think and act in their own lives. He depicts a condition rather than an action. The forces that operate in the play are seen only in their effects. The play is a force in its own right just because its characters seem to have no force of their own. Even the victors are made stupid or ridiculous and deserving of pity as much as scorn. Character has been sacrificed to emotional appeal.[9]

Everything is seen from the point of view of the victims except for the prologue, in which Athena, who has favored the Greeks, and Poseidon, who has favored the Trojans, join in a compact to plague the Greeks, as soon as they sail, with storms and lightning on the homeward voyage. They are not to be punished as conquerors, or for their cruelty, but for sacrilegious disregard of the sanctity of shrines. Other sanctities are not protected by the gods, but in the play itself their force is felt. Euripides is using the old Homeric trick of introducing a scene in heaven to make mortals appear small and to emphasize the folly and irony of their pride of achievement. Conqueror and conquered do not weep together as in Book 24 of the *Iliad*, but they are seen to share the same fate. The common enemy, fortune, should produce a common sympathy.

After the prologue Hecuba is present throughout the play, and the chorus sympathize with her and share her fate. There is much song and dance, which produces an operatic effect. There are moments when the tragic mood is relieved by debate or suspense or hope of recovery or revenge. In the end frustration is universal, and the chorus march with Hecuba to slavery as the towers of Troy blaze in the background, grim symbol of final doom. The art of Euripides is shown in the arrangement of his scenes so as to produce a climax of sorrow and despair. The three Trojan women who have leading parts are the unmarried Cassandra, the widowed mother Andromache, and the aged Hecuba. All three have singing parts. The movement of the drama begins when the chorus speculate about their fate. The herald Talthybius comes to bring the news. Cassandra is awarded to Agamemnon, Polyxena to the dead Achilles, Andromache to his son Neoptolemus, and Hecuba herself to the crafty Odysseus, whom she hates. It is obvious that the captives may be summoned to appear in any order. The important decisions have been made off-stage without explanation or appeal. It is clear that Euripides has secured the privilege of bringing news to his captives at whatever moment he finds most effective. Andromache gives the first clear statement of the death of Polyxena, and the order that Astyanax, her son and Hector's, must

be flung from the battlements, comes to her later through Talthybius at the precise moment when she has resolved to live and
raise up her son to be another Hector. After Andromache's touch-
ing farewell to Astyanax accompanied by denunciation of the
Greeks, but not curses, since they may still refuse burial to the
babe, Menelaus storms in unannounced to seek Helen. Thus Euripides can produce his effects in his own way. There is no diversified
unity of action, but a diversity of moods that are harmonized to
produce one powerful and lasting impression.

Emotion is relieved in such a way as to intensify the sense of
irony. Even from a mortal point of view reflection can see events
in more than one perspective. Cassandra, being a prophetess, can,
like the gods, foresee the future. She knows of the death that awaits
Agamemnon and of the long wanderings of Odysseus. Logic too
can undermine certainty. Cassandra and Andromache both speak
eloquently in support of paradoxes. Cassandra proves that the defeated Trojans are happier than the victorious Greeks. The conqueror loses more than he gains. Andromache proves that the dead
Polyxena is happier than she, who remains alive suffering the more
because of her virtue and her loyalty to the dead Hector. Her ideal
picture of marriage produces the same effect of frustrated bliss that
we noted in the *Hippolytus,* where marriage is not praised. The
tragic effect of beauty strangled in a brutal world is the same. Andromache is even more innocent than Desdemona, but Euripides
is not now interested in poetic justice. He is too much the poet here
to be interested in anything that can be called justice. Hecuba finds
irony in the contrast between past and present, and in her lament
for Astyanax in the contrast between the hope that was and the
reality that is; the grief of the old queen, now a slave, as she decks
her grandson's mangled corpse for burial, is the climax of the
play. Pathos can go no further. Babe condemned to death and age
condemned to life without hope—these do outrage to our most
sacred feelings and convict the universe of cruelty.

Thus the bare statement of the gods, in the prologue, that the
Greeks will be punished for their violations, is reinforced by scene

after scene of pity fused with irony, so arranged that emotion is inhibited or relieved by argument or other distraction at the right moment. The maiden Cassandra is the first victim to appear. In a mad scene she dances joyfully as if her assignment to Agamemnon as a concubine were an honorable marriage to be celebrated and applauded. The contrast between real misery and ideal bliss is sharply underscored by the mad girl's mistaking one for the other. The trick is easy, once it is disclosed, but Euripides apparently did it first and most effectively, for the scene fits his larger purpose. Suddenly, however, he interrupts his emotional appeal and jolts us into a cool mood of almost irrelevant sophistry. Cassandra is sud-denly sane and ready to maintain the incongruous thesis that the defeated are happier than the conquerors. Her rhetorical fireworks frustrate emotion for the moment and press home the ironical sug-gestion that great men and great events are not very important after all. The sorrows of Troy fade into the distance, merged in the tragic doom of all mankind about which nothing can be done. Such universalization of pity inhibits action, makes grief luxurious and tragedy merely aesthetic, a tale of old, unhappy, far-off things and battles long ago. Yet emotion waits in ambush, and thought has been rooted where it may grow and break down old defenses. Euripides has shown us a new perspective so cunningly fused with the old that nothing will seem quite so certain again.

When Cassandra has reverted to the role of prophetess and sung the destined woe of Agamemnon, she leaves the stage to the next victim. Andromache appears, infant in arms, like a madonna. The sanctities of a good woman's love for husband and child are ex-posed in moving lines at the moment of profanation. Androma-che's ideal of married life is Oriental in its suppression of jealousy and speech, as well as in her preference for death if chastity is violated. There are many tales of Chinese and Hindu women for whom marriage was the only sacrament, and Euripides has a distinct bias for the un-Greek woman. His contemporaries con-sidered him antifeminist. Yet Andromache is Greek enough to consider Hector's interest in his son and to consent to live and please a new master for the sake of Astyanax. Chastity may be compromised in exchange for other ends. This difficult decision of Andromache is at once made meaningless by the announcement that the boy has been condemned to death as a possible future menace to the Greeks. The irony of a moment of hope and resolution in a tragic tale is a tactic familiar from the plays of Sophocles. The victim who struggles and hopes makes better sport. The agony of Andromache's farewell to her son is mercifully brief. The impact of disaster upon a good woman enslaved in war is permanently etched.

How about the bad woman, Helen? Euripides discovered before Shakespeare the possibility of mixing comic interludes in tragedy. In fact, Aeschylus has his humorous nurse, and Sophocles his humorous guard in the *Antigone*. Base strutters, such as Xerxes, Aegisthus, and Menelaus of the *Ajax,* cannot be taken very seriously. The Spartans Menelaus and Helen could hardly be glorified in Athens, and Euripides makes the most of his dramatic license to abuse them. Menelaus' final weakness after the bluster of his entrance is made both funny and loathsome. At first he is hot to slay Helen and fulfill the purpose of the long war, but when he sees her, serene and contemptuous in her beauty, he grants her first a hearing, then a stay; and the audience knew that the proud Spartan dame would ultimately rule his palace as before. Hecuba's last hope, that vengeance at least on the woman who had caused the war might relieve her agony, is thwarted. The comic interlude has been used at once to belittle the victors and to torment the victim. The pompous conqueror plays the part of a foolish clown. His vulgarity sharpens the pangs of defeat. The world is left without glory or justice. Andromache's ideal of marriage is lost and in its place it set up the abomination of a union without honor or dignity. The conqueror will not right any wrong, nor attain any joy in his own life. The compensations of defeat that were provided in the *Hecuba* are swept away in the genuinely tragic *Trojan Women*. Euripides sees the devastation wrought by war as clearly as Thucydides. The very things that make life dear are sacrificed by both sides. Euripides was soon to abandon Athens for the court of Archelaus of Macedon. The hypocritical Helen is a triumphant villain, and adds enormously to the bitterness of Euripides' commentary on life. Aristotle does not like either the triumphant villain or the comic vulgarized hero, but admits that Euripides is supremely tragic. He has no hope of eradicating folly or making men better. He shows them what they are like with mingled laughter and tears, and grows unsociable.[10]

After this, Hecuba's lament as she prepares the bruised body of Astyanax for burial becomes a universal lament for all the sanctities of human life. No god from a machine is needed to prophesy the future or order the chorus from the stage. Talthybius will do that; and their slow march to slavery as the towers of Ilium expire in smoke and flame is both spectacular and realistic. The apparent formlessness of the play has permitted a mixture of elements that include a minimum of action and decision. No debates among the Greeks are reported. Fate is sheer and uncompromising. The one decision of Menelaus that we see on-stage is rather the defeat of decision by its opposite. It seems likely that the success of this play is due as much to inspiration as to art. To produce such despair and pity Euripides must have known a mood of deep discontent with a world in which success is dearly purchased by disregard of individual happiness and aspiration. Essentially the *Trojan Women* is the work of a defeated romantic whose exultation in the beautiful moments of life goes hand in hand with a sense of the weakness of beauty in a world of ruthless action. The Latin poet Virgil and the English poets Shelley and Keats will feel the same brooding melancholy in their most poetic moments.

We are trembling on the verge of sentimentality, but in this one play Euripides remains poised on the razor's edge, still saved by his evident sincerity. His pity and terror enlarge the scope of sympathy and produce a moral tension, not merely the luxury of idle tears. He has robbed power and glory of their charm and has buttressed the appeal of innocence and honesty. The small things are chosen to confound the great. The precious things that perish grow more precious by the loss. Many homely details contribute to a total that is more than the sum of its parts. As long as wars are waged, the *Trojan Women* will have a contemporary appeal.

In the *Electra,* produced perhaps two years later (413 B.C.), Euripides retells the story of Aeschylus' *Choephoroe,* and incorporates in the old story his new theme of universal failure and universal pity. This time, however, he mixes virtue and vice in his characters. Sanctities are violated by the avenging Orestes and Electra, while Clytemnestra and Aegisthus overflow with motherly sympathy and pious hospitality. Vengeance is reduced to the low level of assassination. Religion and the state are deprived of their significance and become, if anything, mere excuses for crime. Vacillation between conflicting emotions replaces character as it did in the *Medea,* but the pathological rot has spread further and infected all the leading characters. Only the peasant and the old servant, whose function is that of Eumaeus and Eurycleia of the *Odyssey,* show virtue still shining bright among the lowly. The removal of religion and the state from their old place as civilizing forces, leaves individuals naked to all the winds of passion, ferocity, sophistry, repentance, and despair. Euripides has ceased to depict mad individuals in a sane world; he now depicts the world itself as mad and topsy-turvy. Obviously this inhibits thought and action entirely. Emotion is made exciting in itself, and the more horrible the emotion the better it pleases.

When Electra exults gruesomely over the dead Aegisthus and a moment later weeps for her own wickedness, we are witnessing a final disintegration. Action has disintegrated into spurts of thoughtless explosive violence. Thought has disintegrated into a rhetoric that serves all moods impartially and is no longer part of the psychological motivation. Emotion itself has disintegrated into inconsistent impulses that succeed one another like spells of weather. Only the actor profits, for his technique receives constant exercise and recognition; in the general disintegration the only possible effect on the audience is one of aesthetic gratification. Since it is impossible to take anything in the play seriously, for it is

realistic only in spots, the audience need feel no sense of responsibility. They are safe in their own world, obviously superior in intelligence and charm to the principals, and obviously superior in
fortune to the noble peasant and servant. Theologians have maintained that one of the joys of heaven is to watch the sufferings of
the damned without sympathy. The agony of the wicked is a spectacle to be enjoyed in the *Electra* too. Art has completed its evolution from the service of religion and the state to an independent
status as a source of entertainment and private culture. Drama has
ceased its philosophical contemplation of the universe and has
taken to raking in the muck of psychopathy for museum pieces to
exhibit in a chamber of horrors. Good theater becomes livelier as
it neglects the great issues of life. The serious thinker Plato will
desert and denounce the drama with good reason, and blame the
theater for the general democratic failure to discriminate between
good and popular in art and life.[11]

Euripides preserves the old Aeschylean patterns in vestigial form,
but shrunken to a kind of dramatic shorthand. Apollo is made
responsible for the slaying, though the slayers have no reason to
obey him unless foolish superstition is a reason. Orestes in a debate
with Electra shows that he knows better. Pylades does not speak
to enforce the righteous will of Apollo. It is the disagreeable hate
of Electra that backs up the god and sways Orestes. The invocation
of the dead Agamemnon by his children is short and incongruous.
On the other hand there are many novelties in the plot, such as the
debate between Electra and Clytemnestra, which reappears in the
Electra of Sophocles. Electra is promoted to an equal or even
superior part in the slaying of her mother; again Sophocles follows
Euripides. He will not follow him in making Apollo responsible
for sin, or in exaggerating the horror of the two deaths. The death
of Clytemnestra is quite unnecessary in Euripides from a human
point of view. Orestes, having slain Aegisthus, might have succeeded to his father's throne and ruled peacefully, if the murder
of his mother had not forced him into perpetual exile along with
his sister.

Orestes is made weak. Electra forces upon him a heroic role that is thoroughly quixotic. She on her part is self-centered, and has some of the foolish, petty pride of her mother and her aunt Helen that Euripides is fond of satirizing. She is meticulous about small proprieties, but has no qualms about the crafty murder of her mother. She is wrong when she rebukes her peasant husband for the inadequacy of his hospitality and when she rebukes the old servant for supposing that Orestes would have come secretly in fear of Aegisthus. Orestes had actually come secretly, and he was in fact grateful for humble hospitality. Electra's refusal to accept the arguments of the old servant when he proposes evidence that convinced the Aeschylean Electra, is ungracious, inconsiderate, and mistaken. She is equally ungracious to the peasant who, thanks to a generous disposition and good policy, is her husband in name only.

Instead of being visited by the avenging furies of a murdered mother after their act, Orestes and Electra are both visited by pangs of conscience and bitterly acknowledge their sin of matricide. This is psychologically interesting, but produces the impression that Electra is feverishly irresponsible and that Orestes has no strength of mind. His psychological outburst is a blind alley, an impulsive mood that comes too late and leads to no resolve. Action and feeling are divorced, since the reasons that seemed to justify the act no longer suffice after performance. A wise consistency is essential to morality, as we learn from Aristotle. Euripides voices the protest of the heart against conventional standards, but his characters remain adolescent because they are as impulsive and irresponsible in their repentance as in their rash action. The moral problem is left to be settled by a god from the machine, whose absolution of the guilty pair is not inappropriate after their revulsion of feeling. Castor, brother of Clytemnestra, and fiancé of Electra before he was promoted to the heavens, points out that Clytemnestra deserved to die, but that it was nevertheless wrong for her children to act as executioners. This nice distinction, which has a corollary in the doctrine that a citizen may not attack his motherland even in self-defense, is axiomatic from Amphiaraus in the *Seven* of Aeschylus to Plato. When Euthyphro would merely prosecute his father for murder, Socrates views him with distaste. Castor, however, forgives nephew and niece, because they acted under orders from Apollo, but sentences them to perpetual exile. The court of the Areopagus already exists at Athens to absolve Orestes, when he gets there, not because he was right, but again because Apollo misled him. As in our courts, an act of God relieves human agents of responsibility.

The result of Euripides' innovations is to make his *Electra* a genuine tragedy rather than a success story. This is the more remarkable in that Euripides follows the plot of the *Odyssey* rather closely at first. Orestes, like Odysseus, spies out the land rather than make an open attack on the palace, and is recognized against his will by a faithful servant who sees a scar. Orestes, however, is not sure that he is doing right, while both he and Electra agree in repenting afterward. It is the brothers of Clytemnestra, Castor and Pollux, who as next of kin should avenge her, but they are content with fulfillment of the religious requirement of perpetual exile. Orestes is so belittled by his subordination to Electra and his obvious failure to achieve happiness that he is pitiable rather than heroic. Though he is a mixed character, brave but foolish and impious, he is not a strong character like Shakespeare's Macbeth, who is at least a hardy villain. Macbeth went into crime with his eyes open and went down fighting later. Orestes drifted weakly into matricide.[12]

The slaying of Aegisthus was no doubt justified, though Euripides makes it horrible by letting Orestes slay the usurper while he is the latter's guest in the midst of a religious exercise. Thus there is no clear-cut aspiration on either side, and the effect is to present a melodramatic view of life. In Macbeth the hero is tempted by evil spirits, and by his wife, whereas it is Apollo and a sister who mislead Orestes. When man is led into crime by a god, his case is pitiable indeed. Euripides has written more in sorrow than in anger. He presents a picture of life as confused, of men as vacillating between rashness and despondency, and of events as so mixed in cause and effect that we can only gaze fascinated at the kaleidoscopic shifts of fortune. Frustration is universal, as in O'Neill's *Mourning Becomes Electra.* We have come a long way from Aeschylus' patient optimism. Euripides has brought the gods back, not to justify the righteous, but to excuse the thoughtless and sinful. Chance makes reason useless, and rhetoric makes virtue indistinguishable from vice. The way is paved for pure sensationalism, which is the natural offspring of realism. As characters become less noble, their vicissitudes become more extraordinary. Tragedy is sinking into sentimentality, the enjoyment of moral superiority without any assumption of moral responsibility. Euripides has exploited to the full the old theme of frustration in the moment of triumph that we saw in *Medea, Heracles,* and the *Trojan Women,* but in the *Electra* even sympathy is frustrated, unless we are to shed maudlin tears over those whom no action can help because their folly is irremediable.

In the last great masterpiece of Euripides, the *Bacchae,* there is little appeal to pity; terror is uppermost in the end. The onslaught of terror is, however, delayed till the recognition scene, when Agave, unwilling worshiper of Dionysus, who has been dancing in mad joy to celebrate her triumph as slayer of a young lion, comes slowly to her senses and shrieks as she sees in her hand, not the head of a young lion, but the head of her own son Pentheus. This is almost certainly the greatest recognition scene in literature, for it involves a revulsion of feeling on the part of the audience as well as for Agave. Up to this point Euripides has made the religion of Dionysus seem a joyful, unworldly kind of intoxication. Dionysus has appeared as an idealist defying worldly foes who slander his care-appeasing cult of the grape. The easy grace of his triumphs, the enthusiasm of his worshipers, and the comic weakness of his opponents enlist the audience as followers of Bacchus, the god of pleasing illusions. There is no conflict of god with god, as in the *Hippolytus.* This time the young man who is slain by the god is a hardheaded realist, who sins by misunderstanding and rashness.

He fails to recognize the power and also the character of the god. He is already angry, even violent, when he first appears on the scene. He even attacks the seer, follower of Apollo, who has wisely joined the new religion because he foresees that it will succeed, and his grandfather Cadmus, who believes the seer and is a good enough politician to realize that the religion of Dionysus may make favorable propaganda for the dynasty.

With the death of Pentheus the cruelty of Dionysus and the devastation that may come as an aftermath of happy illusion is borne home. Again Euripides presents a triumph that is sweet to the palate but hard to digest. The *Bacchae* is a play to provoke thought, like the *Oedipus,* not merely tears, like *Electra.* It presents quite as profound a problem as the *Oedipus,* for Dionysus is symbolic of all religious ecstasy. To the convinced devotee religion brings the utmost peace and happiness, but to the skeptic a problem with which he cannot deal honestly. To oppose is to perish, while to accept is to prefer dreams to reality, some other world to the good that can be obtained by reasonable efforts. Dionysus, like the Buddhist gods of Tibet, has both a benign and a terrible aspect. Like Christianity, he preaches love and at the same time inspires crusades and massacres. The terrible aspect of Dionysus is as ingeniously developed in the play as that of Medea was, but he, being altogether a god, feels no pity. The audience, however, may well feel fear as well as pity, if they recognize the truth of Euripides' study of religion. That it is true is well attested by historical examples of the triumph of religion over skeptical tyrants. The god, of course, can show no psychological development; he is a force of nature. Nor need we be concerned about the miracles that he works. The success of religious movements is a miracle in itself, child of faith and begetter of more faith. The miracle of conversion or of delusion, as the case may be, makes other miracle superfluous.

The prologue and the epilogue of the play are both spoken by the god Dionysus, who was also a mortal by birth, grandson of Cadmus and cousin of Pentheus, who opposes the new religion.

For the sake of irony the audience were left in no doubt that Dionysus is really a god, but his followers and opponents have many different views of him, and Pentheus considers him an out-and-out impostor. But an impostor would be less mysterious and overpowering. His moral level is not very different from that of Medea, since he takes vengeance on Cadmus and Agave, who follow him, as well as on Pentheus. His excuse is that acceptance by Cadmus and Agave had come too late to save them. It is bold to present a god in human form on the stage, but not too bold, since human beings have been recognized or advertised as gods both in ancient and modern times; and, in any case, a man who can inspire his followers with fanatical devotion has the power for good or evil that the Greeks recognized as divine. Dionysus, like Medea, has a barbaric quality, since the chorus are Asiatic devotees of an Oriental religion. No doubt the music and dancing were as expressive of religious ecstasy as the words are. The chorus come very near to being a protagonist in the play, for the triumph of the god is their triumph. The power of the god appears in the devotion of his worshipers. He is a force acting through the human imagination. Such forces are real enough, however misguided devotees may be. The god must have been particularly convincing on the Greek stage, since Euripides was reproducing in his plot familiar features of myth and ritual. Hence it is not easy to say where miracle begins or ends. The god is an unmoved mover. The power and confidence that he gives are bad or good according to the issue.[13]

In the prologue, Dionysus announces himself as son of Zeus and Semele, daughter of Cadmus. After the first choral ode, the blind seer Tiresias appears and summons Cadmus from the palace. The two old men are agreed that for reasons of policy they will accept the new religion. Their claim to be inspired revelers is not very convincing, for their words are belied by their ludicrous failure in action to recover their youthful agility. Cadmus has political reasons for upholding the divinity of a member of the family, and worships with all the sincerity of a competent politician. Tiresias the seer is right in his prophecies of the triumph of Dionysus and shows some capacity for theological sophistry. His best effort, however, is the claim that religious tradition is above human questioning. This sounds like a parody of Antigone, when we recollect that Dionysus has introduced his religion in his own short lifetime; but new movements somehow have a way of masquerading as genuine manifestations of old and original gods. Tiresias does not disdain the new wine, old bottle that he is.

Pentheus enters already furious, having taken measures to halt the movement by imprisoning the women. He intends also to slay the impostor who has misled him. He laughs at Tiresias and Cadmus, but has to spare his grandfather. The seer he outrages by ordering the destruction of his place of augury. Tiresias proposes to pray to Dionysus to spare Pentheus and Thebes. There can be no doubt that Pentheus has done all that he can to identify himself with the traditional tyrant of fiction by his self-will and by his denunciation of the seer who would save him. He is at least as hasty and as rash in his accusations as Hippolytus. When Dionysus is brought before Pentheus bound and unresisting, Pentheus again scoffs and orders him to prison. The chorus, dejected for a moment, are soon revived by the voice of Dionysus, who has been miraculously delivered by an earthquake. Pentheus is mystified but still hopes that force will suppress the stranger. Even when a herdsman appears and relates how the Bacchants, led by Pentheus' mother Agave, tore cattle limb from limb and won a victory over armed men, the king is not chastened, but orders out the army. At this point Dionysus takes his captor captive, inspiring him with illusions of success. Pentheus volunteers to spy upon the women as they revel, himself dressed as a woman. As Dionysus sends him to death, he suffers the indignity of mockery. In Aristophanes' *Lysistrata* the women dressed a defeated official as a woman and taunted him. It is bold of Euripides to use a comic scene in tragedy. He had made similar fun of the eunuch in the burlesque *Orestes,* but Pentheus is a hero, and he alone among the heroes of Euripides is treated with such mockery. Since he has himself ridiculed the feminine features of Dionysus, there is some justice in his fate. Still, the use of comedy to make tragedy more tragic is highly significant. According to Plato, Socrates had already maintained that the same man should be good both at tragedy and at comedy.[14]

The comedy becomes tragedy when a messenger relates how the women detected the spy and tore him to pieces under the delusion that he was a young lion. His mother Agave comes bearing the bloody head of her son, singing a song of triumph like Cassandra for her own ruin. Up to this point the audience have shared the victory of superman. No doubt when the Parthians saw the play at their celebration after the battle of Carrhae, an occasion on which the head of Crassus lent a touch of realism to the scene, the triumph of the Orient was even more appreciated. But a Greek audience would presumably transfer its sympathy to Agave as Cadmus slowly brings her to her senses. As the play ends, Dionysus sends Cadmus and Agave into exile. The same ending is effective in *Electra* and *Phoenissae,* but only here is it one and the same god that inspired the crime and that executes justice. This is not so much honoring Dionysus as heightening frustration. The man who would follow reason finds in life a mysterious force that he can neither judge nor control. In the attempt to control it the old men are hypocrites, the young man is honest but soon destroyed. The beauty of religion is matched by its cruelty. Here is a real problem which Euripides presents as no problem. By appearing to accept Dionysus he leaves it to the audience to decide what they will do about him. Or perhaps religion mattered so little to an Athenian audience by this time that their only problem was to enjoy themselves at least in the theater. Certain it is that the art which awakens atavistic terrors of the divine is more effective than a mere record of mishap in war like the *Rhesus.*[15]

It is characteristic of Euripides' later tragedies to present the hero in a state of mental aberration, no longer in possession of his soul. Neither calculation nor passion can be trusted, so that men seem to drift bewitched. Life is seen as too confusing to leave scope for responsible action. We are on our way to the exuberant monstrosity of a Seneca, and have ceased to see life steadily or entire, yet the very vagueness of Euripides' indictment of life makes his appeal to emotion more powerful. He is at his best when he deals with social rather than personal problems like those of Orestes. In the *Trojan Women* and the *Bacchae* the lyric part of the play is brought into focus by the interest of the chorus in the result. The *Hippolytus*, like the *Bacchae*, had its religious side. Like the *Medea*, it dealt with love and jealousy within the family; but Euripides does not mix the beauty and terror of love as he does the beauty and danger of religion. He is the poet of mystery and of desperate detachment from life. Sophocles apparently did not care to pursue the path of tragedy with him after the *Oedipus Tyrannus*. We find plays of Sophocles after the *Oedipus* only in the class of ethical plays or stories of success, promoters of good feeling.

VI
Propaganda, Idealism,
and Romance

IN GREEK plays of pity and terror the strongest
influence comes always from Homer's *Iliad*. In political plays,
which inevitably contain propaganda of some sort, the role of
Athena in the settlement at the end of the *Odyssey*, and the use
of a theatrical Athena to promote civil peace after the victory of
Peisistratus, provide a basis of growth. We have seen that Aeschylus in all extant plays is concerned somehow to uphold an
ideal of civilized living. Since in political plays characters must
represent either ideals or opposition to the political interest that
is dear to the heart of poet and audience, there is little scope for
variety in plot or character unless striking incidents are introduced.
Hence political plays are particularly likely to be episodic and to
include characters who devote themselves to the success of the
state or to some other ideal. The two purely political plays of
Euripides, *Suppliants* and *Heracleidae,* consist chiefly of conventional scenes loosely strung together. The state of Athens gives
aid to suppliants, defeats persecutors, and receives undying gratitude for her noble idealism. The pattern of the *Suppliants* of Aeschylus is so similar that we may safely assume that Euripides was
in these plays reworking old stories. Certainly the plays themselves
show that he was not much interested in the result. The pattern
of Sophocles' *Oedipus at Colonus* is the same again, but Sophocles
had the constructive imagination and poetic vigor to elevate the
old story into one of the great masterpieces of drama.[1]

Before attacking these three plays, which are wholly political

[1] For notes to chapter vi see pages 298-302.

in pattern, it will be well to consider the relation of political plays
to the drama of romance and success. Euripides has two plays,
the *Ion* and the *Andromache*, which are undoubtedly political in
their origin but romantic and domestic in their treatment. In both
the fate of an ancestor of the royal line is in jeopardy. His birth
is illegitimate and only after a chapter of accidents and fierce
domestic strife is his place on the throne assured. The audience,
if they accept the story as historical, will find that their patriotic
interest makes them feel strongly the dangers that threaten their
national hero, and makes them rejoice in his ultimate success.
Naturally, anyone who has endangered the life and success of
the infant can easily be made a vehicle for propaganda against the
nation that he represents. Furthermore, history may be recast in
the interest of propaganda wherever it is desirable. At the same
time the domestic strife and melodramatic moments embodied in
the plot open a field to drama that pure tragedy could hardly
exploit. Since the ending is happy in a political play, its strife
and misunderstandings may be treated less seriously than in such
a play as the *Medea*. The rejected mothers get their way in the
end in Euripides, while the husbands are disposed of somewhat
cavalierly. The action is largely autonomous in that the course of
it is guided by a higher power—some god or chance or philosophy
of history—without much influence from the characters concerned,
who may indeed be merely innocent and passive.

It is only necessary to omit the dynastic interest and such a plot
becomes one of domestic misunderstanding with ultimate happiness for all good characters, such as we find in New Comedy. If
interest, in tragedy, is centered on the family reunions of princes
and heroes, we get the ethical plot of Aristotle with its almost
invariable recognition scenes. The pattern is that of the *Odyssey:*
trouble and deliverance accompanied by the discovery of long absent members of the family. Drama always puts the recognition
scene before the deliverance. Euripides' *Iphigeneia in Tauris* is
a masterpiece of this type, and his *Helen* is a burlesque of it, while
the *Electra* of Sophocles turns the story of Orestes into a heroic

melodrama instead of a tragedy. His treatment is less concerned
with morality than that of Aeschylus or Euripides, but the design
of forces that are involved in a highly dramatic action produces
a work of art as intricate in its technique and as effective in the
theater as anything that we have in Greek between *Oedipus
Tyrannus* and Menander. It is Sophocles' one play of successful
intrigue and as such is remarkable for its adherence to heroic ideals
of conduct. In a play of intrigue or a success play it is generally
not necessary to idealize the hero in order to please the audience.
Experience with moving pictures shows that an audience will take
either the side of the police or that of the bandits without qualms,
as long as the story is exciting. The hero must, of course, be either
bold or clever, preferably both; but thought and emotion must
be kept subordinate to action; and there is hardly any limit to
the amount of good luck that can be tolerated. Aristotle notes
the tendency of tragedy in its later development to use mixed
characters and neglect character in the moral sense. We shall consider vacillating and repentant characters more particularly in the
next chapter.

The *Ion* of Euripides is a mixture of elements. Like the comedies
of Shakespeare, it tolerates threats of death, deceptions, and divine
intervention without taking them too seriously or considering their
moral implications except for temporary effect. Ion was king of
Athens and ancestor of the Ionians. Euripides makes him son
of Apollo, not of Xuthus the Achaean, thus purging out the foreign
influence. Since the Ionians worshiped the Delphic Apollo as
patrôos, or guardian of the male line, it seems reasonable to trace
that line to Apollo. To reconcile divine and human fatherhood
of the same infant is one of the problems that beset theologians.
Euripides shows us Apollo bestowing his child on Xuthus, though
the human father is to be left conveniently ignorant of his wife's
extramarital experience with the god. The princess Creüsa who
bore Ion and abandoned him is a very sympathetic and pathetic
character. As in New Comedy, rape, not seduction, is the verdict.
Since the penalty prescribed for a seducer in Athens was death

at the pleasure of the victim's male relatives, rape was no more serious as a crime. On the other hand, seduction involved a woman as *particeps criminis*. Athenian feeling was, then, just the opposite of ours, and we may expect any Athenian story of an illegitimate babe to begin with rape, not with seduction. They protected the reputation of their women at the expense of their men. Just as in Homer strangers were asked, "Are you merchants or pirates?" so in one tragedy Heracles was asked, "Did you get the girl by persuasion or by force?" The implication is the same in both cases, that one occupation or mode of possession was as respectable as the other.[2]

Apollo does not appear in the play. Hermes in the prologue speaks for him, as does Athena in the epilogue. The scene is before the temple of Apollo at Delphi, and it is through the oracle that Ion is bestowed on Xuthus as his son. The oracle, of course, speaks for Apollo. From the point of view of Creüsa, Apollo has behaved like a villain. After forcing her, he has left her and the babe to suffer what might happen, as far as she knows. Ion considers her story impossible, and is prepared to demand an accounting of Apollo himself through his oracle, after he finally recognizes her as his mother. Athena as goddess from the machine answers his questions and everything is set right. The god has been using his own methods to get his son recognized as legitimate prince at Athens. It is evident that the gods, living on a higher plane, may follow a divine plan that seems to make innocent mortals suffer. In Aeschylus' *Oresteia* such a divine plan is treated very seriously. Euripides treats it quite lightheartedly, getting the greatest possible effect of pathos and irony, but using music, dance, and the enchantment of distance and innocence to produce an aesthetic effect that is as charming as any poetic fancy. It starts thought in a whimsical way, but the most sophisticated would surely be content to note once more the humorous effect of pretending that the old mythical tales really happened. As for action, no effect is produced by a play in which human efforts to get results are foiled, and a better divine plan substituted. The most unsophisticated might, to be sure, depart convinced that simple innocence and devotion to the gods will pay in the end.

After Hermes has explained the situation in a prologue, Ion enters to do service as janitor. With song and dance he sweeps the floor and threatens the birds who would defile the temple. The professional actors particularly appreciated this part. In such an operatic role it is clear that tragedy by no means produces its effect without music and spectacle. Fortunately, Greek lyrics can be very expressive in isolation, but much is inevitably lost without music and dance. The *Ion* comes as close to the spirit of Oriental drama, whether in India or China, as it is well possible for a Greek play to do. Note, however, that the Greek characters are unsuitable for heroic roles from the Hindu point of view, since they act from motives of jealousy and revenge. The *Ion* also has a lively chorus of sightseeing servingwomen, attendant upon the queen, Creüsa. Creüsa would like to ask Apollo what has become of his abandoned son, but Ion, whom the audience know to be that son, points out the danger of arousing the god to wrath by such an implied accusation. When Xuthus arrives and asks the god for a son, he is told that the first comer after his leaving the shrine will be his son. Ion, of course, is bound to be the first comer, and Xuthus embraces him. The recognition scene becomes piquant when Ion misunderstands his sudden affection. Creüsa also misunderstands the god's intention and attempts to poison Ion. When he discovers the attempt and would slay her in return, she is saved by the intervention of the old priestess who had brought him up and who hands over to him the tokens that were exposed with him as a babe. Creüsa recognizes these and there is a happy reunion of mother and son. The intervention of Athena, however, is still required, to make Ion accept his position as prince and successor to Xuthus. Xuthus is eliminated from the royal line, since Ion is his son only by adoption, but Xuthus and Creüsa are to be parents of Dorus and Achaeus, founders of the Dorian and Achaean line. Thus these two nations are happily put into a subordinate position with respect to Athens.[3]

The *Andromache* is a companion piece to the Ion, going even further along the path of melodrama, since it introduces the child Molossus, son of Andromache, to sing in a plaintive duet with his mother. The scholiast notes that the material of the play is comic, inasmuch as it deals with rivalry between women joined to one man. He argues, however, that it may be classed as a tragedy, since it ends with mourning for the dead Neoptolemus. Let us call it a tragicomedy, for the death of Neoptolemus is merely a necessary stage to the establishment of Molossus on the throne as ancestor of the Molossian line of kings, and that was a happy ending and the main theme of the play. It seems to have been written for a Molossian audience, perhaps at the time when the Athenians were allied with King Tharyps against Sparta. In any case, Euripides has used the resources of his art to vilify the Spartans. Molossus and his mother are persecuted by Hermione, daughter of Helen, and by her father Menelaus, who is crafty, mean, cruel, and cowardly. Hermione is a typical proud, unruly Spartan woman, who disregards the commands of her husband Neoptolemus, son of Achilles.

The scene is laid in Phthia. The chorus are women of Phthia, and this may be the play to which Aristotle refers when he names the *Phthiotides* as an example of an ethical play which is not complex. Certainly the play has no recognition scene, nor any misunderstanding that is cleared up. The Spartan villains are intentionally wicked from the start and are defeated by open force, not by trickery or intrigue. The moral has been made perfectly plain for the most unsubtle to understand. Andromache is a noble character and her rescue is demanded morally as well as politically. Just as the *Trojan Women* shows the degradation of Andromache, so in this play she passes with her son, who has only a singing, not a speaking part, from misery and danger to security and happiness. It is Peleus, not she, who joins the chorus in mourning for Neoptolemus, and when Thetis, mother of Achilles and grandmother of Neoptolemus, appears to foretell the future, Andromache receives the promise of a Trojan, Helenus, as husband to make her

happy. Neoptolemus had cast her off on the occasion of his marriage
to Hermione.[4]

The play opens with a scene in which Andromache sits as suppliant at the altar of Thetis. Hermione seeks her life and that
of her son. Neoptolemus is absent, but Andromache finds a fellow
slave who will risk her life to take news to the aged Peleus, grandfather of Neoptolemus. The chorus enter and express sympathy.
Then Hermione appears and denounces Andromache as a rival
who has by magic prevented her from bearing a son. Andromache
replies with countercharges and is threatened with fire if she will
not leave the altar. After a choral ode, however, it is Menelaus who
finds means to make Andromache surrender. He has found Molossus, whom his mother had hidden, and Andromache surrenders
herself to save her son's life. Menelaus keeps his promise not to
slay Molossus, but points out that Hermione is not bound by anything that he has said. Thus Andromache and Molossus bewail
their fate together until the sudden arrival of Peleus turns the
tables. Menelaus is roundly upbraided with more stinging reflec-
tions on Spartan customs, before he goes blustering from the scene.
Now it is the turn of Hermione to despair in fear of her husband.
She would commit suicide before he returns, but her old nurse
calms her. Very opportunely Orestes, her cousin, arrives, and she
elopes with him. He has already planned to slay Neoptolemus
at Delphi. In the next scene Peleus hears from a messenger the
news of Orestes' dastardly assassination of his rival for the hand
of Hermione. The corpse of Neoptolemus soon arrives and is
mourned. His grandmother Thetis, though she is a goddess, is not
an Olympian, and hence can appear in the presence of the dead.
She forbids mourning for the dead, gives direction for burial, and
prophesies the future happiness of Andromache, Molossus, and a
long line of kings, who will preserve the stock of Achilles as well
as that of the Trojan Andromache.

The plot of the *Andromache* is highly episodic, but each scene
leads the action one step further. The action is largely unplanned,
but once we recognize that the fate of Molossus is the theme, we

easily see that he can inherit the throne only by the elimination of any hope of legitimate offspring born to Neoptolemus. It is not enough to save Andromache and get rid of Hermione. As long as Neoptolemus lives, he may marry again. Since he is already parted from Andromache, his death serves only to alienate our sympathy further from the Spartans, who disregard all sanctities in their senseless pride and craft. Thus we have a play the plot of which is centered on the fate of a hero who hardly speaks and certainly does not act. His fate depends upon such men or gods as help the innocent and helpless. The effect is rather that of a pageant or a historical play which deals in episodes, because the audience may be assumed to know the actual story and to be interested more in seeing it again from a new angle than in a complete exposition of it as if it were new. Plays about the American Lincoln have a historical background, but are usually made up otherwise of disconnected scenes. Euripides, however, may have invented most of his plot.

The value of the *Andromache* as propaganda is obvious. The enemies of Molossus and his mother are made ridiculous as well as wicked. The calm devotion of Andromache is contrasted with the silly pride and hysterical despair of Hermione, while Orestes and Menelaus behave abominably. In the *Ion,* Euripides had been content to make Xuthus only mildly ridiculous as a victim of the god's deception. Ion's simple belief in the virtue of Apollo also has its humorous side, since it leads him to condemn others for their more realistic views. In the end, though he gains a kingdom, he has to resign himself to acceptance of gods as they are. They use deplorable means to gain their ends, just like any other irresponsible ruler. It is obvious that the final impression left by the happy ending is not one of pity and terror. The effect that Aristotle values in the ethical plot is *to philanthropon,* the 'comforting'—the strengthening of the ties that bind society together. The bonds of family or state are threatened so that there is temporary fear for them and pity for victims, but deliverance comes in time. Greek philanthropy, it must be remembered, included resistance to injustice and inhumanity and condign punishment of offenders. It involved not only love, but anger and hatred for wickedness and cruelty. In Athenian drama care is taken to identify Athens and democracy with justice and the support of sound principles. Athens fights for the oppressed not only nobly but successfully.[5]

The *Suppliants* and *Heracleidae* show Athens at strife with foreign powers. In the former the wives and children of the slain seven who were defeated in the famous attack on Thebes appeal to Theseus at Athens to secure burial for their dead. The reluctance of the king to involve his state in war is overcome only by an impassioned appeal from his mother Aethra on behalf of the suppliants. The king rebukes the Argive leader Adrastus for his folly in allying himself with men of violence and proposes to hold himself aloof from the consequences of such strife. The middle class are the mainstay of the state, not the rich or the poor. Aethra persuades him that for the sake of his own honor he must uphold the cause of justice, for the refusal of burial to the dead is an offense against right. Theseus agrees to refer the matter to the decision of the people, for he is king of a democratically ruled country. When the decision is made in favor of the suppliants, a blustering Theban herald threatens Athens and denounces democracy, which of course Theseus defends. War follows and the Athenians win an easy victory. The bodies of the dead are brought in for burial. When Evadne, widow of Capaneus, flings herself on his funeral pyre, the acme of self-devotion is reached. Her father Iphis vainly tries to dissuade her from self-immolation. Theseus generously bestows the bones of the dead on Adrastus, but Athena intervenes and bids him first require a solemn oath that Argos will never attack but ever defend Athens. The play evidently is intended to strengthen the ties between Argos and Athens by emphasizing their common interest against Thebes. It is implied that Sparta was incapable of generous action. Political wisdom embodied in sententious tirades is introduced even where it is not particularly relevant. Praise of peace and disapproval of the Argive attack on

Thebes, if they are topical, indicate that the play was produced
at a time when Argos was politically active in international affairs
and even threatening to desert Athens, that is, in the year 421 B.C.
The *Heracleidae* must be dated before 427, if we accept Thucydides' statement that all Attica was ravaged in that year, for
it is evidently designed to fit a situation in which the Spartans
had not ravaged the Tetrapolis, of which Marathon was part.
Actually, the Spartans had scruples against ravaging this district
because of the tradition that the sons of Heracles had found refuge
there and had made it a base in the war against Eurystheus of
Argos in which that tyrant was slain by Heracles' son Hyllus.
Euripides adds to the story the part of Alcmena, aged mother of
Heracles. Eurystheus is not slain in battle, but is taken prisoner.
Athens orders that his life is to be spared, but Alcmena, gloating
ferociously over her son's old enemy, slays him herself. Eurystheus,
in gratitude to Athens, promises that his tomb will be a sure protection for the city against the descendants of Heracles if ever
they become her enemies. The sudden generosity of Eurystheus is
hardly in character, nor can the poet offer any evidence of tomb
or ritual to prove the truth of his fiction. The best Euripides can
do is to make the Argive king order that he be buried without
tomb or ritual. Thus the complete absence of evidence confirms
a tale for which there is no evidence. Sophocles has the same problem in the *Oedipus at Colonus,* for no tomb of Oedipus was exhibited there. Here we have evidence to show that, while Greek
dramatists were delighted, if occasion offered, to connect their
tales with some piece of ritual that seemed to confirm their his-
toricity, they were perfectly capable of inventing fiction that could
not be so confirmed.

Euripides is interested in giving the Tetrapolis better security
than the good-will of the Heracleidae. Hence he makes the tomb
and spirit of the Argive king serve as a defense. It was no doubt
also somewhat humiliating to any part of Attica to be spared by
the kindness of the Spartans. It might even be embarrassing to
be so spared, as Pericles foresaw. Those who were ravaged might

suspect those who were not of profiting too much by unpatriotic friendship with the enemy. Euripides' ingenious addition to the tale makes it possible to attribute this ambiguous security to ghostly influence hostile to Sparta rather than to any mutual friendship. Such ghostly protective influences are enshrined in popular belief in many parts of the world. On the borders of China, Burma, and Siam it is customary to protect growing crops by the angry heads of strangers slain for the purpose. The well-known propensity to anger of European strangers makes their heads particularly popular. Eurystheus had all necessary qualifications as an enemy of the Heracleidae. He could be trusted to hate them forever. The Greek poets, however, not satisfied with hate as a motive, represent their ghostly protectors as being also grateful to Athens for some kind of support that she had given them. The support that Athens gave Eurystheus was no more than a gesture, but it sufficed to rationalize a primitive belief in protection by the angry dead.[6]

Otherwise the plot follows familiar formulae. The scene is Marathon and there is a chorus of old men of Marathon. Demophon, son of Theseus, has to be persuaded to protect the suppliants, led by the aged Iolaus, friend of Heracles. When further action is halted by the need of sacrificing a noble maiden, the daughter of Heracles volunteers to die. The blustering Argive herald, Copreus, had already declared war on Athens. When the maiden has gone to death, Hyllus arrives with an army. Old Iolaus insists on going into battle though he can hardly stand in armor. In the next episode a slave of Alcmena wins freedom by bringing good news of victory, including the miraculous rejuvenation of Iolaus, who has been chiefly responsible for success. The miracle is obviously a reminiscence of the rejuvenation of Laertes in Book 24 of the *Odyssey*. The play ends with the scene already discussed in which the captive Eurystheus, doomed to death by Alcmena, utters a final benediction on Athens and a malediction on the Heracleidae, who as kings of Sparta ungratefully made war on Athens in the days of Euripides.

The difference between the genius of Sophocles and that of

Euripides comes out nowhere more clearly than in a comparison
of the *Heracleidae* with the *Oedipus at Colonus,* which has superficially almost the same plot. The *Heracleidae* is the shortest and
the dullest play of Euripides, while the *Oedipus at Colonus* is the
longest play of Sophocles and has a greatness that baffles the
attempt to analyze it. Still, analysis is our business, and we can
at least note obvious differences of construction. Presumably, the
genius of Euripides did not lend itself to the embodiment of
imaginative ethical ideals. He presents us with spectacular exhibi-
tions of momentary devotion that seem to spring from youthful
ardor or from passion. The lifelong devotion that involves daily
humility and labor is hardly for him. He rebels against the conditions of life and finds consolation in division of the records of
the mind. Whether religion is defeated, as in the *Hippolytus,* or
victorious, as in the *Bacchae,* in his plays it is not helpful to the
community, but destructive of human solidarity. In his happy plays
the moral element tends to be personal or unimportant. He is
at his best romantic—interested in escape, rebellion, or the beautiful
and strange. His characters, being true to themselves, prove false
to other men. Sophocles is at his best in depicting loyalties and
the rational impersonal honesty of purpose that promotes human
solidarity. The *Oedipus at Colonus* is a hymn of praise to old-
fashioned simple honesty and to the mutual strength that is won
by the virtues that make men submissive and united. No gods
enter into the play, but the guidance of the gods is everywhere
taken for granted. Oedipus still trusts the oracle of Apollo that
had ruined him. Now it brings him a personal triumph and peace
in death. He had already attained peace of mind by reflecting on
his moral innocence. Sophocles does not suppose that the righteous
are always happy, but he implies that in the long run there is
nothing better than righteousness; and throughout the play he
points the contrast between the loyalty of Oedipus' daughters to
their father and the hideous self-seeking that rules his sons. No
curse is needed to destroy them but the curse of their own un-
ruliness. So an ideal Athens is represented by Theseus, whom

Oedipus can trust without an oath, and contrasted with Thebes, as represented by the false Creon.

The greatest innovation in Sophocles' plot is that he concentrates on one situation throughout. His suppliant is also the man whose death is shown and whose tomb will serve to protect Athens against Thebes. The only self-immolation is that of Oedipus, who goes willingly to his death by divine decree. There is no miracle of physical rejuvenation, but the moral rebirth of Oedipus is the more striking for being, not miraculous, but the result of intelligent reflection. Yet he honestly faces the fact that he is polluted by the mere physical facts of his life—parricide and incest. He will not allow Theseus to touch him, nor does Theseus insist. Note for comparison the unrestrained generosity of Theseus and the helpless dependence of Heracles in the *Heracles Furens* of Euripides. The two men in Sophocles are proudly equal except in fortune; the two in Euripides are alternately depressed in spirit as in fortune. A Sophoclean hero rules at least the kingdom of his own mind. Antigone and Ismene devote themselves not to death but to life for their father. Their life is one of hunger, exposure to weather and to insult, and of constant uncertainty. The reluctance of the state to accept a suppliant is skillfully shifted by Sophocles from Theseus to lesser representatives. The atmosphere of religious awe is maintained from the start, together with the local patriotic interest.

The scene is at Colonus, native deme of Sophocles, before a precinct of the Eumenides, awful goddesses. Blind Oedipus, guided by Antigone, stops there to rest. First a local stranger, then a chorus of men of Colonus, threaten to expel them. The entrance of Theseus is long delayed. This delay enhances the effect of his generous reception of the fugitives in contrast to the hostility of lesser men. Meanwhile, Ismene has brought news that Creon is coming from Thebes to recapture Oedipus because of an oracle that makes it expedient to secure his burial on Theban soil. Creon, arriving after the departure of Theseus, plays the smiling villain until he knows that Oedipus is aware of the plot.

Then he seizes the girls, who are as necessary to Oedipus as the bow of Philoctetes to its owner; furthermore, when Oedipus curses him, Creon proposes to kidnap the aged hero himself. Theseus arrives and makes short work of him, in spite of his argument that Athens should be grateful to be rid of Oedipus. Creon is doing his dirty work for the state, and therefore seems more ruthless than in the other plays where he appears. He is the kind of functionary who takes on the quality of the regime that he represents. Sophocles does not need to describe the battle by which the girls are recovered. He prefers to linger over the affectionate reunion of father and daughters. He also introduces the episode of Polyneices, who is a suppliant and exile now, like his father, and has the support of Theseus and Antigone in his request for a hearing. But community of fortune is not unity of mind, and Oedipus curses this son too. Old age is no cure for anger.

The final scenes remain in which Oedipus, to the accompaniment of signs from heaven, fortified by his knowledge of the oracles, goes to his desired rest. Sophocles makes a virtue of the unknown tomb, for it enhances the mystery of his fiction. Longinus notes the sublimity of the handling of this incident, for which he might have found a parallel in the death of Moses. This is not tragedy, but solemn religious and political pageantry. The mourning for Oedipus is brief. In this last play of Sophocles, he for the first time departs from the tradition that tragedy must dwell on the theme of death or extreme agony. Oedipus welcomes death, and scenes of lament in the play are reduced almost to vestiges. Milton's *Samson Agonistes* owes much to this drama of Sophocles, but is far more psychological in its treatment. The lofty tone, however, and the implicit acceptance of a religious view of life are the same. It is true that religious beliefs differ from people to people and that the sanctities of one time and place are abhorrent elsewhere. The Delphic oracle was not, in practice, an infallible or even honest guide, nor is Milton's theology universally accepted now any more than in his own time. Yet the charm of simple faith is great, and its advantages to the politician are un-

deniable. Polybius considered that Rome's strength lay in superstition. In picturing his ideal Athens of the past, Sophocles coupled
with it an ideal religious guidance that probably few would have
believed in among his audience. Yet Socrates and Plato, for all
their questioning, clung to religious practices as a moral and political necessity. The religious tone of the *Oedipus* is an essential
element in its political message. Contemporary Athens was more
like Thebes, as Sophocles depicts it torn by civil war, than like his
ideal Athens. He had to idealize the religion that he knew, just
as he idealized the state that he knew. Certain it is that communities and states decline when they no longer have a common
faith, acceptance of which enables men to act with mutual confidence. It often happens that the religious ideal shines brighter
in a naughty world. It is characteristic of Sophocles as of Plato to
combine the religious and the political ideal, and not to despair of
reason.[7]

The greatness of Sophocles' play, as of Milton's, is dependent
upon a marvelous felicity of utterance. Sophocles is not only majestic and impassioned, but lively with a perfect simplicity of united
rhythm and thought. His characters do not declaim or strike attitudes. Their thoughts and feelings flow in verse whose art is a
perfect imitation of nature. Contrast the declamation of Ajax on
the theme, all things change, with Oedipus' simple statement:
"Earth's strength decays; the body weakens; confidence departs;
and falsehood spreads." "Topsoil grows thin; men lack vitamins;
the spirit starves; and life becomes a scramble with no holds
barred," is another way to say it. Man is dependent on the physical universe as well as on the moral health of society; and Sophocles could see that the evolution of political life in his Athens was
as irreversible as time. Yet he has the strength of mind as he
approaches ninety and his own death to enshrine in perfect art the
noble ideal that had made democracy possible. Only in one passage—a wonderful lyric that makes no mention of the blindness
of Oedipus—does he betray the sorrows of old age. When Milton
celebrates the sorrows of his blind hero, it is the loss of light that

strikes him most. Thus the poets pretend to sing the woes of their heroes, each mourning in reality for woes of his own.

Not the least of the virtues of this play is its magnificent exploitation of previous dramatic tradition. It is the capstone of a trilogy, mounted firmly on the twin supports, *Oedipus Tyrannus* and *Antigone*. The majesty of Oedipus derives largely from our knowledge of his previous greatness and downfall as depicted in the earlier play. So too the devotion of Antigone to the obligations of kinship and her passionate appeal for Polyneices gain weight and power because they point clearly forward to her known fate as depicted in the earlier play about her. It is clear that Sophocles sees characters as developing in the intervals of time. The time is much longer in the case of Oedipus, and the development thus becomes plainer to see. Yet Oedipus is still the same in many traits of character. He still sees plainly that in the past he took things too seriously, yet his anger blazes forth against Creon and his own son with the old intensity. This time, however, he is right in his estimate of the situation, and that makes all the difference, for his rage is justified. Creon really is plotting against him. Creon's character had been the same before, potentially, but his situation had been different. Sophocles uses him instead of Eteocles to represent the tyrant state, perhaps because he would not destroy the effect of Aeschylus' *Seven against Thebes* by making Eteocles less a patriot, as Euripides did in his *Phoenissae*. Creon does not support his ruthlessness by reasons of state, as he does in the *Antigone,* but that is because he more appropriately suggests to Theseus the reasons of state that might induce Athens to deny succor to the suppliant. Creon has to use craft in this play since he is on foreign soil. In his own Thebes after the death of Eteocles he will play the part of autocratic leader; he is equally given to necessary cruelty before that when serving Eteocles abroad. He was already a crafty politician in the *Oedipus Tyrannus,* though his need was only personal. Still, we must not forget that Creon is a character in plays, not a real person, and that his character deteriorates according to the chronology of the plays rather than in relation to his own growth of years; yet he does not change abruptly.

The traditional background of heroic myth is equally exploited by Euripides in his masterpiece of tragicomedy, the *Iphigeneia in Tauris*. It is evidently Aristotle's favorite among plays with an ethical plot, and it especially deserves to be classed as ethical in the Greek sense, since it concentrates on *éthos*, the psychological depiction of not too heroic characters with an intimate and charming naturalism that enlists the sympathy of the audience and makes their success seem important. The leading characters have aspirations and sentiments that make it seem intolerable that they should be condemned to live or die without realizing their dreams of escape. Their loyalty to ties of family and to the cause of civilization is a strong motivating force in determining their acts and also in provoking enthusiasm in the audience, who can be trusted to take the side of Greeks against barbarians. Thus the play is itself a force in the direction of consolidating family and Hellenism. It is not specifically political, although Athena as god from the machine connects with an Attic ritual the story of Iphigeneia and her near-sacrifice of her brother. Indeed, it is quite possible that the story may have been suggested as an explanation of the ritual. It would undoubtedly add meaning to the ritual and give it a place in the body of heroic myth that largely determined ordinary Greek attitudes and loyalties. Yet it seems safer to say that the moral forces in the play make it entertaining than to assert that the play itself is important as a moral force. It gives moral satisfaction if we are content to take men and conditions as they are; and moral satisfaction is required for entertainment on a serious level.

This *Iphigeneia* was probably produced at about the same time as the *Trojan Women*. Both plays are remarkable for a moral and psychological realism that makes them masterpieces in two quite different categories. They are a warning that we must not expect the protean Euripides to confine himself to any one shape. Both are also in a remarkable way prefigured in the unsatisfying and rhetorical *Hecuba*. It is as if Euripides had seen that the earlier play was an incongruous mixture of fortune and misfortune, and had by patient study distilled from it the elements of pure tragedy and pure happiness in drama. The elements of the *Trojan Women* that might be mere entertainment or embellishment in another play become in it organic parts of a composite appeal to the deepest feelings of the audience. We are made to feel in a particular way the tragedy of conquest in war for victors and vanquished alike. The glory that Homer celebrates and ꞏthat justifies ruthlessness and submission in the *Hecuba* has vanished. The rhetoric that replaced divine assistance in the *Hecuba* is replaced in the *Trojan Women* by a rhetoric that is an attack on the comfortable assumptions of traditional belief. It gains no end, but makes ends seem not worth gaining. Comedy also is used to humble the proud Menelaus and Helen. Even the mad dance of Cassandra is more than entertainment, for it is a happy dance by an unhappy person and so rends the spirit in twain. It is prefigured in the *Andromache* by the unhappy dance of Hermione when she is bent on suicide, but that is purely enjoyable, since Hermione deserves to suffer. There is not only no glory, but no revenge, in the *Trojan Women*.

Glory and revenge are equally omitted from the *Iphigeneia*. The sufferers are innocent and helpless until an unplanned recognition puts them in the way of helping one another. After the recognition there is a successful intrigue just as in the *Hecuba*, but the intrigue produces satisfaction for the living, not merely for the dead. Iphigeneia dreams as Hecuba does of a loved one, but her loved one is not really dead. Furthermore, the part of the action before the actual recognition of the loved one is devoted, in the later play, to depicting the unhappiness and worthiness of the principal characters, not of an episodic character like Polyxena. Hecuba is shown in her play, to be sure, as unhappy but not as particularly worthy of happiness. The barbarian who must be tricked in Iphigeneia is not wholly unworthy, being an honest savage; and he is not actually unsuccessful against human opponents. It is Athena in the end who defeats him. He is not made ridiculous by frustration. Thus the play in two parts—misery followed by a recognition that leads to action and joy—was brought to perfection.

Aristotle particularly approves of the recognition scene in this play, not only because the recognition was unexpected by both sides, but because it was brought about by circumstances that were in themselves probable if not inevitable. That the recognition converted Orestes from a victim to a protégé of his sister makes it a good example of the recognition that is also a peripety. It seems probable that in this case, as in that of the *Oedipus*, Aristotle may have approved rightly but not for the right reasons, for here, as in the *Oedipus*, the moral and psychological misery of the hero is effectively probed before the recognition comes. Orestes knew that he was a matricide and he seemed to have passed forever from the comfort of family ties. For Oedipus this comfort was suddenly made his chief misery. In both cases moral torment is made vivid in a way that is not usual in Greek as it is in Shakespearean and modern tragedy. The torment of a person without security of family ties is, however, not so serious in modern times, nor indeed so common as it was in ancient Greece. Our plays often show characters in search of a not yet identified husband, wife, or mistress, or in search of personal happiness and integrity. Other modern characters find themselves, it may be, even by parting from the family tie. Hence comes the depreciation of recognitions that are not purely psychological. It is the discovery of love, or the capacity to love, or of courage, or of a sense of values within oneself that is favored in drama at the present day.

The rhetoric that was so prominent in the *Hecuba* is totally absent from the *Iphigeneia*. Rhetoric is normally the enemy of *êthos*, though there is a bastard rhetorical *êthos*, conspicuous in such an author as Lysias, that refers not to the revelation of a sympathetic character, but to the assumption of a sympathetic character that may or may not be genuine. Certainly the character assumed by Medea to deceive the Corinthians in Euripides' play was not genuine. Only when she is sure of their support does she betray her genuine feelings. In the *Iphigeneia* we know the real feelings of the characters from the start, since they speak frankly to their friends or to the audience. Only when the recognition is over does action take the place of psychological interest. As Aristotle tells us, it was the fashion in his time to omit the psychological interest; characters were depicted without *éthos*. The result, as we shall see, was to increase distance, gradually assimilating drama to the dance, by which the audience is entertained without imaginative participation in any moral conflict. In the ethical play proper a large part, often the chief part, of the play is devoted to an assault on the moral sympathy of the audience, so that the culminating action, when it comes, may give them heartfelt satisfaction. In classical tragedy we have seen how the psychological exposition also adds a sense of personal loss to the unhappiness of the outcome. Without *éthos*, characters may be quite clearly indicated in a play and the audience may clearly understand the motivation of their acts, but there will be no lines of force operating to enlist the partisanship of the hearers. In this respect the *Bacchae* is less effective than the *Hippolytus*. In fact, after the high point of *Trojan Women* and *Iphigeneia*, Euripides seems to adopt a mocking reticence that disconnects his art from serious concern with practical life.

He uses gods in *Iphigeneia* as in the *Hippolytus* to bring innocent characters into trouble. Apollo and Artemis are the scapegoats, while Athena is as usual a peacemaker. Apollo's oracle has sent Orestes, accompanied by faithful Pylades, to the Crimea to bring back his sister. Artemis had a temple and a statue there, but Orestes also had a sister Iphigeneia who had been saved from sacrifice at Aulis and transported by Artemis to the land of Thoas, king of the Taurians. There she presided over the sacrifices of shipwrecked Greeks that Artemis, according to the Taurian belief, demanded. Modern writers have other means of motivation for the adventures of their heroes in savage lands; on the other hand, the fate of men exiled by the gods seems harder than that of men who seek gain or excitement. Iphigeneia appears first and relates a dream which she interprets as meaning that her brother Orestes is dead. The living Orestes appears as soon as she is gone and with Pylades faces the task of stealing Artemis' image from her skull-decked temple. They retire to hide as Iphigeneia and the chorus enter with libations for Orestes, who is supposed dead. When Orestes and Pylades are captured and brought before her, she is in a vindictive mood, ready to hate all Greeks. For this her dream provides the psychological motivation, since the supposed death of her brother increases her isolation. Yet her previous pity for victims and the actual sympathy that she betrays in spite of her words show that she is unfit by temperament for her horrid duties. Thus her rescue from physical exile will also be a moral rescue, since she is too good for the company she is forced to keep. Her temporary lapse into savagery of mood is excusable, but it makes the need to save her more intense.

The conversations between Orestes and Pylades are designed to present a picture of mutual and loyal friendship, as each refuses to desert the other in difficulty. Later each in turn offers, when Iphigeneia is willing to spare one to take a message from her to Greece, to be the slain victim rather than the survivor. The scene in which Iphigeneia questions her brother about the state of affairs in Greece, approaching nearer and nearer to the story of their mother and her crime and punishment, is reminiscent of Homer's picture of Helen overlooking the Achaean host at the Scaean gate. There Priam questions Helen about one hero after another until she remembers her husband at Sparta and wonders what has become of her brothers. Orestes in his despair refuses to give his name and is visibly reluctant to tell the story of Clytemnestra's crime and his vengeance. No confession is needed to show his state of mind, for the messenger has told of his madness. Indeed, the story was so familiar to the audience that they could be trusted to supply any background of reminiscence that was needed. By dint of repetition it becomes possible for the poet to produce the effect of depth in brief space. The old stories become greatly compressible by a sort

of shorthand notation that recalls the expanded scenes of other
dramas dealing with the same characters. In the excitement and
tension that ensues as Orestes nears the moment of sacrifice by his
sister, the audience can be trusted, since *they* know that Orestes is
not dead, not to note the inconsistency of her assuming that the
brother to whom she had poured funeral libations was still alive,
as she does, when she asks Pylades to deliver a letter to him. She
has no evidence later than her dream, as far as she knows, but she
could not be sure. The letter, which is easily delivered, discloses her
identity. The scene of joy which follows is melodramatic in the
literal sense, for it is more lyrical than dramatic.

The problem then arises, how to elude the barbarians and save
Orestes from his destined death. Iphigeneia volunteers to die for
him, while he refuses to desert his sister. The proposal to slay Thoas
is rejected by Iphigeneia as too treacherous. She proposes to deceive
the king by a pretense of purifying her two victims at the seaside
in a secret rite that none may behold. Of course, the three make
their escape in their own ship. It would not, however, suit Euripides to let them get away, for he needs an impressive ending that
will bring in Athena to explain the sequel and link myth with
ritual. He ties a new knot by allowing a contrary wind to prevent
egress from the bay so that the fugitives are recaptured. Athena
secures not only their release but that of the chorus of captive
Greek women. This instructive example shows excellently the
technique by which a god from the machine is normally introduced. When there is no god, the action comes slowly or abruptly
to an end with no change of course. On the modern stage it is
customary to let a curtain fall as soon as the action approaches a
foreseen end. The action is cut off almost before it comes to a
natural end. When the god is used, the original action is already
over. In order to provide an excuse for intervention a new situation must be created, as in the ending of the *Odyssey*—some new
force or new direction of force that threatens either to restore the
old tension or to create a new one. As Horace says, there must be
a tangle worthy of a champion; evidently it would be a poor drama-

tist who should use a god to untangle his main thread of argument. The good poet provides a new tangle for the purpose.[8]

We have seen how, in the *Oedipus at Colonus,* Sophocles, using themes and techniques of Euripides with modifications of his own, vastly surpassed him. Aristophanes says in the *Frogs* that Sophocles is content to wait on the sidelines until Euripides has competed with Aeschylus. If Euripides triumphs, Sophocles will enter the lists with him. Our knowledge of the date of the *Philoctetes* makes it certain that Sophocles was the last of the three dramatists to attack this myth. We know the plays of that name by Aeschylus and Euripides chiefly from the essays by Dio Chrysostom in which they are compared with Sophocles' extant *Philoctetes.* In the case of the *Electra* and *Choephoroe* we can make the comparison for ourselves since all three plays are extant. The *Electra* of Euripides was produced before the Athenians suffered disaster in Sicily; his *Orestes* came at least four years later, in 409 B.C., when the ensuing revolution of the Four Hundred had been countered and a moderate democracy established. Since the *Orestes* of Euripides is a sequel to the *Electra* of Sophocles rather than to his own or to the *Choephoroe* of Aeschylus, it is extremely probable that Sophocles produced his play in the interval. Sophocles' play stands out in marked contrast to the other two in that it is a powerful plea against tyranny and celebrates the triumph of an exile who returns to overthrow a lawless usurpation. Orestes slays his mother incidentally as a necessary cruelty. The need to rescue the oppressed by craft and by force is emphasized. Once action starts, it moves more rapidly and ceases more abruptly than the action of any other Greek play. It is easy to conceive the play as an allegory of Athenian democracy and the need of strong measures to restore it. It omits any hint of Furies or of repentance in connection with the action of Orestes. This is precisely the attitude of Homer, who glorifies the action of Orestes, omitting all mention of his vengeance on Clytemnestra. Sophocles is here again, in the words of Aristotle, the most Homeric of the dramatists.

He is also, to quote his own words, producing by style and con-

struction an effect that is most ethical and best. He binds his audience emotionally to the revolutionary cause with repeated and
intense appeals, and makes them participate in the struggle. It
seems almost certain that Sophocles wrote for the restorers of democracy in 410. An unsympathetic audience would get little good
of the play. He shows us the ordeal of virtuous courage leading to
a noble and deserved triumph with no note of misgiving. The
matter of the drama is an affair of state, though all the resources of
art are used to establish the sympathetic *éthos* that draws the
audience to Orestes and Electra. Even Electra's weaker sister Chrysothemis, whom Sophocles presents to us for the first time on the
stage, has a charm and grace equaled only by Homer's Nausicaä.
She too is in imperative need of rescue.[9]

Sophocles' debt to Aeschylus is clear enough. If we wish now to
see what he owes to Euripides, we must take note rather of the
happy *Iphigeneia in Tauris* than of the sad *Electra*. Euripides alone
shows Orestes, in his *Electra,* like Homer's Odysseus, refusing to
reveal himself. Sophocles agrees with Aeschylus not only in making Orestes seek recognition by his sister, but in adopting the palace
as scene of action. Sophocles agrees with the *Iphigeneia* when he
uses the supposed death of the absent brother to increase sympathy
for the sister and provides corroborative detail to illustrate her
worthiness and misery. He even makes Electra see the inevitable
degradation of her own character that must follow from her ignoble environment. Such yearning for a better life consigns her
to moral torment until she is saved. It is true that Sophocles is more
likely than Euripides to prolong the agony of characters who suffer
physically, but in dealing with Electra as with Ajax and Oedipus
he shows that he is master of the art of depicting moral torment
also. He differs in that his characters will always take arms against
a sea of troubles. They are strong even in despair, while Euripides'
characters seem weak even in their most impetuous resolves.

There are even two points in which Sophocles seems to correct
Euripides. The Electra of Euripides had rebuked the old servant
for supposing that Orestes would return from exile by stealth, but

she was wrong, for that was just what Orestes, like Odysseus, did. Sophocles lets Apollo in his oracular response sanction the stealthy return but say nothing of matricide. Apollo is thus relieved of responsibility except by implication for the execution of Clytemnestra by her son, and Orestes by obeying gains credit for piety toward the god and is saved from aspersions on his courage. Sophocles makes Apollo the scapegoat only in order to justify his one story of successful intrigue. Orestes can take matricide in his stride. Sophocles has begged the moral question that looms so large in Aeschylus and even Euripides, but we get as a result a sense of clean-cut issues that is a relief. There are moments when the need to act becomes so strong that swords and pistols are invested with chivalric glamour and to reason why is to poison the atmosphere of loyalty. Sophocles' Orestes is not, like Hamlet, sicklied over with the pale cast of thought. Perhaps Sophocles should not have written that way; but this is nevertheless the theme that inspired his most brilliant technical surprises. Indeed, the speed and tension of his action seem intended to burke all doubts.[10]

The other correction of Euripides is less obvious. Prolonged scenes of joy at moments of danger when caution is most necessary may be taken for granted, as they are in *Iphigeneia in Tauris* and elsewhere. It is Sophocles who provides the first criticism and a remedy for this dramatic improbability. When Orestes and Electra have finished their rejoicing, the doors of the palace are opened to disclose a friend, who rebukes them for their careless happiness and reveals that he himself has stood watch ready to warn them if immediate danger threatened. It is pleasant to see the tables turned on Euripides, who prided himself on making everything plain and explicit in his plays. Sophocles has scored a point in realistic technique.

Euripides is fond of letting slaves and women suggest plans of action and guide plots. Sophocles uses Electra as a motive force to temper the edge of Orestes' resolution. In fact, she takes over from the chorus and the old nurse in Aeschylus their positive contributions to the plot, that is, the frustration of Clytemnestra's libations that were sent to appease the dead Agamemnon after an ominous dream, and the deception of Aegisthus. She also takes over the nurse's lament for her nursling Orestes. This leaves her passive role in Aeschylus to be played by her sister, introduced for the purpose, Chrysothemis. Thus Electra and Chrysothemis provide motivation, while Orestes is the embodiment of action. Chrysothemis' willingness to risk punishment by casting the libations away shows her good-will, while her sudden and excessive certainty and joy, when she guesses from an offering of hair that Orestes has returned, makes it even plainer that she shares the hopes of Electra, though she shrinks from unmaidenly violence. The Electra of Sophocles, being assured of the death of Orestes, has better reason than the Electra of Euripides for refusing to accept the evidence pointing to his return. The old slave acts as the agent of Orestes, yet supplies information and advice. He has something of the role of the pedagogue in New Comedy, who must exercise a sobering influence on his too inconsiderately affectionate charges. He once keeps Orestes from greeting Electra and later scolds both for careless rapture. Pylades has no part to play. It is Electra alone who nerves Orestes to his task when he slays his mother.

The part of Orestes gains greatly in strength by the fact that he appears in the prologue of the play with a plan already adopted, as he explains to the old servant. He has no need to waver or deliberate. Action is to some extent guided by circumstance, but the final goal is fixed. His only weakness is the inability to control his emotion when he sees for himself the sad state of his sister Electra. He makes himself known and endangers his plot as Odysseus would never have done. There is a noble simplicity in his sincere emotion that ranges him with Chrysothemis. His emotion, however, also motivates a new and sterner dedication to the work of deliverance. His purpose does not shift, but he achieves a certainty in the execution of it that would not have been his without a strong appeal to his feelings. The sudden hardening of a young man's mood as he sees the facts of life in crude ugliness is well portrayed.

With the disappearance of Orestes and the old servant from the scene after the prologue, Electra appears, telling her tale of woe. The chorus of women sympathize with her position, but not with her reaction to it. She creates misery for herself by unseasonable rebellion against the murderers of her father with whom she must live. Chrysothemis also sympathizes and admonishes at the same time, warning her of worse punishment that Aegisthus will inflict when he returns. Electra demonstrates not so much constancy as a passionate devotion to her father's memory, and is almost frenzied in her martyr's lust for suffering. Clytemnestra appears in person to illustrate the kind of woman who rules the home of Electra. Electra is like her mother in passionate rebellion and in her heart that plots and executes boldly like a man. She blames her hatefulness on the hateful life that she must lead. She would be better if she could. When the old servant enters with the false news that Orestes is dead, the genuine emotion of Electra in the presence of the imagined disaster, as well as the genuine triumph of Clytemnestra's mood, play their part in the plot of the author against his audience. In fact, misunderstanding on the part of characters when the audience see clearly has always been an effective device in the theater. Frustration is felt all the more keenly when it is based on a mistake that is merely one of life's little ironies. Othello is a doubly tragic figure because his jealousy was unwarranted. He was frustrated not only in his love, but in his vengeance.

It is a nice touch that the false messenger should enter with his news just after Clytemnestra has finished praying to Apollo. The apparent answer to prayer is as delusive as in the *Oedipus,* when a messenger arrived with false comfort just as Jocasta concluded her prayer. Jocasta, however, was a sympathetic character, and it is something of a recantation when Sophocles uses the same device in a way to make Apollo seem friendly, not hostile, to the good, and deaf to base pleas. When now a quarrel arises between the two sisters, Sophocles is repeating a theme from his *Antigone,* contrasting two sisters and isolating a strong, passionate, and masculine sister from a weak. In certain lands, when there is no son left

to carry out the duty of vengeance the eldest daughter will dress
as a man and perform the duty of a son. In the first moment of
despair Electra had resolved to die on the doorstep of her enemies,
an Oriental manner of inflicting ghostly curses on the victim. She
soon recovers her Greek practicality, however, and proposes to
Chrysothemis that they should assassinate Aegisthus themselves.
There is little prospect of success, and the punishment of unsuccessful assassins is a mighty deterrent to one not frenzied in devotion to a lost cause. Electra is clearly unmanageable. The chorus
disapprove as they did when she quarreled with her mother. Such
characters in the early plays of Sophocles were on their way to
death, but Sophocles in his later years preferred the sweet to the
bitter in his endings. He begins with apparent tragedy and ends
by gratifying his audience to the full.

Electra in the *Choephoroe* had been afraid of Orestes when he
first appeared. Thus irony prepared the way for a reversal of her
fear to joy as she recognized her brother. Sophocles greatly elabo-
rates the irony and the reversal by his inclusion of Electra in the
deception that was caused by the false news of Orestes' death. The
contrast between the living Orestes, known to the audience, and
the urn with ashes, upon which Electra bestows her tears, is a
triumph of artifice that could only be effective once in such detail.
The grief of Electra motivates the betrayal of his identity by Orestes and at the same time increases the tense sympathy of the audience. As soon as she has given vent to her joy, the dam bursts and
the play sweeps to its conclusion with no pause for reflection or
feeling. Clytemnestra is not seen on the stage, only Electra, who has
good reasons for vengeance. Since we view the situation through
her eyes, any possible problem for Orestes is banished from our
thought. He is more a savior than an avenger. Clytemnestra had
not merely been unrepentant; she had celebrated her murder with
monthly dance and song, a perpetuation of crime that was a contin-
ual challenge to the avenging gods.

Electra is also allowed a sweet triumph over Aegisthus when she
lures him to his doom with words of double meaning that give him

ironical pleasure and confidence. By making his death the climax of the play and ending the action as suddenly as if a curtain had descended in the modern fashion, Sophocles thrusts the matricide as far into the background as it will go, just as Homer refuses to let us reflect on the moral responsibility of Hector in the *Iliad*. Sophocles also employs a brilliant technique to increase tension. Aegisthus sees a body covered by a sheet and assumes that the corpse of Orestes is before him. He bids someone call Clytemnestra. When Margaret Anglin played Electra, she would at this point put her mouth close to the dead woman's ear beneath the sheet and cry aloud, "Clytemnestra-a-a!" This touch is not in the text of Sophocles, but is fully in the spirit of the play. Clytemnestra does not answer; Aegisthus, raising the sheet, recognizes his dead wife, the living Orestes, and his own approaching doom. The play ends with this recognition.

No Greek play is more carefully constructed or more vividly alive than this. Sophocles had the art to make every least emotion apparent in the rhythm of speech and to interweave character and action so that no action seems accidental. There are those in the play who do not foresee or understand events, but the audience have the truth. No divine assistance is required, but piety is rewarded. The struggles of Electra do not, to be sure, affect the result, but they make it seem worth attaining. When she resolves first to die, then to slay Aegisthus, she is showing her worthiness. Just so in Euripides' play Orestes, Pylades, and Iphigeneia had been willing to die to save one another. The sacrifice was not required, for they all escaped, but the readiness had its moral significance. If Electra had made no resolves and come to no decisions, her weakness might provoke pity, but hardly admiration. There is a remarkable counterpoint in the checkerwork of scenes as presented.

Chrysothemis' willingness to help as long as there is hope is matched by her refusal when hope is absent. The difference in temperament between Chrysothemis and Electra, who agree in purpose, is contrasted with the likeness between Clytemnestra and

Electra, who are bitter enemies. The alternation of joy and grief, of recognition by a friend and recognition by a foe, produces a rich harmony. The same Electra who controls herself when terrors beset her is completely uncontrolled in her moment of joy. Orestes had calculated soundly before he met his sister, but he is young enough not to be able to suppress his feeling at sight of her. He could not calculate the effect of an emotion that he had never felt. Thus the formal artifice of the play is not a substitute for feeling; the harmony of power in a moral pattern that includes spontaneous feeling, consideration of ends and means, and a generous sense of the importance of loyalty and reverence is greatly enhanced in its effect by the nice adjustment of its elements. Again Sophocles has surpassed Euripides in his realistic depiction of strong characters in a familiar plot. At the same time it is clear that Euripides has a genius for seeing life from an unusual angle. His insights are destructive of bad morals rather than constructive of good. It is perhaps not too farfetched to compare him to Shiva the destroyer in Hindu fable. Aeschylus will then be seen as Brahma the creator, while Sophocles' favorite role is that of Vishnu the preserver.

VII
Vacillation, Burlesque,
and Variety

THE REMAINING seven plays that are to be con-
sidered are at first sight rather a collection of odds and ends.
They have in common only the negative trait that they have no
claim to be classed with either group of the plays already considered. Their interest is in the action itself and is secured either
by the natural depiction of characters who move from one state
of mind to another, or by the strangeness and even absurdity of
the mixture of elements in the action, or by the mere fascination
of the shifting spectacle as one moment in the action succeeds
another with no attempt to enlist the spectator permanently for one
side or the other and with no concern for the philosophical interpretation of life. Any philosophy that there is will be superficial or
vestigial, and miracles will be as welcome as any other device to
secure a change in the situation. Gods as well as miracles will be
mere theatrical devices, and any new developments will be episodic rather than fundamental. Such plays neither present nor solve
problems, nor do they present conflicts as involving important
principles. They illustrate the possibilities of human behavior and
experience in an entertaining way.

The *Philoctetes* (409 B.C.) of Sophocles of course goes deeper.
Yet I have included it in this group because the victory of the main
character is an entirely new kind of victory. He wins for his side
the soul of the youthful Neoptolemus, who escapes from the snares
set by the dishonest Odysseus. It is extremely common in modern
drama to make the chief problem a personal one: who wins whom
as wife, husband, or lover? This pattern is found in Greek only

186

in comedy, where a hetaera may have rival lovers, in the *Helen* of
Euripides, and in this one serious tragedy. It can hardly be called a
love story, since it is only the soul of Neoptolemus that is the prize,
not his body, yet the main interest in the play is in Neoptolemus'
discovery that he is more moved by the ideals of Philoctetes than
by any consideration of glory or gain. His romantic attachment to
ideals of honorable conduct is so mixed with a romantic attachment to the old warrior himself that he becomes as self-sacrificing
and affectionate in his friendship as are the daughters of Oedipus
in their filial relation or Orestes in his devotion to Electra. Indeed,
Neoptolemus is won to Philoctetes when he sees his suffering and
his courage much as Orestes was overwhelmed with concern at
sight of his sister's woe. The difference is that Orestes' experience
is merely deepened. He does not shift from one loyalty to another
or from one level of insight to another higher one that requires him
to renounce the past.

For want of a better word let us call Neoptolemus a vacillating
character. We have in the play the familiar contrast between good
and bad, between the political scoundrel Odysseus and the noble
friend and fighter Philoctetes. There is none of the confused
morality of Odysseus' role in the *Ajax*. Neoptolemus is naturally
an honest fighter like his father Achilles, but he is temporarily
lured into the camp of Odysseus. When Philoctetes wins him back
by inspiring him with a new and final devotion to his original ideal,
he is set a final examination, which he passes with flying colors. He
must choose between the glory of capturing Troy and loyalty to
Philoctetes and to his ideals. The taking of Troy is quite unimportant, so Neoptolemus evidently decides, in comparison with the
commanding of his soul, enlisted under the banner of honest
friendship. Achilles had relinquished the honor of winning Troy
in order to honor his dead friend; Neoptolemus will forgo the
same glory with the same loyalty to the old crippled, crabbed Philoctetes. Yet though the play has a psychological pivot, it has not the
psychological interest of the *Iliad* or of *Oedipus Tyrannus,* where
the hero's new insight into himself is portrayed in lively detail. We

see Neoptolemus at two separate stages but not at the moment of change. The result of his decision is depicted, not the decision itself. This is not because Sophocles could not depict such a decision. We have monologues of Ajax and Electra to prove the contrary, and Hector's monologue in Book 22 of the *Iliad* might have served as a model.[1]

Philoctetes is given the leading role in his play, just as Electra was in hers. The young man is secondary. Sophocles is more interested in obstinate endurance in a good cause than he is in conversion. He still holds to the tradition that physical suffering is the proper ground of tragedy. That is the *pathos* that Aristotle also includes in his definition of tragedy as an alternative to death. Where there is no death, there must be wounds or intense physical agony. Euripides is much more interested in psychological torment and often spares us the tedious scenes of lamentation that recur in Sophocles in play after play. The vacillation of Orestes in Euripides' *Electra* from action to repentance has been noted. That is a very different kind of conversion from Sophocles' picture of an emotional experience that confirms or restores virtue. That Euripides could depict a shift from selfishness to loyalty is proved twice, by Admetus in his *Alcestis* (438 B.C.) and by the heroine of *Iphigeneia at Aulis* (401 B.C.). These two are the earliest and the latest extant plays of Euripides, and the *Alcestis* was not produced as a tragedy at all, but as a substitute for the comic and vulgar satyr drama that was expected. Thus the *Alcestis* illustrates elements that only later invaded tragedy proper, and the treatment of which culminated in New Comedy.[2]

Like any heroine of New Comedy, Alcestis is loyal to her husband and in the end wins his loyalty in return. She dies for him and is restored to life by Heracles. A nice contrast is also provided by the vulgar comic reveler Heracles when he suddenly sobers up and intervenes to save Alcestis from the grave and so rewards the hospitality of Admetus. Both Admetus and Heracles are mixed characters, and both rather suddenly become better men. Admetus

[1] For notes to chapter vii see pages 303–308.

has the saving grace of hospitality, and for this he is rewarded by the restoration of his wife. He has learned his lesson and passes the test applied by Heracles. He will in the future be as devoted to his wife as she was to him. The tone of the play is rather that of a charming fairy story, where anything can happen and virtues are exaggerated, than that of realism as far as morals are concerned. Yet the characters seem to be on the level of everyday life rather than above it like the heroes of tragedy. Comedy and sentiment are charmingly mixed with no serious intrusion of philosophy or rhetoric. The happy ending also deprives death of its sting and permits us to class the play as a comedy following the pattern of trouble and deliverance. That the deliverance is superhuman need not trouble us. It is gratifying to imagine a world in which a good woman may be restored to life and thus profit by the repentance of her husband. We are not asked either to believe or disbelieve, but merely to suspend our disbelief for the moment.

There is considerable variety in the succession of scenes. In the prologue, Death comes for Alcestis and is warned by Apollo that for all his heartlessness he will be forced to relinquish his prey. The chorus come to get news of Alcestis and are informed by the serv-ant of her affecting farewell to the scene of her married life. When Admetus had been told that he might live on if he could find a substitute to die for him, all whom he asked thus to serve him had refused except his wife. The next scene shows Alcestis on her deathbed exacting a promise from her husband that in return for her loyalty he will never marry again. Her children are introduced and the boy is given a plaintive farewell song to sing for the heightening of pathos.

The funeral is now Admetus' chief concern, but he is interrupted by two arrivals. Heracles comes expecting hospitality, but refuses to stay when he discovers that a funeral is in hand. In the end he consents to stay when Admetus assures him that the dead woman was no kin. The chorus are shocked at this excess of hospitality, but Admetus justifies his deception. The next arrival is not welcomed. It is Pheres, the father of Admetus. The selfishness of Admetus is well brought out when he reviles his father for not having been the one to consent to die, and is answered in kind. There is a comic reversal of ordinary life when the son disowns the father for his disloyalty. Such impiety could not be allowed in a serious play, but here the quarrel between father and son sets off the nobility of Alcestis.

There is more comedy after the funeral train has departed for the tomb. A servant appears and complains bitterly of the conduct of Heracles, who drinks and sings in a house of mourning. Heracles follows, provided no doubt with a new and comic mask, and expounds the doctrine of pleasure as the goal of life as if it were a profound philosophy. The slave is moved to the point of disclosing the truth that Alcestis is dead. Heracles at once recovers his sober philosophy of benevolence and honor and goes to wrestle with Death at Alcestis' tomb. Next, Admetus returns from burying his wife and proceeds still somewhat comically to go to exaggerated lengths to show his repentance. One thinks of Barrie's repentant husband in *Peter Pan,* who sentences himself to the doghouse. When Heracles now returns from the grave with Alcestis veiled and silent and presents her to Admetus as a prize won in wrestling, Admetus stanchly refuses to have any woman in the house now that Alcestis is gone. Heracles, however, insists that Admetus should take the woman's hand and unveil her face. She is, of course, Alcestis. Admetus has been rewarded for his hospitality and has learned to appreciate the wife who died for him. This play is almost our only example of whimsy in Greek, and it is a very successful example.

There is nothing whimsical about the *Philoctetes.* It is very like the *Electra* in its depiction of a tormented and bitterly obstinate character who is saved by the loyalty of a young man. But it makes a great difference in the later play that the young man had come with no plan of action and that his resolve to support Philoctetes involves the abandonment of his own hope of glory. He is extraordinarily like his father Achilles, who in the *Iliad* (Bk. 9, vv. 312 ff.) looks Odysseus in the eye and declares that he hates like the gates of hell the man who has one thing on his lips and another in his heart. Neoptolemus cannot, like Orestes, take a strong line of his own, since he is involved in the affairs of older and more experienced men. He finds himself in a dilemma. He is commissioned to go with Odysseus to Lemnos and bring back Philoctetes with his bow, which has been declared by an oracle to be essential if Troy is to be captured. Philoctetes suffered from an offensive wound and was marooned in Lemnos by the Achaeans on the way to Troy. His one resource is the bow of Heracles, armed with which he can resist any force. Hence Odysseus must use Neoptolemus, a recent recruit, to deceive Philoctetes and win the bow. The youth prefers not to use fraud, but is finally persuaded that duty requires him to make the sacrifice. Be a liar this once, says Odysseus, and ever after maintain a name for honesty. Neoptolemus, accordingly, pretends to be on his way home after quarreling with the Achaeans, especially Odysseus. He wins the gratitude and confidence of Philoctetes by promising to take him also to his homeland.

When Philoctetes feels a fit of illness coming on, he entrusts the bow to Neoptolemus. The son of Achilles, however, is squeamish about his victory. He is not so much revolted by the stench of Philoctetes' wound as by the corruption of his own sense of honor.

> Nothing remains untainted when a man
> Forsakes his bent and acts against the grain. (Vv. 902 ff.)

He confesses the truth and is denounced by Philoctetes somewhat tenderly, for the old hero had loved the young man, and he sorrows over his defection. Odysseus now takes command and deals with the violent opposition of the hero by ordering his seizure. He makes the concession, however, that Philoctetes may remain behind without his bow. The prospect of certain death does not soften Philoctetes, and Neoptolemus is sicker than ever of his own part in the game. We get almost a tableau in the Aeschylean manner as Neoptolemus ignores the protests of Odysseus and hands the bow to Philoctetes. Odysseus leaves hastily, and Neoptolemus with youthful optimism tries to convert the old man by promising a cure for his wound as well as glory if he will come willingly to Troy. The old man's refusal forces upon Neoptolemus a decision whether he will himself return to the siege of Troy or desert the Achaeans and take Philoctetes home. Here he is unlike his father, for Achilles had deserted only when he personally was insulted. Yet Achilles had ignored glory for loyal friendship, and so does his son. He supports Philoctetes tenderly as the two move to leave the island. We are reminded of the end of the *Heracles Furens,* but Sophocles must somehow restore the course of history, which records the fall of Troy. He does so by the device of a god from the machine, Heracles, who orders the two to go to Troy. The god solves a minor new problem, for the interest of the preceding part of the play had no connection with the fate of Troy. What was important in that part was the final decision of Neoptolemus as he met the last supreme temptation. Though the knot requires a god, it is a very subordinate knot. If we reflect on the difficulties involved in supposing that the Philoctetes of this play could ever collaborate with Odysseus, we see that Heracles has nothing to do with the real play. He is a theatrical convenience to make the plot fit recorded history.

If Sophocles had not had the god in reserve, he could not have kept his moral pattern clear. Many young men and women in Greek tragedy sacrifice their lives for glory or for patriotism. It is something new when honesty prevails over the claims of war. The *Philoctetes,* produced a year after the *Electra,* seems rather like a recantation—an atonement for the crafty hero Orestes and his brutal success. At any rate, it exhibits the other side of the medal. Repentance is also presented in a new way. It is not a futile emotion or a recognition of intellectual error. It is a discovery of the importance of being true to oneself if life is not to be loathsome. Achilles put friendship above glory too late, and the *Iliad* became a tragedy; but there is no tragedy in the *Philoctetes,* only a success story that is purely moral. Other characters in Sophocles who weaken are compelled by circumstance, for instance, Ajax when he laments and deceives, and Creon when he reverses his orders about the burial of Polyneices. Neoptolemus alone repents in the moment of success. The poet shows us doubt and decision, though we see no more of the youth than was visible to Odysseus and Philoctetes. In fact, the whole play is a struggle between two forces. They are represented by two persons, but since the decisive moment is the decision of the young man, it ceases to be a personal conflict and becomes a moral issue. We have an ethical plot in a new sense. There are no women in the play, but it is romantic in a Spartan way, for the love between Neoptolemus and Philoctetes is not tepid or calculating. We might call it a case of all for love or the world well lost, but love in this case includes devotion to right and honor. It is not at odds with them as in Homer when heroes are tempted by good women.

It is a surprise at first to find no political motive in the play, but Athena could hardly come in as the friend of Odysseus without confusing the issue as in the *Ajax*. Sophocles seems to be of the same mind now as Aeschylus and Euripides, who commonly regard the Trojan war as a mistake, a case of imperialism, not patriotism. The intervention of Heracles, to be sure, seems to give divine sanction to the enterprise, but the gods in Greek thought are more likely to represent things as they are than things as they ought to be. At least the god represents poetic justice in one sense, for Neoptolemus, having sacrificed glory to duty, deserved his opportunity to get glory too. He chose virtue, and success with honor is added. Such rewards for virtue are not uncommon in ethical plays and have always been popular in the theater. Heracles addresses himself only to Philoctetes and seems to ignore morality, but that may be attributed to the subtlety of Sophocles.

There is nothing in common between *Philoctetes* and the *Helen* (412 B.C.) of Euripides, unless we think of the *Helen* as a competition for the person of the heroine, but the *Helen* of Euripides belongs in much the same category as the *Alcestis*. It has the same exaggerated effects of virtue and punctilio and tends to be whimsical when it is not on the level of burlesque or mere melodrama. It also depicts a good wife whose separation from her husband requires a miracle to end it. The intervention of the miracle in the middle of the play is a warning not to take it too seriously, while the presence of Menelaus and Helen puts us on our guard to expect the same kind of satire that we get when they appear in the *Trojan Women* and *Orestes*. To be sure, the plot resembles that of *Iphigeneia in Tauris*, for we have the same sequence of unhappiness, recognition, and intrigue leading up to a final escape from a foreign land to Greece. Yet the fact that we are in more or less civilized Egypt and that the king is in love with Helen, and that she uses her charms to befool him, makes a great difference. There is a curious mixture of romance and comedy in the same characters. That Euripides could write romantically of love we know from our scanty information about the *Andromeda*. In that play, as a fragment teaches us, the heroine anticipated the expression of young love that is found in Shakespeare's *Tempest:*

> I am your wife, if you will marry me;
> If not, I'll die your maid: to be your fellow
> You may deny me; but I'll be your servant,
> Whether you will or no.[3]

The situation of Helen is a romantic one. She has been seventeen years in Egypt under the protection of the king, Proteus. Aphrodite had promised her to Paris, but Hera to foil Aphrodite had sent Helen in charge of Hermes to Egypt and had created a false Helen for whom Achaeans and Trojans fought. After Helen has explained this in a prologue, Teucer arrives seeking guidance on his course to Salamis in Cyprus. He cannot suppose that she is Helen, but gives her news that Troy is taken and that Menelaus is reported dead, before he goes hastily on his way. Proteus' successor as king of Egypt, Theoclymenus, was eager to marry Helen. She sought refuge at the tomb of Proteus, which was conveniently placed at the gate of the palace. The chorus suggest that Helen should consult Theonoë, sister of Theoclymenus, who knows everything, to find out the truth about Menelaus. When Helen agrees, the chorus go with her rather unnecessarily. While they are away, Menelaus

enters in rags and tatters, for he has lost all his belongings in a
shipwreck. He has the false Helen with him in Egypt guarded by
his men in a cave, but knows nothing of the real and virtuous one.
His pitiful appeal to the old woman who keeps the door is rather
like a scene from Aristophanes. He, like Teucer, is in danger of
his life, for the king has ordered the death of any Greek who enters
the country. The reason for this is the king's fear that Helen may
find means to escape him.

When Helen returns there is a double misunderstanding. Helen
mistakes her husband for a ravisher at first, but when she does
recognize and embrace him, she is sternly repulsed as a fraud, since
Menelaus assumes that Helen's double is the real Helen. A messenger from the cave arrives, however, and informs him that the
wraith has disappeared after disclosing the truth. It is the turn of
the messenger to mistake Helen for her double, and Menelaus is
at last convinced that she is his wife. A plan is now laid for persuading Theoclymenus that Greek custom requires a ship to make
offerings at sea for the dead Menelaus. Theonoë is persuaded, out
of respect for her dead father and for justice, to further their plan
by giving her brother false information. Helen cuts her hair and
disfigures herself as a mark of mourning, but persuades Theoclymenus that she is now willing to marry him and will do so as
soon as the rites are performed. Menelaus is introduced as the
messenger who has brought the news and is put in charge of the
funeral expedition. Naturally the expedition does not return, and
the king discovers from a messenger that he has been fooled. He
is dashing off to murder his sister for her complicity in the plot,
though the chorus attempt to hold him back, when Helen's
brothers, Castor and Pollux, appear as gods to save Theonoë's life
and end the play.

Since Euripides almost duplicates the story of Iphigeneia, he
takes care to produce a totally different effect. There are, to be sure,
many songs in the play that must have been plaintive or joyful,
and the sentimental situations are treated effectively enough, but
there is also enough absurdity to produce an Aristophanic effect

in places. It is not improbable that contemporary comedies were sometimes not very different in tone from this play that passes as a tragedy. Since it contains a good mixture of sentiment and intrigue, it can hardly be called a burlesque. It is much the same cheerful mixture that we find in many modern musical comedies, for instance those of Gilbert and Sullivan, where absurdity and sentiment are pleasantly mixed. To appreciate all the absurdities we should have to see the play properly staged, but there are several that are obvious even in the reading. I will confine myself to a very few examples.

Menelaus is about as absurd as a man without clothes who covers himself with a barrel, and there are many references to his costume. When Helen and the chorus are absent, he weeps and grovels before the doorkeeper without shame. Later, when he has to appeal to Theonoë in the presence of Helen and the chorus, he refuses to weep or to kneel because such conduct does not become the man whose forces captured Troy. The contrast would certainly provoke laughter. Helen at one point assures Aphrodite that if she were moderate she would be the most agreeable of the gods. This is just what the drunken Heracles had remarked in the *Alcestis,* but the virtuous Helen seems to be stepping out of her role, especially when she adds, with, I suppose, a baby-faced stare, "and I don't deny it." There are many remarks scattered here and there that have the obvious purpose of provoking guffaws. The presence of a tomb at the front door of a palace in Aeschylus' *Choephoroe* occasions no remark, because the tomb is supposed in imagination to be at a distance. When Theoclymenus explains, however, that he has had his father buried at the front door so that he can say hello to him every morning when he goes out, Euripides is making fun of a stage convention. Of the principal characters only Theonoë is allowed to be serious at all times. The other characters are desperately determined to gain their ends and are rather emotional. Menelaus and Helen are strikingly romantic when they plan to die together if they cannot escape. Even Teucer gives way to anger at first sight of Helen. Such sudden emotional shifts were grist for the actors.[4]

It has been pointed out that the plot by which Menelaus escapes with Helen is very like one that is employed in the *Braggart Soldier* of Plautus. While the comedy that results from the confusion between Helen and her double is not much exploited, we are at least moving in the direction of the *Menaechmi*. Thus Euripides provides material not only for the romantic element in New Comedy, but also for the intrigues and burlesques of which we see little in Menander and much in Plautus and Terence. Menander is Sophoclean in his serious concern with character, rather than Euripidean. It would be strange if Euripides did not include some message for contemporary Athens in his musical comedy, as Aristophanes preached a sermon in the parabasis, when the whole play was not a lesson; the *Lysistrata,* for example, was. Euripides in one lyric denounces the folly of war, which will never end if it is to be the arbiter of valor. The messenger also denounces the soothsayers who could not see that the Trojan war was fought for an unreal object. Since the *Helen* was composed when the news of the Sicilian disaster was fresh, both these passages are appropriate comment on political realities. The war was foolish and soothsayers had not helped.[5]

If the *Helen* is like a musical comedy, the *Orestes* (408 B.C.) is rather like an opera of the more absurd sort. It has variety, a strong comic element, some realistic depiction of unpleasant characters, and a happy ending that is as incongruous as the friendship of Orestes and Aegisthus with which, Aristotle tells us, some comedies ended. The punctilio and fury with which honor is pursued provide a resemblance to tragedy of the Restoration period in England, but do not reach the absurdity of a historical play by the Japanese dramatist, Chikamatsu, in which a Chinese general regrets that he cannot take his wife's advice and win the war, because it is dishonorable for a man to be influenced by a woman. The lady thereupon commits suicide, and her husband adopts her plan without further scruple. Aristotle notes that the character of Menelaus in the *Orestes* is too low for tragedy. In fact, all the characters seem to be on the low level of comedy, since they are neither on the level of ordinary life nor on the higher level of tragedy. At any rate, since no one will be moved to tears by the *Orestes,* it seems reasonable to assume that it was meant in places, like the *Helen,* to be a burlesque of tragedy. It is not, of course, as deliberately comic as the burlesques of tragedy that were popular later on the comic stage, but it probably is not very unlike them in tone.[6]

In the *Helen,* Menelaus and Helen are the romantic characters whose miseries and intrigue, illumined by a passionate resolve to stand and die together if escape is impossible, maintain the interest of the story when it is at all serious. The *Orestes* shows us the miseries, intrigues, and desperate loyalty and fanaticism of Electra, Orestes, and Pylades—brother, sister, and friend—after the murder of Clytemnestra. In this play the duty of punishing the criminals falls to the father of Clytemnestra, Tyndareus, and he does not pursue them privately, but prosecutes them before the Argive assembly. He is realistic, pitiless, and unscrupulous. Menelaus and Helen are also realistic and selfish. Helen's daughter Hermione is merely a pawn. Thus we have three realistic old people of ungenerous disposition contrasted with three young people who have romantic ideas of honor and no more scruples about methods than their elders. They differ from their elders in showing no capacity for self-preservation. The assembly of the Argives is brought in as the final arbiter of their fate, in much the same way as the army decides the fate of the young victims in *Hecuba* and *Iphigeneia in Aulis.* Thus the burden of decision is removed to some extent from the characters and put vaguely upon an unpredictable assembly which must be swayed by rhetoric or controlled by intrigue. If Euripides has any political message in this play, it is in his picture of the working of democracy. It is true that the criminals are not sympathetically, but sentimentally, portrayed. Any tears will be purely aesthetic, not moral, and the intellect of the audience may be pleasantly awakened from time to time by some comic touch to reassure it that all is make-believe. The goal is clearly entertainment without effort. If the Athenians were reminded of their own confusion by the confusion in the play, they were perhaps comforted by finding that the imaginary world of Euripides was worse than their own.

At the beginning Orestes is brainsick and Electra is watching at his bedside. Helen has already arrived and sends Hermione with an offering for the dead Clytemnestra. Electra tries to silence the sympathetic chorus, who are as noisy as the police in *Pirates of Penzance*. When Menelaus comes, Orestes appeals for help, but Tyndareus arrives with his threats of prosecution and forbids Menelaus to give aid. After the departure of Tyndareus, Menelaus has to listen to a personal plea from Orestes, but he is firm in his refusal to intervene with force to save his nephew from the democratic administration of law. Pylades now appears and is willing to go to any length for his friend. Orestes and he decide to make a defense before the assembly.

In the next scene Electra hears from a messenger that the assembly has taken the part of Clytemnestra and Tyndareus. Electra and Orestes are condemned to die—with the privilege of suicide in lieu of public execution. When Orestes arrives, brother and sister say a sad farewell to life, and are about to retire for the death scene when Pylades recalls them. He will not survive his friend, but suggests that they should at least slay Helen before they die. Everyone brightens up at this proposal to strike one more blow. Electra improves on the plan by the device of holding Hermione as hostage to deter Menelaus from revenge. Orestes applauds her and congratulates Pylades on the wise resourcefulness of his future wife. This was doubtless very funny. Electra has her familiar place at the door watching while Helen is attacked within. She also lures Hermione within as she had lured Aegisthus in Sophocles' *Electra*. Euripides is doing to Sophocles what Aristophanes had often done to *him*.

A really comic figure now appears, one of Helen's eunuchs who has escaped by climbing out below the roof. He tells of the attack on Helen in lyrics that were no doubt accompanied by barbaric music and wild, terrified dancing. Orestes appears with bloody sword and there is more richly comic writhing by the eunuch.

When Menelaus arrives, Electra has her torch ready to fire the house, as Orestes and Pylades on the roof hold a sword to Hermione's throat. Menelaus storms at the door as Jason and Ion had before him. Orestes has the presence of mind to threaten him with stones from above. We are reminded of the siege scenes that are popular in New Comedy. Menelaus does not yield in order to save his daughter, as the conspirators had planned. He shrieks in terror as the sword hovers, but Apollo intervenes and orders Orestes to marry Hermione. Menelaus is to go back to Sparta and let Orestes reign in Argos. The god reconciles everyone at a stroke, including the Argives, who had sentenced Orestes to death, and Helen, who had not really been slain but had disappeared as she became a goddess.

The operatic nature of this performance is clear enough. There is not only the eunuch; Electra has a long lyric passage, and Orestes a long mad scene in which he fights off phantoms with bow and arrow. The use of rhetoric and the role of the assembly as decisive factor are both reminiscent of the *Hecuba,* but motives are so mixed and unrealistic or ungenerous on each side that moral concern is lost in the excitement. There is a schizophrenic juxtaposition of passion and argument, but no integration of impulse and reason to produce character or any will but willfulness. The possibilities of sensationalism have lately been further exploited by Robinson Jeffers and those of existentialism by Sartre, but the *Orestes* is the low-water mark of Greek tragedy. It provided opportunities for the actors and was no doubt entertaining, but the characters are all irresponsible in one way or another, and they seem to learn nothing in the play. Tyndareus is a model for the angry father of New Comedy, but in New Comedy he would at least appear against a background of normal morality; and his excesses, if any, would be punished by ridicule. Where all the characters are abnormal the effect must inevitably be unrelated to morality. Art has got its divorce from life, and we are ready for the drama that makes the pleasure of the audience its goal. In general a mixture of elements, and a spice of variety in the course of the plot, together with any novelty that can be provided, will give pleasure. In the next century, actors will be more important than poets.[7]

The two remaining plays of Euripides, *Phoenissae* (409 B.C.) and *Iphigeneia at Aulis* (401 B.C.), are both plays of action that present a variety of personal points of view. In the latter, as in the *Orestes,* the outcome is uncertain to the end, but the characters are attractive both when they make noble decisions and when they vacillate because of motives that seem reasonable and natural. In both *Phoenissae* and *Iphigeneia* the chorus are a disinterested company of female sightseers. The audience are not allowed to take a single point of view, for they must sympathize with one character after another, all of whom are intent on their personal roles. In this kind of play we may speak of diffraction of the action. The performance gains in color what it loses in intensity and clarity. The *Iphigeneia* as a whole, however, has an ethical appeal that is lacking in the *Phoenissae,* for in all its action the fate of Iphigeneia is a matter for decision, and the scenes of diffracted action have a common goal. In the end self-devotion is rewarded by divine intervention and salvation. Human nature has risen to dominate experience.

In the *Phoenissae* we remain on the level of experience. The old with their caution are frustrated and the young get their way. They die heroically, two for ambition and one for his city. The patriotic role of Eteocles in Aeschylus' *Seven against Thebes,* which tells the same story, is in the *Phoenissae* taken from him and given to Creon's son Menoeceus. Thus Eteocles can represent ambition and tyranny. The play is highly stylized and largely provided with sung and danced parts. Any action that there is occurs in the distant background, from which emotional crises erupt with little interconnection. The successive scenes are not arranged in an ordered series by cause and effect, but selected and juxtaposed like those of the *Trojan Women.* Their variety does not, however, lead up to a total emotional effect, for emotion is presented behind an aesthetic screen, which sterilizes it for practical purposes.

The previous tragic tradition is exploited by bringing in a multi-plicity of familiar characters. Jocasta and Oedipus are still living. The former delivers a long prologue and reports that she has arranged a secret meeting in Thebes in the hope of reconciling her sons. When she leaves the stage, Antigone, whose role is danced and sung, is conducted by an old servant to a position on the walls whence she can describe the attacking army and its leaders. She is all timid curiosity and burns with affection when she sees her brother Polyneices amid the hostile army. Such danced drama is more characteristic of the Chinese or Hindu theater than of the European. She is led away to avoid the chorus, just as characters motivate their exits in New Comedy by similar references. The chorus in this play are as little concerned with the action as the totally detached choruses of Menander. After the chorus, Polyneices appears without warning and, in a danced part, with drawn sword looks this way and that for hidden foes. Musical justice is done to the theme of the exile's return, and Polyneices reports his adventures and the hardships of exile to his mother. When Eteocles arrives, Polyneices asserts his right to equal authority in the state. Eteocles declares that equality is a mere word. He will be sole sovereign in spite of justice. Jocasta rebukes him for his lawless ambitions and censures Polyneices for resorting to arms against his own city. The brothers are unmoved by their mother and in a long responsive chant challenge each other to battle outside the walls.[8]

Creon, the uncle of Eteocles, asks him about the order of battle and is told to consult the seer Tiresias. The seer requires the sacrifice of Creon's son Menoeceus to save the city. Creon, being unwilling to sacrifice his son, makes plans for him to flee, but the ardent youth tricks his father and goes to a voluntary death. His idealism is contrasted not merely with his father's realistic selfishness, but also with the more ardent selfishness of the opposing brothers. A messenger reports to Jocasta the sacrifice of Menoeceus and the repulse of an Argive attack on the wall. When he further warns her that her sons will fight in single combat, she calls Antigone

to go with her and intervene. Creon arrives with the body of
Menoeceus in time to hear a second messenger report the death
of both brothers in a savage duel. Antigone and Jocasta had arrived
too late, and Jocasta slew herself. Antigone now enters with the
bodies and calls out blind Oedipus. Creon exiles them and they
go lamenting on their way to Athens, where the oracle has told
Oedipus he shall die.

It is obvious that in this play we have a variety show made up
of elements chosen from the storehouse of previous tragedy. The
debate between tyranny and equality was no doubt appropriate
at the moment when Athens seemed likely to fall to the sole rule
of Alcibiades, as the Syracusan democracy shortly afterward fell
to the tyranny of Dionysius. This rhetorical episode in the play
might serve to instruct the audience, while the whole theme of
civil war and its resulting misery was not inappropriate. It is the
same theme that Sophocles presented three years later in the
Oedipus at Colonus. Euripides' characters have, however, no strong
moral appeal. Their world is removed to a distance by the stylized
presentation. The spell of sophisticated art has replaced the appeal
of lifelike intimacy. An audience interested in the play of moral
forces in a unified action might as well hang themselves as try
to find it in this play. That part of the story had been done before
and could be taken for granted. Sensations and emotions are presented in thrilling succession without sense of effort, like a series
of magnificent views observed from the windows of an aerial
tramcar. Something of the joy of living is almost inevitably lost
when sensations are purchased so easily; the theater ceases to be
a source of strength either in moral or political life. The Greeks
assumed as a matter of course that the theater should be such a
source of strength, as we know from the dramatic criticism of two
men as different as Aristophanes and Plato. It might be said that
the theater had become too lively to be lifelike. Aesthetic was still
concerned with motion and emotion but had lost contact with
destiny and duty. Christian moralists later took for granted the
wickedness of actors and the theater.

There is plenty of evidence that Euripides, though he was a reckless innovator at times, was still capable of writing in the old manner. The *Bacchae* is convincing proof of that, while the *Iphigeneia at Aulis* is rather a forerunner of the rise of New Comedy than a decadent specimen of tragedy. Its characters are studied on the level of real life. They take serious things seriously and deal with events as they unfold. Even when they are rhetorical, their reasons for using the resources of art to win an argument are apparent. Euripides, in contrast to Sophocles, seems to have more art than genius in his depiction of human behavior, but he often employs his art to very good advantage, as here. A clever lawyer need not always be on the wrong side. The one urgent problem of morality and expediency, whether Iphigeneia is to be sacrificed as the army insists, is uppermost in the minds of all characters, and is the subject of all appeals. Thus it is largely a story of mental conflict and choice like the *Philoctetes* of Sophocles, but Euripides has achieved variety by using a greater number of characters. There are three vacillating characters: Agamemnon and Menelaus, who repent too late (like Medea and the Orestes of Euripides' *Electra*), and Iphigeneia, who repents, like Neoptolemus, of an ignoble decision in time to settle the issue in such a way that the expedient and the right are no longer in conflict. In the background is the army vaguely reported as determined on the sacrifice. Conflict is threatened by the passionate opposition of Clytemnestra and Achilles, but the army gets its way without actual conflict by reason of Iphigeneia's decision. Her noble act is rewarded by a divine intervention reported by messenger. Artemis substitutes a hind and Iphigeneia disappears. Thus the effect in the end is not tragic but highly ethical. On the other hand, the moral problem is so remote from ordinary life that the realistic characterization in most of the play, though entertaining and instructive, has no particular philosophic significance, and would certainly leave no sting in the mind of the hearer, as great tragic moments do.

The question how far the beginning and the end of the play, as we find them in our texts, derive from Euripides himself, and

how far they have been reworked by others, is of no great importance for us. In any case we have an example of tragedy in its
later development, as it moves in the direction of New Comedy.
Naturally, as New Comedy took over the themes of later tragedy,
tragedy itself might be expected to revert to type. Agamemnon
as henpecked husband offers fewer possibilities of development
than henpecked husbands who are ordinary citizens and are not
tied to any particular official role or official series of events. New
Comedy did not of course discard any interesting situations that
appeared in tragedy, but merely added to them such new connections as might make them more humorous and natural. The *Iphigeneia* has the kind of opening that seems to be normal in Menander, the delayed prologue; but in New Comedy the delayed
prologue is spoken by a mythical or allegorical figure, while in
the *Iphigeneia*, Agamemnon, who has already appeared in action
preceding the prologue, also delivers the set prologue.

We are approaching the point where a whole act precedes the
entrance of the chorus and the prologue consequently can no longer
be defined, as it is in the *Poetics*, as that part of a play which precedes
the entrance of the chorus. It will be remembered that in the
Suppliants and *Persians* of Aeschylus nothing preceded the entrance of the chorus. The set prologue, however, still provides in
Greek drama an exposition of the historical setting and presuppositions of the action. It was Terence who began to use a prologue,
not connected with the action of the play, for the purpose of introducing the comedy and appealing for the favor of the audience
—a prologue, in short, in the modern sense of the term. The ending of the *Iphigeneia* is unusual in that divine intervention is
reported, not presented on the stage. The effect is not very different from that of the reported miraculous disappearance of Oedipus
in the *Oedipus at Colonus*.[9]

The liveliness and realism of the rapidly succeeding scenes in
the *Iphigeneia* are something that we have not seen since the
Oedipus Tyrannus. The action seems to move of itself somehow
out of reach of the characters, yet Iphigeneia herself controls it

at the end and gains in happiness, just as Oedipus at the corresponding point lost control and happiness together. Gods are equally
omitted in both plays, for the pressure of the god's demand in the
later play is felt through the army, just as in the *Oedipus* the plague
brought the people to ask for help and set the drama in motion.
Yet in the later play private interests seem to rule all but the heroine,
so that the sudden intrusion of a public interest at the end is almost
incongruous. Certainly there is far less preparation for Iphigeneia's
change of heart than for that of Neoptolemus in the *Philoctetes*.

The play begins with a scene between Agamemnon and a servant
in which Agamemnon repents of his decision to send for his
daughter Iphigeneia to come to Aulis, ostensibly to marry Achilles,
but really to be sacrificed. He gives the servant a letter that will
countermand her coming, then delivers a formal delayed prologue.
The chorus enter and sing, but are mere sightseers with but little
interest in the action until the Panhellenic spirit appears at the
end. Agamemnon's repentance turns out to have been ineffective,
for his brother Menelaus has intercepted the letter; tempers grow
waspish. The argument between the brothers ends when the arrival of Iphigeneia herself, as well as the interest of the troops in
her presence, is reported. Agamemnon weeps in anguish. It is
now the turn of Menelaus to repent and seek to save the victim.
Again it is too late, for the army demands the sacrifice. In the
Medea, repentance was followed by a new decision that canceled
its effect. In this play, by using more characters Euripides may
show genuine repentance that does not halt the action, because
decision rests first with one character, then with another.

It turns out that Clytemnestra has, contrary to orders, come with
her daughter. Iphigeneia's warm affection for her father rends
his heart much as Philoctetes' trust in Neoptolemus made him
writhe. Clytemnestra presents a more difficult problem, for she
roundly refuses to remain aloof from the supposed wedding ceremony. When Agamemnon has gone, Achilles arrives impatient
for action. Since Clytemnestra thinks of him as a son-in-law, she
accosts him familiarly and is comically misunderstood like Xuthus

in the *Ion*. Indeed, the whole role of Clytemnestra has its comic side, since her pride and insubordination to her husband are emphasized. Achilles is also a rather touchy character, punctilious about honor and ready to die for it like Menelaus in the *Helen* or Pylades in the *Orestes*. Since Achilles' name has been used to trick the women, his honor is involved. When Clytemnestra pleads, he agrees to save her daughter. Later he is interested in Iphigeneia for her own sake and offers to rescue her at the last moment if she repents. He is moved by her nobility of soul, not by her physical charms, he says. His resolute support does not actually affect the result, but it affects the quality of Iphigeneia's decision. She is really choosing her course, since the attractiveness of a rescue by Achilles can hardly be denied. This makes her seem worthier to the audience and worthier to Achilles, who is an ideal witness.

Meanwhile an appeal is made to Agamemnon to change his plan. Clytemnestra, Iphigeneia, and even the infant Orestes, plead eloquently but in vain. Agamemnon goes to prepare the sacrifice while Iphigeneia laments in song. Achilles returns prepared to fight alone against the army. At this moment Iphigeneia becomes the psychological pivot of the action and resolves to go voluntarily to death in a cause that will involve the death of many brave men. A brave woman should not hesitate to devote herself to the same cause. As Aristotle points out, Iphigeneia seems to be an inconsistent character, since her devotion is not foreshadowed and since her impulses move violently with consummate eloquence in opposite directions. Plato notes, however, that such violently opposed successive impulses are characteristic of young men. A young woman might be expected to change her mind even more suddenly. At any rate we have here a notable example of the vacillating character. The effect is highly theatrical and, since it involves a shift from selfishness to nobility, highly ethical. It is perhaps no accident that just at the moment when Athens had succumbed in a war to maintain her empire a new ideal of Panhellenism should be presented in the theater. We think of the efforts of Isocrates to unite the Greeks for an attack on Persia in order to end their constant petty dissensions and of the design of Agesilaus to begin his invasion of Asia with a ceremony at Aulis. In any case, the time had probably passed when a narrow ideal of local patriotism would satisfy an audience in the Athenian theater. It is likely that political motives were hardly more acceptable in tragedy than in comedy in the fourth century.[10]

We have come to the end of the great period of Greek tragedy. The actor is now more important than the poet. New developments will occur in the field of technique—the technique of entertainment. Prizes will not be awarded to poets because of the philosophic or moral value of their instruction, but solely on the evidence of pleasure given to the audience. We know from Plato that applause in the theater ruled the decision of the judges long before applause in the assembly became the criterion of statesmanship. In fact, an earnest reformer like Plato could no more flourish in the theater than in political assemblies. There is a story that is significant, whether true or not, which relates that Plato was so moved by the teaching of Socrates that he burned his plays and dedicated himself to philosophy. The role that he had to play on the stage of life was too important to allow him to devote his talents to imitating other men on the scenic stage. Life itself is a tragedy and demands the best efforts of the genius. To write for the stage would be to prostitute art for the end of pleasure. Plato did, of course, write the Socratic dialogues, which are dramatic compositions of a sort. They are certainly fiction. Yet their purpose was to instruct and inspire. They had to please, too, if they were to be read, but their art had a moral purpose. From now on we may expect Athenians to write philosophy when they wish to improve their fellow citizens, and to write not for the citizens as a public body but for individuals who might be induced to dedicate themselves to the cause of truth and right as a nucleus of political reform. No longer is there hope of salvation coming from the multitude. Salvation must come from the enlightened few. Later the few will hope only to save themselves, not the mass of mankind.

We know from Aristotle's *Poetics* something of the spirit of tragedy in his time. He tells us that modern plays in his day were characterless, and we can see that if the dance technique of acting continued, with its preference for doubt and vacillation rather than strength of mind, which involves less physical movement, plays would result in which misunderstanding and rashness must play a greater part than deliberate choice. Thought would be employed not in the grand manner to dominate experience, but in the manner of the law court for attack and defense. Character would be concealed rather than revealed by such rhetorical pettiness. The total effect, then, would be that of movement on a sensational level with no awareness of moral or philosophical forces as controlling human destiny and happiness. Interest would be chiefly in action for its own sake, with little relation to life. As Aristotle says, heroes were of mixed character in his day. Tragedy was found in the frustration of hopes. In such a tragedy it makes no difference whether the man whose hopes are cut short deserves to succeed or not. The audience will be prepared to enjoy the spectacle of another's misfortune on the assumption that all is lost in death. Homer's heroes found an immortality in glory won by virtue. Aristotle wrote for men who could appreciate virtue in everyday life but were resigned to a sentimental uniformity of pity in their art. In New Comedy, thanks to its preoccupation with lifelike characters and problems, morality was still important.

Before we turn to the development of New Comedy, however, let us consider the one example of post-Aristotelian tragedy that has come down to us. It is true that the date of the *Rhesus* is disputed, but that very fact is an indication of lateness. It is not hard to date approximately any fifth-century play that has come down to us, merely from the internal evidence of technique and its relation to other plays or to political life. The *Rhesus* carries dance technique and vacillation further even than the *Phoenissae* or the *Iphigeneia at Aulis*. It has an intervention by Athena in the middle of the play that is quite unparalleled in other dramas, for Athena represents no force in nature, but is brought in merely to provoke a literary feud. She slays the Muse's son Rhesus, and the Muse withdraws her favor from Athens. It is hardly conceivable that Euripides or Agathon could have written anything of the sort to flatter Archelaus of Macedon in the fifth century. For such a challenge to the literary supremacy of Athens we can discover a much more probable background in the literary activity of Alexandria in the third century. It seems safe to assume that the *Rhesus* belongs to Hellenistic literature and to a tradition that is divorced from Athens or any other local center.

The *Rhesus* has come down to us among the plays of Euripides, but the scholiast points out that it is more Sophoclean than Euripidean. He is thinking of the dialogue between Odysseus and the unseen Athena, which may derive from the *Ajax* of Sophocles, or perhaps of the very active participation of the chorus of Trojan soldiers in the action of the play, for Aristotle considers it characteristic of Euripides to separate his chorus from the play instead of treating it as another actor in the manner of Sophocles. The chorus of the *Rhesus* is, however, not very much like the choruses of *Ajax* and *Oedipus at Colonus* with their local patriotism and unquestioning loyalty. The chorus of the *Rhesus* is as characterless as the rest of the play. Its members question, argue, and sing for the sake of movement and variety, but are as little responsible in their attitude as their betters. If they are taken from life at all, they might be thought to represent the easily moved populace of Alexandria. When they hail Rhesus on his arrival as a god, we seem to hear echoes of the adulation of Hellenistic throngs. Another Hellenistic feature in the play is the prominence given to humble characters like the messenger who reports the arrival of Rhesus, and the charioteer who reports the manner of his death. Hector condescends to argue with both of these men with little concern for dignity or even common sense. He is as mobile as a weathercock.

It must not be supposed, however, that the *Rhesus* is not good theater. It was written precisely to be good theater. That it succeeds was attested when in Gilbert Murray's version it was performed

in the garden of New College, Oxford, a few years ago. It is the
only Greek play whose action takes place in darkness. The resulting multiplied doubt and insecurity of the characters lends itself
particularly well to the dance technique of acting. When the chorus
pursue Odysseus in the dark, it is possible to introduce any amount
of misunderstanding and any number of narrow escapes. We
have only to consider what Chinese actors make of the opportunity
to enact a fight in the dark.

The play opens with the approach of the chorus to bring Hector
information. The situation and story are those of the *Iliad*, Book 10.
The Trojans are bivouacking in the plain near the Achaean camp.
The chorus awaken Hector and demand action. When he protests
at their strange behavior, they are content to report that the Achaean
camp is full of lights and that there is a conference at the tent of
Agamemnon. Hector, who has been steadily scolding the chorus
but imposing no discipline whatever, now gives them an opportunity to rebuke him. He rashly concludes that the Achaeans are
planning to flee in the night, and is about to order a general attack.
The chorus' plea for caution is supported by Aeneas, who arrives
in company with Dolon. Hector speedily resolves to send a spy
to get accurate information before ordering an attack. When he
calls for a volunteer, Dolon offers himself but stipulates that he
is to receive the horses of Achilles as a reward. His hopes are high,
but obviously foolish, and his frustration will be a companion piece
to the frustration of Rhesus himself, who loses life and horses also.
Hector, of course, shares in the frustration of their hopes, but is
saved from complete ruin by the restraint imposed by his advisers
and by the fact that, vain as he is, he has somewhat more common
sense than the two who lose their lives. Dolon proposes to disguise
himself in a wolfskin and to bring back the head of Odysseus
or Diomedes.

Hector is now confronted by a shepherd bringing news of the
arrival of Rhesus with fresh forces from Thrace. Hector objects
to receiving news of war from mere shepherds, and when at last
the shepherd is allowed to deliver his news, Hector objects to

receiving reinforcements when the war is already won, as he thinks. Rhesus arrives while the chorus are singing. They hail him as the god Ares in person. One is reminded of the Macedonians and Romans who announced themselves as new Hermes, new Isis, new Dionysus, or the like, and were so hailed by the throngs. Hector rebukes Rhesus for not coming earlier. Rhesus explains with some eloquence the difficulties and hardships that had delayed his arrival and points out that even after ten years the war remains to be won. He proposes personally to settle the war next day and then to invade Greece in retaliation. When warned of Odysseus, he proposes to impale him as a temple-robber. Hector seems sober and conservative by contrast. Rhesus is given the watchword, warned that Dolon should soon return from his activity as a spy, and assigned a campground apart from the Trojans.

Meanwhile it is time to relieve the guard. When the sentinels go to summon the relief, Odysseus and Diomedes appear, full of terrors and misapprehensions. They are looking for Hector, but find no one in his quarters. Odysseus would return content to have slain Dolon; but Athena at this moment appears and tells the two heroes of the arrival of Rhesus and of his horses. If Rhesus survives the night, he is fated to devastate the Achaean camp. In Homer they had all their information from Dolon, but in the play they have learned from him only the watchword. He had, of course, started on his enterprise before the arrival of Rhesus. Athena's part is now to foil Paris, who has heard rumors of the presence of spies. She appears to him in the guise of Aphrodite and deceives him so that he feels secure and departs. Meanwhile, Rhesus has been slain and Diomedes has made off with the horses. Odysseus is seized by the sentinels but escapes through his knowledge of the watchword.

News of the successful attack on Rhesus is brought by a wounded charioteer, who suspects that Hector has disloyally assassinated his ally. Hector threatens the sentinels with punishment, but the charioteer remains suspicious. Hector in the end bids his servants remove the charioteer and tend his wounds. The stubborn sus-

picion of the loyal charioteer shows a lack of vacillation that is
remarkable in this particular play. At this moment the Muse appears with the body of Rhesus in her arms. The mourning is brief,
but the Muse tells of past and future as the god from the machine
was expected to do. In particular she proposes to withdraw her
favor from Athens because Athena alone has brought about the
death of her son. Since the Muse's enmity to Athens was hardly
conspicuous before the third century before Christ, either there
is an anachronism involved of something like a thousand years,
or we must suppose that the incidents of the play are thought of
as happening only on the stage, so that the feud between Athena
and the Muse would begin when the *Rhesus* was first performed,
rather than at the period of the Trojan war, when Rhesus is supposed to have been slain. At any rate, we may assume that the
author of the play felt that he was in a position to point to scant
productivity at Athens in the field of tragedy in comparison with
other parts of the Greek world. That brings us down very late
for the date of the play, and its technique is sufficiently artificial
to confirm our conclusion about that date.[11]

It is by no means certain or even probable that Hindu and
Chinese drama were influenced by the Greek, but if they were,
it was no doubt such plays as the *Rhesus* that were in fashion in
the period when there was such influence. Certainly the dance
technique and movement of Oriental drama resemble that of the
Rhesus more than they do anything in *Oedipus Tyrannus* for
instance. The happy ending is, however, normal in Oriental drama;
hence we might suspect rather the influence of New Comedy than
that of tragedy. In any case, Greek tragedy had become a mere
source of entertainment and concerned itself no more with morals
and philosophic truth. Still later the wordless dancing of panto-
mime displaced tragedy in popular favor. In fact the actual butchery
of gladiatorial combats in Roman times frankly fed and watered
the passions of the multitude. The Greek use of imaginary pain
and death to clear the mind and free it from obsessions of self-pity
and of self-indulgent fears had no place in such a world.[12]

VIII
The Comedy of Menander

ATHENIAN tragedy was most harsh in its view of
the divine just at the end of the Periclean Age, when the *Oedipus
Tyrannus* of Sophocles and the *Hippolytus* of Euripides appeared.
Both are in great part tragedies of misunderstanding and rashness,
and of peripety, or turning the tables, and in both of them events
seem to be intentionally designed by some god to destroy an innocent victim. Sophocles enhances the spectator's sense of the insecurity of life by bringing no visible god into the argument, and
in his masterpiece there is a confusion of identity that does not
appear in the play of Euripides. In his work there is a misunderstanding of facts and motives that leads Hippolytus to condemn
Phaedra unheard, and Theseus to condemn Hippolytus unheard.
There is also peripety in both plays in the sense that both heroes
are instrumental in bringing about their own downfall. Aristotle
strongly approves both the unhappy ending for tragedy and the
play with complex plot in which events are artfully made to produce results that surprise the characters, while the audience can
see on reflection that causal relations have been such as to make
the result probable or inevitable. This is the kind of plot that is
more philosophical than history, for history as a rule lacks the
neat timing and subtle irony of the productions of art. There is
more poetic justice in fiction than in real life. If Aristotle had not
insisted on treating plot and character as two separate things, he
might have included the play with psychological discovery in his
category of the complex. But for Aristotle psychology belongs to
character, not to plot. Hence a plot that confines itself to psychological motivation is not for Aristotle complex, and it does not provide the kind of surprises that Aristotle prefers both in tragedy

and in comedy. That Aristotle's view was nothing novel or extreme
in his own time becomes obvious as soon as we reflect that in New
Comedy there is nearly always a plot involving mistaken identity,
surprises, and a neat concatenation of events unplanned by any
character. Since Aristotle wrote his *Poetics* before Menander had
come of age, we must include Aristotle in any censure with which
we visit Menander on the score of improbable plots and convenient
coincidences. This is just the sort of thing that Aristotle solemnly
declares to be more philosophical than history.[1]

Aristotle holds that the line between tragedy and comedy should
be vertical, dividing plays with unhappy endings from plays with
happy endings, as well as horizontal, dividing plays with heroic
characters from plays whose characters are caricatured, cheapened,
vulgarized, mechanized, or otherwise made to serve as butts for
laughter. The Greek preference for happy endings in tragedies,
as they called their heroic plays, was rebuked by Aristotle. It is
unfortunate that the second book of his *Poetics,* which dealt with
comedy, has perished. It is clear from what has been said, however,
that Aristotle did not consider laughter the essential element in
comedy. What he requires is a plot, preferably complex, involving
mistaken identity and a turning of the tables so as to bring about
a desired and unexpected happy ending for good characters. Such
an ending does not produce the exaltation and purgation resulting
from tragedy, but it gives pleasure to the spectators and strengthens
their philanthropic motives. They are glad to see the good preserved, and they feel strongly the value of family ties and of the
benevolent generosity that makes civilized living possible. We
have in epic a perfect example of this kind of plot in the *Odyssey,*
pronounced by Aristotle to be ethical and complex. It is ethical
because of the presence of *éthos*—a Greek word that includes many
things for which we require separate terms in English. It means
customs, manners, and morals, at the same time; and it includes
the satisfaction that people feel in the presence of the familiar, the
habitual, and the comforting. A happy ending is not particu-

[1] For notes to chapter viii see pages 309–317.

larly effective unless it brings happiness to characters with whom the audience feels a strong sympathy, not merely because they are good, but because the audience has been flattered into thinking that it inhabits a world filled with just such noble people. Thus, the more realistic the picture, the easier will it be for each member of the audience to identify himself personally with the hero.[2]

It was in fact the *Odyssey* that a Greek publicist first termed a fair mirror of human life, but since Menander's time Menander has won prime consideration as the poet who held up the mirror to life. The phrase "Menander's Mirror" is in current use at the head of a column of literary comment. Aristophanes of Byzantium wrote the line, "O Life, O Menander, which is the copy?" The simplicity, liveliness, and truth of Menander are emphasized by ancient critics who had before them his hundred or more plays. Pliny the Elder calls him the unrivaled literary genius of the plain style. Menander had *éthos* in every sense of the word. He depicted customary life, he stressed the moral qualities of his characters, virtue was rewarded in his endings, and he exerted an uplifting influence on readers and spectators alike. The plural of *éthos* becomes *mores* in Latin, *mœurs* in French, and 'manners' in English. The further we go from the Greek, the less does moral comedy or comedy of manners resemble Menander or the *Odyssey*, until in English comedy of manners we find that we have come full circle and that manners and morals are diametrically opposed conceptions. William of Wykeham was not thinking of that more superficial kind of manners when he took as his motto, "Manners Makyth Man."[3]

Menander's depiction of character was thus neither of the extremes in Aristotle's scale, but a kind of mean. In tragedy men appear superhuman, in comedy infrahuman; only in New Comedy are they lifesize. In tragedy we have found characters who, being inferiors, were made somewhat comic by Aeschylus, Sophocles, or Euripides. In the work of the last-named, Menelaus and even Pentheus are treated with ridicule in spite of their royal status. Euripides for his own day was often quite realistic in his depiction of certain characters; and so Sophocles remarked that Euripides depicted men just as they are, whereas he himself depicted them as they ought to be. There can be no question that the Socrates of Aristophanes was both funnier and less respectable than the real Socrates. In comedy, characters rather resemble mechanical puppets. They are funny because they are moved by springs of action too mechanically. In high tragedy, decisions seem more momentous than in real life. Kings, and philosophic kings at that, were suitable material for tragedy in the days when democracy had not yet made every man an uncrowned king. In real life, of course, some of us take life more tragically than others. Some of us are natural clowns, but it should be noted that the clowns are not necessarily less virtuous than the tragedians. It is only superficially that comic characters are inferior.[4]

Aristotle has confused moral or social inferiority with the belittling effect of jokes. A witty remark is a polite insult, as Aristotle knew. So too, the intent of a comic writer makes a difference, and to laugh at our betters may endear them to us. Laughter may be cruel or rude. There is a certain cruelty in the rule of Plato, apparently approved by Aristotle, that only inferiors should be lampooned. It was in this spirit that the proud Spartans laughed at drunken helots but never at themselves. Menander's laughter is highly civilized, for the most part. His laughter is bestowed on morally inferior characters, and his slaves are sometimes more admirable than the representatives of wealth. In the same way such of his characters as deserve it by their idealism are treated with great seriousness. His mirror is convex and shows men and women larger in the foreground but much smaller in the background. In his lifelike effects there is much that derives from comedy and at the same time far more that derives from Homer and tragedy. The realistic depiction of life, if it includes all levels, is humorous rather than tragic or comic. It will on occasion sink to the level of comedy and even farce, but it must be capable of raising its tone to the range of tragedy in rare moments or it will not be really true to life and will not enthrall its audience. It was

the power that Menander displayed in such moments that made
Caesar and other critics rate him above Terence, the Latin half-
Menander.[5]

There is in Menander much of the liveliness of Aristophanes
and even more variety and vacillation than we have noted in some
later tragedies. We have observed how tragedy became less serious
as the interest of the actor in liveliness and exhibition of versatility
began to prevail in the theater and technique became more important than the accurate and moving presentation of serious
themes. If the *Rhesus* is typical, actors were also dancers. In many
plays of Euripides they were singers as well. There are no singing
actors, as far as we know, in Menander, but we are informed that
the actors particularly enjoyed acting in his plays because of the
opportunity that he provided for a lively and versatile performance.
In producing Menander on the modern stage it is well to remember that in India and China the actor is also a dancer and that,
whether Oriental drama derives from Greek danced drama or not,
there is an element of ballet in late Greek tragedy and New Comedy
that makes them in some degree akin to Asia as much as to modern
Europe. Posture and movement must be rhythmic as well as expressive, with a constant shifting of attitudes and positions that
will produce a kaleidoscopic effect for the eye as well as for the
imagination. The grouping of characters on the stage will often
be static, especially since only one, two, or three speaking characters may appear at once, yet the group effect will contribute to
the impression of contrast or conflict that the poet intends to produce. Besides the constant succession of new characters or familiar
characters in new postures, there will also be occasional scenes of
great activity, in which an angry man pursues his slave or even
a fleeing wife or timid neighbor. Soldiers often lay siege to a house
where some unwilling beauty has taken refuge. Though Menander's characters are realistic, his stage and the acting were stylized
and even symbolic. His plays are, of course, all designed to be
seen in the full light of day, and all his scenes are street scenes.
Any atmosphere or moods must be clearly depicted in his text and

carefully projected by the actors, for the stage manager and the lighting expert probably gave no help at all.[6]

The genius of Menander appears most clearly when we reflect that he uses the very means that made comedy farcical and tragedy unmoral and uses them so skillfully that his characters and their problems seem highly realistic. Vacillation leads to decision, and decision leads to success or failure in a setting of seriously treated situations involving not only family ties but general principles of justice and philanthropy. He achieves variety by multiplying characters and by developing the use of diffused or diffracted action. Rustic or urban slaves, men and women, young and old, all have decisions to make and are shown making them. Yet the unity of the action is preserved because all decisions have an ultimate bearing on the final achievement of a result that was not planned or expected by any one character. The audience are informed beforehand of this result, so that they may derive an ironical satisfaction from observing the blindness of the characters. In this Menander is merely following Homer, who always gives his hearers an Olympian view of what is going on and contrasts with it the blindness of human beings. Since the result is known in advance and is accepted by the audience as highly desirable, the moral characters will be those whose action forwards the good cause, while any characters who oppose the general good will stamp themselves conspicuously as villains. The effect will be particularly striking when the technique of *Oedipus Tyrannus* is employed and an occasional character forwards the cause that he means to oppose, just because he is fundamentally honest though lacking insight in the sphere of other virtues than honesty.[7]

In general, then, New Comedy follows the model of Homer's *Odyssey* in its concern with manners and morals. Its plots all have as their theme the reunion of husband and wife, lover and mistress, father and daughter, or father and son, and so on, as well as the righting of wrongs with removal of misunderstanding. Where misunderstanding has led to unkindness or violence, scenes of repentance make forgiveness possible, and mutual kindness is restored on a more solid basis, as in the *Alcestis* of Euripides. The theme of repentance and forgiveness is markedly absent from the *Odyssey,* which is much less psychological in its plot than the *Iliad.* In fact, however, neither the *Iliad* nor Greek tragedy treats the theme of repentance so fully or so understandingly as Menander. His characters pass through an ordeal very like religious initiation and emerge reformed, purified, and enlightened. This remarkable novelty makes him the most Christian of the Greek dramatists at the same time that it involves him in a preoccupation with aspects of love that made him seem intolerably wicked to the shortsighted fanatics who preached Christianity more fervently than they practiced it. Plutarch, the pagan moralist, considered Menander an extremely effective instrument for the implanting of kindly and civilized principles. Menander's plays were the only theatrical fare, he says, that could draw a philosopher to public performances. We have abundant evidence that boys graduated at an early age from Homer to Menander, and not merely because he provided themes and examples for oratory. He was considered worthy to be placed beside Homer as an educator. Hence it is not surprising to find him coupled with Homer in mosaic and in a double sculptured portrait. Before considering this point further it will be well, however, to examine the actually extant fragmentary plays and observe how they depict the play of forces in civilized human life. They all, like the *Odyssey,* take civilization for granted, but yet, like the *Iliad,* emphasize the need for personal adjustment. As in Aeschylus, suffering brings instruction. The interweaving of plot and character is as subtle and successful as in Sophocles, while serious interest in moral problems and the accurate depiction of imperfect and ordinary men and women leave Euripides far behind.[8]

I propose to consider only the three plays of which we have enough to see how Menander handled his plots. If we had all the hundred-odd plays that Menander wrote before he died in the year 291 B.C., while swimming at Peiraeus, we should have a picture of the domestic life of Greece at that period that would be of the utmost interest because of the variety of characters and topics introduced. Much can indeed be surmised on the basis of Latin adaptations by Plautus and Terence, of which many are extant, and of fragments either preserved on papyrus in the sands of Egypt or quoted by moralists like Plutarch and learned anti- quarians like Athenaeus. Indeed, modern scholars have produced excellent studies of the whole tradition of Menander based on such material. Yet in such scattered remnants and dry bones of an author there is little resemblance to the living works of genius on which the ancient estimates of Menander are based. Nonetheless we must try to see whether we cannot, by a careful study of the three plays in which the interplay of forces is apparent, arrive at a verdict on Menander not unlike the high praise that Plutarch, Quintilian, Aulus Gellius, and others bestowed on him.[9]

The three plays that give us our material were largely preserved in leaves of a codex that were discovered by the Frenchman Lefebvre in 1905. He found them buried in the ruins of an Egyptian city, the ancient Aphroditopolis, city of Aphrodite. Menander de- served well to be so preserved by the goddess of love, for love was a theme in all his plays, as Ovid tells us, and always the love he celebrates was the love of a man for a woman, not the homosexual romantic passion that Plato considered truly creative in the realm of spirit. In tragedy, women had been depicted loving disastrously. Menander shows men in love rather than women, and his men are civilized and enlightened with good effect when they suffer for love of a woman. Tragedy had been too lofty to take note of the tender passion. Gilbert Murray has well said that tragedy dealt with the divine, Old Comedy with public affairs, and New Comedy with private life. Yet in modern times the sentiment or even the passion of love has been found capable of supplying endless themes for tragedy or romance. Love since the thirteenth century has in the European world been pretty thoroughly con- fused with the divine. Love has been made the core of religion, and a religious ecstasy has been imported even into the fictional treatment of carnal and immoral passion.[10]

Menander's plays had to conform to current canons of morality, for they were presented at public expense at festivals whose object was still not merely entertainment. Judging by the plays, it was considered as important in Menander's time as in Homer's to present a noble ideal for the edification of women and to show loyal wives and generous sweethearts rewarded by the abject devotion of the men who began by misunderstanding them. Nothing in the plays encourages women to assume any of the prerogatives of men. Women do not, as in Shakespeare, dress as men or go in pursuit of men unless to regain a father or a brother. Women may be exposed by the vicissitudes of fortune to the perils that beset poor women in the ancient world. Kidnapping and slavery might happen even to the best families in time of war. Noble slaves, however, in Menander as in the *Odyssey,* are encouraged to show their breeding and to behave like gentlemen and ladies. In Menander their original status may be brought to light and restored, or faithfulness in slaves, even in those born in slavery, may be rewarded by freedom. Such rewards were probably not uncommon in real life. A woman slave might be excused for taking the initiative and winning freedom for herself as a reward for the happiness that she brought to others.

A woman who was above slavery but not protected by citizenship and family connections also had to fend for herself as best she could. Such women could expect marriage in the full sense only by a fortunate accident. They had to hold a man's love by their personal charm and loyalty. Women of high class required protection by their families. If they were not properly looked after they might be exposed to violence. They are never represented as being seduced by lovers, but are almost always in some way victims of violence when they are in trouble. Menander's men are as violent and voluble in love as his women are reticent, if not passive. For many situations in Menander's plays parallels can be found in Chinese and Japanese life or literature. Probably in any society where women of good class are expected to be pliant in the company of men and not to challenge the dominance of men in their own sphere of public life it will follow that men are not expected to restrain themselves and that women are. In Menander as in Aeschylus, men have to learn by suffering not to coerce women but to respect and persuade them. In the plays of Menander that we have, women are idealized and men are reformed. For that the men have to begin their career by being sinful. The immorality with which Menander was charged by Christians in ancient times and by some modern scholars springs from this requirement of the plot. The *Confessions* of Saint Augustine show the same feature.[11]

Menander, born about 342 B.C., began to produce plays about the time of Alexander's death in 323. His death at the age of fifty-two is lamented by Plutarch as having cut him off before he had reached the maturity of his powers. It is true that almost all our extant Greek tragedies represent the work of men more than fifty years old, but when we reflect that Shakespeare had become unproductive before he died at fifty-two, we note how much more rapidly life is lived in modern times. We are fortunate in having one play, *Epitrepontes* or *Arbitration,* that illustrates the best work of Menander. It was probably produced somewhat later than the *Perikeiromene* or *Shearing,* which may well illustrate a middle period. It is possible, of course, that the scene of the *Shearing,* Corinth, and the fact that the principals are a soldier and his mistress rather than a man of education and his wife, may account for the failure of the second comedy to rise to corresponding heights. Again, it may be that in the one play the parts accidentally preserved from the ravages of time happen to belong to less exalted characters than in the other. Certainly there was a mixture of jest and earnest in every play of Menander. Where we have chiefly the jests surviving, we can hardly do justice to the main theme.[12]

In the *Samia,* which was produced probably before Menander was thirty years old, there can be no doubt that we have a play in which the principals supply most of the humor and in which the depiction of character is less prominent than the devices that produce lively situations. Trouble in Menander's plays is brought about always by the forces that we saw in Euripides' *Hippolytus* —misunderstanding and rashness. As in Euripides' play, the hero is right in the main but falls into a trap set for him. In the *Samia* there is a double trap for Demeas. His original misunderstanding is confirmed when he attempts to test it, so that his mistake is particularly pardonable. But in this early play we get a concatenation of misunderstandings that spread like a plague from one character to another. There is no concentration on the problem of a single pair of characters, and the principals are shown enough in action to compromise their dignity. It is going too far to call this play farcical, for characters and problems are seriously present in the background, but such a play in representation might be expected to produce more laughter than thought. The later plays show a progressive thoughtfulness and concentration on the psychology of the chief characters. The characters seem largely to determine their own fate by their capacity to rise above circumstances. Circumstances no longer dictate behavior, though good behavior may be circumstantially rewarded. There is still a good deal of laughter, but it is not so much the principals who occasion it.[18]

It is generally assumed that the *Samia* and other plays of Menander were divided into five acts. There was no curtain in the Greek theater, but the actors left the stage at each intermission while a band of revelers amused the audience with song and dance. Such vestigial remains of the old comic chorus were no part of the play, and the playwright was not concerned to supply matter for such interludes. He merely left space for them in his text and put in the mouth of one of his characters at the end of the first act a reference to them that would serve as introduction. The absence of a curtain precluded the building up of a climax with which to end either an act or the whole play. The essential was to empty the stage as plausibly as possible. Since only three speaking actors appeared simultaneously, each actor had to represent several characters. Masks were necessarily employed. It was the part of a good dramatist to enable the audience to imagine what was going on off-stage so as to get the impression of continuous activity on the part of a large number of characters. Menander succeeds admirably in this. Action off-stage is often reported, sometimes by characters looking off through an open door and telling what they see happening inside one of the houses that are always depicted at the back of the stage. Interior scenes were not rolled out as in tragedy.[14]

In the *Samia* there were two houses, that of the wealthy and benevolent Demeas and that of the poor and irascible Niceratus. Thus we have two contrasted old men. Demeas had a concubine, Chrysis, a refugee from Samos. She had lost friends and property and, probably, the evidence to prove her citizenship. Demeas had taken her in when she was homeless in the streets of Athens and had established her as his wife in all but name. Athenian men took hetaeras for pleasure, we are told, concubines for comfort, and wives for legitimate offspring. To allow a mere concubine to bring up children was an unusual favor. Demeas also had a confidential slave Parmeno and an adopted son Moschion. Niceratus' wife does not appear in the scenes of the play that have survived, but both she and a daughter Plangon are important to the action. The old men had arranged a marriage between the two young people, Moschion and Plangon, without consulting them, and preparations for the wedding were made in the house of Demeas.[15]

It so happened that Moschion was delighted to enter into marriage with Plangon, for he had long been intimate with her. She had, in fact, borne him a son in secret. The old men knew nothing of this, and Moschion took steps to preserve the baby and the secret with the help of his father's concubine Chrysis. She had borne a child to Demeas which had conveniently died. Hence when Demeas returned, presumably from a trip abroad, Chrysis presented the babe to him as her own and by wheedling and flattery obtained from the reluctant Demeas permission to keep it. Moschion could not openly acknowledge his paternity without exposing himself to the vengeance of Plangon's father Niceratus. As soon as he was safely married to her, there would be no further difficulty. The baby occupies a central position in the plot, for it is the evidence of Moschion's serious interest in Plangon, and any threat to it is a threat to the family of three that so frequently appears in Greek fiction. The secret baby plays the same part in Greek love stories that the secret marriage does in *Romeo and Juliet*. It persuades us that the union of two young people is important and moral. To the Greeks children were the most sacred bond of matrimony. Without them a marriage could easily be dissolved.[16]

In the part of the play that we have, Demeas' relation to Chrysis and his relation to Moschion are also threatened with disruption as a result of misunderstanding. Demeas is led to believe that his son is guilty of seducing his concubine by evidence as convincing as that which led Theseus to condemn Hippolytus. Probably it is in the second act that he comes from the house and reports his suspicions to the audience. An old woman, who did not know that he had overheard, had referred to the babe as Moschion's son. Furthermore, he had seen Chrysis suckling the infant and had drawn the fallacious conclusion that it must be hers. When Demeas threatened his slave Parmeno with a whipping, he forced a confession that the babe was really Moschion's. Parmeno had naturally assumed that the mother was known to be Plangon, not Chrysis. The benevolent Demeas is transformed before the eyes of the audience into a maniac, intent only upon punishing Chrysis without seeming to implicate his son. He thrusts her out of doors in the most brutal fashion, and of course the infant goes with her. As she sits weeping in the street, Niceratus comes along, hears the tale, and shelters Chrysis in his own house. Moschion probably went to his father to protest against the expulsion of Chrysis. This apparently shameless proceeding no doubt induced Demeas to disclose his suspicion and berate the innocent boy. When Demeas learned the truth, he repented of his treatment of Chrysis, but his repentance is only briefly indicated in an exclamation: "By Hephaestus, to think that I should suspect such things! I do not deserve to live." The oath by Hephaestus, which reminds us of the

old story of that jealous husband, whose jealousy was better
founded, is a light touch that does not add to the seriousness of
the treatment. The reconciliation of Demeas and Chrysis is also
obscured by the demands of a new situation which arises as soon
as Niceratus learns that his daughter has an illegitimate child. He
is for destroying the child at once, and Chrysis barely saves it.[17]

Demeas distracts Niceratus from the pursuit of Chrysis only by
pretending to be himself the father of the child. This new juxtaposition of possible parents is, however, not seriously proposed and
rather leads Niceratus to guess that Moschion is involved. In the
next scene it is the turn of Moschion to be indignant. He proposes
to get revenge on Demeas for undeserved suspicion by pretending
that he is going to enlist in a Macedonian army for service in Asia.
That fathers could really suffer agony under such circumstances is
well shown in the scenes of the *Self-punisher,* which Terence
translated from Menander. We have no more of the play, but it is
clear that Plangon and her father may easily have been the next
victims of misunderstanding and have supposed that Moschion
proposed in earnest to desert his bride. At any rate, we have seen
enough to appreciate how the action of the *Samia* shifts horizon-
tally as one principal after another becomes involved. The marriage is a fixed goal that is no doubt reached in the end. It is probable, indeed, that Demeas also took Chrysis to wife when her
paternity was in some way brought to light in the course of the
play. The fact that Moschion is an adopted son leaves the way open
for the discovery that she is his sister.

The disentanglement of a Greek comedy is misnamed, for
actually the Greek poet likes to leave his characters all thoroughly
joined together by ties of relationship or marriage. Such ties are
threatened with disruption in the early part of the play by misunderstanding and rashness. There are also in every play additional ties that had been so thoroughly disrupted that they were
not known by anyone to exist. Thus the psychological treatment
of family relationships that are known is interwoven with a pattern of discovery. From our fragments we might get the impres-

sion that the *Samia* is purely psychological in its motivation, since no hidden relationships come to light in the course of extant scenes, but it is almost inconceivable that a Greek comedy should not have somewhere one of the recognition scenes that were so precious to Aristotle. It is to the credit of the poet that his play does not depend for interest on our knowledge of such hidden factors. The psychological factors are clearly sketched though not elaborated.[18]

We have seen that in the *Samia* Menander probably spent the first act in setting the stage for Demeas' misunderstanding. We shall find in the two later plays that the misunderstanding occurs before the play begins. In the *Shearing* the first scene showed the husband's jealousy already resulting in action—Polemon cutting off the hair of his consort Glycera. The reconciliation is reserved for the fifth act. In the intervening acts lover and mistress do not meet, though both are shown with psychological clarity in scenes with other characters. By keeping Polemon and Glycera apart Menander is able to represent both as highly voluble forces without any such direct conflict as that between husband and wife in Euripides' *Medea*. It is quite possible, indeed, that there was no altercation even in the first scene. We know from the delayed prologue that in the opening scene the event took place from which the play gets its name, the shearing. To judge by the analogy of other plays this shearing of Glycera must have occurred within the time of the action, but it may have happened off-stage and have been reported to the audience by some character standing at the door of a house and looking in. At any rate the original misunderstanding is merely reported in the prologue as the explanation of Polemon's violent jealousy.

The situation, then, at the beginning of the play is strange enough to have news value, but perfectly possible. In the play the characters act naturally in view of their situations, so that any improbabilities are kept outside of the play, as Aristotle advises. A woman had found twins exposed along with a few objects of clothing and adornment that might serve to identify them if ever their relatives should be able to help them later. Infanticide was neither

criminal nor immoral in ancient Greece. It had the approval of
Plato, though Aristotle recommends the procurement of abortion
as a method of birth control. To expose infants is not, in comedy,
to kill them, but just the opposite, to give them a chance of life,
for infants are exposed only when the alternative is certain death.
Either illegitimacy or poverty might make it impossible for infants
to survive. If they were illegitimate, they might be put out of the
way by any responsible relative; if they could not be fed because of
poverty, they would die a natural death. No approval is expressed
in Menander of the exposure of infants in other cases than these.
In Terence the exposure of a daughter instead of putting her out
of the way at birth is denounced as sentimental weakness that is
really cruel, since the life of such an exposed infant might be one
of slavery and exploitation. Comedy is concerned only with the
restoration of such children to their families, who must of course
have repented or grown rich in the meantime so as to make restoration possible or desirable. Naturally, the greater the misery of the
outcasts before they win recognition, the greater the joy of the
audience at their rehabilitation.[19]

In our play the twins were separated. The boy was adopted by
a rich woman, Myrrhina by name, and appears as Moschion, a
callow youth, who really is in love with love but imagines himself
in love with Glycera and a serious rival of her soldier husband
Polemon. The other foundling had, indeed, been given under stress
of poverty by her protectress and adopted mother to this successful
and wealthy leader of mercenaries. Thus Glycera is a good girl
in an ambiguous position. She has no legal protector and cannot,
considered strictly, be better than a concubine. On the other hand,
Polemon considers her a wife and proposes to exercise the right
of a husband to take private vengeance on anyone who pays court
to her. Yet, by lavishing expensive clothes upon her, and perhaps
in other ways, Polemon to some degree justifies the view of Moschion that Glycera is only a hetaera and hence a beauty to be wooed
and won in fair competition by the best man. Moschion's lack of
experience betrays him and prevents our taking his disappoint-

ment too seriously when Glycera turns out to be only a sister. He began his wooing rather roughly by lurking at the door and invading Glycera's privacy when she came to the door in the process of dispatching her maid on an errand. Glycera obviously is observing the same rule as Penelope in not passing beyond the house door, but, knowing that Moschion was her brother and perhaps supposing that he had discovered that she was his sister, she returned his embrace.

Colonel Polemon, it happened, had returned to barracks near the city and had sent his sergeant Sosias to notify Glycera. Sosias' arrival interrupted the sisterly embrace, but not before he had drawn his own conclusions. Naturally, he informed Polemon that his mistress was showing favor to a rival in his absence. He must have made this disclosure only on the next day, for the play begins when Polemon impetuously demands an explanation and, getting none, cuts off Glycera's hair as a mark of her shame and disgrace. After this brief scene the philosophic abstraction Misapprehension appears and explains the situation. She is responsible, and has made the soldier act out of character in order to start a series of events that would result in a happy ending for everyone. Thus the hero is excused beforehand. Love begets jealousy and rash action when the influence of misapprehension is present.[20]

In the next act the separation of the principals becomes complete when Glycera escapes from Polemon's house to seek refuge with Myrrhina, the wealthy lady next door. No doubt Glycera had to disclose to her the fact that she was the natural sister of Myrrhina's adopted son Moschion. Accordingly Myrrhina was willing to shelter her, though she hoped to keep the relationship a secret. Moschion's slave Davus, however, saw a chance to win credit for himself, and informed the young man that Davus himself had persuaded Myrrhina to take Glycera in and that Moschion's wooing would have the sanction of Myrrhina as well as Glycera. Sosias the sergeant also misunderstood the move and reported to Polemon. Thus we have two houses on the stage to symbolize the union and separation of lover and mistress. It is not impossible

that there was a third house, occupied by Pataecus, a wealthy mer-
chant, but Pataecus may merely have entered and left the stage at
one side, as colonel and sergeant are represented coming and going
to and from their barracks on the other. At any rate Pataecus appears as a neutral, who dissuades Polemon from storming the house
where Glycera has taken refuge. He points out that legally Polemon has no right to use violence because technically he was not
really married to Glycera. Consequently she is a free agent and
must be won by wooing.[21]

Pataecus undertakes to act as agent in the wooing, but finds that
Glycera is quite as voluble and determined as her lover. She has
been insulted, and insults she will not put up with. Let Pataecus
get for her the box that she had left behind. If she had really mis-
behaved with Moschion she would not have gone to his mother's
house for refuge. Pataecus is contrasted with the two principals in
turn with highly humorous effect as both resent and repulse his
well-meant efforts to keep matters on a rational plane. It turns out
in the end that he is the father of Glycera and Moschion. It is his
turn to feel emotion and weep as he recalls the death of his wife
in childbirth and how he exposed the babes for lack of the means
to keep them. Moschion learns the secret by eavesdropping, and a
new family constellation results. Glycera has now a new and much
more powerful protector. Polemon is not merely repentant, but
frightened, for he might easily be prosecuted for his assault on
Glycera's hair. Glycera, however, while she does not repent of her
refusal to submit to violence, is enabled by her new position of
power to accept Polemon as a husband. This she does graciously
and with the dignity befitting the daughter of a citizen, but without manifesting emotion. Polemon is repentant and humble and
promises reform in terms that make it clear that he has learned
a lesson. Moschion is not left out, for his new father proposes to
find him a wife, and presumably allows him to make his own
selection of the lady to be honored. At any rate, he will have no
excuse in future for seeking the company of a hetaera. Glycera returns to the house of Polemon.

Thus we have a problem play of the sort that has been so popular in the modern theater, the problem being who marries whom, or who sleeps with whom. In Menander the problem for Glycera is not psychological, but practical. She must maintain her status as an honest woman who is not to be insulted, though actually she has no basis in the political and economic sphere on which to establish her independence. She consents to be a concubine, but not a hetaera, and ultimately becomes a wife. Since she has acted always in the spirit of an honest wife, this is no more than she deserves.

In the case of Polemon psychology comes to the fore. He is as desperate at the loss of his loved one as Achilles was in Homer at the loss of Patroclus. After his violent punishment of Glycera he lies flat on his back sobbing, a sufficient indication that he was personally interested in his mistress, not merely concerned about his honor. Like Othello, he has loved too well. Misunderstanding had led to jealousy and violence, but violence brought no remedy for his disillusionment. His ideal of Glycera was shattered. His repentance is equally genuine and makes possible the atonement that follows.

Thus we have a play constructed about two principals in such a way that all scenes are somehow connected with the main issue. The humorous touches derive from the serious and lifelike depiction of honest but excited parties to an unnecessary quarrel. The low characters in the play are divided into two camps who make the disagreement of their masters an excuse for their own vituperation and belligerence, as in the first act of *Romeo and Juliet* we see the quarrel of Montague and Capulet through its effect on partisans. There is some unnecessary clowning in Menander as in Shakespeare. There is also a highly sentimentalized recognition scene between Glycera and Pataecus that owes more to the example of tragedy than to observation of life. Both the clowning and the sentimentality seem to be entirely lacking in Menander's masterpiece, the *Arbitration*.

In this, our third play, Menander rises to new heights, for now

the original misunderstanding is put quite outside the play, the
hero and heroine probably did not appear at all except in the fourth
act, and the minor characters and slaves are given a new importance. They do not merely pursue loyally the interest of their masters, but take independent action like their betters. It happens that
in each case their independent action contributes to further the
main theme. In each scene, too, Menander shows us a contrast of
character. On one side is generosity, philanthropy, and concern for
social justice; on the other is a shortsighted selfishness that would
disrupt society and deserves to be defeated. Decisions are made in
every scene, and the plot is so constructed that all generous decisions turn out also to have been expedient. Mean characters are
both stupid and unsuccessful. Any satirical laughter is produced at
their expense. There is no overt quarrel between husband and
wife, but a separation is sought by the husband's confidential slave
and by the wife's father. Husband and wife must rise above the
common level of prudential and self-regarding considerations in
order to disappoint and defeat those who presume to act for them.
The play is kept lively and comic, as in the *Shearing,* by letting inferiors represent the hero and heroine.

The heroine, Pamphila, is passive, misunderstood, and good.
Like Penelope, she clings to her husband when to others the case
seems hopeless. The husband Charisius has a complicated psychological experience. He believes himself superior to others, and is
publicly unmasked, but profits by the lesson. Humiliation leads to
despair, reflection, and resolute action. Charisius, like Achilles,
loses a loved one and passes from grief to anger at the only opponent he can find. He began as a philosopher whose sin was pride.
He ends the play on a new level, having passed through the ordeal
of initiation into the mysteries of love. Like Lynceus in the *Suppliants* of Aeschylus, he is transformed from a ravisher of women
into a considerate and devoted husband. He will not offend again,
because he will not proudly demand of others a superhuman in-
fallibility. Love is a force in his life that destroys self-esteem and
breeds loyalty to a truly rational ideal that is strengthened by love

of wife and child. The importance of personality is abundantly stressed in the play.[22]

Not only is Pamphila represented as deserving happiness when she asserts her personal code of loyalty, but the novel notion is presented that an infant has rights that are entitled to respect. Even the foundling is entitled to claim personal property and a chance to better his condition. The play takes its name from an arbitration that concerns him. The decision of the arbiter may be bad law, as Quintilian hints, but it illustrates all the better Menander's belief in the importance of sympathy, decency, and loyalty to humane principles, regardless of law, prudence, or custom. We begin the play with a husband, wife, and babe thoroughly separated. The baby has been exposed in a thicket with small hope of survival or happiness. Charisius is living apart from his wife and pretending to revel with the harp girl Habrotonon. Pamphila remains alone and deserted except for her father, to whom she dares not confess the truth any more than she had confessed to her husband. Ten months before the play begins she had been present as a spectator at a riotous night festival where, no doubt, as at spring rituals all over the world, the urge to assist and share in the promotion of fertility became licentious. She was violated by a drunken youth and bore a son five months after marriage. When we recollect that she was presumably no more than fifteen years old at marriage, it will not surprise us that she said nothing and allowed the babe to be exposed. The indignities to which an unchaste wife or daughter was exposed at Athens were unlimited. The audience were no doubt informed in a delayed prologue that the father of the babe was Charisius himself, but until this fact was known it helped neither husband, wife, nor child. They must help themselves first.[23]

Charisius had not told his wife of his drunken adventure. It is not likely that it seemed important to him, for Athens was full of women who were fair game for riotous youth, and riotous youth did not always exercise sober judgment before experience brought discretion. Nor did he, like Polemon, publish his outraged honor to the world by violent action. Charisius knew that Pamphila had

had a baby because his slave Onesimus, taking his master's part, had told him. Charisius was proud and reticent and therefore spoke neither to his wife nor to her father Smicrines. Smicrines discovered that something was wrong only when he heard of Charisius' attempt to drown his sorrows in company with Habrotonon, a harp girl for whose hire he paid twelve drachmas a day. Since Smicrines knew nothing of Pamphila's baby, he could hardly be expected to understand the behavior of Charisius. Nor was Charisius' behavior intelligible to the friend in whose house he entertained the harp girl or to Habrotonon herself, for Charisius treated the girl with the most distant discourtesy. He was retaliating against his wife, and his heart was not in the work.

Thus the way was open for would-be rivals to woo Habrotonon. Unfortunately, the part of Chaerestratus in the play is not clear. It was undoubtedly he in whose house Charisius was pretending to revel. Chaerestratus had either a philosophic friend or slave tutor, Simias, who strongly disapproved of the interest both of Chaerestratus and of Charisius in the harp girl, and who tried to restore harmony not only between them but between Smicrines and Charisius. In the end it is probable that Chaerestratus was made by a stern parent to marry for his own good and that Habrotonon found freedom and a protector either in the virtuous Simias or in the stern parent. Even without the scenes in which these characters were important we can appreciate the subtlety of Menander's plot and characterization.

As far as the main theme is concerned we can follow the action act by act. The scene is set with two houses, a house of mirth where Chaerestratus entertains Charisius and the harp girl, and a house of mourning where Pamphila sits and waits. She is cut off from everyone except her father Smicrines and her nurse Sophrona. The latter had presumably assisted with the baby. Each act is different in tone from the preceding, for we see the situation from many angles. At first, the cook or caterer and Charisius' slave Onesimus give us a backstairs view of the impending divorce. No limit need be set to their malicious wit and censoriousness. The more unkind

they are, the more we shall sympathize in serious scenes. Clare
Boothe Luce used the same method in her modern play *The
Women*. When Smicrines appears, Onesimus and the friends of
Charisius resent and resist his attempt to investigate. Simias would
want a reconciliation between husband and wife for moral reasons.
Chaerestratus was presumably interested in getting Habrotonon
for himself, and so would also be glad to see Charisius safely lodged
at home again.

Onesimus, however, really had everything to fear from a reconciliation, for he shared the secret of Pamphila's baby that had been
exposed. He might be sold to the mines or for export only. A
Roman confidential slave who knew too much might be crucified
with tongue torn out, but it is not likely that an Athenian could
have afforded such extravagance, or that he would have been so
unnecessarily brutal. Onesimus had assumed when he reported
Pamphila's plight that his master would reward him for his zeal.
He is fond of philosophic jargon, but the slave is contrasted with
his master, for he has no real understanding of Charisius' generous
nature. He apes philosophy but is a Thersites at heart. The cook is,
as usual, a scurrilous and witty character, ready to take a low view
of anything that happens and to embroider the worst gossip. At
first, Smicrines is restrained by his daughter Pamphila, but is justi-
fiably alarmed when his son-in-law continues to spend money ex-
travagantly and is deaf to all appeals for an explanation. Smicrines was from the Greek point of view ungenerous in being more
anxious to preserve his daughter's dowry than to secure an understanding between husband and wife.

Thus the separation of husband, wife, and baby was made sufficiently clear at the end of the first act. The reëntanglement begins
with the appearance of the baby on the stage in Act II, but for two
acts the baby, while advancing his own status, seems to be driving
deeper the separation between Charisius and Pamphila. The audience are in a position to appreciate the irony of this, since they have
probably been warned in a prologue what to expect, but the play
is equally effective in Gilbert Murray's restored version, where

there is no such warning. It must not be supposed that because the infant makes no conscious decision he is not a force in the play. Babies hardly appear on the stage in comedy after Menander, but their appeal will be clear when we consider how much is made of childbirth and of engaging youngsters in moving pictures, where such scenes can be presented convincingly. There are practical reasons for not introducing babies in realistic stage plays. Babies nevertheless exercise tyrannical power in real life over those who love them, and there is no reason why this power of theirs should not be felt as a force in dramatic imitations of life. They are natural and unsophisticated, and a natural and unsophisticated picture of life will include them.

Actually, the plot of the *Arbitration* seems to be a plot of the baby to secure his lawful place as a citizen of Athens in a home where love and justice reign. His only power is to inspire his elders with sympathy by his silent appeal for love and justice, yet the construction of the play is all founded on him and the theme of his progress. He is even more important than the baby of the *Samia*, for that baby has not lost his parents. They do their best to protect him throughout the play. In the *Arbitration* the baby's whole future and even his life depend on the consideration and honesty of random strangers. The arbitration scene in which the baby first appears is central to the plot and rightly provides a designation for the play. In it we find ourselves escaping from the limitations of the domestic theme that normally circumscribe New Comedy, for principles of justice and philanthropy are stressed and a contrast is provided between those who are and those who are not loyal to them. Thus the theme that inspired all Athenian tragedies about suppliants is still heard in Menander's comedy.

There is also a pronounced pastoral effect in this act, since the slaves who dispute possession of the baby are rustics, one a goatherd and one a charcoal-burner, Davus the stupid import from the cold north and Syriscus whose name bewrays him as Semitic and clever. Though the time has passed when citizen charcoal-burners could determine Athenian policy, as in Aristophanes' *Acharnians*, Menander admits slaves to the realm of justice and virtue. Smicrines, to whom they appeal, is at first shocked like his prototype Theognis at the suggestion that men in goatskins have any concern with civilized practices or with appeals to law. He relents, however, as if by a whim, and because he can see what is right when his money is not at stake, he awards the baby to Syriscus and so assures its ultimate recognition by himself as grandson in the fifth act. The moral is plain: acts in support of right and justice are never wholly disinterested. The whole structure of human welfare depends on individual loyalty to principle even when the individual seems not to be directly concerned. Even slaves may and should preserve the interests of citizens and so serve their own. The natural slave will remain a slave, but the slave who is generous like a free man will ultimately gain freedom. Menander's philanthropic ideal is old-fashioned in a world that has abolished slavery, but he is not far from Christian ideals as preached by Paul of Tarsus. Since that time the individual has grown more important, and the whole is less and less.[24]

Davus had found the baby and some keepsakes. He had let Syriscus have the baby, for Syriscus had a wife who could nurse it, but had kept the property. Syriscus wins his case by claiming the property not for himself but for his charge, and by stressing the babe's right to life, liberty, and personal prowess. The arbitration scene, though it is almost static, will hold an audience entranced by its presentation of the rights of man in miniature. The act ends when Syriscus is confronted by a new attempt, so it seems to him, to defraud the baby. Onesimus, watching as inventory is taken, claims a ring that was exposed with the baby as his master's, who lost it while drunk at a spring festival.

In the third act the plot thickens, for with the ring comes interest in detection and exposure. Was Charisius really father of the babe that was identified only by his ring? Onesimus was afraid to take the risk of exposing him. The slave was at his master's mercy.

Habrotonon, however, was only hired, and she had no reason to love Charisius, for he had scorned her charms. She proposes to wear the ring and to lure Charisius into admitting his responsibility. For that she must pretend that the baby is her own. Onesimus hardly trusts her not to keep the child, for Charisius must buy her freedom and support her if he acknowledges a child by her, but at any rate, Onesimus argues, there will be at least no danger of a reconciliation between Charisius and Pamphila, for she will leave her husband once he raises the harp girl to the status of concubine with children. The trick is played. Charisius falls into the trap. The scandal is immediate. The party breaks up, and as the cook leaves, Smicrines learns from him of the insult to his daughter. Wealthy wives did not tolerate husbands who kept two establishments, and he assumes like Onesimus that Pamphila will now leave home, even though he knows nothing of her own baby.

The intrigue of Habrotonon is as bold and unscrupulous as any in Plautus, but it is justified by the good-will of the harp girl, who thinks that she knows the mother and intends to find her as soon as she is sure of the man. Charisius is in the position of Molière's Tartuffe. His predicament is shocking precisely because he had proudly put on airs as a person of superior virtue. The tables have been neatly turned. He knows now what it is like to be an unwilling parent, as well as his wife does. But conviction of sin may be a salutary prelude to repentance and reform. His psychological discovery of himself, of his wife in a new light, and of a new standard of living that judges worth by qualities, not by accidents, is reserved for the next act. The baby is now secure, though not yet a citizen; but the success of the baby seems to have made the break between the parents irreparable.

The fourth act rises to the level of tragedy or a modern problem play and suddenly makes the happiness of Pamphila and Charisius seem momentous. Pamphila's loyalty is thrown into relief. Of her argument with her father we have only two lines in the Greek, but in them her voice is soft, gentle, and low, very different from the explosive indignation of Glycera in the *Shearing*. Pamphila is determined, however, to exercise her privilege as a married woman and decide for herself whether or not to leave her husband.

She will not be treated by her father as a slave who must obey without argument. Smicrines presents the case as strongly as he can. Charisius will be ruined if he purchases the harp girl, sets her free, and attempts to maintain two establishments. It will be even worse if he keeps two women in one house or himself abandons Pamphila. Smicrines is furious when Pamphila maintains that marriage is a life partnership for better for worse, for richer for poorer. She will remain faithful, no matter what her husband has done. As soon as Smicrines goes, she is rewarded by events, for her baby appears in the arms of the harp girl and is recognized. Habrotonon and Pamphila are allies, not rivals, and the baby's weight is now thrown into the scale of marriage as against divorce. The two women go together into the house of Charisius, where the baby will stay permanently, though Habrotonon will have to leave before the play ends.[25]

Now we see Charisius facing his moral problem. He has perforce accepted responsibility for Habrotonon and her baby. Shall he keep Pamphila too in spite of her premarital experience? It is Onesimus who tells the audience of the storm of emotion that shook the husband when on top of the shattering effect of the discovery of his own delinquency he learned of his wife's resolve to forgive him and uphold a lofty ideal of marriage. Onesimus is more frightened than ever as he sees which way Charisius is moving. He hides as Charisius comes out and lays bare his new mood of repentance. He had overheard Pamphila's argument with her father and now sees that his own philosophy was a matter of study and of being thought, not being, virtuous and wise. Since Smicrines will almost certainly return with stronger forces to remove Pamphila, Charisius at first regards Pamphila as lost.

As he reflects, however, on the treatment that she may expect to receive from her hardheaded, hardhearted father, he forgets himself and resolves to face Smicrines. His abasement finds relief in anger as had that of Achilles. As Charisius strides across the stage in fighting mood, he suddenly spies Onesimus. He berates the slave and would have beaten him if Habrotonon had not intercepted the angry man with news that she had pretended to be wronged merely to entrap him. His rage here is highly comic since atonement has already been made. He is finally persuaded that the baby is still his, though also Pamphila's, and goes within to join wife and son. It should be noted that the identity of the baby's mother does not affect the problem at the moment when Charisius makes his decision. He has learned to value his wife's permanent worth, regardless of accidents. His decision is no doubt made easy to carry out by the discovery that it was he who had wronged Pamphila, but there is no reason to suppose that he would not have carried it out in any case.[26]

It is not so much husband or wife as the baby who profits by the discovery that he can be accepted as the third member of a moral triangle, the firm-based symbol of a Greek matrimonial unit. The fifth act is concerned with the final establishment of his position and a general tucking in of loose ends. We do not know how Habrotonon was removed from her threatening position in the house of husband and wife. She was probably not married off, but put in charge of some elderly and safe protector. We have his remark: "He [Charisius or Chaerestratus?] would not have kept his hands off a girl like that, but I will." Nor is it likely that husband and wife appeared together anywhere in the play. The final triumph of the baby, which removes the last threat to the united family, comes when the grandfather Smicrines is disarmed. Since he, Onesimus, and Sophrona are all inferior either morally or socially, we may descend again to the level of comedy.

Smicrines comes on the stage in a fury of determination to save his daughter willy-nilly. Sophrona provides an outlet for his fury, since she has ventured to remonstrate. He shakes her vigorously, as the rhythm of the lines indicates, and threatens her with an all-night ducking. When he knocks at the door, Onesimus intervenes. His presence is a surprise, for it indicates that Charisius is at home. In the *Alcestis* the drunken Heracles had tried to cheer up a gloomy slave by giving him a lesson in philosophy. Onesimus gives the same kind of lesson to Smicrines. Whether he is drunk or not, his philosophy is a comic mixture of Stoic and Epicurean. One hopes that Epicurus and Zeno were both in the audience when this play was produced, for, starting with the Epicurean doctrine that the gods cannot concern themselves with mortal rewards and punishments, Onesimus concludes that they have given men a mentor that should guide them from within and will bring retribution if it is not obeyed, obviously a Stoic doctrine. The fury of Smicrines is not allayed by this piece of impudence, but Onesimus has a trump, the baby. Sophrona now gets her revenge by joining in the sport of baiting Smicrines until he sees that he is beaten and calms down. Thus the play descends from the tragic level of Act IV before it closes with an empty stage.

There is much that is new in Menander and much that was beyond the power of Latin writers of comedy to assimilate. Menander's vivid and charming pictures of women as unmoved movers are not repeated in ancient literature, as far as we know. His emphasis on the love of good women as a refining fire by which men learn to know themselves and their duty better seems incredibly modern. There is nothing quite like it either in Molière or in Shakespeare. Nor do we find elsewhere the same interest in the lives of humble characters. Slaves in Menander make decisions and are generous or base almost to the same degree as citizens. His use of babies as symbols of married union gives a peculiar color to his dramas.

No other dramatist ever displayed such a varied and moving specimen of human life in so little space, for Menander seems to write a kind of dramatic shorthand. His characters show their quality almost instantly, and they are in the briefest space endowed with traits that make them anything but typical fathers, mothers, slaves, mistresses, or sons and daughters. By a free use of monologues and asides Menander lets us see the action that goes on in the minds of his men and women. Thus the psychology of his people explains their behavior and makes his plays rather a representation of the forces that operate inside them than a depiction of external accidents.[27]

A modern novelist like Dickens writes much more nearly in the spirit of Menander than do writers of either the English comedy of manners or ancient Greek prose fiction. Dickens' criticism of the social and economic pattern of life is, however, foreign to Menander. On the other hand, Menander has a special interest in the problems of family life, the tension between one generation and the next or between one sex and the other. He makes a new use of repentance. Smicrines, to be sure, is made a target for jeers and condemnation rather like Xerxes or Creon. Fathers, however, may feel tender about their children after they have been too harsh and may come to a better understanding. Comedy does not deal with irreparable losses. Men in particular undergo a repentance that is fruitful in better relations with their wives. Orestes and Electra repented too late in Euripides' *Electra.* Lynceus in the Danaid trilogy of Aeschylus, Admetus in the *Alcestis,* and Neoptolemus in the *Philoctetes* changed their minds for the better, but the course of their emotions at the moment of change is not charted with the skill that Menander employs. Thus the pattern of regeneration—sin, repentance, and reform—remained to be exploited by him. He gives us a model of the satyr and of the civilized respectful husband in the same character instead of in two. Such a change involves the growth of personality.

Since Menander was limited to a scant two hours or less in his plays, he could produce his varied and profound impression only · by quickening the tempo of life as he depicted it on the stage. Such increased speed inevitably reduces the scale of events, just as the scale of a mountainous landscape is commonly reduced in stereo-scopic views without changing the proportions. Just as puppies and kittens at play amuse us by their antics and appeal at the same time to our tender feelings, so Menander's men, women, and babies, though they reproduce the contours of life, inspire humorous laughter quite apart from any matter in the plays. Menander's personages are as lively as those of Aristophanes and more lifelike. They are as moral as those of Homer and Sophocles but less heroic, and they are not concerned with physical pain and death. They are concerned with breaches in the texture of civilized living. It is not surprising that Menander's name was used as a label for the blissful life of cities at peace in a fertile land. Menander seems to have written to please himself. At least he did not often win the prizes that were awarded by the plaudits of the multitude, and he did not write for money. He wrote rapidly in a style that was almost classical and at the same time almost conversational in spite of the meter. He increased the respect accorded to Athens at a time when most of her glory was in the past and when her wealth and power were overshadowed by the successors of Alexander. He is said to have refused to visit Alexandria when he was invited by King Ptolemy, and for that reason, if for no other, he must be classed as the last of the great Athenians rather than as a forerunner of Alexandrian literature. Alexandria could hardly hope to challenge the literary supremacy of Athens as long as Menander lived.[28]

When the characters of tragedy ceased to take themselves seriously and became mere idiots dancing in the wind, Menander filled the gap by making comedy a serious and moral commentary on what men do and what they ought to do. His superiority to competitors and imitators was as marked as is that of Shakespeare in English literature.

IX
Aristotle and the
Philosophy of Fiction

It seems safe to say that Aristotle's *Poetics* has received more consideration than any other single work of literary criticism. It is still treated by some scholars as a gospel that is valid today. Original writers do not regard it so highly. Indeed, though it is essential to study Aristotle and Greek fiction together if one is to understand either of them, one result of such study is the conviction that Aristotle is but a pedestrian guide to Greek poetry. Who now will accept his assumption that there is one best form of tragedy or of any other kind of writing? Certainly no one will maintain that Greek writers exhausted the possibilities of tragedy or epic. Relativity, progress, and variety are visible to us in the work of Greek poets and still more in the work of modern writers. We value in Aeschylus and Euripides qualities that are unnoted by Aristotle. We compare Homer and Sophocles with Shakespeare and Occidental with Oriental literature. Our wider horizon inevitably gives us new and wider views, especially since we stand on Aristotle's shoulders.[1]

Since Aristotle preferred a complex plot in tragedy, it is a reasonable conclusion that the *Oedipus Tyrannus* of Sophocles was for him a model tragedy, for there is no other extant Greek tragic plot in which recognition of personal identity leads to disaster. There is, to be sure, recognition of facts in other tragedies. Theseus recognizes the innocence of Hippolytus in Euripides' play and Jason discovers the deceit and power of Medea, but in such cases recognition is rather a result than a cause of the central tragedy.

[1] For notes to chapter ix see pages 317–322.

245

The *Oedipus Tyrannus* has also the most striking self-caused peripety in Greek tragedy. In any case, this play not only conforms to Aristotle's canons, but is most conspicuously cited by him to illustrate his points.

Aristotle follows in the *Poetics* the principles that were dear to him in biology. He looked for distinct species and found the ideal of each species in its most perfect specimen. He did not expect further evolution, nor had he any strong romantic interest in what he took to be merely immature stages of development. The fact that every work of art is unique was little regarded by him. He even discusses a part of the action, the recognition scene, as if it were a separate entity, and as if there were one best kind. He misses the obvious consideration that a scene that is good in one play would not necessarily be good in another, and that to repeat one best scene would be fatal to the interest of artist and reader alike.[2]

Nor was Aristotle much interested in psychological analysis. In his scheme the normal or best character controls his emotions and behaves virtuously in accordance with Greek social standards. The philosopher had little sympathy with or interest in those who did not conform. Aristotle treats works of fiction for the most part by objective analysis—as specimens rather than as channels of power conveyed from the author to the actor or reciter and through him to an audience. Such a view of Homer had appeared in the *Ion* of Plato; he uses as an illustration the power of the magnet, which magnetizes a whole series of links. Aristotle is aware, to be sure, that a writer must feel what he writes if he is to move the hearer, and he believes that the function of tragedy is to produce through emotion an effect in the hearer that he calls *catharsis*. Yet, by speaking of action or myth as the life or soul of tragedy and by treating action as something distinct from character and psychology he seems to give his sanction to the kind of fiction that would move the spectator merely by its choice of incidents, and to the kind of criticism that is more concerned with the arrangement of events in a probable or necessary sequence than in the effect on the audience. He holds that the bald theme of a drama should be strikingly tragic in itself. Actually, the crude disasters of daily life are often poor material for art. It is the psychological and moral insight of Sophocles that makes his *Oedipus* great.

We may either consider a play as an objective depiction of action in which some pattern of cause and effect is the organic clue—what Aristotle calls its life—or as a means of communicating a certain excitement, felt by the poet, from him to his audience. Aristotle seems to want it both ways with no attempt to reconcile form and function in his theory. Hence he can say that Euripides is most tragic in spite of his poor construction, for he does not consider how the supposedly poor construction helps to produce a tragic effect.[3]

It is true that almost any charge that is brought against Aristotle can be met by pointing to some passing observation which shows that he was aware of a point that is not central in his treatment. Furthermore, a whole theory of aesthetics may be erected by a sufficiently determined philosopher on the basis of Aristotle's scattered observations. Yet his inconsistencies and his silences give the impression that he had no carefully considered philosophy of fiction, or indeed any philosophy of art in general. In art as in psychology he stops short of subtlety in his account of inner experience. Certainly the *Poetics* is almost entirely concerned with what we should call technique and not with philosophy of fiction or with the psychology of art. It is a handbook for those who would write Greek tragedy, as the *Rhetoric* is a handbook for orators.

Since Greek tragedy was written in verse, the *Poetics* has something to say about poetry in the chapters on diction, but it is emphatically not a treatise on poetry in the modern sense of the word. One who seeks initiation into the mysteries either of poetry or of philosophy in the *Poetics* of Aristotle will be sadly disappointed. In any case, we have lost so completely, except for Plato, the work of Aristotle's predecessors—poets, sophists, and philosophers—that we frequently lack a context in which to place his statements. What does he mean by *mimêsis, êthos, pathos, catharsis,* and many other words that are used with a variety of meanings in Greek and that have remarkably different meanings in different contexts? There is much that is unexplained in the *Poetics* and much that is explained differently by different scholars. I hope to bring some new considerations to bear and to make some points clearer.

Aristotle classifies tragedy and comedy as subdivisions of drama, and drama as a subdivision of verbal fiction, while fiction itself is a species of *mimêsis* or imitation. Painting, sculpture, dancing, and music are also mimetic arts, according to Aristotle. In drama, comedy is distinguished from tragedy by its treatment of character, though Aristotle elsewhere would prefer to distinguish plays by the kind of plot. It was the second book of the *Poetics* that dealt with comedy, whether comedy of laughter or comedy of happy endings; and that is lost to us. Epic is distinguished from drama by its means of communication—through words alone without actors.

Aristotle does not raise the question how *mimêsis* is related to art in general and to the beautiful. He omits consideration of architecture, which, being functional or formative rather than mimetic, is not included in his classification. The inclusion of music as a kind of mimesis with sculpture, painting, and dancing proves that 'mimetic' did not mean for him what 'representational' does for us. We must note that for Aristotle symbols are presumably mimetic, since he says in the *Rhetoric* that a word is a *mimêsis*. When sounds and gestures are naturally expressive, they may be termed mimetic, though it is a nice question how they are related to conventional symbols. Natural and conventional signs are both means of expression or communication, hence means of representation. It is perhaps idle to wonder whether song and dance that represent no specific feeling or purpose in the performers apart from a general interest in art are more, or less, mimetic than sad songs sung by sad people or gay dances danced by gay people. Art was presumably mimetic in Aristotle's sense when it was either symbolically or expressively representational or communicative. In any case, the two basic elements are, in his view, a natural instinct of mimicry and an equally natural love of harmony and rhythm.[4]

An audience has the pleasure of discovering what is meant by the representation in any mimetic medium as well as the pleasure that belongs to beauty and order. We can learn something of the function of art from Aristotle's acceptance in the *Politics* of a current classification of music as practical, ethical, or enthusiastic. The ethical is probably what we should call educational, communicating to the recipient habits of controlling passion that have value in civilized life. Practical music presumably was an aid in such activities as marching or working. Enthusiastic music gives free rein to emotion, but may relieve tension and so lead later to a more ordered life. Thus both the ethical and the enthusiastic are means of communication and have a certain practical value apart from any pleasure or entertainment that music provides. Of course, music that is subsidiary to serious activity is practical in a special sense. In any case, Aristotle's term *mimêsis* does not exclude consideration of art as functional, expressive, symbolic, or communicative, as well as representational. It begs no questions.[5]

We must note, however, that arts, such as music, dancing, and drama, which require human performers and are temporally extended, are in a different category from arts that produce artifacts, like painting or sculpture. In discussing Greek art we need not take into consideration the modern feat of recording on film the sight and sound of a dramatic performance. That is another matter. Music, dances, and even poems might have in ancient times a definite form though they were retained only in memory and no material notation of that form existed. In such a case there seems to be no artifact. Even where a notation of words, music, or movement exists, there must also be skilled performers if the artist is to communicate the work of his imagination. It is at need possible to dispense with performers only if the reader of notes or the hearer of words is capable of supplying a performance in imagination, interpreting what is seen in terms of sound or what is heard in terms of sight, and responding with the emotion and tension that would accompany performance.

Some secondary creation is required if the original is to be revived. The work of art exists potentially as long as there are means of reviving it, but it can be revived only in the imagination of someone capable of appreciating it. This statement applies also to a painting, or indeed to a game of chess, but in these cases either matter alone or form alone is more obviously the same in each revival. A work of art that requires performers will never be precisely the same at each performance. This is particularly true of drama, where the audience must respond if the actors are not to be ineffective.

The actual sense (or senses) through which the substance of a story or drama is received is not a matter of primary importance. Probably Theophrastus was right in holding that the sense of hearing is most emotional. Music is Dionysiac, while sculpture and painting are Apollonian. Possibly Theophrastus did not take into consideration the muscular senses with their aesthetic of action and tension. Fiction and dramatic performances appeal strongly to the muscular senses as well as to the emotions and to the moral sense, but the imagination must first be stirred through the medium of seeing or hearing, or both. Perception may lead not only to emotion and tension, but to thought and the resolve to act. Fiction as an art seeks a harmony of emotional and tensional excitement and relief. Only the performer in a dance or play has a physical sense of movement, attitude, effort, or accomplishment; accordingly, his muscular senses and feelings will be affected more immediately. On the other hand, he will feel his own part of the performance more keenly than the others, so that his imagination may be out of focus for the total effect.[6]

It does not matter whether a tale is told to the ear alone, as in modern radio broadcasts, or to the eye alone, as in the old silent moving pictures, though there is probably some connection between reason and light, which is so often a symbol of it; and Dionysiac orgies have a natural affinity for night and darkness. When music is combined with spectacle, the music seems to receive less attention, but it still produces effects of emotion and tension. Bodily reactions are notoriously responsive to imagined situations. Football substitutes watching a game have a strong sense of struggle and victory or defeat; the sugar content of their blood has been found to increase just as if they were playing. The sense of struggle is presumably less for spectators who have never had experience of actual combat, but even so some tension will be felt by anyone who is interested at all. One who has not danced himself need not be entirely deaf to musical rhythm or to the contagion of seen dances. In Greek drama the sense of movement, pose, deliberation, decision, struggle, and success or failure is strong. In all that the characters do, moreover, they make clear by their words the course of their thoughts and arguments. Such speech is indispensable if they are to be represented as reasoning. Obviously, a form of art without words cannot represent fully the motives that govern men or any philosophy that animates them. Hence words are needed if drama is to contain any serious treatment of the problems of life or to depict thinking men as free agents in pursuit of happiness.

Aristotle does not consider the psychology of the audience except for the mention of catharsis. He notes that dancers represent characters (*êthos*), incidents (*pathos*), and achievements (*praxis*). These three words are charged with multiple meanings. *Êthos* denotes normality, whether of environment, custom, or ideals. It includes ordinary life, good characters, and happy living, but may be extended from good to any kind of environment or character. When it is used for descriptions of character or for characterization in drama, it refers to bad characters and bad morals as well as good. *Pathos* means anything that happens, with a preference for the accidental, the emotional, and the disastrous. Accident, disease, and passion are all included in the Greek word *pathos*. The word refers equally to external events, to physical hurts, and to psychological storms. The wide range of meaning may produce confusion. Emotions, though they are *pathos,* something that happens to a character, are at the same time an element in *êthos* or characterization, morality, and right living. On the other hand, there is an implied contrast between *êthos,* the normal and desirable, and *pathos,* the abnormal and undesirable.[7]

Praxis, action or achievement, is also difficult to translate, because it has three aspects or tenses, like the English word 'business.' It includes action planned, action in progress, and the outcome of the action. The significance of Aristotle's demand that action in drama should have a beginning, a middle, and an end must not be missed. In its simplest form drama tells how something abnormal happens to a character, what he decides to do about it, and how his decision leads to success or failure, happiness or unhappiness. The sympathetic spectator experiences the need to act, the process of deliberation and decision, and the sense of victory or defeat. Drama so viewed is concerned, like religion and ethics, with ultimate happiness and unhappiness. Tragedy deals with unhappiness, comedy with happy outcomes. Aristotle rightly treats the art of fiction as a composite of all elements that enter into the problem of right living for individuals and communities, as well as the problem of happiness. Its aesthetic is an aesthetic of thought, emotion, and the sense of action or achievement; when it uses words, it may include all the profundities of poetry, science, and philosophy in its representation of human life.[8]

When Aristotle comes to the discussion of epic and drama, he analyzes the objects of representation as *mythos,* story or action, *éthos,* character, and *dianoia,* thought. His omission of *pathos* from this list is justified, for what happens to a character is part of the story or action, and what happens in him is an element of his *éthos.* The addition of thought as an object in drama is equally justified, for words have been added to the means of communication employed by dancers. Gestures or other elements in a representation without words give but an inadequate hint what some character is thinking. Aristotle seems, however, to find thought in the words of a deliberative or argumentative speech only, and does not distinguish between the sincere thought that leads to a decision within a character and the often insincere arguments by which one character seeks to influence another. Sincere thinking which leads to choice should belong to character in Aristotle's scheme, while clever arguments designed to deceive are but means to an end, a part of the action—not ethical, but rhetorical.

In the end, Aristotle refers his readers to the *Rhetoric* for an account of thought that may be useful to dramatists. Yet it is clear in earlier passages that deliberative thought was as much in his mind as argumentation. Aristotle must have expected his readers to turn to the *Ethics* in order to understand *êthos,* and there they would find a treatment of the part played by emotion, reason, and action in producing character and happiness. Character results when emotions are governed by reason. Character is displayed in drama whenever there is an indication of what a man's principles are, what he chooses to do or not to do. Aristotle should have separated thought that is a part of character from thought that is a part of action. Then he might distinguish within character the elements of emotion and reason.[9]

When he later makes a distinction between simple and complex plots he is really separating character and choice from action that is not determined by choice. There are two elements in the plot of a drama, first the action of the characters themselves, and secondly the pattern of events as far as they are not controlled by the characters. Aristotle might better have separated character and environment instead of character and action, for action results partly from the decisions of human actors, partly from the resistance of circumstance. Both characters and environment as presented in fiction are created by the author. When he creates character, psychological interest is uppermost. When he emphasizes the effect of environment, accident, or divine dispensation, he implicitly introduces some philosophical attitude of his own. Either psychological or philosophical depth may make a piece of fiction great. Conflict between individuals may be emphasized, or conflict between groups. Society may be shown in conflict with the individual or engaged in the struggle for social happiness. The individual in turn may be shown in opposition to social or political conditions or in profound opposition to God and nature. The fact that character and action overlap, that a good deal of the action in a drama is bound up with character, indicates a fundamental weakness in Aristotle's list of the objects of representation in drama.[10]

It is not difficult to divine, however, why he makes his distinctions as he does. Evidently he is thinking of Poetics as an art added to other arts or branches of study. He had already dealt with character in the Ethics and with thought or argument in the Rhetoric. The remainder was left for Poetics, which accordingly is in the first instance concerned with stories, plots, or actions, regardless of the connection of thought and character with action. Aristotle insists that the course of events as represented should show probable or necessary causal connection. He also notes the advantage of taking fictional themes from history and legend, since such themes give the impression of historical truth and consequently are more easily accepted as true accounts of life. In Greek poetic fiction the historical element is always prominent, and as a result any great work in it always involves incidentally an interpretation of history.

History as written may contain more or less of psychological and philosophical interpretation. Ideally, it should be possible to represent actual events as causally connected. As a matter of fact, the historian who leaves nothing unexplained may safely be accused of introducing an element of fiction into his history. Yet it is often possible to include a true account of motives and causes in history. As long as history aims solely to inform and fiction merely to entertain, the distinction is clear; but philosophy and psychology have a way of creeping in and obscuring the difference between imagination reconstructing the past and imagination fitting events to a pattern.

Certainly history as now written deals with action, character, and thought through the medium of words. In Aristotle's list of the six parts of tragedy there appear (besides action, character, and thought, the three objects of representation) two means of imitation—music and diction—and one manner of imitation—presentation to the eye, or spectacle. Thus spectacle includes the

arts of the dancer, the actor, the scene painter, and others concerned with production. Aristotle dismisses spectacle as being
less a product of art than the other parts and as involving, in any
case, arts that the poet does not control. Such arts could hardly be
learned from books. Aristotle deals briefly in the *Poetics* with the
art of composition in words, discussing elementary points of grammar and matters of style in his usual observant fashion, but with
no great insight either linguistic or poetic. He is content to leave
music to the specialists.[11]

The six parts of tragedy are thus the spheres of six arts that
contribute to the production of drama. Only four of them play
a part in the writing of epic or of drama as read but not performed. In these there is no music or spectacle, only story, character, thought, and diction. Aristotle is inclined to focus attention on the written words as the real drama. He is hardly fair
to music and spectacle, which had evidently a very important
part in the effect of Greek drama. Nor is diction the mere tool
that Aristotle implies, unless we are to agree that poetry is merely
prose embellished. Even when diction is realistic, it is as much an
object of imitation as character or thought, for it reproduces real
speech as heard in daily life. And if it is imaginative, how are
we to separate form and matter, end and means? Even dramatic
poetry may well be an end in itself.

For Aristotle the unity of a drama is an organic unity, like that
of an animal. The play is a single organic whole if its action, which
is its life or soul, has causal continuity from a beginning in events,
whereby the characters are forced to act, to an ending in success or failure. In either case, the characters are at the end no
longer under compulsion to act. But this way of regarding a
play as something objective is not enough, for a play is also a
medium of communication by which not only knowledge, but
power, passes from the imagination of the author to that of the
audience. It is usual, when we speak of the plot of a play, to mean
by plot the story or action as defined by Aristotle. There are really,
however, three kinds of plot that should be distinguished.

First there is the plot of character against character, which is also called intrigue and is well illustrated by *Agamemnon* and *Medea*. In these plays the action is almost wholly planned by Clytemnestra and Medea. These plays have, as Dr. Johnson said of Restoration drama, "intrigue for plot." In a second kind of play there is action not planned by any character, but only by the poet. In fact, the action of a complex play like the *Oedipus Tyrannus*, so far as it is anyone's plot, is a plot of the poet against his characters. Actually in both these cases the poet's purpose is to interest and influence his audience, so that the plot of the play is really a device of the poet for the purpose of producing a particular effect. The third type of plot, then, is the plot of the poet to enthrall his audience and to make them feel what he feels. Can we refuse to see a plot in a play like the *Trojan Women*, that has neither intrigue nor action in the ordinary sense, yet performs the cathartic function of tragedy extremely well? We must, I think, recognize the third and most important kind of plot, the plot of the author against his audience.

To avoid ambiguity, let us call this third kind of plot the design of the play. From this point of view the play is not an organism like an animal, but is organized like an artifice. It is an attempt to capture the imagination of reader or audience by the power of imaginative art and is a very special kind of communication. For great fiction belongs to the realm of imagination, and imagination may be fraught with power. Men are guided by their imaginations in creative moments, and great imaginative constructions in any field have a way of determining the future of individuals and nations. Plato was aware of this fact in a way that Aristotle seemingly was not. Imagination is an integrating factor in consciously self-directed life. It includes sensations and desires, calculations and plans, inspirations and loyalties, the sense of freedom and resolve, and the sense of triumph or dejection together with the whole gamut of emotion.

Thus the imagination combines all the elements of conscious life; it envisages possibilities and impossibilities as well as actualities; it may restrict itself to the level of sensation or to the realm of disinterested conceptual theory. It may combine sensation and thought, or embrace also the field of emotion, either concentrating on one emotion or balancing contrary emotions. The needs of the body, too, have a way of translating themselves into pictures. The thirsty man sees water everywhere; the hungry man is haunted by visions of beefsteak; and Saint Anthony had a comparable experience. Yet, as far as imagination is sensory, it invents no new elements, though new combinations and analogical extensions are possible. The range of possibilities is infinitely greater by comparison in the realm of conceptual thought. Mathematics seems to be a spontaneous creation of the mind. In this field, as in that of sense, the imagination may be uncontaminated by alien elements from the realm of action. Such purity of mood is, however, unstable, for interruptions demanding action come to all but the select few. The need to act is a felt need that also has its representation in the imagination. Possibilities of motion, impulse, effort, and achievement haunt the imagination when other drives are satisfied. Thus it is through the imagination that men become aware of their own impulsive and compulsive ideal loves or fears. I was once lost for hours on the face of a cliff where every move was dangerous. To feel fear physically would have been fatal. I was aware of my fear, however, the whole time, because my imagination painted me a picture of bare bones bleaching in the forest below that was too vivid to be ignored for a moment.

Thus imagination is a crystal ball into which we may gaze and see the truth about ourselves. Such truth is a kind of Aristotelian god, self-moving and self-contemplating, and possessing power to integrate subordinate powers and functions in subjection to itself. Such integrating constructions on the highest level may be present in connection with religion, art, or philosophy, either separately or in combination. Art is most faithful to the senses, philosophy to conceptual thinking, and religion to the rules of action in a world where we may be happy or unhappy, thwarted or successful. Literature, the art that uses words as a medium, is unique in its ability to include thought and truth in its imaginative constructions. It may, in fact, reduce the sensory medium to a minimum. The books that contain literature are often completely unsatisfying as objects of sense perception, yet contain in symbols the most sublime works of imagination. The greatest achievement of art is to convey a sense of freedom to act, though action must occur in a universe that severely limits the possibility of action. It is only in fiction using the medium of words that art can reproduce for the imagination a sense of creative action. Action is much more than motion. Painting and sculpture may convey a sense of motion, but they lack the element of temporal extension in their composition, so that they can give us motion only as it exists at one instant. Arts the medium of which admits temporal extension, such as music, dancing, drama, and other forms of fiction, are more lifelike in their constant shifting of mood. Dancing and music convey both a sense of motion and an artificial induced emotion in a changing experience and may even symbolically express religious or philosophic concepts. Still, words are needed if any adequate and illuminating process of thought is to be included in a work of art.

Art, then, is able to portray the working of a human mind in active life only in fiction, and such mental activity is one of the two main elements of fiction, as of life. The other is an objective series of events presented as items of sensory experience or as a sequence in thought. Only on the conceptual level of thought do we rise to the contemplation of events as causally connected. Even when fiction concerns itself only with a pattern of events as seen or known but not felt, the mature audience will expect to see causes producing effects somewhat as in life. For comic purposes the effects may be disproportionate to the causes. In tragedy likewise there may be a certain emphasis on irrationality in human fortune in order to stress human weakness and to produce that sense of frustration which is essential to great tragedy. There is a strong imaginative appeal, however, even in sequences that do not involve human actors, as in the subject matter of geology and astronomy. History is often presented in a dramatic pageant as if fate had its own pattern and determined the fortunes of men with cold impartiality. The Shakespearean play *Henry the Eighth* and *The Dynasts* of Thomas Hardy have this effect, reducing human desire and effort till they seem little more significant than the posturing of puppets.[12]

A work of fiction, then, involves the two patterns: that of events and that of human psychology—feeling, thought, and action. Each work of fiction implies in its emphasis and pattern a philosophic attitude toward life. It may be gaily or cynically unphilosophic or profoundly contemplative; in either case a philosophy of life is implied. This is attributable to the imaginative attitude of the author, and if its presentation in art is successful, the audience will revive in their imagination the experience of the author. The author in his presentation will be addressing an ideal audience. It is possible that no actual audience will be capable of appreciating his attempt to communicate. Certainly audiences will react quite differently to the same work of art according to the varying capacity and prepossessions of their own imaginative power. It follows that in order to appreciate a great work of fiction we must somehow attempt to enlarge our imagination until we can become the ideal audience for whom the author wrote. For Shakespeare we must become Elizabethans, for Homer we must become Greeks, for Chikamatsu we must become Japanese. Thus a knowledge of the author's mind and of the mind of those for whom he wrote is essential to the appreciation of fiction, and of poetry too, for that matter. It is well to underscore this point, since much nonsense is uttered and cherished by those who would isolate a work of art from its setting in the history of author and audience. In a work of fiction the morality or immorality of the characters must be appreciated or the philosophic implications will be missed. Homer's moral standards are not ours. If we apply our moral assessment to his characters, we shall never know the joy of understanding his imaginative depiction of life.

Philosophy and morality are embedded in the psychology of author and audience. But besides author and audience, in any work of fiction that has human characters, these characters have their own independent psychology. They laugh and weep, argue or ponder, face their fate with courage or despair, and play their part in the action. They may act on impulse, from habit, in response to the moral demands of society, or as asserters of a personal creed that defies society. The great characters of fiction have ambition and are aware of themselves as free agents. They ponder their own fate and that of mankind in poetic or philosophic mood. Thus the psychology and philosophy of the characters in a work of fiction may assume an importance greater than that of the pattern of events.

We have, then, in fiction two kinds of event, each of which is part of the action of the play: (1) the event that is not planned by any character, or at least not determined by the planned action of a character intending to produce the event; and (2) the event that *is* produced by the plans and foresight of some character. Among the later plays of Euripides are some, such as the *Trojan Women,* in which the characters have so little control over their destiny that the effect of the play is almost entirely emotional. Since Aristotle considered Euripides the most tragic of dramatists, he probably considered the plot in which the characters seem least to determine their own destiny as the most tragic. Greek drama in the end tended to concentrate on a depiction of action divorced from the psychology of the characters. Each character follows his own bent and the action is a resultant, but interest is concentrated on what happens to the characters rather than on what happens in them. In fact, Aristotle speaks of late plays as being largely characterless. It is not likely that any play dispensed with characterization. Aristotle probably meant that the psychology of the personages was not so depicted as to make them seem great or noble. For Aristotle, character results from the control of emotion by thought. When merely emotional figures were depicted in a play, Aristotle would have noted the absence of character that results from failure to control emotion.[13]

Aristotle's insistence that plays should be classified by distinctions of plot rather than by distinctions of character has its bearing on his failure to stress the psychological element in drama. The practical consideration that is involved in his discussion of the relative importance of plot and character in drama is this: if character is taken to be the important element, all serious plays which depict characters of heroic stature will be tragedies, as opposed to satirical or comic plays, which alone will be classed as comedies. By insisting on the importance of plot and distinguishing the tragic plot with unhappy ending from the ethical plot with its happy ending for good characters, Aristotle is enabled to exclude from the category of tragedy all plays with happy endings. Such plays, although they were commonly called tragedies, would thus be included by him among the comedies. It follows that such plays were chiefly discussed in the lost second book of the *Poetics,* which dealt with comedy. Hence, too, Aristotle can define tragedy as a kind of drama that arouses pity and fear, not merely as a kind of drama that deals with serious subjects or noble characters. Thus in the psychology of his audience the failure of the characters in the play is translated into a sense of frustration. Frustration is usually the final stage of the action of a tragedy; for, so far as the action concerns a single character, the beginning of the action is the external event that makes the character think and feel, the middle of the action is the thought, feeling, and decision of the character, and his success or failure after decision is the end of the action. Thus Aristotle lays great stress on the results of action as depicted. In fact, he creates a special category for the complex plot, that in which there is a sudden discovery that reverses the outcome and makes it unexpectedly happy or unhappy for the favored characters.[14]

To the modern critic it seems that Aristotle here again fails to grant due weight to psychology, for he does not include in his reversals any merely psychological discovery. Such a psychological pivot in the *Iliad* as Achilles' grief for Patroclus, and the consequent transfer of his anger from Agamemnon to Hector, does not, according to Aristotle, make the plot complex. It so happens, however, that in extant Greek tragedies there is usually a strong psychological appeal in moments of discovery. It is probably because of this circumstance that Aristotle put the complex play above both tragedy and comedy, since in practice poets produced strong effects in such scenes. His concept of the complex play ceased to be significant when plots were later, by Shakespeare and others, made regularly to hinge on psychological moments of repentance and discovery of self. On the other hand, his distinction of tragedy and comedy according to the outcome, happy or unhappy, is still with us. It is easy to see why the kind of complex plot that Aristotle loved has largely fallen out of fashion, for we prefer our psychology unmixed with either happy or unhappy accidents. Such a writer as Thomas Hardy, however, still emphasized the weakness of man by subjecting his characters to overwhelming and unexpected misfortunes.

It is an important point that Aristotle makes when he finds, as I think he does, the essence of tragedy in the sense of failure that it conveys. When the failure seems to involve all that is best in man, or to include the whole of mankind in one unrelieved picture of frustration, tragedy is most complete. In such tragedy the action is somehow a thing in itself, undetermined by human aspirations or plans. The characters in such a play may be good or bad, but they can hardly appear great. Contrast with this the tragedy of a great character whose failure is due to a slight fault or miscalculation or even to a noble defiance of some person or institution that operates on a lower plane. Here the strength of man is emphasized and failure is redeemed by the splendor of the ideal loyalty that is depicted. The *Oedipus Tyrannus,* Aristotle's preferred tragedy, is a mixture of both types. Aristotle considers that the Sophoclean play with its great central character is better constructed than the more tragic Euripidean, of which there are good examples in the *Trojan Women* and the *Electra.* When there is no strong character in a play, pity may be great, but the effect is likely to be sentimental. The audience may take pleasure in the sad scene and shirk responsibility. A great character is needed for moral stimulus.[15]

It is only in his definition of tragedy that Aristotle regards the psychology of the audience, when he speaks of tragedy as using pity and fear to achieve its catharsis of such emotions. The emotions the catharsis of which is achieved are undoubtedly emotions felt by members of the audience. Aristotle might well have distinguished between the participation of the audience in the life of characters depicted in a play, especially when the portrayal is psychologically profound, and the emotion that is produced in the spectator by the mere sight of another's suffering or failure. He would perhaps have rated the sympathetic experience of the audience as ethical and so secondary to the tragic emotion which he considers essential. Since his account of catharsis was, probably, contained in the lost second book of the *Poetics,* scholars have been much exercised to define the term. It is a word that applies in Greek to any physical or mental process that produces a pure product or a state of health. Winnowing, churning, and the washing of clothes are purely physical. Secretion of semen and separation of other distinct organic products, such as bones, are physiological. The separation of conceptual thinking from emotion is psychological. As Anaxagoras pointed out, the mind must be unmixed in order to perform its function.[16]

Aristotle might conceivably be thinking in the *Poetics* of a physiological purgation at least secondarily, but so far as emotions are psychological, any catharsis of them belongs to the field of psychology. There are some striking passages in Plato that explain with great probability what Aristotle had in mind. In the pseudo-Platonic *Definitions* catharsis is defined as the separation of better from worse. This probably derives from a passage in Plato's *Sophist* in which examples are given such as sifting or winnowing. The means by which separation is effected in such cases is agitation. In the *Timaeus* Plato holds that fire, earth, air, and water in the physical universe are separated by pressure as liquid is separated from solid in the extraction of juice from grapes or oil from olives.[17]

It is, of course, the separation of the rational mind from physical and emotional elements that is most important to the philosopher. Plato says in the *Sophist* that *elenchus*, or logical analysis, is the greatest and most sovereign kind of catharsis or purification. We get further light from the *Timaeus*, where Plato recommends mental catharsis in addition to physical catharsis. The goal is mental as well as physical health. Catharsis is procured by motion or agitation and is of three kinds: internal; external and mild; external and drastic. In the physiological field the best catharsis is procured by motion from within, that is, by gymnastics. The second best is procured by motion superinduced from without upon the body as a whole, for instance riding in carriages or on ships. There is a character in Shakespeare's *Winter's Tale* who goes on a sea voyage to purge melancholy. The least desirable catharsis of the body is the violent and partial motion that is induced by drugs.[18]

Plato does not illustrate the corresponding psychological motions that procure mental health, but it is easy to see what they are. He has mentioned in the *Sophist* the mental gymnastics that are the best catharsis. In the *Laws* he recommends that babies under three years of age should be kept in constant motion as if on shipboard. No doubt he would have approved of cradles and baby carriages, though he mentions only rocking in the arms as a means of procuring internal calm and freedom from fear for the infant soul. He supports the argument by noting the curative use of Corybantic music and dancing for the insane. In both cases, he argues, fear is produced by mental cachexia. "When accordingly anyone treats such disturbed emotional conditions by external agitation, the motion that is brought to bear from the outside overcomes the internal commotion that belongs to fear or madness and so produces an evident peace and calm in the mind in contrast with the violent beating of the heart that had occurred in both cases. This altogether desirable result puts babies to sleep, and in the case of those who stay awake while they dance to the flute in company with the gods to whom severally men do worship with propitious rites, it produces for us a state of mental sanity in place of a condition of mental instability." Plato does not in the *Laws* altogether exclude tragedy or even comedy from his second-best state. In any case, it is clear that any cathartic effect of tragedy, if it is to be fitted into Plato's system of psychiatry, must be comparable to the settling and refining effect of external agitation, such as the sea voyage, rather than to mental exercise or violent, druglike shocks. Drugs and shocks even today are, however, used with success in treating mental depression, and such treatment corresponds to Plato's third kind of physical purgation, that by means of cathartics. The snake pit was once used for shock treatment of insanity.[19]

In view of this background it is likely that Aristotle assumed that for the perfect exercise of reason there must be a separation of rational and irrational elements. There may be some people so emotional that relief from emotion is the important thing. In the case of the sane, however, even if emotions had not threatened the rule of reason, it might be supposed that reason could still be somewhat purified and refined or, as we say, elevated. Emotion has its proper place, but it should not be in control. Minds may wander or become confused. Clarity of mental vision may come as a result of emotional disturbances. Thus the mind is able to see things in proper perspective as from a secure point of vantage. This is at least an intelligible account of the effect of tragedy on some people, and it is what Aristotle might be expected to mean by catharsis or clearing of the mind. The pleasure of a return to mental health by relief from confusing emotion or pain explains why we enjoy tragedies.

There is nothing in this view that conflicts with Aristotle's moral psychology. In the *Eudemian Ethics* vice is said to result from a failure of reason to control irrational impulses. Control seems to involve separation, and in the *De Anima* Aristotle approves the statement of Anaxagoras that the mind must be unmixed in order to prevail, that is, to know. There are, in fact, people who go to plays for a thrill or for a good cry, and modern psychiatrists are still exploring the therapeutic possibilities of dramatic expression. Minds obsessed by a complex actually find release by looking at the obsession as something objective. The objectification of emotion in art is just what is needed to enable a tormented soul to see life steadily and see it whole. There are those who do not enjoy tragedy. It is only the enjoyment of those who do that requires explanation. In their case an elevation of spirit comes with mingled pain and pleasure. It brings a sense of detachment from circumstance that leads to clear vision and power to act without emotional confusion.[20]

It may be asked why Aristotle did not go further and treat of art as a branch of the theoretic life and thus an activity of the highest value in itself apart from results. The answer is, I suppose, that aesthetic was not yet a full-grown branch of philosophy, and that intellectual beauty was for Aristotle as for Plato the highest form of beauty. The study of nature or mathematics led to beautiful results, and that was the kind of beauty with which the philosopher was mainly concerned. Philosophy had learned to use poetry and fiction, but had not yet recognized them as equals and friends rather than rivals and subordinates.[21]

To complete the interpretation of Aristotle's statement about catharsis, we need only observe that the pity and fear which are the means of purgation are artificial pity and fear operating, not blindly, but rationally, through contemplation of remote possibilities rather than through pressure of actualities. There is no reason, however, why they should not induce genuine compassion and caution, since the situations of art presumably have their counterparts in life. The ethical element in Sophocles' *Oedipus Tyrannus* is strongly marked. Oedipus' abnormal fears, which make him a prey to superstition and blindness, might well cause a fear of fear and a strengthening of the view that a calm and resolute mind is the best of oracles, as patriotism in Hector's creed was the best of omens. The emotions that are purged or separated are clearly any fears or griefs that make life hard for the spectator. Perhaps by "that sort of" emotions Aristotle means the emotions in the spectator that enable him to respond to the play when its depicted sorrows strike a responsive note in his breast. Assuming, then, that the figure in Aristotle's mind is one derived from winnowing or churning, that is, clarification by agitation, we may interpret his phrase somewhat as follows: "Tragedy produces its clarifying effect by bringing to bear on the mind imaginary scenes of grief and terror, thus freeing it from preoccupation with similar emotions of its own." [22]

The catharsis of tragedy, then, results in a clarification both of emotion and of thought, for emotion becomes objective in a work of art, and the mind is elevated so that it contemplates its own emotion and thus achieves imaginative freedom. The difference between Plato and Aristotle is that Plato would recognize two planes of reason, one on which the good is operative, and a lower plane that is conceptual or technical, and creative only when subordinated to the rule of *nous,* that is, creative intelligence. Aristotle objects to this separation of the two planes and the objects of thought in them, and treats reason as one in its function, though it may operate in two fields, the theoretical and the practical. [23]

Aristotle recognizes, however, other values in tragedy besides the cathartic and classifies tragedies, as a whole, according to their effect in four classes. The complex tragedy with its emphasis on misapprehension and the unexpected is at the top of his list. Such plays have a strong element of irony, for in them men appear as ignorant of their own good and as working always against themselves. He ranks second the merely tragic play in which a great and obstinate character is thwarted. Such a character is a rebel and is destroyed by self-will, not by the irony of fate. The third class is the ethical, in which success and failure are apportioned with poetic justice. Such plays please the audience but are not properly tragic. His fourth class is one that *we* should rate very high indeed, for it includes the *Prometheus* of Aeschylus. Sophocles spoke of the *onkos,* the majesty or imaginative grandeur of Aeschylus,

and I should read *onkos* for the meaningless letters that appear in
the text of the *Poetics*. Certainly the *Prometheus* has imaginative
grandeur, just the quality that we should define as poetic or even
tragic. Both Sophocles and Aristotle preferred realism.[24]

It remains to note again that Aristotle's philosophy was ill designed to evaluate the function of art and literature in human life.
The later Greek treatise *On the Sublime* marks a great advance
over his methods. Modern literary criticism tends to isolate its
subject matter from the rest of life; but philosophy is related to
fiction much as it is to history. Literary men and historians may
be philosophical, but the phenomena of fiction are as uncon-
trollable by the philosopher as the phenomena of history. I suggest that the historical effects of fiction might be more carefully
studied. Fiction may, in some cases, be said to have a religious
function. Biographical data might well be assembled in a *Varieties
of Literary Experience*. Above all, historical studies of the effect
of works of fiction on national patterns of behavior would help us
to assess the practical and philosophic importance of fiction. Our
object in such studies would not be to ban the kind of fiction that
does not contribute to our philosophic goal, but to attain a better
understanding of imagination as a force that directs individuals
and states. Many biographies of Chinese Communist leaders mention their being awakened by the fourteenth-century novel which
Pearl Buck in her translation calls *All Men Are Brothers*. The
story is rather like our tales of Robin Hood, but in the Chinese
novel banditry is glorified as an end rather than as a means to
the reëstablishment of justice. Japanese fiction glorifies loyalty,
whether to feudal superiors or to a religious code, but it does not
depict any successful resistance to authority, only courage and
patience under persecution, rather as mediaeval stories of martyrs
and saints do. Hindu literature is full of miracles and is emotional
or aesthetic rather than realistically moral.[25]

Religion or philosophy overshadows fiction in the Orient. Only
in Europe did realistic fiction come before philosophy, history, or
organized religion, for Homer was a realist in his depiction of

manners and morals. His greatest character is a free agent, a successful rebel against authority. Homer also contemplates the life of man from the vantage point of tragic irony. He makes his hearer feel the strength and weakness of many noble characters as from within them, yet at the same time forces him to contemplate them with detachment. Thus Homer achieves an elevation of spirit or catharsis that communicates itself to his readers and paves the way for philosophy. The sense of tragedy that he conveys is strong both in the historian Thucydides and in the philosopher Plato. For Aristotle, Homer is the great master of fiction who shows characters acting and suffering without apparently projecting himself into his story. Yet it is clear that Homer had a sure feeling for the values of life and has largely formed the European character as we know it—restless, rebellious, ever in love with some ideal that makes life glorious but short. When Aristotle says that fiction is more philosophic than history, he must be thinking of fiction as written by Homer. Events are nicely timed in both the *Iliad* and the *Odyssey*. Thucydides dramatized his history but omitted individual psychology. When history presents us with great characters as carefully studied as those of fiction, history too becomes a force in national and personal life, for history becomes what Plato terms the *real* tragedy, a work of the imagination which permits a member of the audience at any time to take his place upon the stage and become at once actor and, to some extent, author in a story that is never finished. The part that each man creates for himself may be moulded by his reading of fiction or history or philosophy. In any case, philosophy must take account of fiction and history and must also be present in them if they are to be great and permanent forces.[26]

Notes

ABBREVIATIONS

In these Notes the following abbreviations are used:

AJA American Journal of Archaeology

AJPh American Journal of Philology

CJ Classical Journal

CPh Classical Philology

CQ Classical Quarterly

CW Classical Weekly

HvdStCP Harvard Studies in Classical Philology

JHS Journal of Hellenic Studies

Phil. Philologus

R-E Pauly-Wissowa, Real-Encyclopädie

TAPhA Transactions (and Proceedings) of the American Philological Association

NOTES TO CHAPTER I
The Pattern of Success: Homer's *Odyssey*
Pages 1–26

[1] See Aristotle, *Poetics* 9.3: 51^b 5–10: "For this reason fiction is something more philosophical and more important than history. For fiction rather generalizes, while history relates particular events." It is possible to appreciate fiction without asking whether the author found his plot in actual life or invented it, just as we may enjoy the beauty of a garden or a landscape without knowing whether it was designed by man or is a product of nature. Beauty and art, like beauty and truth, are inextricably intertwined.

[2] It is not the least of the merits of Rhys Carpenter's Sather lectures (*Folk Tale, Fiction, and Saga in the Homeric Epics*, Univ. of California Press, 1946) that, in spite of his interest in the materials that Homer used, he sees clearly that the *Iliad* is an artistic whole. His argument (pp. 181–185) that the *Iliad* and the *Odyssey* cannot be the work of one author because they do not display the same attitude toward dogs was answered by John A. Scott in an article published after Scott's death: *CW* 41 (1947–1948) 226–228. To this article Cora E. Lutz adds a footnote in *CW* 43 (1949–1950) 89 f.

Ronald A. Knox, in a witty essay which purports to prove that the first and second parts of Bunyan's *Pilgrim's Progress* could not have been written by the same man, reduces to an absurdity most of the methods by which the *Iliad* and the *Odyssey* are assigned to separate authors. See the essay, "The Identity of the Pseudo-Bunyan," in *Essays in Satire* (London, 1928).

[3] See Matthew Arnold, *Culture and Anarchy*, chaps. iv and v.

[4] Since the discussion of Aristotle's *Poetics* in chapter ix amounts to a reasoned summary of my statements about it in earlier chapters, it will be convenient to postpone most of my notes to that chapter and to request the interested reader to refer to it for an account of my interpretation of Aristotle.

[5] Hannah More's views on the reading of Scott's prose and poetry are quoted from *Hannah More or Life in Hall and Cottage*, by Mrs. Helen C. Knight (New York, American Tract Society, 1862). Lady Murasaki's work has been brilliantly translated by Arthur Waley and published in various editions since 1926 by Houghton Mifflin (Boston and New York).

273

[6] For Solon see Plato, *Timaeus* 22b. Note Plato, *Epinomis* 987de for the statement that the Greeks improved the learning that they got from barbarians. For revision of religious practices by Solon see F. Jacoby, *CQ* 38 (1944) 73. For Cretan ignorance of Homer see Plato, *Laws* 3.680c. See Pindar, *Nemeans* 7.20–30 and Thucydides 1.9–11. Plato deals severely with Homer and drama in *Republic*, Books 2 and 10. He provides for censorship of tragedy in his second-best state in *Laws* 7.817a–d.

[7] Aristophanes puts into the mouth of Euripides the statement that a poet should be esteemed for his skill and good advice so far as he makes men better citizens (*Frogs* 1009 f.).

[8] Aristotle noted that the *Iliad* and the *Odyssey* alone of epics known to him had dramatic plots (*Poetics* 4.12:48^b 35 f.). For the argument from design see my articles, "The Moral Pattern in Homer," *TAPhA* 70 (1939) 158–190, and "The Divine in Homer," *Crozer Quarterly* 22 (1945) 20–27.

[9] See note 2 to chap. viii for references to fuller discussion of the ethical plot. For the *Orestes* see *Poetics* 25.31: 61^b 21. See also *On the Sublime* 29.2.

[10] See Plato, *Laws* 4.704d–707d, and for Athena, *Od.* 13.416–428. Odysseus considered (6.141–144) whether he should clasp Nausicaä's knees or address her from a distance. Penelope considered (23.85–87) whether she should embrace Odysseus at once or question him first. Caution prevailed in both cases.

[11] Agamemnon and Orestes are introduced in Book 1 and in Book 11 especially. Clytemnestra is mentioned by name in Books 3 and 11 and is cited as a model of evil in women in contrast to Penelope in *Od.* 24.192–202. Orestes is brought in as an example to Telemachus, Agamemnon as a warning to Odysseus, and Clytemnestra as a foil to Penelope.

[12] Penelope's right to stay on in her husband's house as long as his death is not certain, or until she chooses to leave of her own accord, is recognized by Telemachus (2.130–145). It would be sin to coerce her.

[13] The brilliant studies of Milman Parry in the technique of oral poetry enable us to appreciate the methods of Homer; but to conclude that, because the technique of modern Yugoslav epic is comparable to that of the Homeric poems, therefore no Homeric poet existed who was very different in capacity and achievement from modern oral poets, is a non sequitur. On this point see the review by Albert Bates Lord of Samuel Eliot Bassett, *The Poetry of Homer* (Sather Lectures; Univ. of California Press, 1938), in *AJPh* 68 (1947) 219–222, and Lord's article, "Homer, Parry, and Huso," *AJA* 52 (1948) 34–44. This last gives a complete bibliography of Milman Parry at the end. I see no reason to distinguish, as Lord does, between Homer the Poet and Homer the Oral Poet. Rhys Carpenter admires the work of Parry and at the same time speaks of Homer as the direct

spiritual ancestor of Attic tragedy: *op. cit.* (see note 2 above), pp. 6, 78–85, 166 f. Most of Homer's material was no doubt traditional, but the design that is impressed upon it by Homer is as original as the design of Sophocles' *Electra*. The fact that Aeschylus certainly, and Euripides probably, had used the same material before merely throws into relief the great originality of Sophocles.

[14] See *Od.* 19 for the meeting of Odysseus and Penelope.

[15] I have described the Greek attitude toward women and their behavior in an article, "Woman's Place in Menander's Athens," *TAPhA* 71 (1940) 420–459. The continuity of the Greek traditional ideal of feminine propriety is remarkable. There is very little difference between Homer and Menander if we allow for the lower level of the characters of the latter. Women have their sphere of life quite as separate and quite as circumscribed in Homer as later. For an account of monuments to Chinese widows see M. Huc, *A Journey through the Chinese Empire* (New York, 1855), pp. 46 f.

[16] See *Od.* 6.180–185, 18.255, 19.128, 15.16–23.

[17] For the Chinese play see the summary of *Mu Yang Chüan, The Shepherd's Pen*, in L. C. Arlington and Harold Acton, *Famous Chinese Plays* (Peiping, 1937).

[18] I owe the suggestion that Penelope may have recognized Odysseus from the first to A. M. Harmon of Yale University, who presented it in a presidential address delivered before the American Philological Association at Ann Arbor, Michigan, in 1939. The same idea is differently developed by P. W. Harsh, "Penelope and Odysseus in *Odyssey* XIX," *AJPh* 71 (1950) 1–21.

[19] Herodotus (1.60) tells the story how Phya, an unusually tall woman, represented Athena and was declared to be the goddess in person bringing Peisistratus back to Athens, when he made his triumphant return from exile. We need not suppose, as Herodotus does, that the Athenians really identified Phya with the goddess. She symbolized Peisistratus' policy of pacification and unity, and served to advertise his good intentions.

[20] Horace (*Ars Poetica* 191 f.) forbids the employment of a god from the machine unless there is a problem that justifies the interference. It is even more important to note that the problem that brings in the god is normally not the main theme, but a new difficulty that the poet introduces for the purpose. In Greek practice, gods may symbolize some human institution or virtue and so be brought on to point a moral. They often vindicate history or predict the future, which for spectators is, of course, the past. Sometimes they establish rituals, as in *Iphigeneia in Tauris*, where the poet carefully provides a misadventure for his characters in order to justify the

appearance of Athena. The late *Rhesus* might be thought to violate the canon of Horace, but the need to mourn the dead or to vindicate the dying, as Artemis does in the *Hippolytus*, should satisfy a candid critic. The Greek stage had no curtain, and either a funeral procession or an epiphany provides the play with a well-defined ending and removes the actors from the stage.

NOTES TO CHAPTER II
The Tragic Pattern of the *Iliad*
Pages 27–55

[1] For Aristotle see *Poetics* 23.1: 59ᵃ 20, ζῷον ἓν ὅλον. Alcidamas is quoted by Aristotle, *Rhet.* 3.3.4.

[2] It is convenient to refer to the treatise *On the Sublime* under the name of Longinus. *Iliad* and *Odyssey* are compared in chap. ix of Longinus. The author finds an example of sublimity in the *Odyssey* (11.543–567) in the silence of the ghost of Ajax, who is still angry with Odysseus. This is in 9.2: the reference in the next paragraph is to 9.7.

[3] For Sarpedon see *Iliad* 12.322–328; for Penelope, *Od.* 19.328–334; for Achilles, *Iliad* 9.410–416 and *Od.* 11.489–493. Plato criticizes Homer's view of death in *Rep.* 3.386a–388d.

[4] Plato, like Aristotle after him, regarded Homer as the originator and great master of tragedy: *Rep.* 10.595c and 598d. See Arnold's poem *To a Friend* (Oxford, 1909, p. 40).

[5] Simone Weil's essay was later issued as Politics Pamphlet 1: *The Iliad.* It appeared also, translated by Mary McCarthy, in *The Mint*, No. 2 (London, 1948), pp. 84–111. For Agrippa's remark see *Acts* 26:28, and compare Moffatt's translation (New York and London, 1926). See Bertrand Russell, "The Free Man's Worship," *Philosophical Essays* (London, 1910), pp. 59–70, and A. E. Housman *passim*, also Walt Whitman, "I Hear It Was Charged against Me," *Leaves of Grass* (New York, 1925), p. 107.

[6] Albert Schweitzer, *Indian Thought and Its Development* (London and New York, 1936), makes the distinction cited. For Japanese dramas of revenge see "The Soga Revenge," translated in F. A. Lombard, *An Outline History of the Japanese Drama* (London, 1928); and *Chushingura or Forty-seven Ronin* by Takeda Izumo, Miyoshi Shoraku, and Namiki Senryu, translated by Jukishi Inouye (Tokyo, 1937).

⁷ The poet's function is the same as stated in both *Iliad* and *Odyssey*, to instruct future generations by praising the good and exposing the bad: *Iliad* 6.344–358 and *Od.* 24.194–202.

⁸ Achilles stresses the fact that he is disinterested, as far as the justice of the war is concerned. He is seeking glory at the cost of life: *Iliad* 1.152–157 and 9.410–416. J. T. Sheppard brings out well the issue in the dispute of Book 1 in his study of significant epithets: "Zeus-Loved Achilles," *JHS* 55 (1935) 113–123. At *Iliad* 9.116–118 Agamemnon recognizes that Achilles is dear to Zeus. Odysseus makes it clear at 19.171–183 that Agamemnon was originally in the wrong. Achilles' repeated expression αὐτὸς ἀπούρας (1.356; cf. 1.507, 2.240), 'alone he took her,' stresses the self-will of Agamemnon and labels him as the first autocrat. See note 8 to chap. i for references to fuller discussion.

⁹ Andromache begins her temptation of Hector with the words (6.407) φθίσει σε τὸ σὸν μένος, 'it will kill you, that valor of yours.'

¹⁰ Helen's character appears in her conversations with Paris (3.383–447) and with Hector (6.312–368). Amphinomus has enough conscience to be uncomfortable. He protects the beggar (*Od.* 18.394–422) and would not slay Telemachus without the sanction of an oracle (16.394–406). He would not disregard a sign (20.240–247). Odysseus' attempt to warn him in time fails (18.118–157).

¹¹ For the connoisseur of bows see *Iliad* 6.321 f. and *Od.* 21.396–400. Achilles sings at *Iliad* 9.186–189. For the gods as an excuse for one's own fault see *Iliad* 3.64–66 (Paris); 6.357 and *Od.* 4.261 f. (Helen); *Iliad* 19.85–138 (Agamemnon); *Od.* 11.61 (Elpenor, who is termed half-witted at 10.553). No one is so modest in Homer, I believe, as to give the gods credit for his own praiseworthy achievements. It is rudeness when Agamemnon attributes Achilles' prowess entirely to divine assistance (*Iliad* 1.178). Courtesy or policy frequently leads one character to exonerate another by attributing sin or misfortune to the gods' action: Priam to Helen, *Iliad* 3.164; Nausicaä to Odysseus, *Od.* 6.187–190; Odysseus to the ghost of Ajax, 11.558–560; Telemachus of Phemius, *Od.* 1.348; Achilles of Agamemnon, *Iliad* 19.270–275. Homer himself makes Aphrodite a scapegoat for Helen in *Iliad* 3; Telemachus (*Od.* 17.118 f.) and Penelope (23.222) accept this view, though other characters blame Helen severely. Students of theology should note that these are all illustrations of character or technique and that Homer was aware, long before he put the sentiment into the mouth of Zeus in *Od.* 1.32–34, that mortals blame the gods for faults and miseries that they bring upon themselves. The gods themselves, of course, in turn blame fate when they find it inconvenient to do what they are expected to do.

[12] The Vaphio cups are in the National Museum, Athens. Replicas and illustrations are common. There is a good one for our purpose in Chrestos Tsountas and J. Irving Manatt, *The Mycenaean Age* (Boston and New York, 1897), pl. 19, facing p. 216. The vase to which I refer is illustrated in J. D. Beazley, "Attic Black-Figure," *Proc. Brit. Acad.* 14 (London, 1928) pl. 15.

[13] Walter Leaf's statement is found in his *Homer and History* (London, 1915), p. 17.

[14] See Diedrich Mülder's article, "Ilias," in *R-E* 9. He takes the opposite view from Leaf's, maintaining that the gods are always essential machinery. Note Herodotus 2.53.

[15] For Hephaestus see *Iliad* 21.342–382 and 1.571–600.

[16] For Thetis see *Iliad* 1.357–428 and 495–532; 18.35–147 and 380–467; 19.1–39; 24.1–140.

[17] Ares fights in *Iliad* 5 on the Trojan side. At *Iliad* 5.113–120 he is about to avenge his son Ascalaphus, who was slain fighting on the Achaean side. The story of Aphrodite's adultery with Ares is found in *Od.* 8.266–366. The judgment of Paris is referred to at *Iliad* 24.29 f.

[18] Agamemnon refers depreciatingly to Clytemnestra at *Iliad* 1.113–115. He demands recognition by Achilles that he is the more kingly at 9.160. Achilles uses the same word resentfully in his reply at 9.392.

[19] See Aristotle, *Poetics* 6.12: 50ᵃ 15–20 (action).

[20] See *Poetics* 13.1–6: 52ᵇ 28–53ᵃ 17 (double plot, triumphant villain).

[21] See *Poetics* 24.3: 59ᵇ 13–16 (plot of *Iliad*); 11.10: 52ᵇ 11–13. "*Pathos* [as a necessary element, at least in simple tragic plots] is a fatal or painful experience, for example, deaths in plain sight, intense sufferings, inflicting of wounds, and the like." Here the Greek word for suffering implies physical, not mental, agony. Nor are pity and fear, the emotions that according to Aristotle (11.7: 52ᵃ 38 f.) should be roused by tragedy, very accurate terms for the interest in conflict that is important both in ancient and in modern tragedy. The interplay of social and psychological forces or motives in scenes where two characters are opposed, or one character is drawn two ways, is largely ignored by Aristotle. Such scenes seem more important now than the pity and terror that he desiderates. In general, however, Aristotle preferred the same plays as modern critics, even when his reasons are differently put.

[22] For Hector's debates with Polydamas see *Iliad* 12.200–250 and 18.243–313. For Hector's soliloquy and decision see 22.98–130. In the second debate with Polydamas, Homer states plainly that Hector was wrong. In the earlier debate the plain statement made to Hector by Iris, speaking for Zeus and in her own person (11.200–209), justifies Hector's disregard of the omen. Just

so Priam in 24.171–187 receives an order and assurances from Zeus by the mouth of Iris in her own person. Later (217–227) he admits that his mission to Achilles would be too foolhardy to undertake except for her assurance. He would never have heeded a mere prophet or priest in such a case. Homer is careful not to create a precedent for successful disregard of omens, unless, to be sure, Iris appears in her own person to guarantee success. On the other hand, he inculcates a skeptical attitude toward professional interpreters of omens. He is a realist.

23 Since Achilles in the legend had a son old enough to fight within months of the time at which the *Iliad* ends, he must have been by inference at least middle-aged. Homer depicts him, however, as an untried youth who has never known failure. His character grows from Book 1, where he raises the point of honor against Agamemnon, through Book 9, where he proves that he is not merely seeking more compensation, and Books 18 and 19, where he displays not merely anger at another's offense but extreme shame and contrition at his own dishonorable and avoidable plight. His code of honor includes loyalty to a friend; thus friendship is added to honor as a theme. In Book 24, Achilles is generous to a foe; pity or humanity is added to the earlier themes. In a way this is a mere broadening of the base of honor from self to friend to humanity. Plato later ranged honor under the banner of reason or intelligence; clearly he was indebted to Homer for his start.

24 In my interpretation of Book 9 I follow S. E. Bassett, *The Poetry of Homer* (Sather Lectures; Univ. of California Press, 1938), as against C. M. Bowra, *Tradition and Design in the Iliad* (Oxford, 1930). Thetis is quoted by Achilles at 9.410–416.

25 For Gilgamesh see S. N. Kramer, "The Death of Gilgamesh," *Bull. Am. Schools of Oriental Research* 94 (April, 1944) 9. Heracles chose virtue rather than vice or pleasure (Xen. *Mem.* 2.1.21–33). Paris chose Aphrodite and the possession of Helen rather than Hera and her offer of empire over Asia or Athena and her offer of victory in war with Greece (Eur. *Trojan Women* 924–933). Solomon asked God for wisdom only, but God, approving his choice, added riches, wealth, and honor. Death of foes and long life for himself are also mentioned as possible choices (*Chronicles II* 1.7–12).

26 For Socrates see Plato, *Ap.* 28b–d; for Plato see *Epistle VII* 334e: "When a man makes the highest ideals his aim for himself and for his city, and accepts the consequences, in his death there is nothing ignoble or amiss"; for Demosthenes see *Or.* 18, "On the Crown," 199. Demosthenes takes not only this theme from Plato, but also the comparison of the defeated cause to a ship that has foundered because of a storm of unexpected violence (Plato, *Ep. VII* 351d). Plato compared Dion to a helmsman. Demosthenes

can argue that he, not being general, was not even at the helm (194). See Dante, *Inferno* 5.66. At *Iliad* 19.78, Agamemnon begins a long and muddled apology that is as lame as the wounded Agamemnon himself. Agamemnon is ignored later in the *Iliad*. Achilles refers to him contemptuously at 24.654, and Hermes echoes the sentiment at line 687. In the lower world at last Agamemnon recognizes the superiority of Achilles (*Od.* 24.35–97). Achilles refers to son and father in his lament for Patroclus (*Iliad* 19.315–337). He weeps for his father and Patroclus together in the presence of Priam (24.511 f.).

[27] For Lycaon see *Iliad* 21.34–119; for Achilles' love stronger than Hades, 22.376–394.

[28] *Iliad* 19.302. Homer likes to show two views of the same event. Sometimes he uses the Olympians to effect this result; sometimes he contributes information from his own knowledge of what is in the hearts of his characters or of what will happen to them later in his story. When the reader is allowed to know more than the characters, that is the essence of dramatic irony. Events in history may be termed ironical when knowledge of consequences gives the observer better insight than the actors had at the moment of acting. In J. A. K. Thomson, *Irony: An Historical Introduction* (London, 1927), there is a chapter on irony in Homer, but Thomson intentionally avoids definition and detailed analysis. See also G. G. Sedgewick, *Of Irony, Especially in Drama* (Univ. of Toronto Press, 1948). If terms are defined, the distinction between tragedy and irony or between comedy and irony will be clear enough, and it will be clear that tragic irony derives from Homer. See also note 1 to chap. viii, below.

[29] J. L. Myres, "The Last Book of the 'Iliad,' " *JHS* 52 (1932) 264–296, makes clear the pattern of the book and its place in the *Iliad*. He acknowledges a debt to J. T. Sheppard, *The Pattern of the Iliad* (London, 1922). I am indebted to them both as well as to the American unitarians, John A. Scott, Samuel E. Bassett, and George M. Calhoun, not to mention the many others whose articles or books on Homer I have read. The most recent is L. A. MacKay, *The Wrath of Homer* (Univ. of Toronto Press, 1948), in which the view is set forth that the *Iliad* was put together by an Ionian poet, chiefly from two cycles of legend, one centered about Achilles, one about Agamemnon.

NOTES TO CHAPTER III
The Social Consciousness of Aeschylus
Pages 56–87

¹ For the personified curse in Bhasa see A. B. Keith, *The Sanskrit Drama in Its Origin, Development, Theory and Practice* (Oxford, 1924), p. 99. For Plato on magic see *Laws* 11.933a–e. For the importance of kindly feelings on the part of dead and dying see *Laws* 9.865d–866b, 869a, and 11.932a, reading ἵλεῳ for νέοι. The same mistake is found at 2.671ᵇ 10; see *AJPh* 60 (1939) 102.

² For Aeschylean dances see Athenaeus 1.21d–22a. Note *Cho.* 425: ἀπριγδόπληκτα πολυπλάνητα δ᾽ ἦν ἰδεῖν.

³ For Aeschylus' style as swollen note Aristophanes, *Frogs* 940, and Longinus 3.1–4. See Plutarch, *Moralia* 79b, 715e, Longinus 3.2, and Horace, *Ars Poet.* 25–27, for the quotations. Chamaeleon and Sophocles are quoted in Athenaeus 1.22ab. See also note 3 to chap. iv, below.

⁴ See *Apology* 22a–c and *Poetics* 14.20: 54ᵃ 9–12. See also my article, "Aeschylean *onkos* in Sophocles and Aristotle," *TAPhA* 78 (1947) 242–251, for the emendation and interpretation of *Poetics* 18. Plato probably has in mind the Prometheus trilogy of Aeschylus in *Epistle II* 311b. His statement confirms the independent interpretation of H. D. F. Kitto in his *Greek Tragedy* (London, 1939), p. 64 n., and *JHS* 54 (1934) 14–20. I am much indebted to Kitto's book, to H. W. Smyth, *Aeschylean Tragedy* (Sather Lectures; Univ. of California Press, 1924), and to Gilbert Murray, *Aeschylus: The Creator of Tragedy* (Oxford, 1940), as well as to others more numerous than I can mention. I have constantly consulted P. W. Harsh, *A Handbook of Classical Drama* (Stanford Univ. Press, 1944). While Murray's book is packed with information and charm, I find that he overdoes emphasis on Greek interest in the traditional and the occult. The Greeks themselves liked to insist on their own civilization and to contrast it with barbarous superstition. They scrutinized myths and adapted them to serve Progress and Reason. See also D. W. Lucas, *The Greek Tragic Poets* (London, 1950), for an introduction to Greek drama.

⁵ The suppliant plays are: Aeschylus, *Suppliants* and *Eumenides;* Sophocles, *Oedipus at Colonus;* Euripides, *Suppliants* and *Heracleidae.* There are also many scenes of supplication.

⁶ For Medea (amor . . . qui plus pollet potiorque est patre) see Pacuvius,

Medus, fr. 260. The reconstruction of the Danaid trilogy is not undisputed. See Kurt von Fritz in *Phil.* 91 (1936) 121–136, 249–269.

[7] For Plato's account of the corrupting influence of the harem on Persian kings see *Laws* 3.694a–695e. This is a good place to cite the fundamental article of B. E. Perry, "The Early Greek Capacity for Viewing Things Separately," *TAPhA* 68 (1937) 403–427. In Aeschylus' *Persians*, attribution of Greek victory to the gods does not mean that the Greeks did not appreciate the importance of silver mines, of narrow passes, and of tricks of all kinds, as well as of good moral and political institutions. Aeschylus lets Atossa array Xerxes in regal splendor before his entrance because the combination of lamentation with luxurious appointments was particularly relished by the Greeks. There was irony in the contrast. The references to gods in the *Persians* are: Zeus, 827 f.; Poseidon, 750; Athena, 347. That Phoebus Apollo (205 f.) was on the wrong side need surprise no reader of Homer. But were the Greeks different from us when they attributed victory to many different factors at once? Is there anyone who does not claim to be spiritually as well as physically superior when he is victorious? It will be noted that I do not always agree with Perry about Homer. Many seeming inconsistencies vanish when we consider the plot of the *Iliad* or the *Odyssey*. The Phaeacians *are* treated satirically by Homer, as the Persians are by Aeschylus. Those who find Homer unsophisticated are perhaps themselves less sophisticated than they should be.

[8] When I say that Xerxes is a ridiculous figure in the closing scene of the *Persians*, I do not mean that the Athenians necessarily laughed out loud, but only that they enjoyed the spectacle and felt superior. Certainly Aeschylus does not depict Xerxes as greater than ordinary men. By Aristotle's definition he is a comic character. We should have to see the dance ourselves and with Athenian eyes to know just how far the actor of Xerxes' part went in the direction of portraying him as a drunken helot. And even a drunken helot may be viewed with enough disdain to suppress laughter. But I suspect that vulgar spectators may have laughed loudly, even as the vulgar do today when their betters are sympathizing with some passionate outbreak. Smyth (see note 4 above) rebukes an unnamed editor who once spoke of Xerxes as comic, and Kitto (see note 4) seems to agree with Smyth while finding a tragic Xerxes dull. The blinded Thracian king of Euripides' *Hecuba* supplies the best parallel to Xerxes. No Greek was sorry for such barbarians when they brought deserved disaster on themselves. The Greek sense of superiority was flattered, not diminished. Xerxes trying to be a warrior instead of his mother's pet was as funny as Hephaestus limping as he took over the role of Hebe and Ganymede in *Iliad* 1. Such harmless *hybris* is not tragic.

9 The attackers have many un-Hellenic traits. They are noisy, boastful, and irreverent, besides speaking a foreign language, as the chorus asserts in line 170. It may be noted that by the code of Plato (*Laws* 9.869cd) Eteocles would not even require purification if he slew his brother in civil war. See Aristophanes, *Frogs* 1021. For Arjuna's protest against war see *Maha-bharata*, "Bhagavadgita," chap. i (tr. K. T. Telang, *Sacred Books of the East*, Vol. 8; Oxford, 1898). The rest of the *Bhagavadgita* consists of the instruction of Krishna by which Arjuna is persuaded to do his duty as a warrior.

10 "The custom of killing the aged by giving them too greasy food was observed not only by the heathen but also by 'impious Christians'" among the Uighurs in the thirteenth century: W. Barthold, *Turkestan down to the Mongol Invasion* (London, 1928), p. 390.

11 My article "The *Seven against Thebes* as Propaganda for Pericles" is summarized in *TAPhA* 76 (1945) xxxvii, and is printed in *CW* 44 (1950–1951) 49–52. See Plutarch, *Cimon* 8.7 f. for Sophocles' first victory, *Pericles* 7.1–4, 9.2–4 for Pericles' political position, Thucydides 1.127 and Herodotus 1.61 for the curse, Plutarch, *Aristeides* 3.4 for the application of Seven 592–594 to Aristeides, *Themistocles* 23 for the fear of invasion, and *Pericles* 5–8 for characteristics of Pericles that are not unlike those of Eteocles in the play. The oracle is cited in *Seven* 742–749. Eteocles, like Ajax in *Iliad* 17.645–647 (see the comment of Longinus 9.10), makes no prayer for life; he prays only for his city (69–77). Aeschylus depicts Orestes rightly slaying his mother in the *Choephoroe* and Cassandra going with eyes open to her doom in the *Agamemnon*. Though self-devotion is a common theme in tragedy (note Oedipus, Polyxena, Iphigeneia, Alcestis, Macaria, and Menoeceus in tragedies, Codrus and Leonidas in history), the *Seven* is the only play in which the theme is central to the plot. Eteocles is as much elevated by Aeschylus as Xerxes is debased.

12 For Plato see *Rep.* 9.592b. Harsh (see note 4) remarks that the *Prometheus* is the earliest extant play that employs protatic characters, i.e., characters who appear before the chorus and are used merely for exposition. He notes that, in the prologue, characterization by language goes as far as it ever does in Attic tragedy. I pointed out in *AJPh* 58 (1937) 342 f. that Kratos has a habit of catching up a word of Hephaestus and building a retort about it. In line 52 we must, in view of this habit, read with the best manuscript τῷδε δεσμά. Kratos is a forerunner of the more likable humble characters in the *Oresteia*. It is not certain that the *Prometheus* is earlier than the *Oresteia*, but Aeschylus' depiction of tyranny in the *Prometheus* may well reflect an interest in Sicilian tyranny, which was overthrown by 466 B.C.

To suit the character of Oceanus it is necessary to emend line 333 to read πάντων μετασχεῖν ὡς τετολμηκὼς ἐμοί, as I proposed in *CP* 35 (1940) 182 f. Translate: "I envy you, safe as you are from any charge that you are boldly resolute to share with me in everything."

[13] There is a useful discussion of the *Prometheus Unbound* and the concluding play of the trilogy in the edition of George Thomson (Cambridge, 1932).

[14] I know the story of Sogoro only through a translation by George Braithwaite, *Life of Sogoro, the Farmer Patriot of Sakura* (Yokohama, 1897), and Lord Redesdale (A. B. Mitford), "The Ghost of Sakura," *Tales of Old Japan* (London, 1919), pp. 161–191.

[15] If we use the term "diffracted plot" for the action that is furthered by various characters who are not in collusion or even necessarily in sympathy with the outcome, we might speak of the plot of the *Choephoroe* as a "diffused plot." The chorus and the old nurse independently further the plot of Orestes because of their sympathy with and knowledge of his plans. The nurse knows very little, but guesses enough to help.

[16] The observations that Athena converts the Furies by her persistent reasonableness and that in her method she shows herself superior to Apollo, while the whole play is a lesson in moral suasion, are well made by Pearl Wilson, "Note on *Eumenides* 881–891," *CPh* 42 (1947) 122 f.

[17] It will be noted that I do not follow George Thomson (*Aeschylus and Athens: A Study in the Social Origins of Drama*, London, 1941) in his reinterpretation of Aeschylus in the light of social evolution, though I duly appreciate his edition of the *Oresteia* (Cambridge, 1938). For a criticism of Thomson see the review by Gilbert Norwood in *CPh* 37 (1942) 437–441. The social evolution depicted by Aeschylus, like his theology, is largely the product of his imagination and is plausibly invented or adapted for purposes of propaganda. He is hardly more historical than Hesiod is in his genealogies and his account of the four ages. To produce a maximum of enthusiasm in his audience Aeschylus naturally leaves his specific program, if he had one, vague. He is creating an atmosphere favorable to progress and uses methods that are still in favor among modern advocates of religious, political, and educational institutions.

NOTES TO CHAPTER IV
Sophoclean Tragedy
Pages 88–121

[1] The action of the *Trachiniae* is, to be sure, the result of a plot of Nessus the centaur, long since dead. If the spectator or reader were interested in Nessus and his triumph, the plot might be classed as one of intrigue. The plot of Nessus is, however, revealed only by deduction as it succeeds. No interest is aroused in Nessus and the justice of his case. Nessus' blood is not essential to the plot. Many love potions have proved fatal to life or reason when there was no intriguing centaur in the background. Hence the plot of Nessus is merely an additional spice added to the theme of a fatal love potion. It is indeed a delightful example of turning the tables or poetic justice when Nessus, who was slain for lechery and attempted rape by Heracles, wins revenge because Heracles himself is lickerish and brutal. Two oracles are also fulfilled in a way that is surprising and ingenious. The plot is well constructed and leads to an impression, not of successful intrigue, but of the fundamental uncertainty of human events. Nessus had calculated the result, but the odds were heavily against it at any one moment. The danger was too remote to be kept always in mind, even if the formula had not been the secret of Deianeira alone. The poet makes paradox his central aim.

[2] See Plutarch, *Moralia* 79b, and the references in note 3 to chap. iii, above, and note 24 to chap. ix, below. The passage in Plutarch is otherwise discussed by C. M. Bowra, "Sophocles on His Own Development," *AJPh* 61 (1940) 385–401. In his book, *Sophoclean Tragedy* (Oxford, 1944), Bowra emphasizes the thought of Sophocles rather than the dramatic interest of the plays. His understanding of Greek thought is based on wide reading and is usually sound. Though my own interest is in dramatic moments, and though I have written my chapters without reference to his book, I am pleased to find that he often supplies just the evidence that I need for my conclusions. It is obvious that I owe more to him than I knew. But his occasional introduction of divine motivation where Sophocles says nothing of it, and his attribution to the poet of a Job-like and un-Hellenic trust in God, "though he slay me," suggest that in his case, as in that of Glaucus, the gods have not helped his judgment. Note the protest voiced by Gilbert Norwood in his review of Bowra's book in *CPh* 41 (1946) 49–55. With regard to the classification of Sophocles' plays, however, I agree with Bowra. It seems

285

clear that Sophocles has an almost Aeschylean faith in human virtue, but he does not stress progress or institutions as Aeschylus does. Sophocles is Homeric in his depiction of loyalty, whether loyalty is crowned by triumph or by a worthy death. His politicians are inferior. He likes simple, straight-forward characters.

[8] Plutarch's words in *Moralia* 79b are: ὥσπερ γὰρ ὁ Σοφοκλῆς ἔλεγε τὸν Αἰσχύλου διαπεπαιχὼς ὄγκον, εἶτα τὸ πικρὸν καὶ κατάτεχνον τῆς αὑτοῦ κατασκευῆς, τρίτον ἤδη τὸ τῆς λέξεως μεταβάλλειν εἶδος, ὅπερ ἠθικώτατόν ἐστι καὶ βέλτιστον, κτλ. Note that διαπεπαιχώς is an accepted emendation of the impossible reading of the manuscripts, διαπεπωχώς. For Longinus see chap. iii, pp. 90 f. The passage in Longinus rather strengthens the case for this particular emendation, which is, in any case, the most probable paleographically. It may be that Sophocles meant by πικρόν 'harsh' not merely tragedy, but peripety. J. D. Denniston in a note on Eur. *Electra* 418 says that the word is "constantly used of an action which recoils on the doer's head."

With regard to the dates of Sophocles' plays, the *Ajax* probably precedes the *Antigone*, which was produced in 441 B.C. or shortly before, the *Oedipus Tyrannus* is generally placed soon after 430, and the *Trachiniae* is a companion piece. I put it earlier than the *Oedipus*, because Deianeira has traits of Euripides' *Alcestis* (438 B.C.) and Heracles is the most rough, masculine, and unattractive of all Sophocles' characters. For *éthos* he rates approximately zero; he is all *pathos* or suffering when we see him on the stage. Gilbert Murray in the introduction to his translation (*The Wife of Heracles:* Oxford, 1947) assumes that he is not an idealized character. But he is not much worse than Ajax, who is idealized as a masculine, warlike person. Sophocles is interested in contrasts and surprises in the *Trachiniae*. Possibly the theme of destruction wrought by a loving woman was suggested by attacks on Pericles through Aspasia. Of the three plays in which virtue is triumphant, *Philoctetes* was produced in 409, and *Oedipus at Colonus* was finished when Sophocles died in 406. The third, *Electra*, has been plausibly put in 410 by A. S. Owen in *Greek Poetry and Life: Essays Presented to Gilbert Murray* (Oxford, 1936), pp. 145–157. His arguments are convincing even apart from the fact that the theme of the play is one of resistance to usurpation and of successful revolution, just what was happening at Athens in that year. My sequence of discussion is the same as that of Bowra and Webster (*An Introduction to Sophocles*, Oxford, 1936). J. T. Sheppard (*The Wisdom of Sophocles*, London, 1947) puts *Trachiniae* before *Antigone*, finding support in F. R. Earp, *The Style of Sophocles* (Cambridge, 1944). Kitto strangely displaces *Electra* and *Trachiniae*.

[4] For Amphiaraus see *Seven against Thebes* 580–586. Plato expounds as his own the familiar code in *Epistle VII* 331a–d. He would not act as adviser to a man unless his advice was likely to be taken. He would force no free man, not even a son, to take his advice. He would use compulsion in the case of a slave. He would not annoy parents by trying to reform them. In their case compulsion would be impiety. So, too, he would advise his own state only when it might do good. He would not foment a revolution in which citizens would be lost through death or banishment. In the geometrical form of justice a superior has a right to respect and immunity even when he is unjust. Slaves may not retaliate against masters, children against parents, wives against husbands, or citizens against the state.

[5] I refer to Shakespeare's *Coriolanus* and to the *Lord Dewa* of Yamamoto Yuzo (*Three Plays*, tr. Glenn W. Shaw; Tokyo, 1935). These plays lend themselves to comparison with the *Ajax*. Eugene O'Neill's *Hairy Ape* shows a man for whom social adjustment is impossible because of pride.

[6] It should not go unrecorded that the late American secretary of defense, Forrestal, who committed suicide by leaping from a window, had been reading the words of Sophocles' *Ajax* in the translation of W. M. Praed. See *Time*, May 30, 1949, p. 14.

[7] For Japanese belief in the efficacy of the spirit of a dead soldier see D. C. Holtom, *Modern Japan and Shinto Nationalism* (Chicago, 1943), pp. 48–52, and R. O. Ballou, *Shinto: The Unconquered Enemy* (New York, 1945), p. 43. In reports of the recent war there are many references to the banzai charge of Japanese soldiers as an alternative to surrender. For Plato see the citations in note 1 to chap iii, above.

[8] To cast out the dead unburied was not an uncommon practice in the ancient world, if atrocious crimes had been committed. Plato provides that one who willfully murders a parent, brother, sister, son, or daughter shall be cast out unburied: *Laws* 9.873b; and so temple-robbers: 12.960b. Unknown murderers who are detected disregarding a public curse receive the same treatment: 9.874b. Plato even savagely rules that it is impious and criminal for anyone to bury an atheist: 10.909c. When Electra in Sophocles' play (1488 f.) would abandon Aegisthus' body to such undertakers as he deserves, I suppose that she expects birds and dogs to take care of him. At any rate, she has no desire to gloat over her foe's severed head like her counterpart in Euripides.

[9] For Socrates see Plato, *Apology* 41b; for Pindar, *Nemeans* 7.20–27, 8.23–27; for Homer, *Od.* 11.543–567.

[10] The close parallel between the injunction of Pericles, as cited by pseudo-Lysias, *Against Andocides* 6.10, and the statements of Antigone (450–460) and Tiresias (1068–1076), suggests that Sophocles is paraphrasing Pericles.

It was pointed out to me by Professor Max Radin of the University of California that for the history of law the statement of Pericles is of special interest, since it is probably taken from a speech in prosecution that actually influenced a court. It is our guarantee that Sophocles considered the plea of Antigone just and legal, a plea in support of, not against, the right of the state. The unwritten law referred to by Pericles is discussed in Felix Jacoby, *Atthis* (Oxford, 1949).

[11] For the exclusion by the Athenians of any appeal to unwritten law after 403 B.C. see Andocides, *On the Mysteries* 1.89. For Plato see *Epistle VII* 325de. Note Plutarch, *Alc.* 22.4 and *Phocion* 37.3.

[12] There is an interesting study of Kautilya (Chanakya) and Lord Shang, realists of India and China of the third century before Christ, in H. N. Spalding, *Civilization in East and West* (Oxford, 1939).

[13] Since writing this paragraph, I have seen an excellent performance of the *Antigone* of Jean Anouilh by the French clubs of Bryn Mawr and Haverford colleges. It is remarkable how effectively the theme of the old play is transposed into modern theatrical idiom. Those who have seen the French play will have noted how important the characterization of the guards is in sharpening the conflict of ideals. The theme of love is naturally made more vivid in the French play, and the psychology of the heroine receives its due. I must confess that the modern ending, which does not make Creon bewail his fate after the manner of Xerxes, suits my taste. Creon's character gains in consistency thereby, and the treatment of the moral and political problem is improved by the absence of a contrived and sentimental ending. The modern play, like a Messiah, divides sheep from goats; and the goats seem not to have been displeased with it. At least, the German censorship permitted it to be performed during the occupation of France. On fear and conscience as motives in social organization see Plato, *Laws* 4.720b–e, *Rep.* 7.536e, 8.547c, 8.548b, Hypereides, fr. 210, and Dem. 8.51.

[14] See A. A. Milne, *Autobiography* (New York, 1939), pp. 294–299, for his account of the failure of *The Truth about Blayds*.

[15] On seppuku, vulgarly known as harakiri, see *Tales of Old Japan* (see note 14 to chap. iii, above), App. A. Feigned courtesy and compliments to victims of torture or political pressure are reported from Japan as well as in stories of the torture of Jesuit missionaries by Iroquois Indians. There is an unflattering account of the Japanese in Manchuria in Alexandre Pernikoff, *"Bushido," the Anatomy of Terror* (New York, 1943), which must not be confused with the *Bushido* of Inazo Nitobe, who was an idealist.

[16] Some have wanted to soften in translation Haemon's reported spitting in his father's face (1232). But see the passages recently cited by various contributors in *CJ* 41 (1945–1946) 371–374, 43 (1947–1948) 99 f., 44 (1948–

1949), 490. Loud hawking and spitting on the floor by refined Chinese ladies in a public dining room provokes comment from an Englishman in D. E. Morris, *China Changed My Mind* (London, 1948; Boston, 1949). Sticking out the tongue shows disrespect in America, surprise in China, and respect in Tibet. Eructation, to use the language of Don Quixote, after meals is prescribed as a compliment to one's host by the social code of most of Asia, proscribed in Europe. What the ancient Greeks did about this I do not know.

[17] Plato recognized the importance of fear as a deterrent of crimes, and inserted in his works many myths about future punishment of the sinful. In the *Laws* he inclines to a system of punishment by reincarnation. Either the good may be promoted to a higher status in the animal kingdom, while the bad are demoted, or the principle "Be done by as you did" may be introduced, so that one who murders his parents will in his next life be in turn murdered by his children, and so on. When, as in this case, each punishment involves a crime, retribution becomes an endless chain. Plato did not expect his myths to be taken literally. Both systems are found in Hindu and Buddhist thought. See the article "Karma" in James Hastings, *Encyclopaedia of Religion and Ethics*. For the two systems in Plato see *Timaeus* 42bc, *Laws* 10.904a–905d and 9.870de, 872e.

[18] Bowra's mistake in supposing that Athenian custom permitted a concubine and a wife to be kept by a man in the one house, and that a wife who protested would be condemned, is too important to pass unnoticed. The passages that he cites from Lysias (1.31), Isaeus (3.39), and pseudo-Demosthenes (59.122) prove only that some men had concubines, not that they kept them in addition to a wife or in the same house with a wife. Matrimony implies motherhood, *con*cubinage merely sleeping *with* a man, not living *with* another woman. At Athens the concubine might be a mother, but not of citizens. The hetaera might become concubine or wife, but when Charisius accepts Habrotonon the hetaera as a concubine in Menander's *Epitrepontes*, it is assumed by all that his wife will leave him. When she does not, she is following the example of Penelope and being more loyal than circumstances require. A man might, I suppose, keep a wife in Athens and a concubine at the Piraeus for the sake of convenience, but to introduce a concubine or a hetaera into the house with a wife was as scandalous in Athens as it is in Homer and tragedy. It is the sort of thing of which such licentious characters as Alcibiades are accused. Barbarians were different, and barbarian ideals of marriage were as much condemned in Greece as the Continental Sabbath once was in Scotland. In the *Andromache*, Hermione denounces her rival as a barbarian (243). One might as well cite a Frenchwoman's

view of the Sabbath to illustrate Scotch practice as cite Andromache's behavior for evidence of Greek theory. In this particular Hermione was quite
correct; she was unfair only when she blamed Andromache for having
been her husband's concubine. The slave had no choice. But Hermione,
not Andromache, represents the Greek matrimonial code. A tyrant like
Dionysius might even have two wives at once, and Agamemnon might
bring a concubine home from the war, but this was *hybris* and recognized
as such by all good citizens. I have discussed the point more fully in my
article, "Woman's Place in Menander's Athens," *TAPhA* 71 (1940) 420–
459, esp. 427 f.

[19] For Hindu holy men note Durvasas, whose arbitrary curse causes all the
trouble in Kalidasa's *Shakuntala,* and the ascetic sage of the same name
who forces the goddess Sarasvati to descend to earth in the *Harshacarita* of
Bana, chap. i. For Achilles and his psychology in this connection see pages
49–55 in the present work.

[20] Note the correct interpretation of line 677: *Creon.* πορεύσομαι,/σοῦ μὲν
τυχὼν ἀγνῶτος, ἐν δὲ τοῖσδ' ἴσος. "I will go, having found you a stranger to
me, myself an equal among these [the multitude]." Creon's tone is one of
grievance. He is interested in his own privileges, not in any danger to
Oedipus. Creon had proposed to keep the message from Delphi a secret
from the multitude (91 f., where Creon's suggestion is otherwise unnecessary, but shows how punctilious he is). He cheerfully assumes that he is
the equal of Oedipus in all that counts (581, 627), though the problems
of the state disturb him not at all. Oedipus has to warn him that kinship
will not protect him (551 f.). Creon's arguments all beg the question. What
could be more irritating and presumptuous than for Creon to argue that
casting him off was as bad for Oedipus as to be slain (611 f.)? The contrast
in character would be very effective on the stage and would create sympathy
for Oedipus in much the same way as Polonius justifies Hamlet in Shakespeare's play. Creon's procedure in making himself popular by winning
special consideration for those who gained his favor (596–599) resembles
the technique employed by Absalom (*Samuel II* 15: 1–6), and Absalom
was plotting rebellion. Creon's defense was as offensive to Oedipus as can
well be imagined. Perhaps he did like popularity for its own sake, or for the
bribes that came with it, but here, as in other plays, his political ideals are
too low to make Oedipus like him. My interpretation of line 677 was published in *AJPh* 56 (1935) 53. It is as bad to suppose that Sophocles idealizes
Creon in this play as it would be in the *Antigone.*

[21] My indebtedness to J. T. Sheppard, *The Oedipus Tyrannus of Sophocles*
(Cambridge, 1920), is obvious. He says (xiii): "Oedipus is a good man,
and here lies the greatness of his tragedy." But if Oedipus is to appear as a

great man, with the faults as well as the virtues of a great man, Creon should be interpreted as a foil, a small man with no obvious faults, like Oceanus or Polonius, a "stuffed shirt." Creon had already been depicted in the *Antigone* as intent on formal correctness but incapable of taking fire or probing deeply. He was interested in his privileges as a prince, not in mere rights as a citizen. The plots of Sophocles' plays tell us more about his philosophy than his words do. As W. C. Greene says in *Moira* (Harvard Univ. Press, 1944), p. 91: "The dramatist's outlook on life must be sought even more in the plot than in any sentiments which his characters may express." See also *ibid.*, p. 139. Greene, too, sees ultimate tragedy rather than morality in the *Oedipus*. In *HvdStCP* 58–59 (1948) 228–231 appears a summary of a thesis by Cedric H. Whitman, "The Religious Humanism of Sophocles," which supports this principle. Whitman finds that "Sophoclean tragedy . . . emerges as a treatment of the basically tragic nature of heroic morality." He rejects the Aristotelian theory of a tragic flaw or *hamartia*.

[22] Here I am indebted to an article of A. D. Nock, "Religious Attitudes of the Ancient Greeks," *Proc. Am. Philos. Soc.* 85.5 (Sept., 1942) 472–482, for the reference to Plutarch, *Dem.* 20, 1. Nock's article, like Perry's cited in note 7 to chap. iii, emphasizes the Greek ability to mingle points of view that seem incompatible to a reflective observer. They could believe in oracles and at the same time disregard them when it was convenient. They could be pious and yet manipulate or bribe the gods and oracles for their own ends. It is not unusual in modern times to find sincere believers in political or religious creeds who derive inconsistent profits from the institutions that they profess to support for impersonal reasons. Nock says (478): "The gods, like the Greeks, were sensible and not easily shocked."

[23] Tertullian (*Apol.* 9) reports the reaction of the Macedonians. The Persians were accused by the Greeks of practicing incest. For Euripides' argument in defense of Pasiphaë see the fragment of his *Cretans* conveniently edited by D. L. Page (*Greek Literary Papyri: 1. Poetry*) for the Loeb Classical Library. Compare Oedipus' statements in *O.T.* 776–778 about the aspersion cast on his birth:

πρίν μοι τύχη
τοιάδ' ἐπέστη, θαυμάσαι μὲν ἀξία
σπουδῆς γε τῆς ἐμῆς οὐκ ἀξία,

and in *O.C.* 438 f., where he rates his fury when he blinded himself as too severe in its punishment:

κἀμάνθανον τὸν θυμὸν ἐκδραμόντα μοι
μείζω κολαστὴν τῶν πρὶν ἡμαρτημένων,

and in 266 f., where he declares that he was more a sufferer than a sinner:

τά γ' ἔργα μου

πεπονθότ' ἐστὶ μᾶλλον ἢ δεδρακότα

("my acts were more in suffering than in doing").

NOTES TO CHAPTER V
Euripidean Tragedy
Pages 122–155

[1] For Euripides' criticism of social prejudices see Paul Decharme, *Euripides and the Spirit of His Dramas,* tr. James Loeb (London and New York, 1906), pp. 112–118. Note particularly fragment 52 of the *Alexander* (Stobaeus, *Flor.* 86.2). For criticism of Euripides see Gilbert Murray, *Euripides and His Age* (London and New York, 1913; 2d ed., Oxford, 1946); F. L. Lucas, *Euripides and His Influence* (Boston, 1923), and G. M. A. Grube, *The Drama of Euripides* (London, 1941), as well as the works of Harsh and Kitto cited in note 4 to chap. iii. My classification of the dramas of Euripides imposed itself in the attempt to analyze them. The seven tragedies, of which *Hecuba* and *Heracles* are as much stories of partial triumph over evil, "making the best of things," as tragedies, are dealt with chronologically, for all are later than the four tragedies of Sophocles that were discussed in chapter iv. The five plays with happy ending of Euripides and two of Sophocles belong together, for both poets derive their subjects and methods from Homer's *Odyssey* and the plays of Aeschylus. Union in family and state are emphasized in varying proportions. The remaining five plays of Euripides, with the *Philoctetes* of Sophocles, and the *Rhesus,* all show interesting new developments that stand out more clearly when they are considered together.

[2] Sophocles' statement that Euripides depicted men as they are while he himself depicted men as they ought to be (or as they ought to be depicted, it makes no difference) is cited in Aristotle, *Poetics* 25.11: 60[b] 33 f.

[3] Hippolytus and Alcestis die peacefully on the stage, while Ajax commits suicide. For Aristotle's remark see *Poetics* 14.6–9: 53[b] 14–22.

[4] For a wife who was with difficulty persuaded by her husband to return to her family and marry another man see Isaeus 2.8 f. Pericles is said in Plutarch's *Pericles* (24.5) to have joined in giving his rich wife to a new husband at her request. After that, Aspasia became his concubine, mother of

free children, one of whom, Pericles the Younger, later became a citizen and was one of the unlucky generals who won the victory of Arginusae. The two faults that Aristotle notes in the construction of the *Medea*, the miraculous chariot given to Medea by her grandfather Helius (*Poetics* 15.10ᵇ: 54ᵇ 1) and the unexpected arrival of Aegeus (*Poetics* 25.31: 61ᵇ 20 f.), are possibly connected and may indicate a hasty reworking by Euripides of an existing play. If Aegeus originally appeared at the end to succor a Medea whose children had been slain by the Corinthians, not by herself, it was necessary, provided the Corinthians were to be exonerated and a more ferocious Medea introduced who slays her own children, to avoid making Aegeus accessory to the crime. Hence the emphasis in Euripides (731–755) on the oath that Medea makes him swear to give her an asylum. Since the *Medea* is written for a two-actor stage, the report is likely to be true that Euripides took the story from Neophron of Sicyon. Nor is it unlikely that Neophron's play presented the Corinthians in a bad light and that they paid Euripides the reported five talents for recasting the myth. The example of Pindar shows us that myths were manufactured or recast to please generous patrons, and in the *Heracleidae* we have a play of Euripides that seems obviously to be made to order to fit a specific need of a new myth to avert ill fame (see pp. 164–166). For references and discussion of these points I refer the reader to the excellent edition of D. L. Page (Oxford, 1938), Introd., esp. pp. xxiii–xxv and xxx–xxxvi.

⁵ It is usual nowadays to emphasize in Hippolytus the traits that set him apart from other men and make him difficult socially and to imply that Euripides holds him up as a warning against excess. No doubt, ingrown virtue can be very isolating and even disagreeable, but on the other hand there may well be a certain meanness in the everlasting mean, however golden. Hippolytus has a personal ideal that under ordinary circumstances would have kept him happy and forgotten by the world. His disability as a bastard may account for his turning away from the world of women and public life, but it is not necessary to invent a psychology of perversion or inversion to explain his behavior. Nor should we adopt the modern heresy, so strange to the ancient world and the modern Orient alike, that attributes all the sanctity of religion to heterosexual passion and refuses to recognize any virtue that denies the claim of Aphrodite to be supreme goddess. Hippolytus is unkind to Phaedra in that he shames her publicly in spite of her heroic resistance to a really abnormal passion, and she brings him too to public execration and death in spite of innocence. Her words must not, however, be quoted as an unbiased account of Hippolytus any more than those of Theseus at the moment when he regards his son as a Tartuffe. Hippolytus has the freshness of athletic and impulsive adolescence. His

rudeness to Phaedra is a mistake but not unnatural. There is a perfect peripety when she puts him in the same position with herself as victim of injustice.

The play has features that belong to the later tradition of martyrology, such as the refusal to offer incense to a false god and the epiphany of the true god at the end of the story. Certainly denunciation of immorality is common among Christian saints. The language used by Tertullian and Jerome in order to make sex seem nasty makes Hippolytus appear positively modest and discreet. Since tales of martyrdom have always been popular from Peru to Japan, it is not surprising to find the type in Greek tragedy. Antigone and Eteocles are similarly martyrs to ideals of religion and patriotism, but the story of Hippolytus is complicated by his mistake in not being sure that he understood before he spoke irretrievably. He is virtuous and rash, but no less virtuous for that according to Greek notions. Antigone was a deliberate martyr; Hippolytus is a martyr only by mistake—a mistake that would not have occurred except for the irresponsible malice of Aphrodite.

Plato in the *Laws* (8.840ab) cites athletes who abstained from all sexual intercourse during the time of training, and he would prescribe such asceticism for all bachelors in his ideal state. In his *Laws* he finds a place for married love and loyalty in a monogamous system, and no longer as in *Symposium* and *Phaedrus* advocates a romantic ideal of homosexual love or, as in the *Republic,* attempts to abolish monogamy and the private family. Hippolytus professes (1016–1018) to have no higher aim than to be victorious as an athlete and to lead a happy life among friends. Euripides seems to have invented for Hippolytus a devotion to Artemis that combines athletic asceticism and a mystic communion with wild nature. It would not have been easy to glorify him as an adherent of any actual religious or philosophic sect that practiced celibacy, as is clear from Theseus' picture (948–954) of the pedantic vegetarian followers of Orpheus. We know from Aristophanes' account of Socrates in the *Clouds* that the same sect may appear at once as pale pedants and as uninhibited revelers. The early Christians and the Jews have been similarly traduced. Euripides makes asceticism respectable by persuading the Olympian Artemis to sponsor it. Presumably, modern critics do not object to asceticism in life or literature when it appears as a feature of organized Christianity or Buddhism. It seems hardly fair to deny to a pagan the privilege of imagining a religious celibate who deserves praise for his devotion. The nurse denounced Phaedra's virtue as *hybris* (474). Similarly, Phaedra accuses Hippolytus of not knowing *sophrosyne* (730 f.), the very virtue that he exemplifies. Both Phaedra and Hippolytus lost in men's eyes the honor on which they had set most store. They are misunderstood martyrs and illustrate the romanticism of Euripides.

It must be confessed that Euripides does not give us a very clear picture of Hippolytus, probably because he is more interested in paradox than in psychology. There are, however, still some shy people in the world who win a bad reputation because they have not the charm that virtue requires as solvent. Yet even without the favor of Aphrodite, Hippolytus, when he is not embarrassed by the presence of worldly people, is attractive enough. Just as Robinson Jeffers in his *Medea* uses the concept of a sacred passion to bind Medea and Jason, where Euripides was content with the sanctity of a sworn oath, so a modern critic in judging Hippolytus is likely to consider him really impious for preferring to remain celibate, where Euripides is content to make him guilty of an impiety that is merely formal and of which probably most respectable Greek men were habitually guilty. I suspect that a Greek man who sacrificed to Aphrodite would have been, not orthodox, but addicted to gambling and the wrong kind of venery. Plato's attitude toward women is not very different from that of Hippolytus. See notes 10 and 11 to chap. viii for works that explain ancient and modern attitudes toward women and love. For modern feeling note also the statement of S. Radhakrishnan, *Religion and Society* (London, 1947), p. 167: "We must realize that sex union is the great sacrament of life."

Hippolytus finds bliss in a denial of the claims of society, but finds that the world invades his peace and destroys it. His sweet illusion is a child's dream. This theme is the essence of tragedy, according to F. L. Lucas (*Tragedy*, New York, 1928, p. 55), who finds in Turgenev's *A Month in the Country* a perfect illustration of the moment in which it suddenly dawns upon someone that life does not grant the perfect bliss that one had imagined. This is an aspect of the theme of frustrated ideals or defeated illusions, as you choose, a theme that is variously illustrated in Goethe's *Götz von Berlichingen* and in Shakespeare's *Othello*.

⁶ There is an illustration of the first scene of Euripides' *Hippolytus Stephanephorus* in a Pompeian painting, the subject of which seems clear enough, though no student has so far, I believe, identified it. It is reproduced in *Yale Classical Studies* 9 (1944), pl. 8, no. 23, in connection with an article by Christopher M. Dawson, "Romano-Campanian Mythological Landscape Painting." It is described on p. 90, where references are given to *Röm. Mitteilungen* 5 (1890) 264–266, and S. Reinach, *Répertoire de Peintures grecques et romaines* (Paris, 1923), p. 387. Two goddesses or statues are shown side by side. One is receiving a wreath from a young man, who is accompanied by two companions with spears. Two dogs are shown in the foreground, while a stag leaps in the background. A woman, whose figure

does not appear clearly, is shown looking on, but cut off by a stream, in the foreground. The young hunter who neglects one of the two goddesses and presents a wreath to the other is certainly Hippolytus, for whom Phaedra languishes. For a recent study with illustrations of the story of Hippolytus see Kurt Weitzmann, "Euripides Scenes in Byzantine Art," *Hesperia* 18 (1949) 192–195. See also the postscript to the article of Dawson cited above that is found in *Yale Classical Studies* 11 (1950) 300–303.

While I am referring to Dawson's article I will record in passing my conviction that pl. 15, no. 43, discussed on his pp. 101 ff., illustrates the recognition of Orestes and Iphigeneia in *Iphigeneia among the Taurians*, as Sogliano originally suggested. The picture is discussed in P. Hermann, *Denkmäler der Malerei des Altertums* (Munich, 1905), pp. 209 ff., and in Reinach, *op. cit.*, p. 22. The most conspicuous object in the painting is an altar, brands from which are scattered about, and from behind which a goddess is departing, evidently without the expected victim. I do not know why brother and sister might not embrace as fervently as a pair of lovers; lovers do not embrace on the Greek stage any more warmly than brother and sister, as far as I know. Behind Orestes his friend Pylades stands by, while behind his sister a young woman runs away either in terror or to take the news. I suggest that she represents a member of the chorus of the play and that she is frightened by the appearance of Athena above. Possibly the appearance of Athena also accounts for the absence of Scythians from the picture. At any rate, the theme is an interrupted sacrifice, and I know of no case of such a thing combined with a recognition except in the story of Iphigeneia and Orestes.

[7] For Aristotle's statement that a plot in which a hero suffers who does nothing wrong is abominable see *Poetics* 13.2: 52[b] 34–36.

[8] Baroness Shidzué Ishimoto in her autobiography, *Facing Two Ways* (New York, 1935), p. 14, relates that her father named her after Shidzuka, the faithful concubine of Yoshitsune. He had seen and admired, the night before his daughter was born, a No drama that depicted Shidzuka's devotion. Japanese tales are told in as many and flexible forms as the Greek legends were. I know this tale only in the version of James S. De Benneville, which is somewhat different from the form of the story as reported by Baroness Ishimoto. See De Benneville, *Saito Musashi-bo Benkei* (Yokohama, 1910), Vol. II, chap. xiv, pp. 239–260, "The Story of Shizuka."

[9] For the Melian affair see Thuc. 5.84–116.

[10] See *Poetics* 13.3: 52[b] 36–38; 15.1: 54[a] 16 f.; 13.10: 53[a] 29 f.

[11] The *Electra* of Euripides is a perfect example of decadent art, whether we like decadence or not. Each scene is particularly moving in itself, especially Electra's scenes when played by Edith Wynne Matheson, yet no whole or

consistent view of life is obtainable from it. It is strictly sensational. F. P. Chambers has well studied both for ancient and modern times the rise of aestheticism and its effect on art and taste. For the ancient world see his *Cycles of Taste* (Harvard Univ. Press, 1928), and for the modern world, *The History of Taste* (Columbia Univ. Press, 1932).

Plato traces the corruption and failure of democracy to the theater, where the function of the judge was originally to hold up a standard for poets and audience alike. When the judges began to award the prize according to the applause of the audience, whose standard was one of mere entertainment, perhaps pleasure of a vulgar and debasing sort, whether purely aesthetic or mixed, taste and morals deteriorated. Since political assemblies were held in the theater, it is not surprising if the pleas of statesmen were similarly judged by the pleasure that they gave to the hearers or by an unrealistic aesthetic standard. It was more important, as in some trials and elections today, to be a finished orator than to have a good case.

For Plato on theatrocracy see *Laws* 2.658e–659c and 3.700a–701b. I have defended the manuscript reading against emendation; see L. A. Post, *The Vatican Plato and Its Relations,* Am. Philol. Assoc. Monograph 4, 1934, pp. 97 f. Translate: "For the old Greek law might have left [sc. but did not] the decision to the majority of spectators and selected the victor by a show of hands, just as the present law of Sicily and Italy by so doing has corrupted the poets themselves and the tastes of the theatre as well."

[12] For the mixed character, partly virtuous and partly vicious, note Aristotle's statement in *Poetics* 18.16–18: 56ᵃ 19–25. Poets who dramatize a long story are unsuccessful, says he, but those who deal with a reversal of fortune or a simple plot achieve their aim admirably. What they aim at is a combination of tragedy and good feeling, such as occurs when a clever, unscrupulous man like Sisyphus or a bold criminal is overthrown. On the English stage, characters like Macbeth and Sir Giles Overreach illustrate the type. The audience enjoys vicarious participation in successful crime, but salves its conscience in the end by approving the downfall and punishment of the unjust man. Orestes in Euripides may, however, have been classed by Aristotle as a characterless hero, one who acts without any revelation of the springs of action within himself and without engaging the sympathy of the audience. Aristotle notes in *Poetics* 6.14 f.: 50ᵃ 23–29 that most tragedies of his day were lacking in moral interest (ἀήθεις), that is, in characterization in the Greek sense. Such characters said rhetorically or poetically something that met the situation but was not particularly characteristic. There is no strong character and no impression of sincerity in the *Rhesus,* which is post-Aristotelian but well illustrates his meaning.

[18] For the many features of ritual that Euripides introduces in his play see

the recent edition of E. R. Dodds (Oxford, 1944). R. P. Winnington-Ingram's interpretation in *Euripides and Dionysus* (Cambridge, 1948) largely coincides with mine. I did not receive his book in time to be indebted to it.

[14] For the thesis of Socrates see the end of Plato's *Symposium* (223d).

[15] For the Parthian performance of the *Bacchae* after their victory over the Romans at Carrhae (54 B.C.) see Plutarch, *Crassus* 33.

NOTES TO CHAPTER VI
Propaganda, Idealism, and Romance
Pages 156–185

[1] Herodotus (9.27) puts the legends of Euripides' *Suppliants* and *Heracleidae* into the mouth of an Athenian orator speaking in 479 B.C. This might be anachronistic, but it seems certain in any case that the legends were ancient, since the Spartans as a matter of fact up to 427 B.C. spared the Tetrapolis in memory of aid given to the Heracleidae. It is unlikely that recent propaganda would have influenced them.

[2] According to the *Library* of Apollodorus (1.7.3), Xuthus begat Ion. Euripides recasts the legend to please his audience and to create a new pride in their ancestry. A. W. Verrall, on the contrary, implies that Euripides was trying to discredit an established myth; see *Euripides the Rationalist* (Cambridge, 1895). The date of the *Ion* is found to be 418 or 417 by A. S. Owen in the Introduction to his edition (Oxford, 1939). The definite statement that a man might put anyone to death who should solicit his daughter's love is found in Heliodorus 4.6.6. By the law of Solon (Plutarch, *Solon* 23.2) an unchaste daughter or sister might be sold into slavery. Plato in his *Laws* (9.874bc) provides that one who violates a free woman or boy may be slain with impunity by father, brother, or son of the victim. A violator caught in the act might also be slain by the husband, as we know from Lysias 1.30–34, where the statement is made that punishment was heavier in case of seduction, and that it applied even when the woman seduced was only a concubine. In New Comedy it is always assumed that maidens have been violated, not seduced, and that the young man, if caught, is at the mercy of the girl's relatives. For the question addressed to Heracles see *Trag. adesp.* 402 Nauck (Plutarch, *Amatorius* 751d).

[3] For the actors' appreciation of the role of Ion see Demetrius, *On Style* 4.195.

⁴ I have discussed the *Andromache* very briefly in two previous articles: "Aristotle and Menander," *TAPhA* 69 (1938) 1–42, esp. 14 f., and "Dramatic Infants in Greek," *CPh* 34 (1939) 193–208, esp. 199 f.

⁵ For τὸ φιλάνθρωπον see *Poetics* 13.3: 52ᵇ 37 f. It means the comfortable feeling produced by an ethical plot in drama. The ethical in this sense is the normal, including customary, familiar life and the tender feelings that hold family and state together, as well as the actual winning in practice of a victory of familiar sentiments and normal loyalties over disturbing elements in life. Such plays as Thornton Wilder's *Our Town* and Eugene O'Neill's *Ah! Wilderness* are modern examples of the type.

Critics need better terms to distinguish the comedy of feeling from the comedy of wit. Our term "comedy of manners" derives, almost certainly, from Aristotle's ethical plot. But Greek ethical plots, as found in tragedy and the moral comedy of Menander, are at the opposite pole from Restoration comedy, which was dubbed "comedy of manners" by Lamb, Hazlitt, or some other critic of their time. Will some lexicographer not devote himself to studying the history of the term and make it clear that the meaning has been completely reversed between Menander and Etherege? No help is afforded at present, as far as I know, either by dictionaries or in histories of drama and dramatic criticism. On this point see my article, "Menander in Current Criticism," *TAPhA* 65 (1934) 13–34.

⁶ It is not necessary to suppose that the *Heracleidae* has suffered in transmission if we assume that Euripides wrote it rather hastily to order and that he was not greatly interested in it. For a defense of the text about as it stands see G. Zuntz, "Is the *Heracleidae* Mutilated?" *CQ* 41 (1947) 46–52. For Pericles' fear that, if his land were not laid waste by the invaders, it might prejudice the people against him, see Thucydides 2.13.1. For the sparing of the Tetrapolis by the Spartans in the early part of the war and their reason see Diodorus Siculus 12.45.1. The various accounts of the death of Eurystheus are discussed by Sir J. G. Frazer in a note in the Loeb Apollodorus (2.8.1). He notes that the Scythians used the heads of foes to guard their houses (Herodotus 4.103). Head-hunting is still practiced by the wild Wa between Burma and China; see the article "Wa" in the *Encyclopaedia Britannica* (Chicago, 1949). The tradition is not quite dead among the Nagas, and it is apparently impossible to disentangle the motives of headhunters, though the head seems always to embody power, for whatever purpose, in proportion to the quality of the slain man. Nicoll Smith in *Burma Road* (New York, 1940), pp. 283 f., quotes a British administrator as affirming that European heads would be more highly valued than others if the hunters could get them.

⁷ For the relation of Milton's *Samson Agonistes* to Greek drama see W. R.

Parker, *Milton's Debt to Greek Tragedy in Samson Agonistes* (Johns Hopkins Univ. Press, 1937). In the next paragraph my statements derive from F. R. Earp, *The Style of Sophocles* (Cambridge, 1944). I have elsewhere profited from the same author's *The Style of Aeschylus* (Cambridge, 1948).
[8] The notion that the dramatist, when he introduces a god from the machine, is at his wits' end is found in Plato, *Cratylus* 425d. Antiphanes, the comic poet, pointing out how easy it is to write tragedy, compares the poet who "raises a god" to the athlete who raises a finger or fingers to confess himself beaten. His phrase δάκτυλον αἴρειν (fr. 191 Kock, line 15, cited by Athenaeus 6.222c) has been understood neither by translators of Athenaeus nor by editors of comic fragments, though it is explained in Suidas. Holding up a finger or fingers was equivalent to throwing in the sponge in modern boxing. On occasion, to make sure, an athlete might hold up both hands at once like the beaten man in Theocritus (22.128–130), but the unclenched fingers were the essential signal of surrender, just as we still throw up our hands in despair. My attention was called to this idiom by H. L. Crosby in connection with Dio Chrysostom 47.10 when he was preparing his Loeb translation. The Greek dictionaries do not help.

In Harpers' Latin dictionary *tollere digitum* is explained as being equivalent to "cry mercy" with reference to Martial 5.62.4. The gesture is found in ancient representations of boxing bouts. See E. Norman Gardiner, *Athletics of the Ancient World* (Oxford, 1930), illustrations 173, 180, on his pp. 199, 203. Gardiner says "raising a hand," and no doubt the hand is raised with the finger, but the single index finger is clearly designated in the pictures. In the index of Karl Sittl, *Die Gebärden der Griechen und Römer*, references to the gesture are given under *Zeigefinger*, but not under *Finger* or *Hand*. Sittl interprets Antiphanes correctly and cites other passages of Greek authors on his p. 218, but not the passage in Dio Chrysostom. Dio says that he is quoting a letter of Aristotle; I imagine that the letter was a forgery.

The fact is, as study of examples shows, that the poet was rather obligated to provide a problem that would specifically justify the appearance of a god, *dignus vindice nodus:* Horace, *Ars Poetica* 191. The god is needed by the poet, as Aristotle notes (*Poetics* 15.10c: 54b 26), not to solve the main problem of the play, but to predict the future and to connect the action with later history. To bring in a god is, however, to cry quits in one sense. The poet is not baffled, but he has said what he has to say except for the part that only a god could know, and the introduction of the god may be quite as perfunctory as the singing of national anthems sometimes tends to be. Dropping the curtain is also a mechanical ending, but it does not bring discredit to the poet.

Note that *Iphigeneia in Tauris* is not a sequel to the *Electra* either of Euripides or of Sophocles. The date 413, which is preferred by M. Platnauer in his edition (Oxford, 1938), brings it too close to the *Electra* of Euripides. I should put it a year or two earlier.

⁹ The references are to *Frogs* 791–794, and to Dio Chrysostom, *Discourses* 52 and 59. The *Philoctetes* of Euripides was produced in 431, that of Sophocles in 409. Since Owen assigned Sophocles' *Electra* to the year 410 (see note 3 to chap. iv) on independent evidence, the consideration that in that year resistance to usurpers must have seemed particularly important to the Athenians confirms his date and makes it probable that Sophocles wrote with contemporary conditions in mind. Revolutions bring deterioration of morals, as Thucydides noted, but it is even more necessary to act boldly in revolutionary times. Sophocles sternly held, as did Aeschylus, that the death of Clytemnestra was necessary for deliverance. That does not mean that he thought it was an ideally good thing. It is better not to need the surgeon's knife and better not to be in a position where forcible justice or war is the only means of salvation. See Plato, *Laws* 1.628d. Note, however, that J. D. Denniston in the Introduction to his edition of Euripides' *Electra* (Oxford, 1939) still held to the view that Sophocles' play was the earlier.

My suggestion that the *Electra* of Sophocles was propaganda for action against the usurping oligarchs in 411–410, or at least incorporates the spirit of the victorious restored democrats, was written before I had read Jean-Paul Sartre's version of the same story, *Les Mouches*. Different as his play is, it seems equally to represent the spirit of the resistance in France against the Germans and the government that they sponsored during the occupation. Except for the impact of recent history, it probably would not occur to anyone to note in Sophocles' *Electra* the strong sense of urgency and devotion to a cause that appears in it and in no other Greek tragedy. If it is not propaganda in the best sense of the word, then there is no such thing in Greek.

¹⁰ The question whether Orestes and Electra were justified in slaying their mother is not discussed by Sophocles. It has been discussed by modern critics, notably by J. T. Sheppard in *CR* 41 (1927) 2–9 and 163–165, who believes that Sophocles disapproved of the matricide. H. D. F. Kitto, *Greek Tragedy* (London, 1939), p. 133, even sets his ban magisterially on further disagreement: "However great be Sophocles' sympathy with Electra's character, let us hear no more of his condonation of the crime, of his 'happy ending.'" C. M. Bowra, *Sophoclean Tragedy* (Oxford, 1944), pp. 212–260, has fully answered the arguments of Sheppard and Kitto. He makes the point that Clytemnestra was no true mother to Electra and

Orestes, and that Sophocles makes this explicit. This reminds one of Mencius' justification of the slaying of a ruler by a subject in the *Book of Mencius*, 2.8: "I did not hear that a subject slew his ruler, but that a criminal was executed." H. G. Creel in *Confucius, the Man and the Myth* (New York, 1949), p. 221, thinks that the doctrine of the rectification of names that is found in the Confucian *Analects* 13.3, is a later addition and does not represent the views of Confucius himself. Note that Kitto in the new edition (1950) of his book cited above revises his view of the *Electra*.

Since Orestes belonged to the heroic age, he can hardly be expected to be guided by later legal and moral standards, much less to act like a Christian on principles that Sophocles had never heard of. Plato exonerates the man who slays his brother in civil war. The only doubt raised by Sophocles is the doubt whether Orestes should have used lies and trickery to gain his end. Apollo must answer for that. If he was right in ordering the secret return, then all was well done. The death of Clytemnestra was justified by her own arguments. It was just by the verdict of Aeschylus in the *Eumenides*. Clytemnestra had abdicated as wife and mother. She was on the side of Orestes' enemy Aegisthus, whom every consideration of honor and duty required him to overthrow. It seems clear that Sophocles regarded Clytemnestra as justly punished; that, even if he did not, he was not obliged to represent a heroic Orestes as doubtful of his duty; and that, though he recognized the bad effect of a broken family on character, he also found in the victory of Orestes the necessary cure for moral infection.

The only thing that he will not accept without reservation in Orestes' behavior is his deceit. Sophocles emphasized the next year in his *Philoctetes*, in such a way as to make his conviction clear to all, the principle that deceit does not become a hero. Modern critics are amusingly indifferent to the moral taint of deceit while they quibble about an execution that caused Sophocles no qualms whatever. Clytemnestra had ranged herself with the enemy, and to slay an enemy in open fight was in his eyes no crime. We should recall how Sophocles playfully practiced stratagems in his fifties (Athenaeus 13.604d), when he was general, after he had been accused by Pericles of being a better poet than general. Whatever Sophocles the general may have learned about strategy in love and war, the poet was still a believer in honesty, in dealing with friends and foes alike; at least, that was his ideal for dramatic heroes.

NOTES TO CHAPTER VII
Vacillation, Burlesque, and Variety
Pages 186–213

[1] For Achilles' choice of doing honor to Patroclus in preference to gaining further glory for himself by capturing Troy see *Iliad* 22.378–394. For Hector's soliloquy see *Iliad* 22.99–130. Cf. *Ajax* 457–480 and *Electra* 812–822.

[2] Aristotle defines *pathos* as death or wounds or intense physical suffering in *Poetics* 11.10: 52[b] 11–13. For an interesting allegorical interpretation of the *Philoctetes* see Edmund Wilson, *The Wound and the Bow* (Boston, 1941), pp. 272–295.

[3] With the quotation from *The Tempest*, Act III, Scene 1, compare *Andromeda*, fr. 132 Nauck:

$$\text{ἄγου δέ μ', ὦ ξεῖν', εἴτε πρόσπολον θέλεις}$$
$$\text{εἴτ' ἄλοχον εἴτε δμωΐδ'.}$$

[4] It was noted by A. W. Verrall, *Essays on Four Plays of Euripides* (Cambridge, 1905), that King Theoclymenus resembles a Gilbertian monarch (p. 53) and that the play is a jest (p. 48). The mixture of sentiment, burlesque, and strange situations is very like what we find in *The Mikado*. Menelaus speaks grandiloquently in lines 947–953; contrast his appeal to the portress, in which he does not disdain to weep (456). Compare Helen's words to Aphrodite (1105 f.) with those of Heracles in *Alcestis* (790 f.). G. M. A. Grube, *The Drama of Euripides* (London, 1941), p. 342, has noted the comic possibilities of the scene (578) in which Helen tries to prove her identity to Menelaus by a mark that he alone as husband is privileged to see. Moses Hadas considers the play a parody: *A History of Greek Literature* (Columbia Univ. Press, 1950), p. 96. A. Y. Campbell in his edition (Univ. Press of Liverpool, 1950) is chiefly concerned to emend the text. In removing absurdities he greatly changes the tone of the play, for example in such a line as 389, where Menelaus wishes that Pelops had died among the gods, but might be understood to wish that Pelops had died inside the gods (sc., after being eaten). Absurdities are just what should not be removed from the words of Menelaus, especially when a double meaning with comic possibilities is in question.

[5] The messenger points out the folly of trusting any oracle but one's own intelligence (744–757). The chorus points out the folly of making war the criterion of virtue (1151–1157). If competition in bloodshed is to decide

303

the claim of valor, never will strife cease from among the cities of men. These arguments are relevant to the Athenian situation in 412 B.C.

⁶ In the *Orestes* and *Phoenissae* Euripides provided opportunities for the exhibition of Timotheus' new style in music, particularly in the part of the eunuch in the former. No doubt it accords with the new music that all the characters except Pylades are inferior, as is noted in the hypothesis. See S. E. Bassett, "The Place and Date of the First Performance of the *Persians* of Timotheus," *CPh* 26 ('1931) 153–165, and U. von Wilamowitz-Möllendorff, *Timotheus, die Perser* (Leipzig, 1903), p. 100. I know Chikamatsu's *Battles of Kokusenya* only from the summary in W. G. Aston, *A History of Japanese Literature* (New York, 1899), pp. 280–288. For Aristotle see *Poetics* 15.7: 54ᵃ 28 f. and 25.31: 61ᵇ 21. The *Orestes* is also designed to abet the sort of acting that made the aged Mynniscus call his younger rival Callippides a monkey. See *Poetics* 26.4: 61ᵇ 34 f. The comic eunuch, who serves as messenger, singing his news in a tremulous soprano, has no parallel in Greek drama unless we allow the wounded charioteer of the *Rhesus*. Such a feature is enough in itself to demonstrate a late date for a play.

⁷ Aristotle tells us that in his time the actors were more important than the poets in dramatic composition: *Rhetoric* 3.1.4. The evidence that actors influenced our text of the tragedians is cited and discussed by D. L. Page, *Actors' Interpolations in Greek Tragedy* (Oxford, 1934). Only in *Phoenissae* and *Iphigeneia at Aulis* is suspicion strong that scenes have been added or substituted in plays of Euripides. It is not likely that the work of Euripides is seriously perverted, for actors had opportunity to introduce new scenes only when plays were already rather loose in construction and suitable for histrionic display. Sophocles and Aeschylus were for the most part let alone except for the ending of *Seven against Thebes*. I have been content to discuss the plays as they stand in our texts without attempting the impossible task of sifting the genuine from the spurious, believing that the main design of each play is much as Euripides left it.

⁸ In speaking of actors as dancing their parts I have in mind the fact that actors were and are dancers in the Hindu, Chinese, and Japanese theater, to varying degrees. The actor who played the frenzied Hermione (*Andromache* 825–866) or the mad Cassandra (*Trojan Women* 308–340) must have performed frantic gyrations. Hindu dramatists like to introduce a maiden frightened by a bee as an excuse for lithe movement. The Chinese actor, playing the part of a lady with bound feet who must pick something from the ground, makes the most of the opportunity to achieve the difficult feat lingeringly and gracefully. Greek actors may have begun by parodying the airs of great ladies when they played Helen or Clytemnestra; in the end they probably surpassed their originals. The strutting, posing

male is also a good subject for dancing actors, especially when doubt or terror is appropriate; in the end all characters become timid posers.

Polyneices in the scene referred to and Hector in the *Rhesus* flit birdlike from apprehension to apprehension. Menander gives us psychological drama designed for stylized acting. In Aristophanes the train of events does not wait for psychological moods. The acting is stylized, but the lines have a rhythm that belongs to patterned physical movement and encounters. In fact, one who acts an Aristophanic part to the Greek words will discover in the pattern of the verse a guide to the actor's movements on the stage. This was observed in preparing for performances of Aristophanes' *Clouds* and *Peace* at Swarthmore College in 1939 and 1941, in which L. R. Shero had the leading part. He also played Pentheus in a performance of the *Bacchae* at Bryn Mawr College in 1935 that was brilliantly directed by Mrs. Eva Sikelianos. In tragedy the words need little help from sudden gestures or poses; they are frequently rhetorical or poetic rather than chiefly dramatic as in Menander. The later danced roles in tragedy imitate life at two aesthetic removes. They are luxurious and sentimental rather than moral and energetic in their appeal. See also note 6 to chap. viii.

All Greek acting was stylized, but the range of styles is wide. The evidence is chiefly that of the words that have come down to us. Stately acting goes with stately words. Lively acting goes with lively words. Verse does not lend itself to realistic acting except in burlesque for comic ends. This is not a matter that can be mathematically demonstrated, though it is sometimes possible to illustrate the liveliness of Greek characterization by examples. Repeated words with initial and final sounds the same, repeated words with scansion the same, both anapaest and fourth paean, a line with six caesuras, a line beginning with six short syllables, and the more familiar devices that produce smoothness, roughness, a tone of decision, of bombast, or of anticlimax, are found in the armory of Menander, as I have pointed out in *TAPhA* 62 (1931) 228–234 and *AJPh* 62 (1941) 465 f. The liveliest character in Sophocles is Chrysothemis in the *Electra*. Whether the special lilt of her lines can be analyzed I do not know. But Sophocles' characterization is never as lively as Homer's or Menander's. Tragedy abandoned *éthos* in the end, taking entirely to rhetoric and the gliding and undramatic rhythms of danced drama, and even in the great period only Sophocles at his best could combine *éthos* and dignity in his dramatic style without becoming declamatory.

[9] See *Poetics* 12.4: 52^b 19 f. D. L. Page (see note 7 above) has discussed the question how much of the *Iphigeneia at Aulis* was written by Euripides himself, what parts were added after his death to complete the play, what changes were made in later revisions undertaken by or for actors, and what

parts of the play show the effects of extensive corruption or loss of the text with consequent improvisation by mediaeval scribes or editors. Though Euripides left the work unfinished, the form of the plot must have been clear at least to the point where Iphigeneia volunteers to die. Subsequent addition or substitution of lines or scenes has probably not greatly affected the tone of the play. Exaggerated baseness and nobility of character were already characteristic of Euripides. The ending as it now stands is designed to celebrate an attack by a European leader on Asia, but an epiphany of Artemis or some other god might be even more effective as Hellenic propaganda and would give less prominence to the vindictive Clytemnestra. She is not a very good omen for a later leader of Greek hosts against Asia.

[10] See *Poetics* 15.9: 54ᵃ 31–33 and Plato, *Epistle VII* 328b. The question arises how it happens that in this one play we find a glorification of the Trojan war. All patriotic plays except this one appeal only to local patriotism, not to united Greece against Asia. The prophetic mind of Euripides may have foreseen the defeat of Athens from afar and have prepared a play with a message for the next generation. Is it too much to suppose that men like Alcibiades of Athens, Lysander of Sparta, and Archelaus of Macedon were alert to such a possibility, or was Persian support of Sparta in 407 and 405 sufficient to create an occasion in Athens for attacking Asia? But in reality the attack on Asia in the play is not so important as the united effort of Greece. Hence I should regard the final scene of the drama as a last vain attempt by Euripides to reconcile the warring factions within Greece.

But ten years later, when Agesilaus of Sparta actually led a small expedition to Asia, he made the port of Aulis a parade ground, where he attempted to offer special sacrifices. He never forgave the Boeotarchs who prevented him. See Xenophon, *Hellenica* 3.4.3 f., 3.5.5, 7.1.34. In the *Agesilaus* 1.8, Xenophon relates that general enthusiasm greeted Agesilaus' proposal to make war at the expense of Persians rather than Greeks. After Agesilaus, many a ruler was urged by Isocrates and others to lead united Greece against Asia, until in the end Philip and his son Alexander of Macedon made the conquest of Persia a reality. It would be bold to suggest that on any particular occasion the play of Euripides was performed to create and justify the right sentiments, but it would be even bolder to suppose that the play was never so performed. In this case, too, Euripides anticipated the sentiment of a later century.

[11] The latest discussion of the date of the *Rhesus* that I know assigns it to the fourth century before Christ: J. Geffcken, "Der Rhesos," *Hermes* 71 (1936) 394–408. The arguments of Geffcken hold equally well for the third century, where G. Hermann placed it: *Opuscula* (Lipsiae, 1828) III, 262–310. There seems little doubt that Euripides wrote a *Rhesus* and that our play

passed as his at some time in the Alexandrian period. Since we do not know when the substitution was made or how much our play owes to the genuine play of Euripides, it seems impossible to discover which play the scholar Dicaearchus (*ca.* 347–*ca.* 287 B.C.) discussed. At any rate, he cited a prologue which differs from that of our play. Still a third prologue, in which Hera addresses Athena, summoning her to assist the Achaeans, is quoted in the Greek introduction. It is quite possible that the play was as much refashioned from time to time as the prologue. These matters are discussed in the Introduction to an edition (Cambridge, 1916) by W. H. Porter, who defends the play as Euripidean, holding that Gilbert Murray may have been right in thinking it a pro-satyric drama written by the youthful Euripides in imitation of Aeschylus and revised by another hand for reproduction after the poet's death.

It seems most unlikely to me that any play written for production at Athens would have ended with an epiphany in which Athena and, by implication at least, Athens are resentfully rebuked by the Muse and deprived of her favor. It is certainly an anachronism for the Muse to declare (941 f.) at the time of the Trojan war that the Muses especially honor Athens. The reference to Musaeus as an Athenian citizen betrays the learned writer, who knows that the Museum Hill was supposed to hold the tomb of Musaeus (Pausanias 10.12.11). A. S. Way (Loeb Classical Library) translates line 949: "No new sage will I bring to thee (sc., to Athens)." It is possible, with Porter and Murray, to make the words mean: "I shall not call in any other poet (sc., to compose a dirge)." This seems unlikely in view of the later statement (976) that the Muses together will lament Rhesus, as they will Achilles. It went without saying that the Muses required no mortal to write poetry for them. They were dispensers of poetry, not receivers.

There seems to be no good reason for introducing Athena into the middle of the action except the desire to motivate hostility of the Muse to Athens. The fact that Pindar knew (Bergk, fr. 220 [181] = Schol. *Iliad* 10.435) of an intervention of Athena against Rhesus was no compelling reason for her appearing at this point in the play. Hence we have a right to expect an explicit statement by the Muse of her enmity. No doubt the author of the *Rhesus* is imitating plays, such as the *Psychostasia* of Aeschylus and the *Hippolytus* of Euripides, in which divinities quarrel, with threats of retaliation. In fact, the Muse's threat against Thetis (978 f.) is so irrelevant here that it points to reminiscence of the *Psychostasia*. In that play a prophecy by Eos of the death of Achilles, who had slain her son Memnon, would have been appropriate. Such pointless intrusions as this smack of Alexandria; and the activity of the actors required in the performance of the *Rhesus*—

often not clearly indicated in the text, but deduced by scholars—belongs to a late period of tragedy. Satyric drama may have been on occasion almost as lively as comedy, but our only pro-satyric drama, the *Alcestis* of Euripides, is no livelier than contemporary tragedy, as far as acting goes. The *Rhesus* is much more like the *Helen* and the *Orestes* in its appeal to the eye. If it is Euripidean, it is very late Euripidean and very much revised to suit a later century.

¹² On the question whether Hindu drama derives from Greek, see also note 6 to chap. viii, and observe that A. B. Keith, *The Sanskrit Drama* (Oxford, 1924), after consideration of the evidence, gives a verdict in favor of the independence of Hindu drama. Both Hindu and Chinese drama are operatic, including much song and dance, and the possibility is still not excluded that the Greeks in India may have contributed to the rise and development of Hindu drama. We know that they had a decisive influence on Buddhist sculpture because in that field we have contemporary artifacts to prove it. The influence of Indian sculpture on Chinese Buddhist sculpture is equally certain. In the great period of Chinese drama, the thirteenth century, when the Mongols were supreme, it seems unlikely that there was influence from abroad, though Chinese literary men turned to dramatic composition when they were unwilling to hold political office under Kublai Khan or other conquerors.

But before this, danced drama was especially favored and encouraged by the T'ang emperor Hsüan Tsung (713–756 A.D.), and many novelties were introduced from abroad. At this period the Mohammedans had not yet reached the borders of China with their puritanical attitude toward drama, and Buddhism formed a link between India and China before their arrival. After 751, Islam largely dominated Turkestan, and in the tenth century Turks ruled China, but drama, I am told, has no place in Islam. Hence it is not likely that drama in China was much influenced from abroad after the eighth century until modern times. For the development of drama in China see the chapter by Hsiung Shih-i in *China*, edited by H. F. MacNair (Univ. of California Press, 1946), pp. 375–385, which supplies much-needed and long-desired information.

¹ History sometimes produces effects that look as if they were designed: for instance, when the statue of Mitys fell upon the slayer of Mitys (*Poetics* 9.12: 52ᵃ 7–9). The effects of art are presumably always designed, but the design need not include a moral pattern. Aristotle perhaps considered only certain types of fiction as being more philosophical than history. In any case, it seems obvious that so far as fiction embodies a philosophy that is not exemplified in history it substitutes artifice for truth and should be more pleasing to the immature than to the genuine philosopher who tries to see things as they are. But Aristotle also allows the artist to depict things as they ought to be or as they are thought to be (*Poetics* 25.11: 60ᵇ 32–35). Presumably, philosophic fiction in his sense presents things as they ought to be. Yet we are confronted by the *Oedipus Tyrannus*, which shows things as they ought not to be, a pattern of events seemingly designed to accomplish a particular disaster. Such fiction is more artistic and artificial than history, but not more philosophic unless it is philosophical to emphasize the irony of fate—the alluring deceitfulness and cruelty of life. When events seem to be intent on punishing bad men, we have poetic justice; when they lure great men to defeat themselves, the effect is what is now termed ironical.

It would not do to assume offhand that there is more irony in art than in history. The most we can say is that irony in drama may be underlined by the author so that even the least intelligent observer will be impressed. History, however, may also be written so as to bring out the irony of events. To do so would presumably be as philosophical as to emphasize poetic justice. Irony in drama is interestingly discussed in A. R .Thompson, *The Dry Mock* (Univ. of California Press, 1948). It is worth noting that in *Oedipus Tyrannus* there is no ironical character human or divine except perhaps Tiresias, but verbal irony is used to give emphasis. In Euripides we find gods used to convey a sense of irony, but Euripides' gods are not realistically convincing. The ironical character in drama, whether god or man, produces quite a different effect from that of the impersonal irony of fate. In *Othello,* Iago is an ironical character behaving like the offended god of a Greek tragedy, but, being mortal, he is punished in the end with poetic

309

justice. From Iago's point of view there is irony in his defeat in the moment of success, for he has brought punishment upon himself. The audience, who do not admire Iago, will find more irony in the fate of Othello, since he kills because he loves too well.

There is a further complication when an author presents his characters in such a way that the irony of their fictional fate is not apparent to the ordinary observer. Thomas Hardy, Anatole France, and Sophocles make their irony clear. In Thompson's view Ibsen is doubly ironic because he conceals his irony. If he was an ironist in spite of himself and perhaps even without knowing it, we have a case of irony multiplied by irony: the ironical author is himself a victim of the irony of fate.

There is no reason why the ironist should take a tragic view of life. The Olympian view of man that Homer gives us through the eye of Zeus can be tragic, but it has its comic side. The gods have their sport with men, and Homer makes the gods ridiculous. There is no snobbery in his treatment of the divine; he can see the absurdity involved in worshiping the upper classes. What could be more ironical than the rule of the universe in the hands of such frivolous tipplers! Comic irony at its best involves good sport without death or serious injury. Any suffering is represented as being merely necessary and salutary castigation of vice or bad manners. When the mistaken zeal of others is viewed from the vantage point of knowledge without action, then there is irony in the view. Mistakes may quite well lead by divine guidance, as Misapprehension points out in the delayed prologue of Menander's *Perikeiromene*, to a happy outcome. In such a case, irony is combined with comedy as elsewhere with tragedy. If the spectator sees a surprise coming for a character in comedy and laughs at the surprise, that is ironic. If the spectator is himself surprised and laughs, that is the laughter of paradox, which is a simpler matter. See also note 28 to chap. ii above.

[2] It must be confessed that my statement of Aristotle's meaning owes something to combination and deduction. Alfred Gudeman in his edition of the *Poetics* (Berlin and Leipzig, 1934), p. 317, held, as I do, that the ethical tragedy of *Poetics* 18 is a play with a happy ending. My view of the meaning of *éthos* and the *philanthropon* in the *Poetics* is set forth in my articles, "Aristotle and Menander," *TAPhA* 69 (1938) 1–42, and "Aeschylean *onkos* in Sophocles and Aristotle," *ibid.* 78 (1947) 242–251. The statement that plays should be classified by plot, not by character or anything else, occurs in *Poetics* 18.3: 56ᵃ 7–10.

[3] The references in this paragraph are to Alcidamas, quoted by Aristotle, *Rhet.* 3.3.4: 06ᵇ 12 f.: καλὸν ἀνθρωπίνου βίου κάτοπτρον; Aristophanes Byz. p. 249 Nauck (Syrianus, *in Hermoginem Comm.*, ed. H. Rabe, II 23):

'Ω Μένανδρε καὶ βίε, πότερος ἄρ' ὑμῶν πότερον ἀπεμιμήσατο; and Pliny *N.H.* 30.7: litterarum subtilitati sine aemulo genitus. Note also for appreciation of Menander's realism Manilius 5.476: qui vitae ostendit vitam chartisque sacravit; Quintilian 10.1.69: omnem vitae imaginem expressit, and Aulus Gellius 2.23.12; illud Menandri de vita hominum media sumptum simplex et verum et delectabile. I have dealt briefly with the absurdity of applying the term "comedy of manners" indiscriminately to Menander and to writers like Wycherley and Etherege in my article, "Menander in Current Criticism," *TAPhA* 65 (1934) 13-34.

[4] For Sophocles' remark see *Poetics* 25.11: 60ᵇ 33 f.

[5] See Aristotle, *Rhetoric* 2.12.16: 89ᵇ 11 f.: ἡ γὰρ εὐτραπελία πεπαιδευμένη ὕβρις ἐστίν. Plato's prescription for comedy is found in *Laws* 7.816de, but for καινὸν read ταπεινὸν, as I proposed in *AJP* 60 (1939) 97. Aristotle assigns low characters to comedy by definition (*Poetics* 2.1-7: 48ᵃ 1-18). I have twice discussed what Caesar meant by attributing to Menander a *vis* (not *vis comica*, for *comica* modifies *virtus*) that he did not find in Terence. See "The Art of Terence," *CW* 23 (1929-1930) 121-128, and the more accurate study in "The 'Vis' of Menander," *TAPhA* 62 (1931) 203-234. Caesar's words are preserved at the end of Suetonius' life of Terence:

> Tu quoque, tu in summis, o dimidiate Menander,
> Poneris, et merito, puri sermonis amator.
> Lenibus atque utinam scriptis adiuncta foret vis,
> Comica ut aequato virtus polleret honore
> Cum Graecis neve hac despectus parte iaceres.
> Unum hoc maceror ac doleo tibi desse, Terenti.

There is a discussion of the verses of Caesar by L. Alfonsi in *Rivista di Filologia Classica* 74 (1946) 32-43. I have not seen the work of A. de Lorenzi, *Quaderni filologici* II: *Dimidiatus Menander alla luce della polemica antiatticista di Cicerone* (Napoli, 1948).

[6] For the preference of actors for the lively, dramatic style of Menander's verse see Demetrius, *On Style* 4.193. Aristotle points out that in the dramatic competition of his day actors were more important than poets, *Rhet.* 3.1.4: 1303ᵇ 33 f. He also tells us that Mynniscus, who had acted with Aeschylus, called Callippides, who was popular a half century later, a monkey because of his exaggerated mimicry, *Poetics* 26.4: 61ᵇ 34 f. For some comments on a modern production of Menander see my review of Gilbert Murray, *Two Plays of Menander* (New York, 1945), in *CW* 41 (1947-1948) 202-205. Greek acting was always stylized. As it became more animated it approached nearer to dancing. Where we find lyric meters in the actors' parts in Euripides and in Plautus, we may safely assume that any acting was

rhythmical. That the audience were alert to hiss and interrupt the actor who did not keep time, we know from Cicero, *Paradoxa Stoicorum* 3.26: histrio si paulum se movet extra numerum . . . exsibilatur, exploditur. In Menander we find no lyric meter, but the rhythm of the metrical words is a sufficient clue to the movement of the actor. A sense of life and movement is implicit in the arrangement of the words. In such a tragedy, however, as the *Rhesus* the rhythm is smooth and the language is a mere accompaniment to the actor's art. Such drama may be entertaining and artistic, but it produces no illusion of life, any more than modern musical comedy does.

    A. L. Kroeber, *Configurations of Culture Growth* (Univ. of California Press, 1944), pp. 448 f., suggests that Greek drama may have provided the original stimulus for Hindu drama, as Chinese did for Japanese, though the actual pattern of the drama was from the start independent. He calls such transfer of an idea from one culture to another stimulus diffusion, concept diffusion, or stimulus transmission. See particularly his article, "Stimulus Diffusion," *Am. Anthropologist,* 42 (1940) 1–20. In Hindu language, drama is dancing and the actor is a dancer.

[7] Smicrines, for instance, in the *Arbitration,* is in general an unsympathetic character. When, however, he consents to arbitrate between Syriscus and Davus, his honesty saves the day, so that he is partly responsible for the happy ending, in which his project of divorcing his daughter from her husband is frustrated.

[8] For Plutarch's praise of Menander see his *Comparison of Aristophanes and Menander,* which may be found in Volume 10 of the Loeb *Moralia* with a translation by H. N. Fowler, or in J. D. Denniston, *Greek Literary Criticism* (London and New York, 1924). See also Plutarch, *Convivial Questions* 7.8: "What literature is best for reading aloud at dinner?" Here is found the assertion (712b) that a symposium could be handled better without wine than without Menander. I have discussed Menander's morality in more than one article. See notes 2, 3, and 5 above and the criticism in my book, *Three Plays of Menander* (London and New York, 1929), which had previously appeared as an article entitled "The Genius of Menander," *Quarterly Review* 250 (1928) 353–367. For the coupling of Homer and Menander in sculpture as in primary education see my "Notes on Menander," *AJPh* 62 (1941) 460 f. There are scholars who identify the portraits in question not as Menander but as Virgil. See Rhys Carpenter, "Observations on Familiar Statuary in Rome," *Memoirs of the American Academy in Rome* 18 (1941) 96–104. Inscriptions make certain the significance of a pair of mosaics found at Antioch, which represent Achilles with Briseïs and Menander with Glycera. See *Antioch-on-the-Orontes III* (Princeton Univ. Press, 1941), p. 176, no. 110, with pl. 50 and pp. 248–251 (cf. pp.

168 ff., no. 131, with pl. 63). According to an inscription on the base of a herm *Epigr. Gr.* Kaibel (Berlin, 1878) 1085, lines 11 f., Aristophanes of Byzantium placed Menander next to Homer in literary merit. Ovid (*Tristia* 2.370; see note 10 below) assures us that Menander was read by boys and girls. Boys who studied Menander are mentioned by Statius, *Silvae* 2.1.113–116; Ausonius, *Epistles* 22.46 f.; and Apollinaris Sidonius, *Epistles* 4.12.1. Quintilian (10.1.69–72) recommends Menander highly to the educator and considers him far superior to other writers of comedy.

⁹ There is need of a good study of Menander in English. Ph. E. Legrand's *Daos,* translated under the title *The New Greek Comedy* by James Loeb (London and New York, 1917), deals with New Comedy in general, combining Greek and Latin writers. G. Capovilla, *Menandro* (Milan, 1924), is the only book entirely given over to exposition and criticism of Menander, I believe. There are bibliographies in the excellent editions of Christian Jensen (Berlin, 1929) and Alfred Körte (Leipzig, 1938). T. B. L. Webster has recently discussed Menander's plays in a series of articles in the *Bulletin of the John Rylands Library:* 29 (1945–1946) 143–159, 369–391; 30 (1947) 115–143, 347–400; 31 (1948) 180–223. These articles with others are now published in a book, *Studies in Menander* (Manchester Univ. Press, 1950). The article on Menander by Körte, *R-E* 15.707–761, is the best introduction for scholars.

¹⁰ Note Ovid, *Tristia* 2.369 f.:

Fabula iucundi nulla est sine amore Menandri
Et solet hic pueris virginibusque legi.

Gilbert Murray in his *Aristophanes* (Oxford, 1933) includes a chapter on Menander, from which I paraphrase his remark. This chapter is an expansion of his contribution to Powell and Barber, *New Chapters in Greek Literature,* Second Series (Oxford, 1929). For the great change that came into literature and life with a new confusion of religion and love see Denis de Rougemont, *Love in the Western World* (New York, 1940, but published also in England under the title *Passion and Society,* and originally in French at Paris as *L'Amour et l'Occident*). For Menander's interest in religion note his *Theophorumene.* For his interest in philosophical conversion note the second Didot fragment in Körte's edition (Leipzig, 1938), p. 145. For the subject of conversion in the pagan world see A. D. Nock, *Conversion* (Oxford, 1933). The treatment of love in ancient authors as an initiation into a new life, that may be higher and better, deserves further study. Much is suggested along this line by Hermann Fränkel's treatment of Ovid in his Sather lectures, *Ovid: A Poet between Two Worlds* (Univ. of California Press, 1945).

[11] For the position of women in ancient Greece see my article, "Woman's Place in Menander's Athens," *TAPhA* 71 (1940) 420–459, where references in support of my statements will be found. To say, as a scholar did recently, that women in Athens were either citizens or slaves, is a great mistake. Many citizens had noncitizen concubines or daughters, who were certainly not slaves, to say nothing of metics and freedwomen. A woman might in legal status be slave, free, or citizen; in relation to a man she might be hetaera or concubine, or wife. Only a citizen could be a wife, but hetaera or concubine might be either slave or free, or for that matter a citizen. Concubines with children were normally free. For the remarkable revolution carried through by Menander in the literary treatment of love and women see also my earlier article, "Feminism in Greek Literature," *Quarterly Review* 248 (1927) 354–373.

[12] See Plutarch, *Comparison* (as in note 8 above). The dates given are necessarily not exact. My translations from Menander (see note 8) are now revised and reprinted in Oates and O'Neill, *The Complete Greek Drama* (New York, 1938). My version of the *Arbitration* was revised again and reprinted in Oates and Murphy, *Greek Literature in Translation* (New York, 1944). Gilbert Murray's *Two Plays of Menander* (Oxford and New York, 1945) is an excellent translation of *Perikeiromene* and *Epitrepontes* with restoration of the missing parts. The reader of this will not, however, be able to distinguish Menander from Murray. The Loeb translation of F. P. Allinson (revised 1930) is less dramatic in its diction and makes Menander seem much less serious and natural in English than in Greek. It is also in a few details out of date, but is otherwise accurate. It has the advantage of including many fragmentary plays and fragments of lost plays.

[13] Misunderstanding, *Agnoia,* speaks the delayed prologue of the *Perikeiromene.* Polemon in that play (lines 440 f.) and Smicrines in the *Epitrepontes* (706, 752 f. Körte; 630, 676 f. Jensen) are guilty of *propeteia*, rashness, moving too soon. In my article "Aristotle and Menander," *TAPhA* 69 (1938) 1–42, esp. 20–22, I have suggested that the *hamartia*, or tragic error, that Aristotle prescribes for the hero of tragedy amounts to misunderstanding and rashness. Certainly Oedipus misunderstood the oracle and his whole situation and was overquick to act. Achilles in the *Iliad* fails in foresight and prudence. Demeas in the *Samia* of Menander and Charisius in the *Epitrepontes* both jump to conclusions that are mistaken, but in the latter play moral and psychological forces are emphasized. Obviously *hamartia* is a very inadequate formulation of the many varieties of maladjustment or rebellion that occur in literature.

[14] The five acts of tragedy are first found in Seneca, among writers whose works are extant in complete form. Horace sets five acts as a limit in his

Ars Poetica 189. Menander's plays seem to have been divided into five acts, not by relevant choral odes or by a curtain, but by unintegrated comic interludes. Only at the end of the first act is a reference made by some character to the approach of the revelers who provide entertainment between acts. Since no more than three speaking actors appear on the stage at once in any scene, it is clear that Menander wrote for actors who by rapid shifting of costumes and masks could take many parts each. Being limited to three actors, he was obliged to remove one set of characters from the stage before he could bring another on. The scene could not be changed in the course of a play and always represented a building or buildings, usually two houses, with a street in front where all the action occurs. Menander with great skill suggests the presence of numerous characters and many events that occur off-stage. Thus amid the diversity of scenes he preserves the illusion of a single action that affects many lives. For the Greek theater, its actors, and its masks see Margarete Bieber, *The History of the Greek and Roman Theater* (Princeton and London, 1939), and the article "Maske," *R-E* 14.2 (1930) 2070–2120, and A. W. Pickard-Cambridge, *The Theatre of Dionysus in Athens* (Oxford, 1946).

[15] The quotation is from the writer of the speech *Against Neaera,* Dem. 59. 122. See also note 11 above.

[16] For the importance of infants in Greek family life and in realistic drama see my article, "Dramatic Infants in Greek," *CPh* 34 (1939) 193–208.

[17] The reminiscence of Hephaestus' role as jealous husband in the song of Demodocus (*Odyssey* 8.266–366) is obvious, though treatises on oaths or religion in New Comedy have more than once missed the point. Similarly, oaths by Helius indicate a detective mood, for it was Helius who detected the lovers Ares and Aphrodite in the story.

[18] Aristotle discusses recognition scenes in *Poetics* 16.

[19] For exposure of infants as sentimental weakness note Terence, *Heautontimorumenos* 634–641. In modern Japan it has been reported that contractors paid for girl babies but charged a small fee for taking male infants off their parents' hands and ending their lives; but I am now unable to cite the source of this report.

[20] It must have been Sosias who saw the embrace of Moschion and Glycera, for Polemon would not have waited till morning to take action. It was Moschion who hoped to talk later with Glycera. See my note in *AJPh* 62 (1941) 462–464.

[21] For the scene between Pataecus and Polemon see my note in *CQ* 23 (1929) 211. For an appreciation of the scene with Glycera see my note on *Perikeiromene* 307–310 in my article cited in the preceding note.

[22] It is sometimes stated that Greek literature does not depict the development

of character, and that personality wins no recognition before the appearance of Christian influence in Augustine and the Middle Ages. I am reminded of a remark that accompanies a sketch by James Thurber in *Men, Women and Dogs* (New York, 1943), p. 152: "She built up her personality, but she's undermined her character." It seems likely that bad characters like Alcibiades in the ancient world had abundance of personality. It is extremely probable that Charisius in the *Arbitration* was presented, possibly in a new mask, as a reformed character; but there is little use in arguing such points, for definitions are not easily agreed upon in this field.

[23] It should be noted that when Charisius later repents he does not set up a standard of continence for men, whether married or not. He repents of the rashness by which he had incurred responsibility as father of an infant. His plight, he says (505 Körte, 531 Jensen), is the same as Pamphila's. She was an involuntary mother, he was an involuntary father. There were, to be sure, philosophers who recommended continence to men, but that is not the question at issue in Menander's play. It was the expense of a harp girl that shocked Smicrines. Charisius had no reason to repent, nor did anyone feel strongly about his conduct, until the baby appeared. Quintilian (10.1.70) names *Epitrepontes* among plays that contain *mala iudicia*.

[24] For the view that those who are clothed in skins have no concern with justice see Theognis 53–58. The letter in the New Testament addressed by Saint Paul to Philemon about the slave Onesimus shows the apostle's attitude toward slavery.

[25] Pamphila's lines (510 f. Körte, Z^1 p. 35 Jensen) are as smooth and serious as her father's reply is raucous and staccato. These lines need only to be read in the original to make the dramatic situation vivid. In lines 706 f. (630 f. Jensen) Smicrines' jolting rhythm emphasizes his jolting violence to Sophrona.

[26] To argue that Charisius' problem did not exist because he was really the father of his wife's child is like arguing that Othello's problem did not exist because his wife was really not unfaithful to him. The irony of a scene in which we see the agony of a character who suffers because he is mistaken is the most powerful weapon of the dramatist, whether the ending is happy or unhappy. It is only armchair critics who maintain such perverse arguments; the actual spectator puts himself in the place of the mistaken Othello or Charisius.

[27] For the use of monologue in New Comedy to report to the audience what has happened off-stage and what is going on in the mind of a character see Wolfgang Schadewald, *Monolog und Selbstgespräch* (Berlin, 1926).

[28] The phrase *libertatem Menandri* occurs in Statius, *Silvae* 3.5.93; but see the interpretation of A. W. Van Buren in *AJPh* 50 (1929) 372 f. An epi-

gram on a herm makes Menander say that he taught men to be happy. See the reference in note 8: ἀνθρώπους ἱλαρὸν βίον ἐξεδίδαξα: "I taught mankind the whole lesson of gracious, gladsome living." Menander is said to have won the first prize only eight times, although he wrote some 108 plays, of which the titles of about 98 are mentioned by ancient writers.

For his speed in writing the words of a play, once he had conceived characters and plot, see Plutarch, *Moralia* 347ef. To a friend who asked whether he had finished his play for presentation at the approaching Dionysia, he replied: "Certainly I have finished my comedy, since the distribution of scenes and parts is complete, but I must write the lines to be spoken." Philemon was often preferred to him by the judges (Quintilian 10.1.72; Aulus Gellius 17.4.1), and Menander is said to have asked him if he was not ashamed of his victories. According to Pliny (*N.H.* 7.111), Menander declined invitations to visit the court of Ptolemy in Egypt. This theme is embroidered in the fictitious correspondence between Menander and Glycera that we owe to Alciphron (4.18, 19).

NOTES TO CHAPTER IX
Aristotle and the Philosophy of Fiction
Pages 245–269

[1] The editions, translations, and essays of Lane Cooper uphold the authority of Aristotle with little if any adverse criticism but much interpretation. See the Introduction to his *Aristotle on the Art of Poetry* (Cornell Univ. Press, rev. 1947), p. xviii: "Aristotle's fundamental assumptions, and the generalizations upon which he mainly insists, are as true of any modern literature as they are of his own." See also Lane Cooper, *An Aristotelian Theory of Comedy* (New York, 1922). There is excellent criticism of Aristotle in F. L. Lucas, *Tragedy in Relation to Aristotle's "Poetics"* (London and New York, 1928). I have learned much, not only from these two writers, but from the editions of S. H. Butcher (London, 4th ed., 1907), I. Bywater (Oxford, 1909), and A. Gudeman (Berlin and Leipzig, 1934). For an estimate of the importance of Aristotle today see William C. Greene, "The Greek Criticism of Poetry: A Reconsideration," in *Perspectives of Criticism* (Harvard Univ. Press, 1950).

[2] The principle is well illustrated by C. I. Lewis in *An Analysis of Knowledge and Valuation* (La Salle, Ill., 1947), p. 496: "One could not by select-

ing from amongst Beethoven's symphonies the three movements which are rated highest, and juxtaposing these, create a better symphony than Beethoven ever wrote."

[3] See Plato, *Ion* 533d–536d and Aristotle, *Poetics* 17.3: 55ª 30–32 (emotion); 6.2: 49ᵇ 24–28 (catharsis); 6.19: 50ª 38 f. (myth); 14.2: 53ᵇ 3–7 (bald theme); 13.10: 53ª 26–30 (Euripides).

[4] See *Poetics* 1–5 and *Rhetoric* 3.1.8: τὰ γὰρ ὀνόματα μιμήματά ἐστιν. Much the same criticism of Aristotle appears in Francis Fergusson, *The Idea of a Theater* (Princeton Univ. Press, 1949). See Fergusson's discussion of the distinctions between plot and action, form and purpose, in his Appendix. His further remarks on the histrionic sensibility are particularly good. There is no reason to suppose that kittens are merely copying their elders when they play. They assume roles of attack and defense that are at once recognized by other kittens. The human young are notorious copycats, but in their play, too, spontaneous originality is not excluded. The possible failure of histrionic sensibility with consequent misunderstanding is illustrated by the report of a three-year-old son of mine on an experience that left him somewhat aggrieved. "Carol and Billy were the mother and father, and I was the baby. When I didn't want to play any more, I began to cry; but they thought that I was just being a baby and went on playing." Much conflict in serious matters obviously is a matter of wanting or not wanting to play some particular game in science, religion, or politics.

[5] *Politics* 8.7.4: τὰ μὲν ἠθικὰ τὰ δὲ πρακτικὰ τὰ δ' ἐνθουσιαστικά.

[6] Theophrastus, fr. 91 (Plutarch, *de Auditu* 38d: Loeb *Moralia* I 206): τὴν ἀκουστικὴν αἴσθησιν Θεόφραστος παθικωτάτην εἶναί φησιν πασῶν. I. A. Richards in his *Principles of Literary Criticism* (London and New York, 1925), pp. 112 f., emphasizes the importance of attitudes or tendencies to act. I have called them tensions and include in them the readiness to act that needs only a sign to precipitate activity.

[7] See *Poetics* 6.2: 49ᵇ 27 f. (catharsis); 1.6: 47ª 27 f. (dancers).

[8] See *Poetics* 7.1–7: 50ᵇ 21–34 (complete action); 6.12: 50ª 15–20 (happiness).

[9] See *Poetics* 6.9 f.: 50ª 7–12 (parts); 19.1–6: 56ª 33–56ᵇ 8 (thought). From *Poetics* 6.23: 50ᵇ 7 f. we might expect Aristotle to send his pupils to the *Politics* for some of the thought required in plays, but, as he says, it was in the older plays that characters spoke like statesmen. Yet political plays appear among the works of Euripides. Praise of the middle class in the *Suppliants* finds an echo in the *Politics*.

[10] See *Poetics* 6.24: 50ᵇ 8–10 (*éthos*).

[11] For the parts of tragedy see note 9 above; for the spectacle, *Poetics* 6.27 f.: 50ᵇ 15–20; and for diction, *Poetics* 20–22.

[12] G. R. Stewart in his recent novels *Storm* and *Fire* has subordinated the

human actors to a plot which is in each case the history of a natural event. Human actors are similarly dwarfed in the *Persians* of Aeschylus.

[13] See *Poetics* 13.10: 53ª 26–30 (Euripides); 6.14 f.: 50ª 23–29 (plot without character).

[14] See *Poetics* 18.3: 56ª 7–10 for classification of tragedy by plot. It is true that Aristotle has already eliminated comedy from consideration by a distinction based on character (*Poetics* 2), but he recognizes that Menelaus in the *Orestes* of Euripides is properly a comic character (15.7: 54ª 28 f.) and that some tragedies have the happy ending that is proper for comedy (13.11–13: 53ª 30–39). Hence in modern terminology a play, however serious, is called a comedy if only it has a happy ending.

It is a puzzle that Aristotle prefers as the best kind of tragic material the sort of discovery that prevents an unhappy ending in *Iphigeneia in Tauris* (*Poetics* 14.19: 54ª 4–9). Such a play is, like the *Odyssey*, ethical and complex (24.1–3: 59ᵇ 7–16)—complex because it has a recognition scene, and ethical presumably because it has a happy ending. Though Aristotle does not explicitly define the ethical plot as one with a happy ending, no other kind of plot fits the term in his scheme. See my articles, "Aristotle and Menander," *TAPhA* 69 (1938) 1–42, and "Aeschylean *onkos* in Sophocles and Aristotle," *ibid.* 78 (1947) 242–251. Alfred Gudeman expressed the same view before me in his edition of the *Poetics* (see note 1 above), p. 317, without giving reasons. The New Comedy was ἠθική or moral in two senses. It depicted characters realistically, neither nobler than ordinary men as in tragedy nor inferior as in Aristophanic comedy, and it showed good characters winning happiness, as the *Odyssey* does. In classifying tragedies (*Poetics* 18) Aristotle puts all complex plots in one class, whether the ending is happy or unhappy. This leaves very few plots to be classed as merely ethical.

[15] Aristotle preferred the complex play with unhappy ending (*Poetics* 13) because it causes most pity and fear. My comparison of *Oedipus* with Euripidean tragedy is not taken from any explicit statement in the *Poetics;* it is an interpretation of his recognition of Euripides as most tragic in spite of his poor management in other respects (13.10).

[16] Aristotle in the *Politics* (8.7.4: 41ᵇ 38) promised to explain in the *Poetics* what he meant by catharsis. Since he does not do so in the extant book on tragedy and epic, we may suppose that the lost second book, which dealt presumably with invective, satire, and comedy, contained the missing explanation. If that is so, Aristotle must have connected catharsis with comedy. Since, however, it is inferior characters who are pilloried in comedy as a rule, it is hard to see why any theory of catharsis is necessary. Ridicule of inferior characters should have a moral effect. Plato provides in *Laws*

7.816de that comedy should be confined entirely to inferiors whether as performers or as objects of ridicule. But at Athens poets had the privilege of ridiculing and misrepresenting the leading men of the state. Such occasional indulgence of ridicule and invective against chosen leaders could be justified better as catharsis of anger, envy, or malice than as moral instruction. Some tragedy and some comedy was ethical. In fact, the much-abused term "comedy of manners" presumably derives from a Greek classification of New Comedy as ethical or moral comedy in contrast to the scurrilous and abusive comedy of Aristophanes.

It is important to note that catharsis is not limited, like the English word 'purgation,' to the elimination of waste and impurities. We speak of refining oil, clarifying butter, screening coal, cleaning grain, extracting cod-liver oil, pressing grapes or olives, purifying the blood, and clearing the mind of confusion or error. These would be instances of catharsis in Greek, and no figure of speech is involved in speaking of catharsis of the mind. Anaxagoras is quoted with approval by Aristotle, De Anima 3.4: 429ᵃ 18 f.: ἀνάγκη ἄρα ἐπεὶ πάντα νοεῖ ἀμιγῆ εἶναι: "Since the mind knows everything, it must be unmixed." For the theory that admixture of bodily humors causes mental illness see Plato, Timaeus 87a. The philosopher's need to separate mind from body is emphasized by Plato in many passages of the Phaedo (e.g., 67a), and philosophy is spoken of as a catharsis (82d). In Hippocrates, De Generatione 1, the secretion of semen is attributed to agitation or churning of the blood. In this case it is the pure concentrated essence that is eliminated. Catharsis in Greek means separation without implying that the inferior product is either valueless or discarded. In Plotinus, catharsis is elevation of mind and separation of the higher life from the lower. See Hazel E. Barnes, "Katharsis in the Enneads of Plotinus," TAPhA 73 (1942) 358–382.

[17] The references are to Def. 415d, Soph. 226b–227a, and Tim. 53a.
[18] The references are to Soph. 230d and Tim. 88c–89b. There is abundant material on catharsis in E. Howald, "Eine vorplatonische Kunsttheorie," Hermes 54 (1919) 187–207, but he does not interpret catharsis as I do. There is a careful study of the expression κάθαρσις παθημάτων by Franz Dirlmeier in Hermes 75 (1940) 81–92. He establishes the meaning as relief or freedom from emotions and concludes that we are dealing with a genitive of separation. It occurs to me that after catharsis, meaning or implying 'separation,' the genitive may still be objective. The idea of separation is in the word, not in the construction. We may speak either of a separation of emotion from the mind or of a relieving of the mind from emotion. Greek can use the objective genitive with the same impartiality as English between thought and emotion.

[19] The reference is to *Laws* 7.790c–791b. A recent fictional account of insanity by M. J. Ward was entitled *The Snake Pit* (New York, 1946). Drastic therapies are reported by E. A. Strecker, *Fundamentals of Psychiatry* (Philadelphia, 1942), pp. 115 f.

[20] The references are to *E.E.* 2.2.5 and *De Anima* 3.4: 429ᵃ 18–20. For participation in drama as a method of psychiatric treatment see J. L. Moreno, *Psychodrama* (New York, 1946).

The novelty in my interpretation is in the recognition that catharsis to the Greeks implied primarily separation rather than elimination. Tragic catharsis does not get rid of emotion or of excess emotion, nor does it merely refine emotion. It rids the mind of emotional confusion or lack of control by making the emotion objective, by separating it from the rational mind, which is the self. The thinker is aware of his emotion without identifying himself with it. It still moves him, but he is not overpowered by it. He controls his emotion and becomes a free, integrated person, not a schizophrenic. For much the same view as mine see E. P. Papanoutsos, "La Catharsis aristotelicienne," *Eranos* 46 (1948) 77–93.

[21] Aristotle's protreptic to the study of biology as something *kalon* 'beautiful,' in *Part. An.* 1.5: 44ᵇ 22–45ᵃ 37, shows how important the Quest for intellectual beauty was in motivating Greek scientific studies. The patterns of nature are to Aristotle as beautiful as the patterns of art. The Greeks also found beauty in moral acts. There is no Greek word for beauty that refers chiefly to sensuous beauty. I heartily subscribe to the remark of W. Somerset Maugham in *A Writer's Notebook* (New York, 1949), p. 366, to the effect that there is a greater beauty in the moral courage with which men confront the essential irrationality of the universe than in any work of art. For a critique of aesthetic theories see M. C. Nahm, *Aesthetic Experience and Its Presuppositions* (New York and London, 1946).

[22] The statement about catharsis that I have freely interpreted is found in Aristotle's definition of tragedy, *Poetics* 6.2: 49ᵇ 27 f.: δι' ἐλέου καὶ φόβου περαίνουσα τὴν τῶν τοιούτων παθημάτων κάθαρσιν.

[23] For a statement with different emphasis of the essential difference between Plato and Aristotle see Erich Frank, "The Fundamental Opposition of Plato and Aristotle," *AJPh* 61 (1940) 34–53 and 166–185. The division between the idea of the good and subordinate ideas corresponds to a division in the mind's function between creative intelligence and scientific knowledge.

[24] I have discussed Aristotle's classification of tragedies in *Poetics* 18 twice. My recent article, "Aeschylean *onkos* in Sophocles and Aristotle," *TAPhA* 78 (1947) 242–251 contains the proposal to read ὄγκος for οης in *Poetics* 18.7: 56ᵃ 2. It also defends the interpretation of the meaning of Aristotle's

term "ethical" tragedy that appeared earlier in my article, "Aristotle and Menander," *ibid.* 69 (1938) 1–42.

[25] The revolutionary influence of *Shui Hu Chuan* is frequently attested. According to the preface of Pearl M. Buck, who published a translation under the title *All Men Are Brothers* (New York, 1933), an edition has been issued by the Communists of China with a preface in which it is termed the first Communist literature of China. Pingying Hsieh in *Girl Rebel* (New York, 1940), p. 50, gives it credit for decisive influence in her life. It was a forbidden book under the Manchus and no doubt inspired the secret societies that helped Sun Yat Sen in his early days. See the account of his life by Lyon Sharman (New York, 1933), p. 85. The Japanese fiction to which I refer is exemplified in the free adaptations by James S. De Benneville, *Saito Musashi-bo Benkei* (Yokohama, 1910), *Oguri Hangwan Ichidaiki* (Philadelphia, 1916), *The Yotsuya Kwaidan* or *O'Iwa Inari* (Philadelphia, 1917), *Bakemono Yashiki* (Yokohama, 1921), and in the *Life of Sogoro, the Farmer Patriot of Sakura,* tr. George Braithwaite (Yokohama, 1897). I have in mind the Sanskrit dramas of Kalidasa and the great epics *Mahabharata* and *Ramayana* as examples of Hindu fiction.

[26] For Plato's rejection of tragedy in favor of creative activity in political life see *Laws* 7.817[b]: "All our polity is framed as a mimesis of the fairest and best life, which is in reality, so we assert, the truest tragedy." For the whole theme see the article of Helmut Kuhn, "The True Tragedy: Greek Tragedy and Plato," *HvdStCP* 52 (1941) 1–40 and 53 (1942) 37–88. I repeat in this chapter much of what I said in "The Divine in Homer," *Crozer Quarterly* 22 (1945) 20–27. See *Poetics* 9.3: 51[b] 5 f.

Index

INDEX

Bushido, 288
Butcher, S. H., 317
Bywater, I., 64, 317

Caesar on Menander, 218
Calhoun, G. M., 280
Callippides, 304, 311
Campbell, A. Y., 303
Capovilla, G., 313
Carpenter, Rhys, 273 f., 312
Catharsis, 246, 263–267, 269, 319–321
Chambers, F. P., 297
Character, 253; absence of, 260; contrast of, 113, 290; studied in Euripides, 124–126, 140. *See also* Characterization, Characters
Characterization, 89, 216 f., 260
Characters: inferior, 101, 126, 197, 242; mixed, 104, 149, 188; realistic, 185, 189, 197, 204; romantic, 198; vacillating, 130
Children, in drama, 96, 127, 130, 143, 157, 161, 189, 207, 225–227, 234, 237, 241
China and the Chinese, 8, 32, 41, 45, 60, 63, 136, 222, 322
Chinese drama, 23, 202, 211, 213, 308; novel, 268
Choice, 253; moral, 51, 72, 204. *See also* Decision
Chorus: as actor, 115, 155; as foil, 71 f.; as protagonist, 66, 152; as sightseers, 206; as tempter, 107; characterless, 210; counterparts of, in Homer, 56 f.; detached, 201, 206; in Aeschylus, 59; in Menander, 224; leaves stage empty, 96, 194; number of members of, 66; role of, 128; shift of attitude of, 104
Christianity, 151, 203, 238; and Menander, 220; influence of, 33
Comedy, 248, 261; as element in tragedy, 69 f., 139, 144, 152–154, 160 f., 163, 173, 190, 194–200, 206 f.; Latin writers of, 242; level of, in Menander, 241; *Odyssey* as, 16; of manners, 216, 243, 299; theory of, 215; tragic element in, 239; use of term, 13. *See also* New Comedy
Communists, Chinese, 322
Complex plot, *see* Plot
Concubine as insult to wife, 80, 239
Conflict, theme of, 133

Confucius, 32, 302
Contemporary allusions, *see* History, references to
Contrast, moral, 26, 37–39, 67, 187, 233
Conversion, 85; as theme, 188
Cooper, Lane, 317
Corinthians, and legend of Medea, 293
Creel, H. G., 302
Crosby, H. Lamar, 300
Curse, 114, 167, 183; in Aeschylus, 71 f.; in Homer, 58; in Plato's *Laws*, 58; in Sophocles, 88, 96, 103, 112

Dance, 152, 159 f., 202, 213, 258; comic, 199; in Aeschylus, 60; mad, 173. *See also* Danced drama
Danced drama, 60, 308
Dante, 52
Darkness, scenic, 211
Dawson, Christopher M., 295
Death, on stage, 292; theme of: absent from Aeschylus, 87; in Homer, 28 f., 126 f.
De Benneville, James S., 296, 322
Decadence of theater, 203, 209
Decharme, Paul, 292
Decision, 204, 219; depicted in Sophocles, 188; off stage, 141, 198; scene of, 83, 192
Delphic oracle, 82, 86, 109, 111, 167, 169; as scapegoat, 175, 180
Democracy, 170; defense of, in tragedy, 164; in Aeschylus, 86; not recommended in *Odyssey*, 26
Demosthenes, 52, 114
Denniston, J. D., 286, 301
Detection, theme of, 238
Dianoia, 252
Dicaearchus, 307
Dickens, Charles, 243
Diction, 254 f.
Dio Chrysostom, 300
Dirlmeier, Franz, 320
Distance, aesthetic, 175, 201, 203
Dodds, E. R., 298
Double plot, *see* Plot
Dream: in Homer, 40; in tragedy, 82, 88, 173, 176

Earp, F. R., 286, 300
Eccyclema, 80